THE
BEST OF POPE

EDITED
WITH AN
INTRODUCTION

BY

GEORGE SHERBURN

PROFESSOR OF ENGLISH
HARVARD UNIVERSITY

REVISED EDITION

THE RONALD PRESS COMPANY
NEW YORK

A Volume of a series in English edited by
ERNEST BERNBAUM

CONTENTS

Contents

INTRODUCTION

IT IS one of the ironies of literary fate that Mr. Pope, once the poet of dukes, bishops, and statesmen, should now be commemorated chiefly by Grubean academics whom he might delightedly have consigned to his *Dunciad*. The low ebb of his reputation, to be sure, seems to have passed with the days of Bowles and De Quincey; and now after a long period of neglect it is possible to write more sympathetically of the satirist who was a poetic sensation two centuries ago. His personality was early the object of hostile comment, and for over a century his theories of poetry have been far from the mode; these two facts have assisted in making him an author whom people habitually quote and seldom read. Nevertheless he remains one of the great figures in the history of English poetry, so great that any generation with an interest in aesthetic theories and in fine workmanship must study him and his poems. The problem is to understand the man justly and to appreciate his works.

I

It must have been about the year 1706 that George Granville sent a friend the following invitation to meet Wycherley:

Name your Day, and I will bring you together; I shall have both your Thanks. Let it be at my Lodging. I can give you no *Falernum* that has outliv'd twenty Consulships, but I can promise you a Bottle of the good old Claret that has seen two Reigns: Horatian Wit will not be wanting when you two meet. He shall bring with him, if you will, a young Poet, newly inspir'd, in the neighbourhood of *Cooper's Hill*, whom he and Walsh have taken under their Wing; his name is Pope; he is not above Seventeen or Eighteen Years of Age and promises Miracles; If he goes on as he has begun, in the Pastoral way, as Virgil first try'd his Strength, we may hope to see *English* Poetry vie with the Roman, and this Swan of *Windsor* sing as sweetly as the Mantuan.

It was very much "under the wing" of these wits of Dryden's day that Pope achieved his first "miracles." How did the "newly inspir'd" youngster come by such patrons? He was not of distinguished family—a notable innkeeper of Andover was his great grandfather; his grandfather, an Oxonian, was a prosperous pluralist and chaplain successively to the Marquess and the Bishop of Winchester; the father was content to sign himself "Alexander Pope of London, Merchant." This worthy dealer in linens (wholesale) had, in those days when change was common, turned Roman Catholic, and this fact may explain the poet's seemingly small knowledge of his father's family. It may have been mere convenience that caused him later to claim relationship with the Earls of Downe, but sincere if mistaken beliefs in such connections are not uncommon.

Pope was born in 1688 hardly more than a stone's throw from the spot where

> London's column pointing at the skies
> Like a tall bully lifts its head, and lies.

But while the poet's interest was usually focussed on London life, the city was never long his place of residence. At the age of twelve, after intermittent experiences in various Catholic schools, he was taken by his father to live on a small place just purchased near Binfield and Windsor Forest. For about sixteen years in this

Paternal Cell,
A little House, with Trees a-row,
And, like its Master, very low,

he steeped himself in poetry—in Milton, Dryden, and especially in the Latin classics. These last were to him living masterpieces; he largely escaped the pedantry of grammar and archaeology, which would have come upon him in the schools. His appetite and industry in these studies were excessive and partly because of them, partly from inherent constitutional weaknesses (both parents were past forty-five when he was born) his health was permanently impaired. In 1716, when the already disproportionate taxes on Roman Catholics seemed about to be increased, the Binfield home was sold. There followed a brief residence at Chiswick, and in 1718 when Homer had made the poet prosperous, he acquired the villa at Twickenham which for the rest of his life was to be the celebrated scene of his hospitalities.

It is perhaps natural that in an age when literary fame helped to make Prior a plenipotentiary, Addison a Secretary of State, and even Dick Steele a knight, Pope (debarred by religion from civic recognition) should have attained a social popularity unparalleled in letters except perhaps by the brief career of Laurence Sterne. His friends were usually the most distinguished and socially desirable people in England. How did this merchant's son, residing in a secluded spot, form these acquaintances that were first to aid and later to adorn his fame? Was it by means of his pleasant voice, attractive eyes, his quick wit, or was it what we more vaguely call "social charm"?

During the Binfield period (1700-16), three groups of famous friends may be noted, all important in the poet's career. The first includes the chief surviving wits and poets of Dryden's day. Walsh, Wycherley,

Granville, Cromwell, Congreve and Betterton—among others—were early loud in their praises of his *Pastorals*. As a result Tonson in 1706 solicited the privilege of publishing them: but they appeared only in 1709, and one doubts if the praise upon publication equalled that which these elderly wits had bestowed upon these "miracles" beforehand.

During the dramatic last four years of Queen Anne (1710-14) authors lived in the hope of success through political writing, and Pope, while aloof from such hopes, could not avoid being involved in that bitterness between Whig and Tory which thrust apart even such close friends as Swift and Addison. If from his elderly friends Pope had learned the importance of artistic conscience, of brilliance and finish, he was to learn from his second group of friends, only briefly attached to him, to regard literature as a school of taste and morals. This second group included the newly celebrated essayists—Steele, Addison, Budgell, Philips, and others. Among these Pope was intimate only with Steele, whom he assisted largely in the *Guardian* and less clearly in the *Spectator*. It was the newly prevalent spirit of aesthetic and moral reform (marked in this group) that had led Pope to his second important publication, his *Essay on Criticism* (1711). In this work he first openly indulged in personal satire. Steele and Addison had in the *Tatler* aimed certain jibes at the able but eccentric critic, John Dennis. Pope (whose early friends had most of them been intimate with Dennis) should have known better than to print such lines as

> Fear not the anger of the wise to raise;
> Those best can bear reproof, who merit praise.
> 'Twere well might critics still this freedom take,
> But Appius reddens at each word you speak,
> And stares, tremendous, with a threat'ning eye,
> Like some fierce Tyrant in old tapestry.

Dennis (Appius) immediately retorted with astonishing virulence; Pope was so unwise as to continue the warfare (in spite of Addison's real or pretended disapproval, wits of the day loved to see Dennis in a rage), and a lifelong feud resulted. The original animus of the quarrel is obscure: it may have been personal, or it may have been that to Pope as to others Dennis represented a false ideal in criticism. Evidence is lacking. Pope was young and (as always) reckless. "Fools rush into my head, and so I write," was his later excuse: obviously the brilliant, caustic idea tempted him to unwise, if somewhat honest, utterance.

His connection with Addison was probably closest in 1713 when the young Papist was used to disguise the partizan tendency of *Cato* with a prologue which brought him some fame. At about this time Addison encouraged Pope in his arduous and ambitious project of translating the *Iliad,* but quarrels with Ambrose Philips and probably others of Addison's "Little Senate," together with a tighter drawing of party lines, gradually excluded Pope from this circle. By 1715, if not before, he and Addison were definitely hostile—though there was never an open break between them.

The fundamental cause of estrangement from Addison and his group was the fact that Pope had already become a member of a more brilliant group—which had the fortune to be Tory. Addison, with the sound advice "not to be content with the praise of half the nation"—especially, one suspects, with that of the Tory half—let the young poet go to the rival faction. Here Swift, Arbuthnot, Parnell, Gay, Bolingbroke, and the Earl of Oxford, offered Pope a lasting warmth of friendship and a wealth of intellectual stimulation hitherto lacking in his experience. Under these influences he attained aesthetic and intellectual maturity—defined the proper objects of satire, and acquired

philosophy. Unsurpassable as were such things as
The Rape of the Lock (1712-14) and *Eloisa to Abelard*
(1717), they are to be associated with the more trivial
spirit of the *Tatler* and *Spectator*. They won him fame
as poet; the later works made him an influence on the
thought and civilization of his race. Without this
third group of friends such an achievement might have
been denied him.

Their influence began operation at once in a series
of projected prose satires by the Scriblerus Club, as
the group called themselves; but few of their produc-
tions—most of which were done in collaboration—
were published till years later. The immediate preoccupation of Pope was the translation of the *Iliad*.
This work, begun at a moment (1713) when the family fortunes seemed threatened, was destined to bring
financial independence as well as added fame. Pope
hereupon entered on a long decade of drudgery—
translating the *Iliad,* and, with the help of Broome and
Fenton, the *Odyssey*—and editing the plays of Shakespeare besides. In fame and fortune the period was
prolific. Of happiness it was less productive.

From the moment of announcing his purpose with
the *Iliad* he was attacked frequently by the Little Senate at Button's coffee house, whom Addison would
not or could not silence. Indeed, it is now known
that in 1715 Addison revised the attacks of his friends
Burnet and Duckett on Pope—softening the extreme
and injudicious parts concerning the poet's deformity,
which Addison thought cruel or ineffective. Attacks
were particularly frequent in 1715 when the first volume of the *Iliad* appeared and in 1717 when Gay's
satirical farce *Three Hours after Marriage* (in which
Pope and Arbuthnot collaborated) was cried down.
The attacks on the *Iliad* were motivated, ostensibly, by
Pope's ignorance of Greek and his presumption in

thinking himself competent to translate the greatest of all poets. If, furthermore, in his translation he used such lines as

> The priest may pardon, and the God may spare,

there was immediate outcry against his religion. Many of the attacks had nothing to do with Homer but concerned indiscreet bits of satire or indecency written by Pope in the coffee houses or taverns and never intended for the eyes of any except the right people. Too frequently Edmund Curll or some other scavenger-publisher saw these dubious morsels through the press—to Pope's discomfiture. Under the shelter of his great fame some of them still live to prejudice delicate readers against him. The constant succession of attacks that wore out his patience, and the general freedom of the day so far as indecency was concerned, are too often neglected in extenuation of his at times unlovely conduct.

A particularly trying moment came in 1726 when the reaction to his *Shakespeare* and his *Odyssey* was sharpest. There was loud clamor concerning incompetence and the high cost of cheap book-making; and this time the sting was intensified by some measure of truth in the charges. It was now known that Pope had hired Fenton and Broome at a relatively cheap rate (though doubtless the best they ever received for poetry) to translate a number of books of the *Odyssey;* and his incompetence as editor of Shakespeare was conclusively proved by Lewis Theobald in a two-hundred page review of Pope's work—chiefly of his work on *Hamlet*. This volume was called

Shakespear Restor'd: Or, a Specimen of the many Errors, as well committed as unamended by Mr. Pope. Design'd not only to correct that Edition, but to restore the true Reading of that Poet in all the Editions hitherto publish'd.

There have been few Shakespearean scholars in any day who could view with equanimity a similar announcement of an equally superior and thorough review of their work. Certainly Pope could not do so Weary of attacks he had earlier half decided that when Homer was translated he would write no more; later (1729) inspired possibly by the success of Young's *Universal Passion,* he told Fenton that all his future poems would be in the epistolary vein of Horace. The attacks of the past decade on his politics, his religion, his poetic ability and his moral character, confirmed him in this last decision. Visits of Swift from Ireland in 1726 and 1727 lent further determination, and thereafter a new phase of Pope's career was manifest. Belinda, Eloisa, and the "Unfortunate Lady" were far in the past: his genius was now to be devoted to the service of satire.

In the period of 1727-44 three sorts of work may be distinguished: the *Dunciad,* the satires and epistles in the vein of Horace, and the *Essay on Man.* The *Dunciad* with its various revisions lies across the whole period — in many respects Pope's greatest achievement and in many respects his greatest tactical error. Apparently begun some years before 1726 and discarded, the poem at Swift's suggestion was reworked—with Lewis Theobald as King of the Dunces. Pope erred in thinking that by this one effort he could annihilate all the small enemies who had pestered him for years. "This poem will rid me of these insects," he wrote; but his opponents were firmly entrenched in the periodical press of the day and were certain of the benevolent attitude of the Walpole government, which wished to scare both Swift and Pope out of party-writing. And a very few of them were too able to be thus annihilated. The effect of the poem was naturally sensational. Pope's aristocratic friends were

astonished that he should expose himself to the inevitable filthy retorts and that he should forget their
code, which limited combats to persons of equal station. He found no active allies of importance. The
Earl of Oxford wrote Swift: "Mr. Pope stands by
himself *Athanasius contra mundum.* There is never
a newspaper comes out but he is favoured with a letter, a poem, an epigram, even to a distich, from the
numerous herd of dunces and blockheads that are in
and about London". . . For the most part the dunces
expanded in this sunlight of dubious publicity: bad
advertising is better than none, and so for the most of
them the *Dunciad* proved harmless. To such victims
as took themselves and their scholarly or literary abilities seriously there came a more quiet but more per-
manent reaction of settled grievance. Mrs. Elizabeth
Thomas ("Corinna") remarked: "He has opened
Pandora's box, which perhaps he may never be able
to shut again." This prophetic utterance indicates the
nature of Pope's tactical error in the *Dunciad.*

In its less fortunate and less significant phase the
Dunciad had grown out of personal animus; in its
more important aspects it was a climax in the warfare of the *bel esprit* against the dull poet or the
pedant. It thus continued the tradition of Swift's
Battle of the Books (1704) and of the popular *Chef
d'œuvre d'un inconnu* (1714). In the 1729 edition
"with notes variorum" this burlesque of scholarship
was indulged with reckless disregard for accuracy.
Later most of these notes were dropped, and pedantry
not proving a very popular motif, the dulness of bad
poets came to be stressed. Theobald was not sufficiently in the public eye to make a good hero, and (possibly under the influence of Warburton) Pope decided
to depose Theobald and substitute Cibber, whose career
as laureate had come as an anticlimax after a notable

career in the theatre. In the spring of 1742 appeared
The New Dunciad, obviously a fourth book destined
to be added to the original three. This addition was
duly accomplished in 1743, with extensive revision of
the whole poem—of which Colley Cibber now became
the hero. Various slashing passages concerning the
heavy pedantry of editorial scholarship were mutilated
in an attempt to adapt Books I and III to Cibber; but
the genuine worth of the new Book IV has generally
been regarded as ample compensation for other losses.
The dignified rich melody of the conclusion of the
poem makes it one of the most magnificent passages
in Pope.

It has been commonly thought that Pope published
his own letters in order to show the public a better
side of his personality than the *Dunciad* had exhibiteu.
The episode of this publication is highly obscure, but
it seems certain that the project first occurred to Pope
before 1728. Evidently he was proud of his ability
as a letter-writer; it may very likely be that compliments of his correspondents put the idea of publication into his head. But there were difficulties: decorum forbade the publication of one's own letters.
To Pope, however, letters were a part of one's literary
output; and in cases of similar embarrassment concerning literary gems which a modest-seeming author
wished to get before the public there were two standard subterfuges: one could get the work pirated, or
one could print an authorized edition and announce it
as done to forestall piracy. If Pope had done the
second alone, nobody would have believed his excuse.
Hence after some years of intermittent intrigue with
his enemy, Edmund Curll, editions (1735) by Curll
were brought out, were pronounced unauthentic by
Pope, and ultimately replaced by the authorized edition
of 1737.

If Pope had at the start of his effort devised the whole intrigue that followed, all the world would pay homage to the "creative imagination" there displayed; but the truth probably is that he stumbled from device to device, and it is certain that he had many lessons from earlier episodes in the career of Curll, in such concealments as attended the printing of *Gulliver,* and in the somewhat similar "quarrel" between Voltaire and the publisher Nicolas Prevost over the London editions of the *Henriade* (1728). As in the case of Voltaire much of Pope's scheming (for instance, getting the letters taken before the House of Lords) was merely for the sake of publicity. What the Victorians were naïve enough to think basely deceitful in this process, Pope was shrewd enough to think good advertising. It is certain, however, that the excessive complexity of the intrigues is one of the facts in Pope's career that in the last century counted most harshly against him. It is also to be regretted that Pope manipulated the text of his letters until the historian can have little confidence in it. It has not, however, been proved that these manipulations are in general made for purposes more subtle than this same aim of sales. Pope naturally saw that letters to or from Addison or Wycherley would interest the public more than letters to John Caryll. To remake for purposes of interest letters to Caryll into letters to more famous men is of course not honest; but there is nothing particularly subtle or clever in Pope's tricks of this sort. It is inexcusable and even maddening that he should have done such a thing; but it is also inexcusable that editors with Victorian consciences should Bowdlerize the text of his letters while rebuking the poet for textual sins. The episode of Pope's letters is an unhappy one, and the full story remains yet to be told—if ever it can be unravelled.

The "satires and epistles," on the whole, came somewhat more graciously out of Pope's life. The first of
the series to be published appeared in December, 1731,
under the title *An Epistle to the Right Honourable
Richard Earl of Burlington.* It is now the fourth of
the "Moral Epistles." For it the Dunces were lying
in wait. They played up the possible portrayal of the
Duke of Chandos as Timon; and were severe on
Pope's shamelessness in thus attacking a peer who had
earlier made him a lavish present of money. Stories
of Pope's pecuniary ingratitude to persons satirized by
him were told more than once during his career (notably in connection with the passage in Moral Essay, II,
lines 115-50, supposed to refer to Sarah, Duchess of
Marlborough), but not one gift from such a person
can be proved, and Pope's general aversion to presents of money is well established. With regard to
Chandos, however, the Dunces scored. Although Pope
disclaimed the identification of Timon as Chandos and
in 1734 tried to make amends in the first of the Moral
Essays (line 54), when Theobald's Shakespeare came
out in 1735 Chandos was down as subscribing for four
sets — which indicates a suspicious enthusiasm for
Pope's enemy. The general attitude of even Pope's
friends is well seen in a letter by the Earl of Bath to
Lady Kaye (December 27, 1731):

The censures on Mr. P. . . are universal and severe; none
to take his part, and all out of envy or, you may suppose, judgment, running him down. He has wrote too many things that
have afforded me much pleasure, for me to join in this clam-
orous throng, nor dare I speak my opinion of so powerful a
man, but under your Ladyship's roof . . . I hope he'll not be
so intimidated as never to write again, for tho' his enemies
are powerful in their tongues, they are not so in their pens.
[*Hist. MSS. Com., Dartmouth MSS., I, 327-28*]

From such a reception of this Essay Pope saw what
he had to expect—not so much from hostile readers

as from hostile journalists. In consequence, when the four epistles of the *Essay on Man* appeared (1733-34), they were strictly anonymous, and during the months in which they appeared, other poems avowedly by Pope were published probably to lessen suspicion as to his authorship of the *Essay on Man*. The ruse worked, and the immediate reception of the poem was most cordial. Neither the heterodoxy nor the inconsistency of the thinking, while recognized, was offensive, until Professor Jean Pierre de Crousaz of Lausanne attacked them in an *Examen* (1737). In 1738 Pope printed an Imitation of Horace, Epistle I of Book I, addressed to Bolingbroke, who is thought largely to have inspired the *Essay on Man*. Here Pope frankly confesses his incongruous eclecticism:

> But ask not, to what Doctors I apply?
> Sworn to no Master, of no Sect am I:
> As drives the storm, at any door I knock:
> And house with Montaigne now, or now with Locke.
> Sometimes a Patriot, active in debate,
> Mix with the World, and battle for the State,
> Free as young Lyttelton, her cause pursue,
> Still true to Virtue, and as warm as true:
> Sometimes with Aristippus, or St. Paul,
> Indulge my candor, and grow all to all;
> Back to my native Moderation slide,
> And win my way by yielding to the tide.

At the end of the epistle Pope further confesses that

> . . . no Prelate's Lawn with hair-shirt lin'd
> Is half so incoherent as my Mind,

and reproaches Bolingbroke laughingly for offering no aid:

> Is this my Guide, Philosopher, and Friend?
> This, he who loves me, and who ought to mend?
> Who ought to make me (what he can, or none;)
> That Man divine, whom Wisdom calls her own.

Help came, however, not from Bolingbroke, but from the opposite party. The Reverend William Warburton, formerly friendly to Theobald, now (1738) published a series of letters, ultimately collected as *A Critical and Philosophical Commentary on Mr. Pope's Essay on Man* (1742), which blamed Crousaz for basing his attack upon a faulty French translation and which demonstrated to Pope's surprise and satisfaction that he had builded better than he knew and that his poem was not hostile to Christianity. Bolingbroke's absences in France made Pope's acceptance of Warburton's defense the easier: Warburton became his literary adviser and upon his death the official editor of his works. This intimacy naturally galled Bolingbroke, but Pope's dependence on Warburton, even coupled with other grounds of complaint, would hardly justify Bolingbroke's abuse of Pope's memory after the poet's death.

In politics as well as in philosophy Pope had been allied with Bolingbroke during the 'thirties. He had, to be sure, other political guides, for the leaders of the Patriot group who opposed Sir Robert Walpole, were his personal friends. Cobham, Marchmont, Chesterfield, Wyndham, Lyttelton, Murray, and many others gathered in the celebrated grotto at Twickenham to plan for Walpole's downfall. Pope's poems are full of compliments to them and of caustic satire on the Court party. The King, the Queen, and Lord Hervey were most violently attacked. In 1728, six months after the coronation of George II Pope dared print in the *Dunciad:*

> Still Dunce the second rules like Dunce the first,

and nine years later he amplified his charges against the King in the *Epistle to Augustus*. Walpole, of course, is frequently scored off, but at times Pope, like

Fielding, seems inclined to be conciliatory towards Sir Robert—who for his part kept a constant, wary eye on the poet, paid for attacks on him, and more than once made slight gestures as if meditating public prosecution. But Walpole's methods were covert, as we see from the diary of William Oldys, who records, July 31, 1749, a visit to the widow of a late scribbler, Thomas Odell:

> Saw several of her late husband's papers, mostly Poems in favour of the Ministry, and against Mr. Pope. One of them printed by the late Sir Robert Walpole's encouragement, who gave him ten guineas for writing, and as much for the expense of printing it; but through his advice it was never published, because it might hurt his interest with Lord Chesterfield and some other noblemen who favoured Mr. Pope for his genius.

The possibility that many of Pope's lesser (and noisier) Dunces may have been similarly subsidized has been too little considered; Pope was active in politics throughout the 'thirties—and perhaps earlier—and his occasional pose of disinterested observer should deceive no one.

Of political principles, Pope, like most of the Patriots, had few. He and Bolingbroke both preached against "party" government, and the whole group affected to glow with a noble passion to "save the country"—from Sir Robert Walpole! Frequently Pope is severe on venality. This is not said to be peculiar to the Walpole regime (see Moral Epistle, III, 35-38), but is most commonly predicated of it. "Not to be corrupted is the shame," was the cry of one of his later poems, and that was the cry of his group. Aside from these "party" ideas Pope's political wisdom is vague. He was naturally a monarchist, but he would express republican sentiments as well as any Whig.

> For Forms of Government let fools contest,
> Whate'er is best administered. is best.

This genteel superficiality, so characteristic of the age, is perhaps adequate for a poet, but one wonders what views Pope would have embodied in his projected epic of *Brutus,* "in which all the great principles of true and false governments and religions should be chiefly delivered in feigned examples."

Many of Pope's Horatian epistles are so admirably applied to himself that autobiographic charm must be added to the interest one finds in their politics and philosophy. In this later period of his career the poet is distinctly the dignified and elegant amateur— playing at philosophy, statecraft, and even gracing his satire with an urbanity befitting subjects far above the Dunces. He is, in spite of some alarms with regard to possibly seditious lines, perfectly sure of himself and his position. He can now speak of himself without fearing a charge of egotism. Lord Hervey had stung him to defense of his family by the line

> Hard as thy heart and as thy birth obscure,

and more than once (most notably in the *Epistle to Dr. Arbuthnot*) Pope replied. In the Imitation of the *Second Epistle of the Second Book of Horace* he writes:

> Bred up at home, full early I begun
> To read in Greek the wrath of Peleus' son.
> Besides, my Father taught me from a lad,
> The better art to know the good from bad:
> (And little sure imported to remove,
> To hunt for Truth in Maudlin's learned grove,)
> But knottier points we knew not half so well,
> Depriv'd us soon of our paternal Cell;
> And certain Laws, by suff'rers thought unjust
> Deny'd all posts of profit or of trust:
> Hopes after hopes of pious Papists fail'd
> While mighty William's thund'ring arm prevail'd.

Such lines are gracious allusions to past bitterness that drove his father from the City, where Pope was born, and from Binfield, where the family had been so happy. More truly characteristic of the poet (who was a notable *gourmet*) is the passage in the *Second Satire of the Second Book of Horace* (1734), which describes the culinary resources of the villa at Twickenham:

> Content with little, I can piddle here
> On brocoli and mutton, round the year;
> But ancient friends (tho' poor, or out of play)
> That touch my bell, I cannot turn away.
> 'Tis true, no Turbots dignify my boards,
> But gudgeons, flounders, what my Thames affords:
> To Hounslow-heath I point and Bansted-down,
> Thence comes your mutton, and these chicks my own:
> From yon old walnut-tree a show'r shall fall;
> And grapes, long ling'ring on my only wall,
> And figs from standard and espalier join;
> The dev'l is in you if you cannot dine:
> Then cheerful healths (your Mistress shall have place),
> And, what's more rare, a Poet shall say Grace.

Such delight in victuals and drink fits in well with Gay's charming "Receipt for Stewing Veal" (doubtless inspired by Pope and once printed by Curll as his) and with the tradition that Pope's death was hastened from eating potted lampreys. His appetites were only spasmodically restrained by considerations of health, and he was by no means typically valetudinarian. Dr. Arbuthnot thought much of Pope's ill health was brought on by habitual association on equal terms with persons of superior vitality. This side of his character, though never stressed by biographers is obvious in his "Farewell to London" (1715), and in the following passages from letters by William Kent the artist:

June 27, 1738. Pope is very busy; he last night came to me about 8 o'clock in liquor, and would have more wine.

Nov. 28, 1738. Have not seen Pope but once these two months before last Sunday morning; and he came to town the night before; the next morning he came before I was up. I would not get up, and sent him away to disturb someone else; he came back and said he could meet with nobody. I got drest and went with him to Richardson, and had great diversion; he shewd three pictures of Lord Bolingbroke. . . Another Pope in a morning gown with a strange view of the garden to shew the obelisk as in mourning to his mother's death. The son of Richardson and Pope agreed that Pope's head was Tizianesco; the old boy grew warm and said, We have done our best. My service to Mr. Bethell, and tell him his friend, Pope, is the greatest glutton I know. He now talks of the many good things he can make; he told me of a soup that must be seven hours a making; he dined with Mr. Murray and Lady Betty, and was very drunk last Sunday night. He says if he [Bethel?] comes to town he'll teach him how to live and leave off his roasted apples and water. [*Hist. MSS. Com., Spencer MSS., II, 19*].

In 1738 Pope was fifty years old and he was destined to live only six years more. He had had an active, busy life, working harder than most of his more robust contemporaries, and "playing" with them on almost equal terms. Not ill health merely but rather zest for life gives pathos to the couplet that originally read:

> The soul uneasy and confin'd at home
> Rests and expatiates in a life to come.

Nature gave him a weak constitution; in his adult life he suffered—at times acutely—from spinal trouble, and his health was worn further by trying to live, not wildly, but as a gentleman of his day liked to live. He died, aged fifty-six, in the year 1744 of dropsy and asthma.

II

Pope's conception of the art of poetry differs fundamentally from that of the nineteenth century and the present day. Poetry for him was the best vehicle of moral instruction. It was the *best* vehicle because it

utilized "the passions" as well as the reason, and the
co-operation of passion and reason was regarded essential to moral welfare. He and his contemporaries recognized the validity of Horace's dictum as to poets
(aut prodesse aut aut delectare volunt), but they rele-
gated delight to a secondary place: poets delighted in
order to instruct. It follows that Pope's art was concerned with meanings, not with surfaces; with ideas
rather than with images. He was early charged with
being "an eternal writer of amorous, pastoral madri-
gals," but his own boast was:

> That not in Fancy's maze he wander'd long,
> But stoop'd to truth, and moralized his song.

He was, then, no "imagist"; he even spoke slightingly
of such triviality, though he recognized the importance
of "images" as an ornament to poetry. But human
motives and duties—and errors!—were the burden of
his song; and when he wrote of outdoor nature, as
for once in *Windsor Forest,* he used the landscape as
the natural setting for the genteel activities of the
sportsman. Landscape for its own sake apart from
humanity is not for him poetic material. He neglects
the pictorial and strives rather to present the essential
quality of objects.

Another important divergence of the aesthetic of
his day from that of ours is its impersonality. Ideal
conduct for a Chesterfield consisted not in self-expres-
sion or 'self-realization', but in perfect conformity with
a fine pattern of behavior—in 'decorum'. The poet
similarly expressed not his personal feelings; for self-
expression was by no means his object. He rather
gave precepts for and illustrations of conduct for men
in general. In his imitations of Horace, as we have
seen, he showed a true gift for autobiography; but
it was like the autobiography which Anatole France

has given us in *Le livre de mon ami* and other volumes about "Pierre"—always charming but not always
self-consistent and never quite authentic as fact. It is
art, not history. Pope has been accused more than
once of insincerity in his praise of retirement and
content:

> Blest, who can unconcern'dly find
>   Hours, days, and years slide soft away,
> In health of body, peace of mind,
>   Quiet by day,
>
> Sound sleep by night; study and ease,
>   Together mixt; sweet recreation;
> And Innocence, which most does please
>   With meditation.
>
> Thus let me live, unseen, unknown,
>   Thus unlamented, let me die,
> Steal from the world, not a stone
>   Tell where I lie.

Even the last lines, in the first person, had best be interpreted in the light of the classical theories of universality and ideality, and not in the light of later
theories of self-revelation in poetry. The lines are
simply Pope's expression of an ideal theme, they may
or may not be what *he* always thought, but they certainly are

> What oft was thought, but ne'er so well express'd.

Pope's art so far is true neo-classic. The poet follows or imitates nature, and nature is what is normal
and universal in human experience: it is common
sense, not the particular sense of the individual. In
practice, however, and in theory at times Pope differs
from Aristotle in a tendency to be realistic rather than
idealistic in his attitude towards human nature. The
perfect hero of the modern romance seemed to Pope

morally impracticable: "we but read (so the 'Essay on Homer' tells us) with a tender weakness what we can neither apply nor emulate." Homer's heroes with their boastfulness and "unmanaged roughness" he finds preferable. In a note to the *Odyssey*, he takes the obvious position that "perfection is not to be found in human life, and consequently ought not to be ascribed to it in poetry." The life and tastes of Pope's readers invite him to the use of materials such as make him seem at times a journalistic rather than a 'classical' poet. Ultimate values seem frequently lost in that welter of topical fact that is the despair of annotators.

So much for the materials of poetry. The methods are also typically neo-classical. Three terms mainly concern us here: invention, imitation, and "the rules." Like other men of his day Pope praises invention as the superlative excellence of poetry. But while to many the term was in connotation logical and purely rationalistic (as it had been when to the ancient rhetoricians it meant simply the finding of arguments), Pope associated the term with the ideas conveyed by such words as *amazing, vast, fire, heat;* he also calls it the *vivida vis animi*. It is in such terms that he speaks of genius, and so we are perhaps justified in thinking that he tended to regard invention as a process of imaginative creation. It was certainly associated with inspiration. But invention was not "creative imagination," for it worked harmoniously with imitation. In fact, invention is chiefly regarded as the source of those 'bold strokes' that pleased dangerously, or of the nameless graces "beyond the reach of art" that Pegasus himself so quaintly "snatched" in the *Essay on Criticism*. It is in tendency irrational and inexplicable, allied with the *je ne sais quoi* of art.

Imitation, at first sight inconsistent with invention, is not hostile to it. This would obviously be true if imitation were limited to the Aristotelian sense in which imitation of nature is a representation of life idealized. But even in the neo-classic process of imitating at second-hand "natural" authors, invention finds a place to work:

> Imitation does not hinder invention: we may observe the rules of nature, and write in the spirit of those who have best hit upon them; without taking the same track, beginning in the same manner, and following the main of their story almost step by step; as most of the modern writers of epic poetry have done after one of these great poets. [From a note prefixed to Pope's *Odyssey,* Book I.]

Imitation here is evidently imitation of the spirit and general method of the ancients. It is such imitation that leads Pope to write, not 'lyrics' or 'poems', but the more specifically classical *genres* of pastoral, (mock-) epic, and satire.

In this process the much misunderstood "rules" play an important part. Pope calls them, in the passage just quoted, the "rules of nature," and in the *Essay on Criticism* makes it clear that they depend for authority on reason and nature and not on Horace or Aristotle. "I am saucy enough," Pope says in the "Postcript" to the *Odyssey,* "to think that one may sometimes differ from Aristotle without blundering"; but he never thinks one may thus happily differ from 'nature'.

> The rules of old discovered, not devised,
> Are Nature still, but nature methodized.

They are principles of common sense that embody the best experience of the ancients and enable modern genius to work wisely in the light of the ancients. But genius is the *sine qua non;* the rules alone and slavish imitation would never enable one to make poetry.

Another phase of imitation meets us as we pass to

considerations of the language of poetry. The fundamental principle here is propriety. Pope has commonly been blamed as responsible for the artificial and tumid diction affected by the poets of his century. Probably his attempt (with eyes cast towards *Paradise Lost?*) to establish in English an epic style worthy of Homer may have misled both himself and his followers, but in his later works he achieves notable distinction in the use of proper words in proper places, in the avoidance of the 'low' words and 'glittering' wit which the *Essay on Criticism* had proscribed. The *Epistle to Dr. Arbuthnot* as well as others of his epistles is a remarkable poetic example of the language of real life—which in the sensible days of Mr. Pope was the language of gentlemen and not that of peasants.

Commonplaces baldly stated, to be sure, would not make poetry; nature must be "to advantage dressed," but substantially all Pope has to say about this advantage is found in the couplet:

> Expression is the dress of thought, and still
> Appears more decent as more suitable.

In the fourth "Moral Essay," lines 50-54, he is explicit on the danger of "over-dressing" nature, and his practice usually accords with his theory. It is through neatness and justice of language, through an astonishing accuracy of verbal marksmanship that Pope achieves his best effects. At times, as every one knows, he displays an un-English tendency to use Latin constructions or arrangements of modifiers, and of course at his worst he exhibits the indulgence of his day in the rococo. This last quality is less frequently seen after 1731 than most critics imagine.

Pope's versification (or "numbers") has caused fully as much variety of judgment as his diction. He is

here, first of all, an apostle of "correctness"—or at
least of precision. In a letter to Walsh (October 22.
1706), he sets down a very rigid set of specifications
concerning verse, which (like all poets with programs
and with common sense) he freely disregarded at
times. He did practise the principles laid down as to
tone quality and as to the avoidance, in general, of
the Alexandrine and the triplet. He tended to place
the cesura near the middle of the line, but sometimes
it falls after the first foot, or before the last. The
expletives and successive monosyllables, condemned on
principle, he had too much sense to bother about when
actually writing. Concerning hiatus he was sensitive,
but nevertheless hiatus occurs. In fact, this letter,
written when Pope was eighteen, has perhaps had too
much consideration as a program. The letter, furthermore, says nothing as to the point where Pope's 'correctness' is most notable—which is making the metrical
accent and the speech accent of words practically always identical.

It is true that the closed couplet was Pope's metrical unit, and also that such a unit is a more rigid pattern than any other great English poet has used. Within the couplet, however, and especially within successive
couplets, Pope is most skilful in varying the placing
and the length of the pauses. Examples of lack of
variety—especially in somewhat tedious parallelisms
such as open Canto IV of the *Rape of the Lock* and in
the monotonous antithesis of lines 9-14 of Canto II—
come readily to mind; but if one studies the more
mature effects found in the story of Sir Balaam
("Moral Essays," III), one finds, within the narrow
limits self-imposed, an astonishing variety of effect
gained by manipulation of pauses and of inflectional
tune. Undoubtedly it is unwise and even dangerous
to impose such limits, but it is true that Pope's art

as well as that of his great musical contemporaries,
Handel and Bach, succeeds, in large part, because of
this rigidly exact and entire control of the elements
of rhythm.

In rhyme Pope is much less an artist. Swift was
pleased with the first volume of Pope's Homer; yet
when he wrote to say so, he had to add: "I am angry
at some bad rhymes and triplets; and pray in your next
do not let me have so many unjustifiable rhymes to
war and *gods*." Both justness and variety are frequently lacking in his rhymes. He repeats the same
rhymes too closely; and even allowing for changes in
pronunciation since his day (which would justify the
large class of *join: shine* rhymes, among others) he is
too often careless and inexact in his sound identities.
It follows that for Pope rhyme is a habit rather than
an excellence. It may be worth while to add that he
had no animosity towards blank verse, as his correspondence with Atterbury shows; indeed, his projected
epic of Brutus—meditated probably as early as 1718—
was actually begun in that metre.

The art of Pope, so far as sound goes, depends on
tactful and subtle manipulation of pauses and on what
we nowadays call "tone color." By this last quality
is not meant merely the onomatopœic effects so ably
preached in lines 364-73 of the *Essay on Criticism,*
and so skilfully exemplified in such passages as that
in the *Rape of the Lock,* Canto II, lines 123-36, where
Ariel threatens punishments for careless sylphs. These
admirable lines are a *tour de force,* but there are finer
achievements in the nice harmonies of tone and matter
in more complex passages such as the conclusion of the
Dunciad and the lines in the first epistle of the *Essay
on Man* concerning the lamb, the "poor Indian," and
the "vast chain of being." Here Pope reaches a rich-

ness of tone which fused with the weighty matter of his utterance makes him a truly great poet.

But, some one urges, how about those other passages in which the shrill spite of the satirist is so grating? There are indeed such. One can only regret that certain vicious couplets about Lady Mary Wortley Montagu, for example, were ever penned—no matter if some of them are highly just. These passages, however, seldom exceed the brief stab of a single couplet, and the frequency of their appearance is easily exaggerated. Many critics have talked both of the "white heat" of Pope's rage and of his "cold venom distilling drop by drop." By a tactful choice of single passages these conflicting metaphors can be convincingly illustrated. It is true that as one glides over the smooth versification of a satire by Pope one comes suddenly to a new tone in the verse: the poet's voice is raised; it becomes tense—not shrill perhaps, but certainly tense and burning. Is this the "white heat" of the poet's rage? If we examine the portraits of Atticus and Sporus in the *Epistle to Dr. Arbuthnot,* the answer may be too readily affirmative. Are there not other passages, however, similar in tone but too impersonal to be inspired by rage or infected with emotional venom? There seems to be this sudden access of a tense precision and eloquent vibration in the tones of the poet when he begins the story of Sir Balaam, or when he apostrophizes the Ancients in the *Essay on Criticism* or Bolingbroke at the end of the *Essay on Man.* There is the same flaming elevation in the many passages where he defends his chosen instrument of satire as effective in virtue's cause, or where in the *Epilogue to the Satires* the black trumpet announces

That NOT TO BE CORRUPTED IS THE SHAME.

Personal rage or spite will not explain all of these

passages, and it is well to remember that it *alone* would explain none of them. This varying tone is part of the art necessary in poems loosely built and liable to disintegration. Such passages held attention; one expected them as one awaited an aria after a recitative in Handel. Eighteenth century art depended not on long crescendoes leading to orgastic climaxes but on balance and alternation of tone.

That these passages originate as frequently in aesthetic intention as in personal anger is further suggested by the sure brilliance and vehemence of individual couplets that frequently stab through the moral commonplaces surrounding them. The 'critic-learning' of France moves Pope suddenly to

> The rules, a nation born to serve obeys;
> And Boileau still in right of Horace sways.

Other examples are

> Be thou the first true merit to befriend:
> His praise is lost, who stays till all commend.

> And spite of Pride, in erring Reason's spite,
> One truth is clear, WHATEVER IS, IS RIGHT.

> Yes, I am proud; I must be proud to see
> Men not afraid of God, afraid of me!

> What nothing earthly gives, or can destroy,
> The soul's calm sunshine, and the heart-felt joy,
> Is Virtue's prize.

It is interesting, finally, to see this same vibrant quality flash out in the opening couplets of various poems. The *Essay on Man* begins with a trumpet call:

> Awake, my St. John! leave all meaner things
> To low ambition, and the pride of Kings.

The First Satire (To Fortescue) begins with true
English bluntness:

> There are, (I scarce can think it, but am told,)
> There are, to whom my Satire seems too bold.

And perhaps the best known beginning is that of the
Epistle to Bathurst:

> Who shall decide, when Doctors disagree,
> And soundest casuists doubt, like you and me?

Such couplets as these come from a man who was
no mere peevish invalid; he wrote vigorously and
lived vigorously for the most part. There is in every
one of these couplets, as in his keenest satirical portraits, a firm control joined with a flashing brilliance
and a joyous satisfaction in superlatively fine utterance. These traits do not coexist with rage and venom.

Critics who have insisted on the shrillness and malice
of Pope have been misled usually in one of two ways:
they mistake the genesis of satire or they cannot accept an aesthetic that makes emotionalized truth rather
than emotionalized experience the material of poetry.

The nature of satire depends, to be sure, on the
nature of the satirist. It is easy but wrong to identify
satire and malice. Just before Pope's time such men
as Otway, Temple, Tillotson, Blackmore, Dennis, and
others, had opposed satire; and the personalities found
in the verses of Boileau, Dryden, and Pope certainly
did not win supporters for the *genre.* Shortly after
Pope set up as a modern Horace, his young friend
Lyttelton addressed to him the question

> Why wouldst thou force thy Genius from its End?
> Form'd to delight, why striv'st thou to offend?
> When every soft, engaging Muse is thine,
> Why court the least attractive of the Nine?

This disparagement of satire is common and natural in any age, and yet it is safe to predict that in any age in which the *nouveau riche* thrives, the bitter medicine of satire will also thrive. It was the religious, social, and political abnormality of the time that warped Pope into a satirist.

Similar influences operate in the twentieth century, and they, rather than any doctrine of innate malignancy, explain the work of the numerous satirical biographers and novelists of the present day. Judged from their printed works these authors of our century seem less lovely than Pope. They habitually vilify the dead, and they satirize by preference innocuous, complacent virtue. They delight in imagining a satire that "resembled nothing so much as spoonfuls of boiling oil, ladled out by a fiendish monkey at an upstairs window upon such of the passers-by whom the wretch had a grudge against." It is thus that the man who brilliantly ruined the art of biography by writing his *Queen Victoria,* misinterprets the rationale of Pope's satire. And yet Mr. Strachey and, in general, his imitators in the art of satiric prose have the reputations of being amiable and even delightful men. Their conception of the satirists *qui ante nos fuerunt* is, however, traditionary rather than imaginative. They exaggerate and misjudge the difference between Pope and themselves. None of the intimates of Pope regarded him as a fiendish monkey, and if the Dunces did, why should we take their word for it? Supposing the "Eminent Victorians" were all alive, would Mr. Strachey wish us to accept their views of certain contemporary satirists? Or should we wish to?

The personality of the satirist must be anatomized: we must see what breeds these hard hearts. Any literary artist must be one whose eager mind is stored with images or concepts that find release naturally in words. It is further generally recognized that such release comes mysteriously, perhaps at moments when the artist is overwhelmed by a more or less definite consciousness of being perfectly poised in life, perfectly at peace in its green pastures, beside its still waters. His cup, like that of the Psalmist, runneth over. This sort of release results in such eighteenth-century masterpieces as the *Songs of Innocence,* or perhaps is better seen in the ever beautiful aria (*Largo*) from the *Xerxes* of Handel, or in the so-called "Air for the G String" by Bach. But perhaps release comes in moments when the artist keenly feels maladjustment, disillusionment, or aspiration. The cup tastes bitter; or, tasting well, serves only to make one yearn for Olympian nectar, untasted by mortals. Obviously the first type of mind is the ideal of the modern "classicist," who believes steadily in "the soul's calm sunshine and the heart-felt joy"—though, like Pope, he seldom achieves it.

The second type of mind must be more carefully considered. If it is accompanied with emotional and delicately sensuous qualities, it may compose odes to nightingales, full of aspiration for the unheard melodies of ideal sweetness: it becomes "romantic." If it is accompanied with a clear-eyed intellectuality that feels most keenly either "the slings and arrows of outrageous fortune," or, perhaps more impersonally, the absurdity and cheapness of a new "aristocracy," the approach of an age of sophisters, economists, and pedants—the release is bound to be satire. Disparity between the ideal state and the grossness of actual existence stings one to such utterance. The resultant satire will evince an almost sadistic appetite for "justice," an appetite which is aesthetic rather than intellectual and which springs from elements probably not fundamentally malicious. It may be also, as in the case of Pope,

that this clear-eyed disillusionment comes to a mind
capable of perceiving severally the maladies of existence without being able to integrate them and draw
up a single coherent indictment against them all. This
but intensifies the maladjustment of the mind.

Pope's case is evidently complex. He suffers from
a sense of personal injustice; he is, throughout his
career as a satirist, an energetic member of the
"patriot" group that opposed Walpole; and he feels a
vehement contempt for such *nouveaux riches* as Timon,
Ward, or Peter Walter. (Incidentally *nouveaux riches*
of his day were almost to a man Whigs and as such
the objects of Pope's dislike.) It is only through
consideration of specific passages and lack of attention to the animus of whole poems that one can fail
to see that most of Pope's satires and epistles are inspired by politics. Personal enmities creep in; but
frequently—as in the case of Lord Hervey—they are
made more bitter by complications in national politics,
and form a part of the patriot opposition. In the
Dunciad and especially in the *Epistle to Dr. Arbuthnot*
personal considerations predominate.

The personal history of Pope's satirical period has
not always been well understood. Many people think
of him as leaping to a reply when attacked; but the
truth is that in most cases he paused before a retort.
Theobald, for example, attacked Pope in 1726; two
years later the *Dunciad* appeared. The castigation of
most of the Dunces in the *Dunciad* marked an exasperated end of years of forbearance on the side of
Pope. After initial errors in attacking Dennis (1711),
Philips (1713), and later Curll (1716), little came
from Pope's pen in the way of personal attack for
twelve years. Meanwhile between 1711 and 1727 over
fifty attacks on Pope were printed, besides almost a
dozen things by Pope that the poet did not wish printed

—including indecent squibs, personal letters, and such
a piece as the satirical portrait of Addison (1722).
These attacks came from at least seventeen different
authors. At least seven newspapers printed anonymous attacks in this period. So far as we know Pope
had attacked something like half of these seventeen
authors; but in most cases (for instance, Dennis and
Gildon) the provocation he offered was slight compared with the return in satire that it yielded. He
may have printed retorts never identified as his; but
as matters stand, all the known facts make the case
for forbearance during the years 1716-26 overwhelmingly in Pope's favor, and overwhelmingly against the
Little Senate at Button's, Curll's authors, and the
(probable) hirelings of such Whig ministers as Walpole. Pope felt increasing annoyance at the petty insults of his enemies, and had a fixed conviction (acquired first from the Scriblerus Club?) that dullness
and pedantry would soon ruin literature. Hence the
Dunciad—which was not a wanton or unprovoked attack, though it was reckless and ill-judged. Convictions
as well as grievances gave it soil.

On the whole, critics will be less ready to accept the
picture of the satirist as a "fiendish monkey" than they
would have been twenty years ago, simply because we
now have so many satirists who seem amicable as well
as caustic, and who in incisive prose aim to serve the
public good rather than their own private malice. And
it may be suggested that a satirist who hunts living
game is not necessarily less sportsmanlike than one
who attacks the dead.

The other error, suggested some pages back, is the
failure to regard as aesthetic, poetry that grows from
enthusiasm for abstract truths rather than from some
emotion derived from experience of life at first hand.
Joseph Warton, one of Pope's justest critics, called

him the poet of reason—and did not mean it as a mortal insult. It is possible for critics to see that the genesis of *Paradise Lost* is largely a glowing perception of certain abstract truths. It ought to be possible to see the same genesis in some of Pope's work; for Pope and Milton belong to the same school, though the one worked in what was called the "greater poetry" (epic, tragedy, great ode) and the other in the "lesser poetry." If one cannot see this glow of intellectuality in the satires and epistles, one ought at least to be aware of it in the *Essay on Man*—which in many respects is Pope at his best.

Here Pope has been criticized for drawing his material from Bolingbroke instead of using the results of his own thinking. The ideas of the poem are none of them peculiar to Bolingbroke; they are the ideas of most of the *esprits forts* of the time, and if Pope had not avowed his debt to Bolingbroke he would have seemed almost as close to Shaftesbury as to St. John. Just as the *Rape of the Lock* and the account of Timon's villa characterize perfectly phases of the social life of the time, so the *Essay on Man* represents the intellectual life most characteristic of the day. With regard to the universe Pope has the mechanistic and optimistic notion of a vast chain of being, linked by benevolence into a harmony where every individual has his natural place fixed. With regard to man himself Pope holds to a belief in the limited scope of reason, in the power of the passions to determine conduct, and in the duty of avoiding that cosmic pride which sinned against accord with "order," or the universal harmony. With regard to the attributes of the deity Pope is in general silent: his study, at least for the moment, is man. These ideas were the common property of the day; Bolingbroke's task was to arouse Pope's enthusiasm for them so that he would write.

There seems little probability in the statement made by Lord Bathurst in his old age, years after the deaths of Pope and Bolingbroke, to the effect that Pope merely versified prose that Bolingbroke wrote.

The point is that Pope, using ideas from whatever source, sublimated them into great poetry. The achievement is easily seen if we consider certain inspired phrases in which the emotion is cosmic rather than personal. Concerning the mortal sin against "order" or universal law Pope is more than once eloquent. The results of the sin are cataclysmic:

> Let Earth unbalanc'd from her orbit fly,
> Planets and Suns run lawless through the sky;
> Let ruling Angels from their spheres be hurl'd,
> Being on being wreck'd and world on world;
> Heav'n's whole foundations to their centre nod,
> And Nature tremble to the throne of God.

Irrationality causes man to act to no purpose—

> Or, meteor-like, flame lawless thro' the void,
> Destroying others, by himself destroy'd.

Scientific pride is urged, ironically:

> Instruct the planets in what orbs to run,
> Correct old time, and regulate the Sun.

The impartial deity

> Sees with equal eye, as God of all,
> A hero perish or a sparrow fall,
> Atoms or systems into ruin hurl'd
> And now a bubble burst and now a world.

For this grandiose imagery Pope's imagination was inflamed by abstract truths. He is just as fervent in quieter passages such as that in the first epistle on "blindness to the future" (lines 77-98) or that on the chain of being (233-46) or even that on the origin of religion (III, 215-40). The *Essay* as a whole is almost uniquely successful in evoking a sense of cosmic reverence in the face of truths than can be only half conceived by man.

It is possible, however, that we are wrong in stressing these emotionally inflamed passages; after all, the art of Pope and of his day was at its best an art of superb clarity and incisiveness rather than of emotional agitation; and Pope's own delight lay probably in the fine and compact brilliance that marks numberless epigrammatic couplets throughout his works. Such art is essentially cultural as well as intellectual. At its best it belongs with the work of the great musicians of Pope's day, Handel and Bach, or with the exquisite realism of Hogarth. Unlike more democratic art which has succeeded it, it cannot be appreciated without study; there never was a time when it could be grasped without intellectual effort. It is a sad limitation to one's taste in literature to insist on art that primarily thrills the senses without affecting the mind, and it is a sad error to see in Pope only the journalistic passages that make footnotes essential—or only the malicious passages that indicate personal spite.

PASTORALS

WITH A DISCOURSE ON PASTORAL

WRITTEN IN THE YEAR 1704

Rura mihi et rigui placeant in vallibus amnes,
Flumina amem, sylvasque, inglorius !—VIRG.

POEMS OF POPE

A DISCOURSE ON PASTORAL POETRY *

THERE are not, I believe, a greater number of any sort of verses, than of those which are called Pastorals ; nor a smaller, than of those which are truly so. It therefore seems necessary to give some account of this kind of Poem, and it is my design to comprize in this short paper the substance of those numerous dissertations the Criticks have made on the subject, without omitting any of their rules in my own favour. You will also find some points reconciled, about which they seem to differ, and a few remarks, which, I think, have escaped their observation.

The original of Poetry is ascribed to that Age which succeeded the creation of the world : and as the keeping of flocks seems to have been the first employment of mankind, the most ancient sort of poetry was probably *pastoral*. It is natural to imagine, that the leisure of those ancient shepherds admitting and inviting some diversion, none was so proper to that solitary and sedentary life as singing ; and that in their songs they took occasion to celebrate their own felicity. From hence a Poem was invented, and afterwards improved to a perfect image of that happy time ; which by giving us an

* Written at sixteen years of age.

3

esteem for the virtues of a former age, might recommend them to the present. And since the life of shepherds was attended with more tranquillity than any other rural employment, the Poets chose to introduce their Persons, from whom it received the name of Pastoral.

A Pastoral is an imitation of the action of a shepherd, or one considered under that character. The form of this imitation is dramatic, or narrative, or mixed of both, the fable simple, the manners not too polite nor too rustic : the thoughts are plain, yet admit a little quickness and passion, but that short and flowing ; the expression humble, yet as pure as the language will afford ; neat, but not florid ; easy, and yet lively. In short, the fable, manners, thoughts, and expressions are full of the greatest simplicity in nature

The complete character of this poem consists in simplicity, brevity, and delicacy ; the two first of which render an eclogue natural, and the last delightful.

If we would copy Nature, it may be useful to take this Idea along with us, that Pastoral is an image of what they call the golden age. So that we are not to describe our shepherds as shepherds at this day really are, but as they may be conceived then to have been ; when the best of men followed the employment. To carry this resemblance yet farther, it would not be amiss to give these shepherds some skill in astronomy, as far as it may be useful to that sort of life. And an air of piety to the Gods should shine through the Poem, which so visibly appears in all the works of antiquity : and it ought to preserve some relish of the old way of writing ; the connection should be loose, the narrations and descriptions short, and the periods concise. Yet it is not sufficient, that the sentences only be brief, the whole Eclogue should be so too. For we cannot suppose Poetry in those days to have been the business of men, but their recreation at vacant hours.

But with a respect to the present age, nothing more conduces to make these composures natural, than when some Knowledge in rural affairs is discovered. This may be made to appear rather done by chance than on design, and sometimes is best shewn by inference; lest by too much study to seem natural, we destroy that easy simplicity from whence arises the delight. For what is inviting in this sort of poetry proceeds not so much from the Idea of that business, as of the tranquillity of a country life.

We must therefore use some illusion to render a Pastoral delightful; and this consists in exposing the best side only of a shepherd's life, and in concealing its miseries. Nor is it enough to introduce shepherds discoursing together in a natural way; but a regard must be had to the subject; that it contain some particular beauty in itself, and that it be different in every Eclogue. Besides, in each of them a designed scene or prospect is to be presented to our view, which should likewise have its variety. This variety is obtained in a great degree by frequent comparisons, drawn from the most agreeable objects of the country; by interrogations to things inanimate; by beautiful digressions, but those short; sometimes by insisting a little on circumstances; and lastly, by elegant turns on the words, which render the numbers extremely sweet and pleasing. As for the numbers themselves, though they are properly of the heroic measure, they should be the smoothest, the most easy and flowing imaginable.

It is by rules like these that we ought to judge of Pastoral. And since the instructions given for any art are to be delivered as that art is in perfection, they must of necessity be derived from those in whom it is acknowledged so to be. It is therefore from the practice of Theocritus and Virgil (the only undisputed authors of Pastoral), that the Criticks have drawn the foregoing notions concerning it.

Theocritus excels all others in Nature and simplicity. The subjects of his Idyllia are purely pastoral; but he is not so exact in his persons, having introduced reapers and fishermen as well as shepherds. He is apt to be too long in his descriptions, of which that of the Cup in the first pastoral is a remarkable instance. In the manners he seems a little defective, for his swains are sometimes abusive and immodest, and perhaps too much inclining to rusticity ; for instance, in his fourth and fifth Idyllia. But 'tis enough that all others learnt their excellencies from him, and that his Dialect alone has a secret charm in it, which no other could ever attain.

Virgil, who copies Theocritus, refines upon his original : and in all points where judgment is principally concerned, he is much superior to his master. Though some of his subjects are not pastoral in themselves, but only seem to be such ; they have a wonderful variety in them, which the Greek was a stranger to. He exceeds him in regularity and brevity, and falls short of him in nothing but simplicity and propriety of style ; the first of which perhaps was the fault of his age, and the last of his language.

Among the moderns, their success has been greatest who have most endeavoured to make these ancients their pattern. The most considerable Genius appears in the famous Tasso, and our Spenser. Tasso in his *Aminta* has as far excelled all the Pastoral writers, as in his *Gierusalemme* he has out-done the Epic Poets of his country. But as this Piece seems to have been the original of a new sort of poem, the pastoral Comedy, in Italy, it cannot so well be considered as a copy of the ancients. Spenser's *Calendar*, in Mr. Dryden's opinion, is the most complete work of this kind which any Nation has produced ever since the time of Virgil. Not but that he may be thought imperfect in some few points. His Eclogues are somewhat too long, if we compare them with the ancients. He is sometimes too allegorical, and treats of matters of religion in a pastoral style, as the Mantuan had done before him. He has employed the Lyric measure, which is contrary to the practice of the old Poets. His Stanza is not still the same, nor always well chosen. This last may be the reason his expression is sometimes not concise enough : for the Tetrastic has obliged him to extend his sense to the length of four lines, which would have been more closely confined in the Couplet.

In the manners, thoughts, and characters, he comes near to Theocritus himself ; 'tho', notwithstanding all the care he has taken, he is certainly inferior in his Dialect : For the Doric had its beauty and propriety in the time of Theocritus ; it was used in part of Greece, and frequent in the mouths of many of the greatest persons : whereas the old English and country phrases of Spenser were either entirely obsolete, or spoken only by people of the lowest condition. As there is a differ-ence betwixt simplicity and rusticity, so the expression of simple thoughts should be plain, but not clownish. The addition he has made of a Calendar to his Eclogues, is very beautiful ; since by this, besides the general moral of innocence and simplicity, which is common to other authors of Pastoral, he has one peculiar to himself ; he compares human life to the several Seasons, and at once exposes to his readers a view of the great and little worlds, in their various changes and aspects. Yet the scrupulous division of his Pastorals into months, has obliged him either to repeat the same description, in other words, for three Months together ; or, when it was exhausted before, entirely to omit it : whence it comes to pass, that some of his Eclogues (as the sixth, eighth, and tenth for example) have nothing but their Titles to distinguish them. The reason is evident, because the year has not that variety in it to furnish every month with a particular description, as it may every season.

Of the following Eclogues I shall only say, that these four comprehend all the subjects which the Criticks upon Theocritus and Virgil will allow to be fit for pasto-ral : That they have as much variety of description, in respect of the several seasons, as Spenser's : that in order to add to this variety, the several times of the day are observ'd, the rural employments in each season or time of day, and the rural scenes or places proper to such employments ; not without some regard to the several ages of man, and the different passions proper to each age.

But after all, if they have any merit, it is to be attributed to some good old Authors, whose works as I had leisure to study, so I hope I have not wanted care to imitate.

SPRING:

THE FIRST PASTORAL, or DAMON

To Sir William Trumbal

FIRST in these fields I try the sylvan strains,
Nor blush to sport on Windsor's blissful plains :
Fair Thames, flow gently from thy sacred spring,
While on thy banks Sicilian Muses sing ;
Let vernal airs through trembling osiers play,　　　　　5
And Albion's cliffs resound the rural lay.

　YOU, that too wise for pride, too good for power,
Enjoy the glory to be great no more,
And carrying with you all the world can boast,
To all the world illustriously are lost !　　　　　10
O let my Muse her slender reed inspire,
Till in your native shades you tune the lyre :

　Spring, etc.—These Pastorals were written at the age of sixteen,
and then passed through the hands of Mr. Walsh, Mr. Wycherley,
George Granville, afterwards Lord Landsdown, Sir William Trumbal,
Dr. Garth, Lord Hallifax, Lord Somers, Mr. Mainwaring, and others.
All these gave our author the greatest encouragement, and particularly
Mr. Walsh (whom Mr. Dryden, in his postscript to Virgil, calls the
best critic of his age). "The author (says he) seems to have a particular genius for this kind of poetry, and a judgment that much exceeds
his years. He has taken very freely from the ancients. But what he
has mixed of his own with theirs is no way inferior to what he has
taken from them. It is not flattery at all to say that Virgil had written
nothing so good at his age. His preface is very judicious and learned"
(*Letter to Mr. Wycherley, Ap.* 1705).
　Sir William Trumbal.—Our author's friendship with this gentleman
commenced at very unequal years ; he was under sixteen, but Sir
William above sixty, and had lately resigned his employment of Secretary of State to King William.
　In your native shades.—Sir W. Trumbal was born in Windsor Forest,
to which he retreated, after he had resigned the post of Secretary of
State to King William III.

So when the Nightingale to rest removes,
The Thrush may chant to the forsaken groves,
But, charmed to silence, listens while she sings,   15
And all th' aërial audience clap their wings.
  Soon as the flocks shook off the nightly dews,
Two Swains, whom Love kept wakeful, and the Muse,
Poured o'er the whitening vale their fleecy care,
Fresh as the morn, and as the season fair :   20
The dawn now blushing on the mountain's side,
Thus Daphnis spoke, and Strephon thus replied.

DAPHNIS

  Hear how the birds, on every bloomy spray,
With joyous musick wake the dawning day !
Why sit we mute when early linnets sing,   25
When warbling Philomel salutes the spring ?
Why sit we sad when Phosphor shines so clear,
And lavish nature paints the purple Year ?

STREPHON

  Sing then, and Damon shall attend the strain,
While yon' slow oxen turn the furrowed Plain.   30
Here the bright crocus and blue vi'let glow ;
Here western winds on breathing roses blow.
I'll stake yon' lamb, that near the fountain plays,
And from the brink his dancing shade surveys.

DAPHNIS

  And I this bowl, where wanton Ivy twines,   35
And swelling clusters bend the curling vines :
Four figures rising from the work appear,
The various seasons of the rolling year ;
And what is that, which binds the radiant sky,
Where twelve fair Signs in beauteous order lie ?   40

Purple Year ?—Purple here used in the Latin sense, of the brightest, most vivid colouring in general, not of that peculiar tint so called. [*Ver purpureum.* Virg. *Ecl.* ix. 40.]

DAMON

Then sing by turns, by turns the Muses sing,
Now hawthorns blossom, now the daisies spring,
Now leaves the trees, and flowers adorn the ground,
Begin, the vales shall every note rebound.

STREPHON

Inspire me, Phœbus, in my Delia's praise   45
With Waller's strains, or Granville's moving lays ,
A milk-white bull shall at your altars stand,
That threats a fight, and spurns the rising sand.

DAPHNIS

O Love ! for Sylvia let me gain the prize,
And make my tongue victorious as her eyes ;   50
No lambs or sheep for victims I'll impart,
Thy victim, Love, shall be the shepherd's heart.

STREPHON

Me gentle Delia beckons from the plain,
Then hid in shades, eludes her eager swain ;
But feigns a laugh, to see me search around,   55
And by that laugh the willing fair is found.

DAPHNIS

The sprightly Sylvia trips along the green,
She runs, but hopes she does not run unseen ;
While a kind glance at her pursuer flies,
How much at variance are her feet and eyes !   60

STREPHON

O'er golden sands let rich Pactolus flow,
And trees weep amber on the banks of Po ;
Blest Thames's shores the brightest beauties yield,
Feed here my lambs, I'll seek no distant field.

Granville.—George Granville, afterwards Lord Landsdown, known for
his poems, most of which he composed very young, and proposed
Waller as his model.

DAPHNIS

Celestial Venus haunts Idalia's groves ;   65
Diana Cynthus, Ceres Hybla loves ;
If Windsor-shades delight the matchless maid,
Cynthus and Hybla yield to Windsor-shade.

STREPHON

All nature mourns, the Skies relent in showers,
Hushed are the birds, and closed the drooping flowers ;
If Delia smile, the flowers begin to spring,
The skies to brighten, and the birds to sing.   71

DAPHNIS

All nature laughs, the groves are fresh and fair,
The Sun's mild lustre warms the vital air ;
If Sylvia smiles, new glories gild the shore,   75
And vanquished nature seems to charm no more.

STREPHON

In spring the fields, in autumn hills I love,
At morn the plains, at noon the shady grove,
But Delia always ; absent from her sight,
Nor plains at morn, nor groves at noon delight.   80

DAPHNIS

Sylvia's like autumn ripe, yet mild as May,
More bright than noon, yet fresh as early day ;
Even spring displeases, when she shines not here ;
But blest with her, 'tis spring throughout the year.

STREPHON

Say, Daphnis, say, in what glad soil appears,   85
A wond'rous Tree that sacred Monarchs bears :

A wond'rous Tree that sacred Monarchs bears.—An allusion to the
Royal Oak, in which Charles II. had been hid from the pursuit after
the battle of Worcester.

Tell me but this, and I'll disclaim the prize,
And give the conquest to thy Sylvia's eyes.

DAPHNIS

Nay tell me first, in what more happy fields
The Thistle springs, to which the Lily yields :   90
And then a nobler prize I will resign ;
For Sylvia, charming Sylvia, shall be thine.

DAMON

Cease to contend, for, Daphnis, I decree,
The bowl to Strephon, and the lamb to thee :
Blest Swains, whose Nymphs in every grace excel ;   95
Blest Nymphs, whose Swains those graces sing so well !
Now rise, and haste to yonder woodbine bowers,
A soft retreat from sudden vernal showers,
The turf with rural dainties shall be crowned,
While opening blooms diffuse their sweets around.   100
For see ! the gathering flocks to shelter tend,
And from the Pleiads fruitful showers descend.

The Thistle springs, to which the Lily yields.—Alludes to the device
of the Scots monarchs, the thistle worn by Queen Anne ; and to the
arms of France, the fleur de lys.

SUMMER:

THE SECOND PASTORAL, or ALEXIS

To Dr. Garth

A Shepherd's Boy (he seeks no better name)
Led forth his flocks along the silver Thame,
Where dancing sun-beams on the waters played,
And verdant alders formed a quiv'ring shade.
Soft as he mourned, the streams forgot to flow,   5
The flocks around a dumb compassion show,
The Naiads wept in every watery bower,
And Jove consented in a silent shower.
   Accept, O Garth, the Muse's early lays,
That adds this wreath of Ivy to thy Bays;   10
Hear what from Love unpractised hearts endure,
From Love, the sole disease thou canst not cure.
   Ye shady beeches, and ye cooling streams,
Defence from Phœbus', not from Cupid's beams,
To you I mourn, nor to the deaf I sing,   15
The woods shall answer, and their echo ring.
The hills and rocks attend my doleful lay,
Why art thou prouder and more hard than they?
The bleating sheep with my complaints agree,
They parched with heat, and I inflamed by thee.   20
The sultry Sirius burns the thirsty plains,
While in thy heart eternal winter reigns.

Dr. Samuel Garth, author of *The Dispensary*, was one of the first friends of the author, whose acquaintance with him began at fourteen or fifteen. Their friendship continued from the year 1703 to 1718, which was that of his death.

The woods shall answer, and their echo ring, is a line out of Spenser's *Epithalamion*.

Where stray ye, Muses, in what lawn or grove,
While your Alexis pines in hopeless love ?
In those fair fields where sacred Isis glides,   25
Or else where Cam his winding vales divides ?
As in the crystal spring I view my face,
Fresh rising blushes paint the watery glass ;
But since those graces please thy eyes no more,
I shun the fountains which I sought before.   30
Once I was skilled in every herb that grew,
And every plant that drinks the morning dew ;
Ah, wretched shepherd, what avails thy art,
To cure thy lambs, but not to heal thy heart !

Let other swains attend the rural care,   35
Feed fairer flocks, or richer fleeces shear :
But nigh yon' mountain let me tune my lays,
Embrace my Love, and bind my brows with bays.
That flute is mine which Colin's tuneful breath
Inspired when living, and bequeathed in death ;   40
He said ; Alexis, take this pipe, the same
That taught the groves my Rosalinda's name :
But now the reeds shall hang on yonder tree,
For ever silent, since despised by thee.
Oh ! were I made by some transforming power   45
The captive bird that sings within thy bower !
Then might my voice thy listening ears employ,
And I those kisses he receives, enjoy.

And yet my numbers please the rural throng,
Rough Satyrs dance, and Pan applauds the song :   50
The Nymphs, forsaking every cave and spring,
Their early fruit, and milk-white turtles bring ;
Each am'rous nymph prefers her gifts in vain,
On you their gifts are all bestowed again.
For you the swains the fairest flowers design,   55
And in one garland all their beauties join ;
Accept the wreath which you deserve alone,
In whom all beauties are comprised in one.

Colin.—The name taken by Spenser in his *Eclogues*, where his mistress
is celebrated under that of Rosalinda.

See what delights in sylvan scenes appear !
Descending Gods have found Elysium here.   60
In woods bright Venus with Adonis strayed,
And chaste Diana haunts the forest-shade.
Come, lovely nymph, and bless the silent hours,
When swains from shearing seek their nightly bowers
When weary reapers quit the sultry field,   65
And crowned with corn their thanks to Ceres yield.
This harmless grove no lurking viper hides,
But in my breast the serpent Love abides.
Here bees from blossoms sip the rosy dew,
But your Alexis knows no sweets but you.   70
Oh deign to visit our forsaken seats,
The mossy fountains, and the green retreats !
Where'er you walk, cool gales shall fan the glade ;
Trees, where you sit, shall crowd into a shade ;
Where'er you tread, the blushing flowers shall rise,   75
And all things flourish where you turn your eyes.
Oh ! how I long with you to pass my days,
Invoke the Muses, and resound your praise !
Your praise the birds shall chant in every grove,
And winds shall waft it to the powers above,   80
But would you sing, and rival Orpheus' strain,
The wond'ring forests soon should dance again ;
The moving mountains hear the powerful call,
And headlong streams hang listening in their fall !

But see, the shepherds shun the noonday heat,   85
The lowing herds to murm'ring brooks retreat,
To closer shades the panting flocks remove ;
Ye Gods ! and is there no relief for Love ?
But soon the sun with milder rays descends
To the cool ocean, where his journey ends.   90
On me love's fiercer flames for ever prey,
By night he scorches, as he burns by day.

AUTUMN:

THE THIRD PASTORAL, or HYLAS AND ÆGON

To Mr. Wycherley

BENEATH the shade a spreading Beech displays,
Hylas and Ægon sung their rural lays,
This mourned a faithless, that an absent Love,
And Delia's name and Doris' filled the Grove.
Ye Mantuan nymphs, your sacred succour bring ;　　5
Hylas and Ægon's rural lays I sing.
　Thou, whom the Nine with Plautus' wit inspire,
The art of Terence, and Menander's fire ;
Whose sense instructs us, and whose humour charms,
Whose judgment sways us, and whose spirit warms !　10
Oh, skilled in Nature ! see the hearts of Swains,
Their artless passions, and their tender pains.
　Now setting Phœbus shone serenely bright,

Thou, whom the Nine.—Mr. Wycherley, a famous author of comedies ;
of which the most celebrated were the *Plain-dealer* and *Country-Wife*.
He was a writer of infinite spirit, satire, and wit. The only objection
made to him was that he had too much. However, he was followed
in the same way by Mr. Congreve ; though with a little more correctness.
　The art of Terence, and Menander's fire.—This line evidently alludes
to that famous character given of Terence by Cæsar :
　　　Tu quoque, tu in summis, ô *dimidiate Menander*,
　　　Pomeris, et merito, puri sermonis amator ;
　　　Lenibus atque utinam scriptis adjuncta foret *vis Comica*.
So that the judicious critic sees he should have said—*with Menander's
fire*. For what the poet meant, in this line, was, that his friend had
joined to Terence's art what Cæsar thought wanting in Terence, namely
the *vis comica* of Menander. Besides,—*and Menander's fire* is making
that the characteristic of Menander which was not. His character
was the having art and *comic spirit* in perfect conjunction, of which
Terence having only the first, he is called the *half of Menander*.

17

And fleecy clouds were streaked with purple light ;
When tuneful Hylas with melodious moan,   15
Taught rocks to weep, and made the mountains groan.
    Go, gentle gales, and bear my sighs away !
To Delia's ear, the tender notes convey.
As some sad Turtle his lost love deplores,
And with deep murmurs fills the sounding shores ;   20
Thus, far from *Delia*, to the winds I mourn,
Alike unheard, unpitied, and forlorn.
    Go, gentle gales, and bear my sighs along !
For her, the feathered quires neglect their song ;
For her, the limes their pleasing shades deny ;   25
For her, the lilies hang their heads and die.
Ye flowers that droop, forsaken by the spring,
Ye birds that, left by summer, cease to sing,
Ye trees that fade when autumn-heats remove,
Say, is not absence death to those who love ?   30
    Go, gentle gales, and bear my sighs away !
Cursed be the fields that cause my Delia's stay ;
Fade every blossom, wither every tree,
Die every flower, and perish all, but she.
What have I said ? where'er my Delia flies,   35
Let spring attend, and sudden flowers arise ;
Let opening roses knotted oaks adorn,
And liquid amber drop from every thorn.
    Go, gentle gales, and bear my sighs along !
The birds shall cease to tune their evening song,   40
The winds to breathe, the waving woods to move,
And streams to murmur, e'er I cease to love.
Not bubbling fountains to the thirsty swain,
Not balmy sleep to lab'rers faint with pain,
Not showers to larks, nor sun-shine to the bee,   45
Are half so charming as thy sight to me.
    Go, gentle gales, and bear my sighs away !
Come, Delia, come ; ah, why this long delay ?
Through rocks and caves the name of Delia sounds,
Delia, each cave and echoing rock rebounds.   50
Ye powers, what pleasing frenzy soothes my mind !

Do lovers dream, or is my Delia kind ?
She comes, my Delia comes !—Now cease my lay,
And cease, ye gales, to bear my sighs away !
    Next Ægon sung, while Windsor groves admired :   55
Rehearse, ye Muses, what yourselves inspired.
    Resound, ye hills, resound my mournful strain !
Of perjured Doris, dying I complain :
Here where the mountains less'ning as they rise
Lose the low vales, and steal into the skies :   60
While lab'ring oxen, spent with toil and heat,
In their loose traces from the field retreat :
While curling smokes from village-tops are seen,
And the fleet shades glide o'er the dusky green.
    Resound, ye hills, resound my mournful lay !   65
Beneath yon' poplar oft we passed the day :
Oft on the rind I carved her am'rous vows,
While she with garlands hung the bending boughs :
The garlands fade, the vows are worn away ;
So dies her love, and so my hopes decay.   70
    Resound, ye hills, resound my mournful strain !
Now bright Arcturus glads the teeming grain,
Now golden fruits on loaded branches shine,
And grateful clusters swell with floods of wine ;
Now blushing berries paint the yellow grove ;   75
Just Gods ! shall all things yield returns but love ?
    Resound, ye hills, resound my mournful lay !
The shepherds cry, " Thy flocks are left a prey "—
Ah ! what avails it me, the flocks to keep,
Who lost my heart while I preserved my sheep.   80
Pan came, and asked, what magic caused my smart,
Or what ill eyes malignant glances dart ?
What eyes but hers, alas, have power to move !
And is there magic but what dwells in love ?
    Resound, ye hills, resound my mournful strains !   85
I'll fly from shepherds, flocks, and flowery plains.—
From shepherds, flocks, and plains, I may remove,
Forsake mankind, and all the world—but love !
I know thee, Love ! on foreign Mountains bred,

Wolves gave thee suck, and savage Tigers fed.   90
Thou wert from Ætna's burning entrails torn,
Got by fierce whirlwinds, and in thunder born !
    Resound, ye hills, resound my mournful lay !
Farewell, ye woods ! adieu the light of day !
One leap from yonder cliff shall end my pains,   95
No more, ye hills, no more resound my strains !
    Thus sung the shepherds till th' approach of night,
The skies yet blushing with departing light,
When falling dews with spangles decked the glade,
And the low sun had lengthened every shade.   100

   Departing light.—There is a little inaccuracy here ; the first line
makes the time after sunset ; the second, before.

WINTER:

THE FOURTH PASTORAL, or DAPHNE

To the Memory of Mrs. Tempest

LYCIDAS

THYRSIS, the music of that murm'ring spring,
Is not so mournful as the strains you sing.
Nor rivers winding through the vales below,
So sweetly warble, or so smoothly flow.
Now sleeping flocks on their soft fleeces lie,   5
The moon, serene in glory, mounts the sky,
While silent birds forget their tuneful lays,
Oh sing of Daphne's fate, and Daphne's praise !

THYRSIS

Behold the groves that shine with silver frost,
Their beauty withered, and their verdure lost.   10
Here shall I try the sweet Alexis' strain,
That called the list'ning Dryads to the plain ?
Thames heard the numbers as he flowed along,
And bade his willows learn the moving song.

Mrs. Tempest.—This lady was of an ancient family in Yorkshire, and particularly admired by the author's friend, Mr. Walsh, who, having celebrated her in a pastoral elegy, desired his friend to do the same, as appears from one of his letters, dated Sept. 9, 1706 : " Your last eclogue being on the same subject with mine on Mrs. Tempest's death, I should take it very kindly in you to give it a little turn as if it were to the memory of the same lady." Her death having happened on the night of the great storm in 1703, gave a propriety to this eclogue, which in its general turn alludes to it. The scene of the pastoral lies in a grove, the time at midnight.

LYCIDAS

So may kind rains their vital moisture yield,   **15**
And swell the future harvest of the field.
Begin ; this charge the dying Daphne gave,
And said : " Ye shepherds, sing around my grave !
Sing, while beside the shaded tomb I mourn,
And with fresh bays her rural shrine adorn."   20

THYRSIS

Ye gentle Muses, leave your crystal spring,
Let Nymphs and Sylvans cypress garlands bring ;
Ye weeping Loves, the stream with myrtles hide,
And break your bows, as when Adonis died ;
And with your golden darts, now useless grown,   25
Inscribe a verse on this relenting stone :
" Let nature change, let heaven and earth deplore,
Fair Daphne's dead, and love is now no more ! "
'Tis done, and nature's various charms decay,
See gloomy clouds obscure the cheerful day !   30
Now hung with pearls the dropping trees appear,
Their faded honours scattered on her bier.
See, where on earth the flowery glories lie,
With her they flourished, and with her they die.
Ah what avail the beauties nature wore ?   35
Fair Daphne's dead, and beauty is no more !
    For her the flocks refuse their verdant food,
Nor thirsty heifers seek the gliding flood.
The silver swans her hapless fate bemoan,
In notes more sad than when they sing their own ;   40
In hollow caves sweet Echo silent lies,
Silent, or only to her name replies ;
Her name with pleasure once she taught the shore,
Now Daphne's dead, and pleasure is no more !
    No grateful dews descend from evening skies,   45
Nor morning odours from the flowers arise ;
No rich perfumes refresh the fruitful field,

Nor fragrant herbs their native incense yield.
The balmy Zephyrs, silent since her death,
Lament the ceasing of a sweeter breath ;   50
Th' industrious bees neglect their golden store ;
Fair Daphne's dead, and sweetness is no more !
  No more the mounting larks, while Daphne sings,
Shall listening in mid air suspend their wings ;
No more the birds shall imitate her lays,   55
Or hushed with wonder, hearken from the sprays ;
No more the streams their murmur shall forbear,
A sweeter music than their own to hear,
But tell the reeds, and tell the vocal shore,
Fair Daphne's dead, and music is no more !   60
  Her fate is whispered by the gentle breeze,
And told in sighs to all the trembling trees ;
The trembling trees, in every plain and wood,
Her fate remurmur to the silver flood ;
The silver flood, so lately calm, appears   65
Swelled with new passion, and o'erflows with tears ;
The winds and trees and floods her death deplore,
Daphne, our grief ! our glory now no more !
  But see ! where Daphne wond'ring mounts on **high**
Above the clouds, above the starry sky   70
Eternal beauties grace the shining scene,
Fields ever fresh, and groves for ever green !
There while you rest in Amaranthine bowers,
Or from those meads select unfading flowers,
Behold us kindly, who your name implore,   75
Daphne, our Goddess, and our grief no more !

LYCIDAS

  How all things listen, while thy Muse complains !
Such silence waits on Philomela's strains,
In some still evening, when the whisp'ring breeze
Pants on the leaves, and dies upon the trees.   80

Lament the ceasing, etc.—" I wish that his fondness had not over-
looked a line in which the zephyrs are made to lament in silence."—
Johnson.

To thee, bright goddess, oft a lamb shall bleed,
If teeming ewes increase my fleecy breed.
While plants their shade, or flowers their odours give,
Thy name, thy honour, and thy praise shall live !

Thyrsis

But see, Orion sheds unwholesome dews,   85
Arise, the pines a noxious shade diffuse ;
Sharp Boreas blows, and Nature feels decay,
Time conquers all, and we must Time obey.
Adieu, ye vales, ye mountains, streams and groves,
Adieu, ye shepherd's rural lays and loves ;   9c
Adieu, my flocks, farewell ye sylvan crew,
Daphne, farewell, and all the world adieu !

MESSIAH:

A SACRED ECLOGUE

IN IMITATION OF VIRGIL'S "POLLIO"

ADVERTISEMENT

IN reading several passages of the Prophet Isaiah, which foretell the coming of Christ and the felicities attending it, I could not but observe a remarkable parity between many of the thoughts, and those in the *Pollio* of Virgil. This will not seem surprising, when we reflect, that the Eclogue was taken from a Sibylline prophecy on the same subject. One may judge that Virgil did not copy it line by line, but made use of such ideas as best agreed with the nature of pastoral poetry, and disposed them in that manner which served most to beautify his piece. I have endeavoured the same in this imitation of him, though without admitting any thing of my own; since it was written with this particular view, that the reader, by comparing the several thoughts, might see how far the images and descriptions of the Prophet are superior to those of the Poet. But as I fear I have prejudiced them by my management, I shall subjoin the passages of Isaiah, and those of Virgil, under the same disadvantage of a literal translation.

YE Nymphs of Solyma! begin the song:
To heavenly themes sublimer strains belong.
The mossy fountains, and the sylvan shades,
The dreams of Pindus and th' Aonian maids,
Delight no more—O thou my voice inspire   5

Who touched Isaiah's hallowed lips with fire !
   Rapt into future times, the Bard begun :
A Virgin shall conceive, a Virgin bear a Son !
From Jesse's root behold a branch arise,
Whose sacred flower with fragrance fills the skies :   10
Th' Æthereal spirit o'er its leaves shall move,
And on its top descends the mystic Dove.
Ye Heavens ! from high the dewy nectar pour,
And in soft silence shed the kindly shower !
The sick and weak the healing plant shall aid,   15
From storms a shelter, and from heat a shade.
All crimes shall cease, and ancient fraud shall fail ;
Returning Justice lift aloft her scale ;
Peace o'er the World her olive wand extend,
And white-robed Innocence from heaven descend.   20
Swift fly the years, and rise th' expected morn !
Oh spring to light, auspicious Babe, be born !
See Nature hastes her earliest wreaths to bring,
With all the incense of the breathing spring :
See lofty Lebanon his head advance,   25
See nodding forests on the mountains dance :
See spicy clouds from lowly Saron rise,
And Carmel's flowery top perfumes the skies !
Hark ! a glad voice the lonely desert cheers ;
Prepare the way ! a God, a God appears :   30
A God, a God ! the vocal hills reply,
The rocks proclaim th' approaching Deity.
Lo, earth receives him from the bending skies !
Sink down ye mountains, and ye valleys rise,
With heads declined, ye cedars homage pay ;   35
Be smooth ye rocks, ye rapid floods give way !
The Saviour comes ! by ancient bards foretold :
Hear him, ye deaf, and all ye blind, behold !
He from thick films shall purge the visual ray,
And on the sightless eye-ball pour the day :   40

He from thick films shall purge the visual ray.—The sense and language show that, by *visual ray*, the poet meant the *sight*, or, as Milton calls it, *the visual nerve.*

'Tis he th' obstructed paths of sound shall clear,
And bid new music charm th' unfolding ear :
The dumb shall sing, the lame his crutch forego,
And leap exulting like the bounding roe.
No sigh, no murmur the wide world shall hear,   45
From every face he wipes off every tear.
In adamantine chains shall Death be bound,
And Hell's grim Tyrant feel th' eternal wound.
As the good shepherd tends his fleecy care,
Seeks freshest pasture and the purest air,   50
Explores the lost, the wand'ring sheep directs,
By day o'ersees them, and by night protects,
The tender lambs he raises in his arms,
Feeds from his hand, and in his bosom warms ;
Thus shall mankind his guardian care engage,   55
The promised father of the future age.
No more shall nation against nation rise,
Nor ardent warriors meet with hateful eyes,
Nor fields with gleaming steel be covered o'er,
The brazen trumpets kindle rage no more ;   60
But useless lances into scythes shall bend,
And the broad falchion in a plough-share end.
Then palaces shall rise ; the joyful Son
Shall finish what his short-lived Sire begun ;
Their vines a shadow to their race shall yield,   65
And the same hand that sowed, shall reap the field.
The swain in barren deserts with surprise
See lilies spring, and sudden verdure rise ;
And starts, amidst the thirsty wilds to hear
New falls of water murm'ring in his ear.   70
On rifted rocks, the dragon's late abodes,
The green reed trembles, and the bulrush nods.
Waste sandy valleys, once perplexed with thorn,
The spiry fir and shapely box adorn :
To leafless shrubs the flowering palms succeed,   75
And od'rous myrtle to the noisome weed.
The lambs with wolves shall graze the verdant mead,
And boys in flowery bands the tiger lead ;

The steer and lion at one crib shall meet,
And harmless serpents lick the pilgrim's feet.   80
The smiling infant in his hand shall take
The crested basilisk and speckled snake,
Pleased the green lustre of the scales survey,
And with their forky tongues shall innocently play.
Rise, crowned with light, imperial Salem, rise !   85
Exalt thy towery head, and lift thy eyes !
See, a long race thy spacious courts adorn ;
See future sons, and daughters yet unborn,
In crowding ranks on every side arise,
Demanding life, impatient for the skies !   90
See barb'rous nations at thy gates attend,
Walk in thy light, and in thy temple bend ;
See thy bright altars thronged with prostrate kings,
And heaped with products of Sabæan springs !
For thee Idume's spicy forests blow,   95
And seeds of gold in Ophir's mountains glow.
See heaven its sparkling portals wide display,
And break upon thee in a flood of day !
No more the rising Sun shall gild the morn,
Nor evening Cynthia fill her silver horn ;   100
But lost, dissolved in thy superior rays,
One tide of glory, one unclouded blaze
O'erflow thy courts : the light himself shall shine
Revealed, and God's eternal day be thine !
The seas shall waste, the skies in smoke decay,   105
Rocks fall to dust, and mountains melt away ;
But fixed his word, his saving power remains ;—
Thy realm for ever lasts, thy own MESSIAH reigns !

IMITATIONS

A virgin shall conceive—All crimes shall cease, etc.
   Virg. *E.* iv. 6.
      " Jam redit et Virgo, redeunt Saturnia regna ;
      Jam nova progenies cælo demittitur alto.
      Te duce, si qua manent sceleris vestigia nostri,
      Irrita perpetua solvent formidine terras—
      Pacatumque reget patriis virtutibus orbem."

" Now the virgin returns, now the kingdom of Saturn returns, now a new progeny is sent down from high heaven. By means of thee, whatever reliques of our crimes remain, shall be wiped away, and free the world from perpetual fears. He shall govern the earth in peace, with the virtues of his father."

Isaiah, ch. vii. 14.—" Behold a virgin shall conceive and bear a son." Ch. ix. v. 6, 7.—" Unto us a child is born, unto us a Son is given ; the Prince of Peace : of the increase of his government, and of his peace, there shall be no end : Upon the throne of David, and upon his kingdom, to order and to establish it, with judgment, and with justice, for ever and ever."

See Nature hastes, etc.
    Virg. *E.* iv. 18.

> " At tibi prima, puer, nullo munuscula cultu,
> Errantes hederas passim cum baccare tellus,
> Mixtaque ridenti colocasia fundet acantho—
> Ipsa tibi, blandos fundent cunabula flores."

" For thee, O child, shall the earth, without being tilled, produce her early offerings ; winding ivy, mixed with Baccar, and Colocasia with smiling Acanthus. Thy cradle shall pour forth pleasing flowers about thee."

Isaiah, ch. xxxv. 1.—" The wilderness and the solitary place shall be glad, and the desart shall rejoice and blossom as the rose." Ch. lx. 13. —" The glory of Lebanon shall come unto thee, the fir-tree, the pine-tree, and the box together, to beautify the place of thy sanctuary."

Hark ! a glad voice, etc.
    Virg. *E.* iv. v. 46.

> " Aggredere o magnos, aderit jam tempus, honores,
> Cara deum soboles, magnum Jovis incrementum—
> Ipsi lætitia voces ad sydera jactant
> Intonsi montes, ipsæ jam carmina rupes,
> Ipsa sonant arbusta, Deus, deus ille Menalca ! "
>
> *E.* v. v. 62.

" Oh come and receive the mighty honours : the time draws nigh, O beloved offspring of the gods, O great encrease of Jove ! The uncultivated mountains send shouts of joy to the stars, the very rocks sing in verse, the very shrubs cry out, A god, a god ! "

Isaiah, ch. xl. 3, 4.—" The voice of him that crieth in the wilderness, Prepare ye the way of the Lord ! make strait in the desart a high way for our God ! Every valley shall be exalted, and every mountain and hill shall be made low, and the crooked shall be made strait, and the rough places plain." Ch. xliv. 23.—" Break forth into singing, ye mountains ! O forest, and every tree therein ! for the Lord hath redeemed Israel."

The swain in barren deserts, etc.
    Virg. *E.* iv. v. 28.

> " Molli paulatim flavescet campus arista,
> Incultisque rubens pendebit sentibus uva,
> Et duræ quercus sudabunt roscida mella."

" The fields shall grow yellow with ripen'd ears, and the red grape shall hang upon the wild brambles, and the hard oaks shall distill honey like dew."

Isaiah, ch. xxxv. 7.—" The parched ground shall become a pool, and the thirsty land springs of water : In the habitations where dragons lay, shall be grass, and reeds, and rushes." Ch. lv. 13.—" Instead of the thorn shall come up the fir-tree, and instead of the briar shall come up the myrtle-tree."

The lambs with wolves, etc.

Virg. *E.* iv. v. 21.

" Ipsæ lacte domum referent distenta capellæ
Ubera, nec magnos metuent armenta leones—
Occidet et serpens, et fallax herba veneni
Occidet.'—

" The goats shall bear to the fold their udders distended with milk ; nor shall the herds be afraid of the greatest lions.   The serpent shall die, and the herb that conceals poison shall die."

Isaiah, ch. xi. 6, etc.—" The wolf shall dwell with the lamb, and the leopard shall lie down with the kid, and the calf and the young lion and the fatling together : and a little child shall lead them.—And the lion shall eat straw like the ox.   And the sucking child shall play on the hole of the asp, and the weaned child shall put his hand on the den of the cockatrice."

Rise, crowned with light, imperial Salem, rise !—The thoughts of Isaiah, which compose the latter part of the poem, are wonderfully elevated, and much above those general exclamations of Virgil, which make the loftiest parts of his *Pollio.*

" Magnus ab integro sæclorum nascitur ordo !
—toto surget gens aurea mundo !
—incipient magni procedere menses !
Aspice, venturo lætentur ut omnia sæclo ! " etc.

The reader needs only to turn to the passages of Isaiah, here cited. [Cited at bottom of text.]

WINDSOR FOREST

To the Right Honourable George,
Lord Lansdown

Non injussa cano : Te nostræ, *Vare*, myricæ,
Te *Nemus* omne canet ; nec Phœbo gratior ulla est
Quam sibi quæ *Vari* præscripsit pagina nomen.
Virg. Ecl. vi. 10–12.

Thy forests, Windsor ! and thy green retreats,
At once the Monarch's and the Muse's seats,
Invite my lays. Be present, sylvan maids !
Unlock your springs, and open all your shades.
Granville commands ; your aid, O Muses, bring !   5
What Muse for Granville can refuse to sing ?
The Groves of Eden, vanished now so long,
Live in description, and look green in song :
These, were my breast inspired with equal flame,
Like them in beauty, should be like in fame.   10
Here hills and vales, the woodland and the plain,
Here earth and water seem to strive again ;
Not Chaos-like together crushed and bruised,
But, as the world, harmoniously confused :
Where order in variety we see,   15
And where, though all things differ, all agree.
Here waving groves a chequered scene display,
And part admit, and part exclude the day ;
As some coy nymph her lover's warm address
Nor quite indulges, nor can quite repress.   20

Windsor Forest.—This poem was written at two different times:
the first part of it, which relates to the country, in the year 1704, at
the same time with the Pastorals; the latter part was not added till
the year 1713, in which it was published.

There, interspersed in lawns and opening glades,
Thin trees arise that shun each other's shades.
Here in full light the russet plains extend :
There wrapt in clouds the blueish hills ascend.
Even the wild heath displays her purple dyes,   25
And 'midst the desert fruitful fields arise,
That crowned with tufted trees and springing corn,
Like verdant isles the sable waste adorn.
Let India boast her plants, nor envy we
The weeping amber or the balmy tree,   30
While by our oaks the precious loads are born,
And realms commanded which those trees adorn.
Not proud Olympus yields a nobler sight,
Though gods assembled grace his tow'ring height,
Than what more humble mountains offer here,   35
Where, in their blessings, all those gods appear.
See Pan with flocks, with fruits Pomona crowned,
Here blushing Flora paints th' enamelled ground,
Here Ceres' gifts in waving prospect stand,
And nodding tempt the joyful reaper's hand ;   40
Rich Industry sits smiling on the plains,
And peace and plenty tell, a STUART reigns.
    Not thus the land appeared in ages past,
A dreary desert, and a gloomy waste,
To savage beasts and savage laws a prey,   45
And kings more furious and severe than they ;
Who claimed the skies, dispeopled air and floods,
The lonely lords of empty wilds and woods :
Cities laid waste, they stormed the dens and caves,
(For wiser brutes were backward to be slaves :)   50
What could be free, when lawless beasts obeyed,
And even the elements a tyrant swayed ?
In vain kind seasons swelled the teeming grain,
Soft showers distilled, and suns grew warm in vain ;
The swain with tears his frustrate labour yields,   55
And famished dies amidst his ripened fields.
What wonder then, a beast or subject slain
Were equal crimes in a despotic reign ?

Both doomed alike, for sportive Tyrants bled,
But while the subject starved, the beast was fed.   60
Proud Nimrod first the bloody chase began,
A mighty hunter, and his prey was man :
Our haughty Norman boasts that barb'rous name,
And makes his trembling slaves the royal game.
The fields are ravished from th' industrious swains, 65
From men their cities, and from Gods their fanes :
The levelled towns with weeds lie covered o'er ;
The hollow winds through naked temples roar ;
Round broken columns clasping ivy twined ;
O'er heaps of ruin stalked the stately hind ;   70
The fox obscene to gaping tombs retires,
And savage howlings fill the sacred quires.
Awed by his Nobles, by his Commons curst,
Th' Oppressor ruled tyrannic where he durst,
Stretched o'er the Poor and Church his iron rod,   75
And served alike his Vassals and his God.
Whom even the Saxon spared and bloody Dane,
The wanton victims of his sport remain.
But see, the man who spacious regions gave
A waste for beasts, himself denied a grave !   80
Stretched on the lawn his second hope survey,
At once the chaser, and at once the prey :
Lo Rufus, tugging at the deadly dart,
Bleeds in the Forest like a wounded hart.
Succeeding monarchs heard the subjects' cries,   85
Nor saw displeased the peaceful cottage rise.
Then gathering flocks on unknown mountains fed,
O'er sandy wilds were yellow harvests spread,
The forests wondered at th' unusual grain,

The fields are ravished, etc.—Alluding to the destruction made in the New Forest, and the tyrannies exercised there by William I.

Himself denied a grave !—The place of his interment at Caen in Normandy was claimed by a gentleman as his inheritance, the moment William's servants were going to put him in his tomb : so that they were obliged to compound with the owner before they could perform the king's obsequies.

Bleeds in the Forest.—The oak under which Rufus was shot was standing till within a few years.

2

And secret transport touched the conscious swain.   90
Fair Liberty, Britannia's Goddess, rears
Her cheerful head, and leads the golden years.
  Ye vig'rous swains ! while youth ferments your blcod,
And purer spirits swell the sprightly flood,
Now range the hills, the gameful woods beset,   95
Wind the shrill horn, or spread the waving net.
When milder autumn summer's heat succeeds,
And in the new-shorn field the partridge feeds,
Before his lord the ready spaniel bounds,
Panting with hope, he tries the furrowed grounds ;   100
But when the tainted gales the game betray,
Couched close he lies, and meditates the prey :
Secure they trust th' unfaithful field beset,
'Till hovering o'er 'em sweeps the swelling net.
Thus (if small things we may with great compare)   105
When Albion sends her eager sons to war,
Some thoughtless Town, with ease and plenty blest,
Near, and more near, the closing lines invest ;
Sudden they seize th' amazed, defenceless prize,
And high in air Britannia's standard flies.   110
  See ! from the brake the whirring pheasant springs,
And mounts exulting on triumphant wings :
Short is his joy ; he feels the fiery wound,
Flutters in blood, and panting beats the ground.
Ah ! what avail his glossy, varying dyes,   115
His purple crest, and scarlet-circled eyes,
The vivid green his shining plumes unfold,
His painted wings, and breast that flames with gold ?
  Nor yet, when moist Arcturus clouds the sky,
The woods and fields their pleasing toils deny.   120
To plains with well-breathed beagles we repair,
And trace the mazes of the circling hare :
(Beasts, urged by us, their fellow-beasts pursue,
And learn of man each other to undo).
With slaught'ring guns th' unwearied fowler roves,   125
When frosts have whitened all the naked groves ;
Where doves in flocks the leafless trees o'ershade,

And lonely woodcocks haunt the watery glade.
He lifts the tube, and levels with his eye ;
Straight a short thunder breaks the frozen sky :   130
Oft, as in airy rings they skim the heath,
The clam'rous lapwings feel the leaden death :
Oft, as the mounting larks their notes prepare,
They fall, and leave their little lives in air.

  In genial spring, beneath the quiv'ring shade,   135
Where cooling vapours breathe along the mead,
The patient fisher takes his silent stand,
Intent, his angle trembling in his hand :
With looks unmoved, he hopes the scaly breed,
And eyes the dancing cork, and bending reed.   140
Our plenteous streams a various race supply,
The bright-eyed perch with fins of Tyrian dye,
The silver eel, in shining volumes rolled,
The yellow carp, in scales bedropped with gold,
Swift trouts, diversified with crimson stains,   145
And pikes, the tyrants of the watery plains.

  Now Cancer glows with Phœbus' fiery car :
The youth rush eager to the sylvan war,
Swarm o'er the lawns, the forest walks surround,
Rouse the fleet hart, and cheer the opening hound.   150
Th' impatient courser pants in every vein,
And, pawing, seems to beat the distant plain :
Hills, vales, and floods appear already crossed,
And ere he starts, a thousand steps are lost.
See the bold youth strain up the threat'ning steep,   155
Rush through the thickets, down the valleys sweep,
Hang o'er their coursers' heads wit' eager speed,
And earth rolls back beneath the flying steed.
Let old Arcadia boast her ample plain,
Th' immortal huntress, and her virgin train ;   160
Nor envy, Windsor ! since thy shades have seen
As bright a Goddess, and as chaste a Queen ;
Whose care, like hers, protects the sylvan reign,

Chaste a Queen.—Queen Anne.

The Earth's fair light, and Empress of the main.
   Here too, 'tis sung, of old Diana strayed,   165
And Cynthus' top forsook for Windsor shade :
Here was she seen o'er airy wastes to rove,
Seek the clear spring, or haunt the pathless grove :
Here armed with silver bows, in early dawn,
Her buskined Virgins traced the dewy lawn.   170
   Above the rest a rural nymph was famed,
Thy offspring, Thames ! the fair Lodona named ;
(Lodona's fate, in long oblivion cast,
The Muse shall sing, and what she sings shall last).
Scarce could the Goddess from her nymph be known,
But by the crescent and the golden zone.   176
She scorned the praise of beauty, and the care ;
A belt her waist, a fillet binds her hair ;
A painted quiver on her shoulder sounds,
And with her dart the flying deer she wounds.   180
It chanced, as eager of the chase, the maid
Beyond the forest's verdant limits strayed,
Pan saw and loved, and, burning with desire,
Pursued her flight ; her flight increased his fire.
Not half so swift the trembling doves can fly,   185
When the fierce eagle cleaves the liquid sky ;
Not half so swiftly the fierce eagle moves,
When through the clouds he drives the trembling doves ;
As from the god she flew with furious pace,
Or as the god, more furious, urged the chase.   190
Now fainting, sinking, pale, the nymph appears ;
Now close behind, his sounding steps she hears :
And now his shadow reached her as she run,
His shadow lengthened by the setting sun ;
And now his shorter breath, with sultry air,   195
Pants on her neck, and fans her parting hair.
In vain on father Thames she calls for aid,
Nor could Diana help her injured maid.
Faint, breathless, thus she prayed, nor prayed in vain ;
" Ah, Cynthia ! ah—though banished from thy train,
Let me, O let me, to the shades repair,   201

My native shades—there weep, and murmur there."
She said, and melting as in tears she lay,
In a soft, silver stream dissolved away.
The silver stream her virgin coldness keeps,   205
For ever murmurs, and for ever weeps ;
Still bears the name the hapless virgin bore,
And bathes the forest where she ranged before.
In her chaste current oft the goddess laves,
And with celestial tears augments the waves.   210
Oft in her glass the musing shepherd spies
The headlong mountains and the downward skies
The watery landscape of the pendant woods,
And absent trees that tremble in the floods ;
In the clear azure gleam the flocks are seen,   215
And floating forests paint the waves with green,
Through the fair scene roll slow the ling'ring streams,
Then foaming pour along, and rush into the Thames.
   Thou, too, great father of the British floods !
With joyful pride survey'st our lofty woods ;   220
Where tow'ring oaks their growing honours rear,
And future navies on thy shores appear.
Not Neptune's self from all her streams receives
A wealthier tribute than to thine he gives.
No seas so rich, so gay no banks appear,   225
No lake so gentle, and no spring so clear.
Nor Po so swells the fabling Poet's lays,
While led along the skies his current strays,
As thine, which visits Windsor's famed abodes,
To grace the mansion of our earthly gods :   230
Nor all his stars above a lustre show,
Like the bright Beauties on thy banks below,
Where Jove, subdued by mortal Passion still,
Might change Olympus for a nobler hill.
   Happy the man whom this bright court approves, 235
His Sovereign favours, and his Country loves :
Happy next him, who to these shades retires,

Still bears the name.—The river Loddon.

Whom Nature charms, and whom the Muse inspires :
Whom humbler joys of home-felt quiet please,
Successive study, exercise, and ease.   240
He gathers health from herbs the forest yields,
And of their fragrant physic spoils the fields :
With chymic art exalts the mineral powers,
And draws the aromatic souls of flowers :
Now marks the course of rolling orbs on high ;   245
O'er figured worlds now travels with his eye ;
Of ancient writ unlocks the learnèd store,
Consults the dead, and lives past ages o'er :
Or wand'ring thoughtful in the silent wood,
Attends the duties of the wise and good,   250
T' observe a mean, be to himself a friend,
To follow nature, and regard his end ;
Or looks on heaven with more than mortal eyes,
Bids his free soul expatiate in the skies,
Amid her kindred stars familiar roam,   255
Survey the region, and confess her home !
Such was the life great Scipio once admired :—
Thus Atticus, and Trumbal thus retired.
    Ye sacred Nine ! that all my soul possess,
Whose raptures fire me, and whose visions bless,   260
Bear me, O bear me to sequestered scenes,
The bowery mazes, and surrounding greens :
To Thames's banks, which fragrant breezes fill,
Or where ye Muses sport on Cooper's Hill.
(On Cooper's Hill eternal wreaths shall grow,   265
While lasts the mountain, or while Thames shall flow.)
I seem through consecrated walks to rove,
I hear soft music die along the grove :
Led by the sound, I roam from shade to shade,
By god-like Poets venerable made :   270
Here his first lays majestic Denham sung ;
There the last numbers flowed from Cowley's tongue.

    There the last numbers flowed from Cowley's tongue.—Mr. Cowley died
at Chertsey, on the borders of the Forest, and was from thence conveyed to Westminster

Oh early lost ! what tears the river shed,
When the sad pomp along his banks was led ?
His drooping swans on every note expire,   275
And on his willows hung each muse's lyre.
   Since fate relentless stopped their heavenly voice,
No more the forests ring, or groves rejoice ;
Who now shall charm the shades where Cowley strung
His living harp, and lofty Denham sung ?   280
But hark ! the groves rejoice, the forest rings !
Are these revived ? or is it Granville sings ?
'Tis yours, my Lord, to bless our soft retreats,
And call the Muses to their ancient seats ;
To paint anew the flowery sylvan scenes,   285
To crown the forests with immortal greens,
Make Windsor-hills in lofty numbers rise,
And lift her turrets nearer to the skies ;
To sing those honours you deserve to wear,
And add new lustre to her silver star !   290
   Here noble Surrey felt the sacred rage,
Surrey, the Granville of a former age :
Matchless his pen, victorious was his lance,
Bold in the lists, and graceful in the dance :
In the same shades the Cupids tuned his lyre,   295
To the same notes, of love, and soft desire :
Fair Geraldine, bright object of his vow,
Then filled the groves, as heavenly Mira now.
   Oh wouldst thou sing what heroes Windsor bore,
What Kings first breathed upon her winding shore,   300
Or raise old warriors, whose adored remains
In weeping vaults her hallowed earth contains !
With Edward's acts adorn the shining page,
Stretch his long triumphs down through every age,

Here noble Surrey.—Henry Howard, Earl of Surrey, one of the first
refiners of the English poetry ; who flourished in the time of Henry
VIII.

Heavenly Mira.—The Mira of Granville was the Countess of New-
burgh. Towards the end of her life Dr. King, of Oxford, wrote a very
severe satire against her, in three books, 4to, called *The Toast.*

Edward's acts.—Edward III. born here.

Draw monarchs chained, and Cressi's glorious field, 305
The lilies blazing on the regal shield :
Then, from her roofs when Verrio's colours fall,
And leave inanimate the naked wall ;
Still in thy song should vanquished France appear,
And bleed for ever under Britain's spear. 310
    Let softer strains ill-fated Henry mourn,
And palms eternal flourish round his urn.
Here o'er the martyr-king the marble weeps,
And, fast beside him, once-feared Edward sleeps :
Whom not th' extended Albion could contain, 315
From old Belerium to the northern main,
The grave unites ; where e'en the great find rest,
And blended lie th' oppressor and th' opprest !
    Make sacred Charles's tomb for ever known
(Obscure the place, and uninscribed the stone), 320
Oh fact accurst ! what tears has Albion shed,
Heavens, what new wounds ! and how her old have bled !
She saw her sons with purple deaths expire,
Her sacred domes involved in rolling fire,
A dreadful series of intestine wars, 325
Inglorious triumphs and dishonest scars.
At length great Anna said, " Let Discord cease ! "
She said ! the world obeyed, and all was Peace !
    In that blest moment from his oozy bed
Old father Thames advanced his rev'rend head. 330
His tresses dropped with dews, and o'er the stream
His shining horns diffused a golden gleam :
Graved on his urn appeared the moon, that guides
His swelling waters and alternate tides ;
The figured streams in waves of silver rolled, 335
And on their banks Augusta rose in gold.
Around his throne the sea-born brothers stood,
Who swell with tributary urns his flood ;
First the famed authors of his ancient name,
The winding Isis, and the fruitful Thame . 340

Henry mourn.—Henry VI.
Once-feared Edward sleeps.—Edward IV.

The Kennet swift, for silver eels renowned ;
The Loddon slow, with verdant alders crowned ;
Cole, whose dark streams his flowery islands lave ;
And chalky Wey, that rolls a milky wave :
The blue, transparent Vandalis appears ;   345
The gulfy Lee his sedgy tresses rears ;
And sullen Mole, that hides his diving flood ;
And silent Darent, stained with Danish blood.

  High in the midst, upon his urn reclined
(His sea-green mantle waving with the wind),   350
The god appeared : he turned his azure eyes
Where Windsor-domes and pompous turrets rise ;
Then bowed and spoke ; the winds forget to roar,
And the hushed waves glide softly to the shore.

  Hail, sacred peace ! hail, long-expected days,   355
That Thames's glory to the stars shall raise !
Though Tiber's streams immortal Rome behold,
Though foaming Hermus swells with tides of gold,
From heaven itself though sevenfold Nilus flows,
And harvests on a hundred realms bestows ;   360
These now no more shall be the Muse's themes,
Lost in my fame, as in the sea their streams.
Let Volga's banks with iron squadrons shine,
And groves of lances glitter on the Rhine,
Let barb'rous Ganges arm a servile train ;   365
Be mine the blessings of a peaceful reign.
No more my sons shall dye with British blood
Red Iber's sands, or Ister's foaming flood :
Safe on my shore each unmolested swain
Shall tend the flocks, or reap the bearded grain ;   370
The shady empire shall retain no trace
Of war or blood, but in the sylvan chase ;
The trumpet sleep, while cheerful horns are blown,
And arms employed on birds and beasts alone.
Behold ! th' ascending Villas on my side   375

  His diving flood.—The Mole sinks through its sands, in dry summers,
into an invisible channel underground at Mickleham, near Dorking,
Surrey.

2 a

Project long shadows o'er the crystal tide.
Behold ! Augusta's glitt'ring spires increase,
And Temples rise, the beauteous works of Peace.
I see, I see, where two fair cities bend
Their ample bow, a new Whitehall ascend !   380
There mighty Nations shall inquire their doom,
The World's great Oracle in times to come ;
There Kings shall sue, and suppliant States be seen
Once more to bend before a BRITISH QUEEN.

Thy trees, fair Windsor ! now shall leave their woods,
And half thy forests rush into thy floods,   386
Bear Britain's thunder, and her Cross display,
To the bright regions of the rising day ;
Tempt icy seas, where scarce the waters roll,
Where clearer flames glow round the frozen Pole :   390
Or under southern skies exalt their sails,
Led by new stars, and borne by spicy gales !
For me the balm shall bleed, and amber flow,
The coral redden, and the ruby glow,
The pearly shell its lucid globe infold,   395
And Phœbus warm the ripening ore to gold.
The time shall come, when, free as seas or wind,
Unbounded Thames shall flow for all mankind,
Whole nations enter with each swelling tide,
And seas but join the regions they divide ;   400
Earth's distant ends our glory shall behold,
And the new world launch forth to seek the old.
Then ships of uncouth form shall stem the tide,
And feathered people crowd my wealthy side,
And naked youths and painted chiefs admire   405
Our speech, our colour, and our strange attire !
O stretch thy reign, fair Peace ! from shore to shore,
Till Conquest cease, and Slavery be no more ;
Till the freed Indians in their native groves
Reap their own fruits, and woo their sable loves,   410

And Temples rise.—The fifty new churches.
Unbounded Thames, etc.—A wish that London may be made a free
port.

Peru once more a race of kings behold,
And other Mexico's be roofed with gold.
Exiled by thee from earth to deepest hell,
In brazen bonds shall barb'rous Discord dwell ;
Gigantic Pride, pale Terror, gloomy Care,   415
And mad Ambition, shall attend her there :
There purple Vengeance bathed in gore retires,
Her weapons blunted, and extinct her fires :
There hateful Envy her own snakes shall feel,
And Persecution mourn her broken wheel :   420
There Faction roar, Rebellion bite her chain,
And gasping Furies thirst for blood in vain.
    Here cease thy flight, nor with unhallowed lays
Touch the fair fame of Albion's golden days :
The thoughts of gods let Granville's verse recite, 425
And bring the scenes of opening fate to light.
My humble Muse, in unambitious strains,
Paints the green forests and the flowery plains,
Where Peace descending bids her olives spring,
And scatters blessings from her dovelike wing. 430
Even I more sweetly pass my careless days,
Pleased in the silent shade with empty praise ;
Enough for me, that to the list'ning swains
First in these fields I sung the sylvan strains.

ODE ON ST. CECILIA'S DAY

[MDCCVIII]

I

DESCEND, ye Nine ! descend and sing ;
The breathing instruments inspire,
Wake into voice each silent string,
And sweep the sounding lyre !
 In a sadly-pleasing strain
 Let the warbling lute complain :   5
  Let the loud trumpet sound,
  Till the roofs all around
  The shrill echoes rebound :
While in more lengthened notes and slow,   10
The deep, majestic, solemn organs blow.
 Hark ! the numbers soft and clear,
 Gently steal upon the ear ;
 Now louder, and yet louder rise
 And fill with spreading sounds the skies ;   15
Exulting in triumph now swell the bold notes,
In broken air, trembling, the wild music floats ;
 Till, by degrees, remote and small,
  The strains decay,
  And melt away,   20
 In a dying, dying fall.

II

By Music, minds an equal temper know,
 Nor swell too high, nor sink too low.
If in the breast tumultuous joys arise,
Music her soft, assuasive voice applies ;   25

44

Or when the soul is pressed with cares,
   Exalts her in enlivening airs.
Warriors she fires with animated sounds ;
Pours balm into the bleeding lover's wounds :
   Melancholy lifts her head,   30
   Morpheus rouses from his bed,
   Sloth unfolds her arms and wakes,
   Listening Envy drops her snakes ;
Intestine war no more our Passions wage,
And giddy Factions hear away their rage.   35

III

But when our Country's cause provokes to Arms,
How martial music every bosom warms !
So when the first bold vessel dared the seas,
High on the stern the Thracian raised his strain,
   While Argo saw her kindred trees   40
   Descend from Pelion to the main.
   Transported demi-gods stood round,
  And men grew heroes at the sound,
   Enflamed with glory's charms :
Each chief his sevenfold shield displayed,   45
And half unsheathed the shining blade :
And seas, and rocks, and skies rebound,
To arms, to arms, to arms !

IV

But when through all th' infernal bounds,
Which flaming Phlegethon surrounds,   50
   Love, strong as Death, the Poet led
   To the pale nations of the dead,

Transported demi-gods, etc.—Few images in any poet, ancient or modern, are more striking than that in Apollonius, where he says that when the *Argo* was sailing near the coast where the Centaur Chiron dwelt, he came down to the very margin of the sea, bringing his wife with the young Achilles in her arms, that he might show the child to his father Peleus, who was on his voyage with the other Argonauts.— Apollon. *Rhod.* v. 553.

What sounds were heard,
What scenes appeared,
  O'er all the dreary coasts !   55
    Dreadful gleams,
    Dismal screams,
    Fires that glow,
    Shrieks of woe,
    Sullen moans,   60
    Hollow groans,
  And cries of tortured ghosts !
But hark ! he strikes the golden lyre ;
And see ! the tortured ghosts respire,
  See, shady forms advance !   65
  Thy stone, O Sisyphus, stands still,
  Ixion rests upon his wheel,
    And the pale spectres dance !
The Furies sink upon their iron beds,
And snakes uncurled hang list'ning round their
      heads.   70

v

  By the streams that ever flow,
  By the fragrant winds that blow
    O'er th' Elysian flowers ;
  By those happy souls who dwell
  In yellow meads of Asphodel,   75
    Or Amaranthine bowers ;
  By the heroes armèd shades,
  Glitt'ring through the gloomy glades,
  By the youths that died for love,
  Wand'ring in the myrtle grove,   80
Restore, restore Eurydice to life :
Oh take the husband, or return the wife !
  He sung, and hell consented
    To hear the Poet's prayer :
  Stern Proserpine relented,   85
    And gave him back the fair.
    Thus song could prevail

O'er death, and o'er hell,
A conquest how hard and how glorious !
  Though fate had fast bound her   90
  With Styx nine times round her,
Yet music and love were victorious.

VI

But soon, too soon, the lover turns his eyes :
Again she falls, again she dies, she dies !
How wilt thou now the fatal sisters move ?   95
No crime was thine, if 'tis no crime to love.
  Now under hanging mountains,
  Beside the fall of fountains,
  Or where Hebrus wanders,
  Rolling in Mæanders,   100
    All alone,
    Unheard, unknown,
    He makes his moan ;
    And calls her ghost,
    For ever, ever, ever lost !   105
  Now with Furies surrounded,
  Despairing, confounded,
  He trembles, he glows,
  Amidst Rhodope's snows ;
See, wild as the winds, o'er the desert he flies ;   110
Hark ! Hæmus resounds with the Bacchanals' cries—
    Ah see, he dies !
Yet even in death Eurydice he sung,
Eurydice still trembled on his tongue,
    Eurydice the woods,   115
    Eurydice the floods,
Eurydice the rocks, and hollow mountains rung.

VII

  Music the fiercest grief can charm,
  And fate's severest rage disarm :

Music can soften pain to ease,   120
  And make despair and madness please :
    Our joys below it can improve,
    And antedate the bliss above.
  This the divine Cecilia found,
And to her Maker's praise confined the sound.   125
When the full organ joins the tuneful quire,
  Th' immortal powers incline their ear,
Borne on the swelling notes our souls aspire,
While solemn airs improve the sacred fire ;
  And Angels lean from heaven to hear.   130
Of Orpheus now no more let Poets tell,
To bright Cecilia greater power is given ;
  His numbers raised a shade from hell,
    Hers lift the soul to heaven.

ODE ON SOLITUDE

HAPPY the man whose wish and care
    A few paternal acres bound,
Content to breathe his native air,
            In his own ground.

Whose herds with milk, whose fields with bread, 5
    Whose flocks supply him with attire,
Whose trees in summer yield him shade,
            In winter fire.

Blest, who can unconcern'dly find
    Hours, days, and years slide soft away,   10
In health of body, peace of mind,
            Quiet by day,

Sound sleep by night ; study and ease,
    Together mixt ; sweet recreation ;
And Innocence, which most does please   15
            With meditation.

Thus let me live, unseen, unknown,
    Thus unlamented let me die,
Steal from the world, and not a stone
            Tell where I lie.   20

Ode on Solitude.—This was a very early production of our author, written at about twelve years old [Pope].

THE DYING CHRISTIAN TO HIS SOUL

[WRITTEN 1712]

I

VITAL spark of heavenly flame !
Quit, oh quit this mortal frame :
Trembling, hoping, ling'ring, flying,
Oh the pain, the bliss of dying !
Cease, fond Nature, cease thy strife,   5
And let me languish into life.

II

Hark ! they whisper ; Angels say,
Sister Spirit, come away.
What is this absorbs me quite ?
Steals my senses, shuts my sight,   10
Drowns my spirits, draws my breath ?
Tell me, my Soul, can this be Death ?

III

The world recedes ; it disappears !
Heaven opens on my eyes ! my ears
With sounds seraphic ring :   15
Lend, lend your wings ! I mount ! I fly !
O Grave ! where is thy Victory ?
O Death ! where is thy Sting ?

The Dying Christian, etc.—This ode was written in imitation of the famous sonnet of Hadrian to his departing soul ; but as much superior in sense and sublimity to his original as the Christian religion is to the Pagan.

AN ESSAY ON CRITICISM

WRITTEN IN THE YEAR MDCCIX

AN ESSAY ON CRITICISM

PART I.

Introduction. That 'tis as great a fault to judge ill, as to write ill, and a more dangerous one to the public.
That a *true Taste* is as rare to be found, as a *true Genius*.
That most men are born with some Taste, but spoiled by false *Education*.
The multitude of *Critics*, and causes of them.
That we are to study our own *Taste*, and know the *Limits* of it.
Nature the best guide of Judgment.
Improved by *Art* and *Rules*, which are but *methodised Nature*.
Rules derived from the Practice of the *Ancient Poets*.
That therefore the *Ancients* are necessary to be studied, by a Critic, particularly *Homer* and *Virgil*.
Of *Licences*, and the use of them by the Ancients.
Reverence due to the *Ancients*, and praise of them.

'TIS hard to say, if greater want of skill
Appear in writing or in judging ill ;
But, of the two, less dang'rous is th' offence
To tire our patience, than mislead our sense.
Some few in that, but numbers err in this,   5
Ten censure wrong for one who writes amiss ;
A fool might once himself alone expose,
Now one in verse makes many more in prose.
   'Tis with our judgments as our watches, none
Go just alike, yet each believes his own.   10
In Poets as true genius is but rare,
True Taste as seldom is the Critic's share ;
Both must alike from Heaven derive their light,
These born to judge, as well as those to write.
Let such teach others who themselves excel,   15
And censure freely who have written well.

Authors are partial to their wit, 'tis true,
But are not Critics to their judgment too ?
   Yet if we look more closely, we shall find
Most have the seeds of judgment in their mind :   20
Nature affords at least a glimm'ring light ;
The lines, though touched but faintly, are drawn right.
But as the slightest sketch, if justly traced,
Is by ill-colouring but the more disgraced,
So by false learning is good sense defaced :   25
Some are bewildered in the maze of schools,
And some made coxcombs Nature meant but fools.
In search of wit these lose their common sense,
And then turn Critics in their own defence :
Each burns alike, who can, or cannot write,   30
Or with a Rival's, or an Eunuch's spite.
All fools have still an itching to deride,
And fain would be upon the laughing side.
If Mævius scribble in Apollo's spite,
There are who judge still worse than he can write.   35
   Some have at first for Wits, then Poets past,
Turned Critics next, and proved plain fools at last.
Some neither can for Wits nor Critics pass,
As heavy mules are neither horse nor ass.
Those half-learned witlings, num'rous in our isle,   40
As half-formed insects on the banks of Nile ;
Unfinished things, one knows not what to call,
Their generation's so equivocal :
To tell 'em, would a hundred tongues require,
Or one vain wit's, that might a hundred tire.   45
   But you who seek to give and merit fame,
And justly bear a Critic's noble name,
Be sure yourself and your own reach to know,
How far your genius, taste, and learning go ;
Launch not beyond your depth, but be discreet,   50
And mark that point where sense and dulness meet.
   Nature to all things fixed the limits fit,
And wisely curbed proud man's pretending wit.
As on the land while here the ocean gains,

In other parts it leaves wide sandy plains ;
Thus in the soul while memory prevails,
The solid power of understanding fails ;
Where beams of warm imagination play,
The memory's soft figures melt away.
One science only will one genius fit ;
So vast is art, so narrow human wit :
Not only bounded to peculiar arts,
But oft in those confined to single parts.
Like kings we lose the conquests gained before,
By vain ambition still to make them more ;
Each might his sev'ral province well command,
Would all but stoop to what they understand.
First follow Nature, and your judgment frame
By her just standard, which is still the same :
Unerring NATURE, still divinely bright,
One clear, unchanged, and universal light,
Life, force, and beauty, must to all impart,
At once the source, and end, and test of Art.
Art from that fund each just supply provides,
Works without show, and without pomp presides :
In some fair body thus th' informing soul
With spirits feeds, with vigour fills the whole,
Each motion guides, and every nerve sustains ;
Itself unseen, but in the effects, remains.
Some, to whom Heaven in wit has been profuse,
Want as much more, to turn it to its use ;
For wit and judgment often are at strife,
Though meant each other's aid, like man and wife.
'Tis more to guide, than spur the Muse's steed ;
Restrain his fury, than provoke his speed ;
The wingèd courser, like a gen'rous horse,
Shows most true mettle when you check his course.
Those RULES of old discovered, not devised,
Are Nature still, but Nature methodised ;
Nature, like liberty, is but restrained
By the same laws which first herself ordained.
Hear how learned Greece her useful rules indites,

55
60
65
70
75
80
85
90

When to repress, and when indulge our flights :
High on Parnassus' top her sons she showed,
And pointed out those arduous paths they trod ;   95
Held from afar, aloft, th' immortal prize,
And urged the rest by equal steps to rise.
Just precepts thus from great examples given,
She drew from them what they derived from Heaven.
The generous Critic fanned the Poet's fire,   100
And taught the world with reason to admire.
Then Criticism the Muses' handmaid proved,
To dress her charms, and make her more beloved :
But following wits from that intention strayed,
Who could not win the mistress, wooed the maid ;   105
Against the Poets their own arms they turned,
Sure to hate most the men from whom they learned.
So modern 'Pothecaries, taught the art
By Doctor's bills to play the Doctor's part,
Bold in the practice of mistaken rules,   110
Prescribe, apply, and call their masters fools.
Some on the leaves of ancient authors prey,
Nor time nor moths e'er spoiled so much as they.
Some drily plain, without invention's aid,
Write dull receipts how poems may be made.   115
These leave the sense, their learning to display,
And those explain the meaning quite away.
    You then whose judgment the right course would steer,
Know well each ANCIENT's proper character ;
His fable, subject, scope in every page ;   120
Religion, Country, genius of his Age :
Without all these at once before your eyes,
Cavil you may, but never criticise.
Be Homer's works your study and delight,
Read them by day, and meditate by night ;   125
Thence form your judgment, thence your maxims bring,
And trace the Muses upward to their spring.
Still with itself compared, his text peruse ;
And let your comment be the Mantuan Muse.
    When first young Maro in his boundless mind   130

A work t' outlast immortal Rome designed,
Perhaps he seemed above the critic's law,
And but from Nature's fountains scorned to draw :
But when t' examine every part he came,
Nature and Homer were, he found, the same.   135
Convinced, amazed, he checks the bold design ;
And rules as strict his laboured work confine,
As if the Stagirite o'erlooked each line.
Learn hence for ancient rules a just esteem ;
To copy nature is to copy them.   140
    Some beauties yet no Precepts can declare,
For there's a happiness as well as care.
Music resembles Poetry, in each
Are nameless graces which no methods teach,
And which a master-hand alone can reach.   145
If, where the rules not far enough extend,
(Since rules were made but to promote their end)
Some lucky Licence answer to the full
Th' intent proposed, that Licence is a rule.
Thus Pegasus, a nearer way to take,   150
May boldly deviate from the common track ;
From vulgar bounds with brave disorder part,
And snatch a grace beyond the reach of art,
Which without passing through the judgment, gains
The heart, and all its end at once attains.   155
In prospects thus, some objects please our eyes,
Which out of nature's common order rise,
The shapeless rock, or hanging precipice.
Great wits sometimes may gloriously offend,
And rise to faults true Critics dare not mend.   160
But though the Ancients thus their rules invade,
(As Kings dispense with laws themselves have made)
Moderns, beware ! or if you must offend
Against the precept, ne'er transgress its End ;
Let it be seldom, and compelled by need ;   165
And have, at least, their precedent to plead.
The Critic else proceeds without remorse,
Seizes your fame, and puts his laws in force.

I know there are, to whose presumptuous thoughts
Those freer beauties, even in them, seem faults.　　170
Some figures monstrous and mis-shaped appear,
Considered singly, or beheld too near,
Which, but proportioned to their light, or place,
Due distance reconciles to form and grace.
A prudent chief not always must display　　175
His powers in equal ranks, and fair array,
But with th' occasion and the place comply,
Conceal his force, nay seem sometimes to fly.
Those oft are stratagems which error seem,
Nor is it Homer nods, but we that dream.　　180
　　Still green with bays each ancient Altar stands,
Above the reach of sacrilegious hands ;
Secure from Flames, from Envy's fiercer rage,
Destructive War, and all-involving Age.
See, from each clime the learned their incense bring !
Hear, in all tongues consenting Pæans ring !　　186
In praise so just let every voice be joined,
And fill the general chorus of mankind.
Hail, Bards triumphant ! born in happier days ;
Immortal heirs of universal praise !　　190
Whose honours with increase of ages grow,
As streams roll down, enlarging as they flow ;
Nations unborn your mighty names shall sound,
And worlds applaud that must not yet be found !
Oh may some spark of your celestial fire,　　195
The last, the meanest of your sons inspire,
(That on weak wings, from far, pursues your flights ;
Glows while he reads, but trembles as he writes)
To teach vain Wits a science little known,
T' admire superior sense, and doubt their own !　　200

　　Secure from Flames, from Envy's fiercer rage, destructive War, and all-involving Age.—The poet here alludes to the four great causes of the ravage amongst ancient writings. The destruction of the Alexandrine and Palatine libraries by *fire ;* the fiercer rage of Zoilus and Mævius and their followers against wit ; the irruption of the barbarians into the empire ; and the long reign of ignorance and superstition in the cloisters.

PART II

OF all the Causes which conspire to blind
Man's erring judgment, and misguide the mind,
What the weak head with strongest bias rules
Is *Pride*, the never-failing vice of fools.
Whatever nature has in worth denied,   205
She gives in large recruits of needful pride ;
For as in bodies, thus in souls, we find
What wants in blood and spirits, swelled with wind :
Pride, where wit fails, steps in to our defence,
And fills up all the mighty Void of sense.   210
If once right reason drives that cloud away,
Truth breaks upon us with resistless day.
Trust not yourself ; but your defects to know,
Make use of every friend—and every foe.
A *little learning* is a dang'rous thing ;   215
Drink deep, or taste not the Pierian spring :
There shallow draughts intoxicate the brain,
And drinking largely sobers us again.
Fired at first sight with what the Muse imparts,
In fearless youth we tempt the heights of Arts,   220
While from the bounded level of our mind
Short views we take, nor see the lengths behind ;
But more advanced, behold with strange surprise
New distant scenes of endless science rise !
So pleased at first the tow'ring Alps we try,   225
Mount o'er the vales, and seem to tread the sky,
Th' eternal snows appear already past,
And the first clouds and mountains seem the last ;

But, those attained, we tremble to survey
The growing labours of the lengthened way,   230
Th' increasing prospect tires our wand'ring eyes,
Hills peep o'er hills, and Alps on Alps arise !
   A perfect Judge will read each work of Wit
With the same spirit that its author writ :
Survey the WHOLE, nor seek slight faults to find   235
Where nature moves, and rapture warms the mind :
Nor lose, for that malignant dull delight,
The gen'rous pleasure to be charmed with Wit.
But in such lays as neither ebb, nor flow,
Correctly cold, and regularly low,   240
That shunning faults, one quiet tenour keep ;
We cannot blame indeed——but we may sleep.
In wit, as nature, what affects our hearts
Is not th' exactness of peculiar parts ;
'Tis not a lip, or eye, we beauty call,   245
But the joint force and full result of all.
Thus when we view some well-proportioned dome,
(The world's just wonder, and even thine, O Rome !)
No single parts unequally surprise,
All comes united to th' admiring eyes ;   250
No monstrous height, or breadth, or length appear ;
The Whole at once is bold, and regular.
   Whoever thinks a faultless piece to see,
Thinks what ne'er was, nor is, nor e'er shall be.
In every work regard the writer's End,   255
Since none can compass more than they intend ;
And if the means be just, the conduct true,
Applause, in spight of trivial faults, is due ;
As men of breeding, sometimes men of wit,
T' avoid great errors, must the less commit :   260
Neglect the rules each verbal Critic lays,
For not to know some trifles, is a praise.
Most Critics, fond of some subservient art,
Still make the Whole depend upon a Part :
They talk of principles, but notions prize,   265
And all to one loved Folly sacrifice.

Once on a time, La Mancha's Knight, they say,
A certain bard encount'ring on the way,
Discoursed in terms as just, with looks as sage,
As e'er could Dennis of the Grecian stage ;   270
Concluding all were desperate sots and fools,
Who durst depart from Aristotle's rules.
Our Author, happy in a judge so nice,
Produced his Play, and begged the Knight's advice ;
Made him observe the subject, and the plot,   275
The manners, passions, unities ; what not ?
All which, exact to rule, were brought about,
Were but a Combat in the lists left out.
" What ! leave the Combat out ? " exclaims the Knight ;
Yes, or we must renounce the Stagirite.   280
" Not so by Heaven " (he answers in a rage),
" Knights, squires, and steeds, must enter on the stage."
So vast a throng the stage can ne'er contain.
" Then build a new, or act it in a plain."
    Thus Critics, of less judgment than caprice,   285
Curious not knowing, not exact but nice,
Form short Ideas ; and offend in arts
(As most in manners) by a love to parts.
    Some to *Conceit* alone their taste confine,
And glitt'ring thoughts struck out at every line ;   290
Pleased with a work where nothing's just or fit ;
One glaring Chaos and wild heap of wit.
Poets like painters, thus, unskilled to trace
The naked nature and the living grace,
With gold and jewels cover every part,   295
And hide with ornaments their want of art.
True Wit is Nature to advantage dressed,
What oft was thought, but ne'er so well expressed ;
Something, whose truth convinced at sight we find,
That gives us back the image of our mind.   300
As shades more sweetly recommend the light,
So modest plainness sets off sprightly wit.
For works may have more wit than does 'em good,
As bodies perish through excess of blood.

Others for *Language* all their care express, 305
And value books, as women men, for Dress :
Their praise is still,—the Style is excellent :
The Sense, they humbly take upon content.
Words are like leaves ; and where they most abound,
Much fruit of sense beneath is rarely found : 310
False Eloquence, like the prismatic glass,
Its gaudy colours spreads on every place ;
The face of Nature we no more survey,
All glares alike, without distinction gay :
But true expression, like th' unchanging Sun, 315
Clears and improves whate'er it shines upon,
It gilds all objects, but it alters none.
Expression is the dress of thought, and still
Appears more decent, as more suitable ;
A vile conceit in pompous words expressed, 320
Is like a clown in regal purple dressed :
For diff'rent styles with diff'rent subjects sort,
As several garbs with country, town, and court.
Some by old words to fame have made pretence,
Ancients in phrase, mere moderns in their sense ; 325
Such laboured nothings, in so strange a style,
Amaze th' unlearned, and make the learnèd smile.
Unlucky, as Fungoso in the play,
These sparks with awkward vanity display
What the fine gentleman wore yesterday ; 330
And but so mimic ancient wits at best,
As apes our grandsires, in their doublets drest.
In words, as fashions, the same rule will hold ;
Alike fantastic, if too new, or old :
Be not the first by whom the new are tried, 335
Nor yet the last to lay the old aside.
But most by Numbers judge a Poet's song ;
And smooth or rough, with them is right or wrong :
In the bright Muse though thousand charms conspire,
Her voice is all these tuneful fools admire ; 340
Who haunt Parnassus but to please their ear,
Not mend their minds ; as some to Church repair,

Not for the doctrine, but the music there.
These equal syllables alone require,
Though oft the ear the open vowels tire ;   345
While expletives their feeble aid do join ;
And ten low words oft creep in one dull line :
While they ring round the same unvaried chimes,
With sure returns of still expected rhymes ;
Where'er you find " the cooling western breeze,"   350
In the next line, it " whispers through the trees : "
If crystal streams " with pleasing murmurs creep,"
The reader's threatened (not in vain) with " sleep : "
Then, at the last and only couplet fraught
With some unmeaning thing they call a thought,   355
A needless Alexandrine ends the song
That, like a wounded snake, drags its slow length along.
Leave such to tune their own dull rhymes, and know
What's roundly smooth or languishingly slow ;
And praise the easy vigour of a line,   360
Where Denham's strength, and Waller's sweetness join.
True ease in writing comes from art, not chance,
As those move easiest who have learned to dance.
'Tis not enough no harshness gives offence,
The sound must seem an Echo to the sense :   365
Soft is the strain when Zephyr gently blows,
And the smooth stream in smoother numbers flows ;
But when loud surges lash the sounding shore,
The hoarse, rough verse should like the torrent roar :
When Ajax strives some rock's vast weight to throw,
The line too labours, and the words move slow ;   371
Not so, when swift Camilla scours the plain,
Flies o'er th' unbending corn, and skims along the main.
Hear how Timotheus' varied lays surprise,
And bid alternate passions fall and rise !   375
While, at each change, the son of Libyan Jove
Now burns with glory, and then melts with love,
Now his fierce eyes with sparkling fury glow,
Now sighs steal out, and tears begin to flow :
Persians and Greeks like turns of nature found,   380

And the world's victor stood subdued by Sound !
The power of Music all our hearts allow,
And what Timotheus was, is DRYDEN now.
    Avoid Extremes ; and shun the fault of such,
Who still are pleased too little or too much.   385
At every trifle scorn to take offence,
That always shows great pride, or little sense ;
Those heads, as stomachs, are not sure the best,
Which nauseate all, and nothing can digest.
Yet let not each gay Turn thy rapture move ;   390
For fools admire, but men of sense approve :
As things seem large which we through mists descry,
Dulness is ever apt to magnify.
    Some foreign writers, some our own despise ;
The Ancients only, or the Moderns prize.   395
Thus Wit, like Faith, by each man is applied
To one small sect, and all are damned beside.
Meanly they seek the blessing to confine,
And force that sun but on a part to shine,
Which not alone the southern wit sublimes,   400
But ripens spirits in cold northern climes ;
Which from the first has shone on ages past,
Enlights the present, and shall warm the last ;
Though each may feel increases and decays,
And see now clearer and now darker days.   405
Regard not then if Wit be old or new,
But blame the false, and value still the true.
    Some ne'er advance a Judgment of their own,
But catch the spreading notion of the Town ;
They reason and conclude by precedent,   410
And own stale nonsense which they ne'er invent.
Some judge of authors' names, not works, and then
Nor praise nor blame the writings, but the men.
Of all this servile herd the worst is he
That in proud dulness joins with Quality.   415
A constant Critic at the great man's board,
To fetch and carry nonsense for my Lord.
What woful stuff this madrigal would be,

In some starved hackney sonneteer, or me ?
But let a Lord once own the happy lines, 420
How the wit brightens ! how the style refines !
Before his sacred name flies every fault,
And each exalted stanza teems with thought !
  The Vulgar thus through Imitation err ;
As oft the Learned by being singular ; 425
So much they scorn the crowd, that if the throng
By chance go right, they purposely go wrong ;
So Schismatics the plain believers quit,
And are but damned for having too much wit.
Some praise at morning what they blame at night ; 430
But always think the last opinion right.
A Muse by these is like a mistress used,
This hour she's idolised, the next abused ;
While their weak heads like towns unfortified,
'Twixt sense and nonsense daily change their side. 435
Ask them the cause ; they're wiser still, they say ;
And still to-morrow's wiser than to-day.
We think our fathers fools, so wise we grow ;
Our wiser sons, no doubt, will think us so.
Once School-divines this zealous isle o'er-spread ; 440
Who knew most Sentences, was deepest read ;
Faith, Gospel, all, seemed made to be disputed,
And none had sense enough to be confuted :
Scotists and Thomists, now, in peace remain,
Amidst their kindred cobwebs in Duck-lane. 445
If Faith itself has diff'rent dresses worn,
What wonder modes in Wit should take their turn ?
Oft, leaving what is natural and fit,
The current folly proves the ready wit ;
And authors think their reputation safe, 450
Which lives as long as fools are pleased to laugh.
  Some valuing those of their own side or mind,
Still make themselves the measure of mankind :
Fondly we think we honour merit then,

Duck-lane.—A place where old and second-hand books were sold
formerly, near Smithfield.

3

When we but praise ourselves in other men.   455
Parties in Wit attend on those of State,
And public faction doubles private hate.
Pride, Malice, Folly, against Dryden rose,
In various shapes of Parsons, Critics, Beaus ;
But sense survived, when merry jests were past ;   460
For rising merit will buoy up at last.
Might he return, and bless once more our eyes,
New Blackmores and new Milbourns must arise :
Nay should great Homer lift his awful head,
Zoilus again would start up from the dead.   465
Envy will merit, as its shade, pursue ;
But like a shadow, proves the substance true ;
For envied Wit, like Sol eclipsed, makes known
Th' opposing body's grossness, not its own,
When first that sun too powerful beams displays,   470
It draws up vapours which obscure its rays ;
But even those clouds at last adorn its way,
Reflect new glories, and augment the day.
    Be thou the first true merit to befriend ;
His praise is lost, who stays, till all commend.   475
Short is the date, alas, of modern rhymes,
And 'tis but just to let them live betimes.
No longer now that golden age appears,
When Patriarch-wits survived a thousand years :
Now length of Fame (our second life) is lost,   480
And bare threescore is all even that can boast ;
Our sons their fathers' failing language see,
And such as Chaucer is, shall Dryden be.
So when the faithful pencil has designed
Some bright Idea of the master's mind,   485
Where a new world leaps out at his command,
And ready Nature waits upon his hand ;
When the ripe colours soften and unite,
And sweetly melt into just shade and light ;
When mellowing years their full perfection give,   490

Parsons.—The parson alluded to was Jeremy Collier ; the critic was the Duke of Buckingham.

And each bold figure just begins to live,
The treach'rous colours the fair art betray,
And all the bright creation fades away !
 Unhappy Wit, like most mistaken things,
Atones not for that envy which it brings.   495
In youth alone its empty praise we boast,
But soon the short-lived vanity is lost :
Like some fair flower the early spring supplies,
That gaily blooms, but even in blooming dies.
What is this Wit, which must our cares employ ?   500
The owner's wife, that other men enjoy ;
Then most our trouble still when most admired,
And still the more we give, the more required ;
Whose fame with pains we guard, but lose with ease,
Sure some to vex, but never all to please ;   505
'Tis what the vicious fear, the virtuous shun,
By fools 'tis hated, and by knaves undone !
 If Wit so much from Ign'rance undergo,
Ah let not Learning too commence its foe !
Of old, those met rewards who could excel,   510
And such were praised who but endeavoured well :
Though triumphs were to generals only due,
Crowns were reserved to grace the soldiers too.
Now, they who reach Parnassus' lofty crown,
Employ their pains to spurn some others down ;   515
And while self-love each jealous writer rules,
Contending wits become the sport of fools :
But still the worst with most regret commend,
For each ill Author is as bad a Friend.
To what base ends, and by what abject ways,   520
Are mortals urged through sacred lust of praise !
Ah ne'er so dire a thirst of glory boast,
Nor in the Critic let the Man be lost.
Good-nature and good-sense must ever join ;
To err is human, to forgive, divine.   525
 But if in noble minds some dregs remain
Not yet purged off, of spleen and sour disdain ;
Discharge that rage on more provoking crimes,

Nor fear a dearth in these flagitious times.
No pardon vile Obscenity should find,   530
Though wit and art conspire to move your mind ;
But Dulness with Obscenity must prove
As shameful sure as Impotence in love.
In the fat age of pleasure, wealth and ease,
Sprung the rank weed, and thrived with large increase :
When love was all an easy Monarch's care ;   536
Seldom at council, never in a war :
Jilts ruled the state, and statesmen farces writ ;
Nay wits had pensions, and young Lords had wit :
The Fair sate panting at a Courtier's play,   540
And not a Mask went unimproved away :
The modest fan was lifted up no more,
And Virgins smiled at what they blushed before.
The following licence of a Foreign reign
Did all the dregs of bold Socinus drain ;   545
Then unbelieving priests reformed the nation,
And taught more pleasant methods of salvation ;
Where Heaven's free subjects might their rights
        dispute,
Lest God himself should seem too absolute :
Pulpits their sacred satire learned to spare,   550
And Vice admired to find a flatt'rer there !
Encouraged thus, Wit's Titans braved the skies,
And the press groaned with licensed blasphemies.
These monsters, Critics ! with your darts engage,
Here point your thunder, and exhaust your rage !   555
Yet shun their fault, who, scandalously nice,
Will needs mistake an author into vice ;
All seems infected that th' infected spy,
As all looks yellow to the jaundiced eye.

PART III

Rules for the Conduct of *Manners* in a Critic. 1. *Candour.* *Modesty. Good-breeding. Sincerity,* and *Freedom* of advice. 2. When one's Counsel is to be restrained. Character of an *incorrigible Poet.* And of an *impertinent Critic.* Character of a *good Critic.* The *History* of *Criticism,* and Characters of the best Critics: *Aristotle, Horace, Dionysius, Petronius, Quintilian, Longinus.* Of the Decay of Criticism, and its Revival. *Erasmus. Vida. Boileau. Lord Roscommon,* etc. Conclusion.

LEARN then what MORALS Critics ought to show, 560
For 'tis but half a Judge's task, to know.
'Tis not enough, taste, judgment, learning, join ;
In all you speak, let truth and candour shine :
That not alone what to your sense is due
All may allow ; but seek your friendship too.   565
   Be silent always when you doubt your sense ;
And speak, though sure, with seeming diffidence :
Some positive, persisting fops we know,
Who, if once wrong, will needs be always so ;
But you, with pleasure own your errors past,   570
And make each day a Critic on the last.
   'Tis not enough, your counsel still be true ;
Blunt truths more mischief than nice falsehoods do ;
Men must be taught as if you taught them not,
And things unknown proposed as things forgot.   575
Without Good Breeding, truth is disapproved ;
That only makes superior sense beloved.
   Be niggards of advice on no pretence ;
For the worst avarice is that of sense.
With mean complacence ne'er betray your trust,   580
Nor be so civil as to prove unjust.
Fear not the anger of the wise to raise ;
Those best can bear reproof, who merit praise.
   'Twere well might critics still this freedom take,
But Appius reddens at each word you speak,   585

And stares, tremendous, with a threat'ning eye,
Like some fierce Tyrant in old tapestry.
Fear most to tax an Honourable fool,
Whose right it is, uncensured, to be dull;
Such, without wit, are Poets when they please,   590
As without learning they can take Degrees.
Leave dangerous truths to unsuccessful Satires,
And flattery to fulsome Dedicators,
Whom, when they praise, the world believes no more,
Than when they promise to give scribbling o'er.   595
'Tis best sometimes your censure to restrain,
And charitably let the dull be vain:
Your silence there is better than your spite,
For who can rail so long as they can write?
Still humming on, their drowsy course they keep,   600
And lashed so long, like tops, are lashed asleep.
False steps but help them to renew the race,
As, after stumbling, Jades will mend their pace.
What crowds of these, impenitently bold,
In sounds and jingling syllables grown old,   605
Still run on Poets, in a raging vein,
Even to the dregs and squeezings of the brain,
Strain out the last dull droppings of their sense,
And rhyme with all the rage of Impotence.
   Such shameless Bards we have; and yet 'tis true,
There are as mad abandoned Critics too.   611
The bookful blockhead, ignorantly read,
With loads of learnèd lumber in his head,
With his own tongue still edifies his ears,
And always list'ning to himself appears.   615
All books he reads, and all he reads assails,
From Dryden's Fables down to Durfey's Tales.
With him, most authors steal their works, or buy;

   And stares, tremendous, etc.—This picture was taken to himself by
John Dennis, a furious old critic by profession, who, upon no other provocation, wrote against this essay and its author, in a manner perfectly
lunatic: for, as to the mention made of him in v. 270, he took it as a
compliment, and said it was treacherously meant to cause him to overlook this *abuse* of his *person*.

Garth did not write his own Dispensary.
Name a new Play, and he's the Poet's friend,   620
Nay showed his faults—but when would Poets mend ?
No place so sacred from such fops is barred,
Nor is Paul's church more safe than Paul's churchyard :
Nay, fly to Altars ; there they'll talk you dead :
For Fools rush in where Angels fear to tread.   625
Distrustful sense with modest caution speaks,
It still looks home, and short excursions makes ;
But rattling nonsense in full volleys breaks,
And never shocked, and never turned aside,
Bursts out, resistless, with a thund'ring tide.   630
   But where's the man, who counsel can bestow,
Still pleased to teach, and yet not proud to know ?
Unbiased, or by favour, or by spite ;
Not dully prepossessed, nor blindly right ;
Though learned, well-bred ; and though well-bred, sincere,
Modestly bold, and humanly severe :   636
Who to a friend his faults can freely show,
And gladly praise the merit of a foe ?
Blest with a taste exact, yet unconfined ;
A knowledge both of books and human kind :   640
Gen'rous converse ; a soul exempt from pride ;
And love to praise, with reason on his side ?
   Such once were Critics ; such the happy few,
Athens and Rome in better ages knew.
The mighty Stagirite first left the shore,   645
Spread all his sails, and durst the deeps explore :
He steered securely, and discovered far,
Led by the light of the Mæonian Star.
Poets, a race long unconfined, and free,
Still fond and proud of savage liberty,   650
Received his laws ; and stood convinced 'twas fit,
Who conquered Nature, should preside o'er Wit.
   Horace still charms with graceful negligence,

Garth did not write, etc.—A common slander at that time in prejudice of that deserving author. Our poet did him this justice, when that slander most prevailed ; and it is now dead and forgotten.

And without method talks us into sense,
Will, like a friend, familiarly convey   655
The truest notions in the easiest way.
He, who supreme in judgment, as in wit,
Might boldly censure, as he boldly writ,
Yet judged with coolness, though he sung with fire :
His Precepts teach but what his works inspire.   660
Our Critics take a contrary extreme,
They judge with fury, but they write with fle'me :
Nor suffers Horace more in wrong Translations
By Wits, than Critics in as wrong Quotations.
    See Dionysius Homer's thoughts refine,   665
And call new beauties forth from every line !
    Fancy and art in gay Petronius please,
The scholar's learning, with the courtier's ease.
    In grave Quintilian's copious work, we find
The justest rules, and clearest method joined :   670
Thus useful arms in magazines we place,
All ranged in order, and disposed with grace,
But less to please the eye, than arm the hand,
Still fit for use, and ready at command.
    Thee, bold Longinus ! all the Nine inspire,   675
And bless their Critic with a Poet's fire.
An ardent Judge, who zealous in his trust,
With warmth gives sentence, yet is always just :
Whose own example strengthens all his laws ;
And is himself that great Sublime he draws.   680
    Thus long succeeding Critics justly reigned,
Licence repressed, and useful laws ordained.
Learning and Rome alike in empire grew ;
And Arts still followed where her Eagles flew ;
From the same foes, at last, both felt their doom,   685
And the same age saw Learning fall, and Rome.
With Tyranny, then Superstition joined,
As that the body, this enslaved the mind ;
Much was believed, but little understood,

Fle'me.—Earlier spelling of *phlegm*, from Old French *fleume.*

And to be dull was construed to be good ; 690
A second deluge Learning thus o'er-run,
And the Monks finished what the Goths begun.
   At length Erasmus, that great injured name,
(The glory of the Priesthood, and the shame !)
Stemmed the wild torrent of a barb'rous age, 695
And drove those holy Vandals off the stage.
   But see ! each Muse, in LEO's golden days,
Starts from her trance, and trims her withered bays,
Rome's ancient Genius, o'er its ruins spread,
Shakes off the dust, and rears his rev'rend head. 700
Then Sculpture and her sister-arts revive ;
Stones leaped to form, and rocks began to live ;
With sweeter notes each rising Temple rung ;
A Raphael painted, and a Vida sung.
Immortal Vida : on whose honoured brow 705
The Poet's bays and Critic's ivy grow :
Cremona now shall ever boast thy name,
As next in place to Mantua, next in fame !
   But soon by impious arms from Latium chased,
Their ancient bounds the banished Muses passed ; 710
Thence Arts o'er all the northern world advance,
But Critic-learning flourished most in France :
The rules a nation, born to serve, obeys ;
And Boileau still in right of Horace sways.
But we, brave Britons, foreign laws despised, 715
And kept unconquered, and uncivilised ;
Fierce for the liberties of wit, and bold,
We still defied the Romans, as of old.
Yet some there were, among the sounder few
Of those who less presumed, and better knew, 720
Who durst assert the juster ancient cause,
And here restored Wit's fundamental laws.
Such was the Muse, whose rules and practice tell,
" Nature's chief Master-piece is writing well."
Such was Roscommon, not more learned than good, 725
With manners gen'rous as his noble blood ;
To him the wit of Greece and Rome was known,

   3 *a*

And every author's merit, but his own.
Such late was Walsh—the Muse's judge and friend,
Who justly knew to blame or to commend ;   730
To failings mild, but zealous for desert ;
The clearest head, and the sincerest heart.
This humble praise, lamented shade ! receive,
This praise at least a grateful Muse may give :
The Muse, whose early voice you taught to sing,   735
Prescribed her heights, and pruned her tender wing,
(Her guide now lost) no more attempts to rise,
But in low numbers short excursions tries :
Content, if hence th' unlearned their wants may view,
The learned reflect on what before they knew :   740
Careless of censure, nor too fond of fame ;
Still pleased to praise, yet not afraid to blame,
Averse alike to flatter, or offend ;
Not free from faults, nor yet too vain to mend.

THE RAPE OF THE LOCK

AN HEROI-COMICAL POEM

Nolueram, Belinda, tuos violare capillos ;
Sed juvat, hoc precibus me tribuisse tuis.

MART. Epigr. XII. 84.

Nolueram, etc.—It appears, by this Motto, that the following Poem was written or published at the Lady's request. But there are some further circumstances not unworthy relating. Mr. Caryl (a Gentleman [1] who was Secretary to Queen Mary, wife of James II., whose fortunes he followed into France, author of the Comedy of *Sir Solomon Single*, and of several translations in Dryden's Miscellanies) originally proposed the subject to him in a view of putting an end, by this piece of ridicule, to a quarrel that was risen between two noble Families, those of Lord Petre and of Mrs. Fermor, on the trifling occasion of his having cut off a lock of her hair. The author sent it to the Lady, with whom he was acquainted ; and she took it so well as to give about copies of it. That first sketch (we learn from one of his Letters [2]) was written in less than a fortnight, in 1711, in two Canto's only, and it was so printed ; first, in a Miscellany of Bern. Lintot's, without the name of the author. But it was received so well that he made it more considerable the next year by the addition of the machinery of the Sylphs, and extended it to five Canto's.

This insertion he always esteemed, and justly, the greatest effort of his *skill* and *art* as a Poet.

[1] He was a *nephew* of that " Gentleman."
[2] Really from his Notes.

To Mrs. Arabella Fermor

MADAM,—It will be in vain to deny that I have some regard for this piece, since I dedicate it to You. Yet you may bear me witness, it was intended only to divert a few young Ladies, who have good sense and good humour enough to laugh not only at their sex's little unguarded follies, but at their own. But as it was communicated with the air of a Secret, it soon found its way into the world. An imperfect copy having been offer'd to a Bookseller, you had the good-nature for my sake to consent to the publication of one more correct: This I was forc'd to, before I had executed half my design, for the Machinery was entirely wanting to compleat it.

The Machinery, Madam, is a term invented by the Critics, to signify that part which the Deities, Angels, or Dæmons are made to act in a Poem: For the ancient Poets are in one respect like many modern Ladies: let an action be never so trivial in itself, they always make it appear of the utmost importance. These Machines I determined to raise on a very new and odd foundation, the Rosicrucian doctrine of Spirits.

I know how disagreeable it is to make use of hard words before a Lady; but 'tis so much the concern of a Poet to have his works understood, and particularly by your Sex, that you must give me leave to explain two or three difficult terms.

The Rosicrucians are a people I must bring you acquainted with. The best account I know of them is in a French book call'd *Le Comte de Gabalis*, which both in its title and size is so like a Novel, that many of the Fair Sex have read it for one by mistake. According to these Gentlemen, the four Elements are inhabited by Spirits, which they call Sylphs, Gnomes, Nymphs, and Salamanders. The Gnomes or Dæmons of Earth delight in mischief; but the Sylphs, whose habitation is in the Air, are the best-condition'd creatures imaginable. For they say, any mortals may enjoy the most intimate familiarities with these gentle Spirits, upon a condition very easy to all true Adepts, an inviolate preservation of Chastity.

As to the following Canto's, all the passages of them are as fabulous as the Vision at the beginning, or the Transformation at the end; (except the loss of your Hair, which I always mention with reverence). The Human persons are as fictitious as the airy ones; and the character of Belinda, as it is now manag'd, resembles you in nothing but in Beauty.

If this Poem had as many Graces as there are in your Person, or in your Mind, yet I could never hope it should pass thro' the world half so Uncensur'd as You have done. But let its fortune be what it will, mine is happy enough, to have given me this occasion of assuring you that I am, with the truest esteem, MADAM,

Your most obedient, Humble Servant,

A. POPE.

THE RAPE OF THE LOCK

CANTO I

WHAT dire offence from am'rous causes springs,
What mighty contests rise from trivial things,
I sing—This verse to CARYL, Muse ! is due :
This, even Belinda may vouchsafe to view :
Slight is the subject, but not so the praise,　　　　　5
If She inspire, and He approve my lays.
　Say what strange motive, Goddess ! could compel
A well-bred Lord t' assault a gentle Belle ?
O say what stranger cause, yet unexplored,
Could make a gentle Belle reject a Lord ?　　　　　10
In tasks so bold, can little men engage,
And in soft bosoms dwells such mighty Rage ?
　Sol through white curtains shot a tim'rous ray,
And oped those eyes that must eclipse the day :
Now lap-dogs give themselves the rousing shake,　　　15
And sleepless lovers, just at twelve, awake :
Thrice rung the bell, the slipper knocked the ground,
And the pressed watch returned a silver sound.
Belinda still her downy pillow prest,
Her guardian SYLPH prolonged the balmy rest :　　　20
'Twas He had summoned to her silent bed
The morning-dream that hovered o'er her head ;
A Youth more glitt'ring than a Birth-night Beau,
(That even in slumber caused her cheek to glow)
Seemed to her ear his winning lips to lay,　　　　　25

John Caryll.—A gentleman of an ancient Catholic family in Sussex, and till his death in 1736 a most intimate friend of Pope's.

And thus in whispers said, or seemed to say.
  Fairest of mortals, thou distinguished care
Of thousand bright Inhabitants of Air !
If e'er one vision touched thy infant thought,
Of all the Nurse and all the Priest have taught ;   30
Of airy Elves by moonlight shadows seen,
The silver token, and the circled green,
Or virgins visited by Angel-powers,
With golden crowns and wreaths of heav'nly flowers ;
Hear and believe ! thy own importance know,   35
Nor bound thy narrow views to things below.
Some secret truths, from learnèd pride concealed,
To Maids alone and Children are revealed :
What though no credit doubting Wits may give ?
The Fair and Innocent shall still believe.   40
Know, then, unnumbered Spirits round thee fly,
The light Militia of the lower sky :
These, though unseen, are ever on the wing,
Hang o'er the Box, and hover round the Ring.
Think what an equipage thou hast in Air,   45
And view with scorn two Pages and a Chair.
As now your own, our beings were of old,
And once inclosed in Woman's beauteous mould ;
Thence, by a soft transition, we repair
From earthly Vehicles to these of air.   50
Think not, when Woman's transient breath is fled,
That all her vanities at once are dead ;
Succeeding vanities she still regards,
And though she plays no more, o'erlooks the cards.
Her joy in gilded Chariots, when alive,   55
And love of Ombre, after death survive.
For when the Fair in all their pride expire,
To their first Elements their Souls retire :

As now your own, etc.—He here forsakes the Rosicrucian system :
which, in this part, is too extravagant even for poetry ; and gives a
beautiful fiction of his own, on the Platonic Theology of the continuance of the passions in *another state*, when the mind, before its
leaving *this*, has not been purged and purified by philosophy ; which
furnishes an occasion for much useful satire.

The Sprites of fiery Termagants in Flame
Mount up, and take a Salamander's name. 60
Soft yielding minds to Water glide away,
And sip, with Nymphs, their elemental Tea.
The graver Prude sinks downward to a Gnome,
In search of mischief still on Earth to roam.
The light Coquettes in Sylphs aloft repair, 65
And sport and flutter in the fields of Air.
  Know further yet ; whoever fair and chaste
Rejects mankind, is by some Sylph embraced :
For Spirits, freed from mortal laws, with ease
Assume what sexes and what shapes they please. 70
What guards the purity of melting Maids,
In courtly balls, and midnight masquerades,
Safe from the treach'rous friend, the daring spark,
The glance by day, the whisper in the dark,
When kind occasion prompts their warm desires, 75
When music softens, and when dancing fires ?
'Tis but their Sylph, the wise Celestials know,
Though Honour is the word with Men below.
  Some nymphs there are, too conscious of their face,
For life predestined to the Gnomes' embrace. 80
These swell their prospects and exalt their pride,
When offers are disdained, and love denied :
Then gay Ideas crowd the vacant brain,
While Peers, and Dukes, and all their sweeping train,
And Garters, Stars, and Coronets appear, 85
And in soft sounds, Your Grace salutes their ear.
'Tis these that early taint the female soul,
Instruct the eyes of young Coquettes to roll,
Teach Infant-cheeks a bidden blush to know,
And little hearts to flutter at a Beau. 90
  Oft, when the world imagine women stray,
The Sylphs through mystic mazes guide their way,
Through all the giddy circle they pursue,
And old impertinence expel by new.
What tender maid but must a victim fall 95
To one man's treat, but for another's ball ?

When Florio speaks what virgin could withstand,
If gentle Damon did not squeeze her hand ?
With varying vanities, from every part,
They shift the moving Toyshop of their heart ;　　　100
Where wigs with wigs, with sword-knots sword-knots
　　　strive,
Beaux banish beaux, and coaches coaches drive.
This erring mortals Levity may call ;
Oh blind to truth ! the Sylphs contrive it all.
　　Of these am I, who thy protection claim,　　　105
A watchful sprite, and Ariel is my name.
Late, as I ranged the crystal wilds of air,
In the clear Mirror of thy ruling Star
I saw, alas ! some dread event impend,
Ere to the main this morning sun descend,　　　110
But heaven reveals not what, or how, or where :
Warned by the Sylph, oh pious maid, beware !
This to disclose is all thy guardian can :
Beware of all, but most beware of Man !　　　114
　　He said ; when Shock, who thought she slept too long,
Leaped up, and waked his mistress with his tongue.
'Twas then, Belinda, if report say true,
Thy eyes first opened on a Billet-doux ;
Wounds, Charms, and Ardors were no sooner read,
But all the Vision vanished from thy head.　　　120
　　And now, unveiled, the Toilet stands displayed,
Each silver Vase in mystic order laid.
First, robed in white, the Nymph intent adores,
With head uncovered, the Cosmetic powers.
A heav'nly image in the glass appears,　　　125
To that she bends, to that her eyes she rears ;
Th' inferior Priestess, at her altar's side,
Trembling begins the sacred rites of Pride.

In the clear Mirror.—The language of the Platonists, the writers of
the intelligible world of spirits, etc.
　Th' inferior Priestess.—There is a small inaccuracy in these lines.
He first makes his heroine the chief priestess, and then the goddess
herself.

Unnumbered treasures ope at once, and here
The various off'rings of the world appear ;   130
From each she nicely culls with curious toil,
And decks the Goddess with the glitt'ring spoil.
This casket India's glowing gems unlocks,
And all Arabia breathes from yonder box.
The Tortoise here and Elephant unite,   135
Transformed to combs, the speckled, and the white.
Here files of pins extend their shining rows,
Puffs, Powders, Patches, Bibles, Billet-doux.
Now awful Beauty puts on all its arms ;
The fair each moment rises in her charms,   140
Repairs her smiles, awakens every grace,
And calls forth all the wonders of her face ;
Sees by degrees a purer blush arise,
And keener lightnings quicken in her eyes.
The busy Sylphs surround their darling care,   145
These set the head, and those divide the hair,
Some fold the sleeve, whilst others plait the gown ;
And Betty's praised for labours not her own.

CANTO II

Not with more glories, in th' etherial plain,
The Sun first rises o'er the purpled main,
Than, issuing forth, the rival of his beams
Launched on the bosom of the silver Thames.
Fair Nymphs, and well-drest Youths around her shone,
But every eye was fixed on her alone.   6
On her white breast a sparkling Cross she wore,
Which Jews might kiss, and Infidels adore.
Her lively looks a sprightly mind disclose,
Quick as her eyes, and as unfixed as those :   10
Favours to none, to all she smiles extends ;
Oft she rejects, but never once offends.
Bright as the sun, her eyes the gazers strike,
And, like the sun, they shine on all alike.

Yet graceful ease, and sweetness void of pride,   15
Might hide her faults, if Belles had faults to hide :
If to her share some female errors fall,
Look on her face, and you'll forget 'em all.
   This Nymph, to the destruction of mankind,
Nourished two Locks, which graceful hung behind   20
In equal curls, and well conspired to deck
With shining ringlets the smooth iv'ry neck.
Love in these labyrinths his slaves detains,
And mighty hearts are held in slender chains.
With hairy springes we the birds betray,   25
Slight lines of hair surprise the finny prey,
Fair tresses man's imperial race ensnare,
And beauty draws us with a single hair.
   Th' advent'rous Baron the bright locks admired ;
He saw, he wished, and to the prize aspired.   30
Resolved to win, he meditates the way,
By force to ravish, or by fraud betray ;
For when success a Lover's toil attends,
Few ask, if fraud or force attained his ends.
   For this, ere Phœbus rose, he had implored   35
Propitious heaven, and every power adored,
But chiefly Love—to Love an Altar built,
Of twelve vast French Romances, neatly gilt.
There lay three garters, half a pair of gloves ;
And all the trophies of his former loves ;   40
With tender Billet-doux he lights the pyre,
And breathes three am'rous sighs to raise the fire.
Then prostrate falls, and begs with ardent eyes
Soon to obtain, and long possess the prize :
The powers gave ear, and granted half his prayer,   45
The rest, the winds dispersed in empty air.
   But now secure the painted vessel glides,
The sun-beams trembling on the floating tides :
While melting music steals upon the sky,
And softened sounds along the waters die ;   50
Smooth flow the waves, the Zephyrs gently play,
Belinda smiled, and all the world was gay.

All but the Sylph—with careful thoughts opprest,
Th' impending woe sat heavy on his breast.
He summons strait his Denizens of air ;   55
The lucid squadrons round the sails repair :
Soft o'er the shrouds aërial whispers breathe,
That seemed but Zephyrs to the train beneath.
Some to the sun their insect-wings unfold,
Waft on the breeze, or sink in clouds of gold ;   60
Transparent forms, too fine for mortal sight,
Their fluid bodies half dissolved in light,
Loose to the wind their airy garments flew,
Thin glitt'ring textures of the filmy dew,
Dipt in the richest tincture of the skies,   65
Where light disports in ever-mingling dyes,
While every beam new transient colours flings,
Colours that change whene'er they wave their wings.
Amid the circle, on the gilded mast,
Superior by the head, was Ariel placed ;   70
His purple pinions opening to the sun,
He raised his azure wand, and thus begun.
    Ye Sylphs and Sylphids, to your chief give ear !
Fays, Fairies, Genii, Elves, and Dæmons, hear !
Ye know the spheres and various tasks assigned   75
By laws eternal to th' aërial kind.
Some in the fields of purest Æther play,
And bask and whiten in the blaze of day.
Some guide the course of wand'ring orbs on high,
Or roll the planets through the boundless sky.   80
Some less refined, beneath the moon's pale light
Pursue the stars that shoot athwart the night,
Or suck the mists in grosser air below,
Or dip their pinions in the painted bow,
Or brew fierce tempests on the wintry main,   85
Or o'er the glebe distil the kindly rain.
Others on earth o'er human race preside,
Watch all their ways, and all their actions guide :
Of these the chief the care of Nations own,
And guard with Arms divine the British Throne.   90

Our humbler province is to tend the Fair,
Not a less pleasing, though less glorious care ;
To save the powder from too rude a gale,
Nor let th' imprisoned essences exhale ;
To draw fresh colours from the vernal flowers ;   95
To steal from rainbows e'er they drop in showers
A brighter wash ; to curl their waving hairs,
Assist their blushes, and inspire their airs ;
Nay oft, in dreams, invention we bestow,
To change a Flounce, or add a Furbelow.   100
    This day, black Omens threat the brightest Fair,
That e'er deserved a watchful spirit's care ;
Some dire disaster, or by force, or slight ;
But what, or where, the fates have wrapt in night.
Whether the nymph shall break Diana's law,   105
Or some frail China jar receive a flaw ;
Or stain her honour or her new brocade ;
Forget her prayers, or miss a masquerade ;
Or lose her heart, or necklace, at a ball ;
Or whether Heaven has doomed that Shock must fall.
Haste, then, ye spirits ! to your charge repair :   III
The flutt'ring fan be Zephyretta's care ;
The drops to thee, Brillante, we consign ;
And, Momentilla, let the watch be thine ;
Do thou, Crispissa, tend her fav'rite Lock ;   115
Ariel himself shall be the guard of Shock.
    To fifty chosen Sylphs, of special note,
We trust th' important charge, the Petticoat :
Oft have we known that seven-fold fence to fail,
Though stiff with hoops, and armed with ribs of whale;
Form a strong line about the silver bound,   121
And guard the wide circumference around.
    Whatever spirit, careless of his charge,
His post neglects, or leaves the fair at large,
Shall feel sharp vengeance soon o'ertake his sins,   125
Be stopped in vials, or transfixed with pins ;
Or plunged in lakes of bitter washes lie,
Or wedged whole ages in a bodkin's eye :

Gums and Pomatums shall his flight restrain,
While clogged he beats his silken wings in vain ;   130
Or Alum styptics with contracting power
Shrink his thin essence like a rivelled flower :
Or, as Ixion fixed, the wretch shall feel
The giddy motion of the whirling Mill,
In fumes of burning Chocolate shall glow,   135
And tremble at the sea that froths below !
　He spoke ; the spirits from the sails descend ;
Some, orb in orb, around the nymph extend ;
Some thrid the mazy ringlets of her hair ;
Some hang upon the pendants of her ear :   140
With beating hearts the dire event they wait,
Anxious, and trembling for the birth of Fate.

CANTO III

Close by those meads, for ever crowned with flowers,
Where Thames with pride surveys his rising towers,
There stands a structure of majestic frame,
Which from the neighb'ring Hampton takes its name.
Here Britain's statesmen oft the fall foredoom   5
Of foreign Tyrants and of Nymphs at home ;
Here thou, great Anna ! whom three realms obey,
Dost sometimes counsel take—and sometimes Tea.
　Hither the heroes and the nymphs resort,
To taste awhile the pleasures of a Court ;   10
In various talk th' instructive hours they past,
Who gave the ball, or paid the visit last ;
One speaks the glory of the British Queen,
And one describes a charming Indian screen ;
A third interprets motions, looks, and eyes ;   15
At every word a reputation dies.
Snuff, or the fan, supply each pause of chat,
With singing, laughing, ogling, *and all that.*
　Mean while, declining from the noon of day,
The sun obliquely shoots his burning ray ;   20

The hungry Judges soon the sentence sign,
And wretches hang that jury-men may dine ;
The merchant from th' Exchange returns in peace,
And the long labours of the Toilet cease.
Belinda now, whom thirst of fame invites,   25
Burns to encounter two advent'rous Knights,
At Ombre singly to decide their doom ;
And swells her breast with conquests yet to come.
Straight the three bands prepare in arms to join,
Each band the number of the sacred nine.   30
Soon as she spreads her hand, th' aërial guard
Descend, and sit on each important card :
First Ariel perched upon a Matadore,
Then each, according to the rank they bore ;
For Sylphs, yet mindful of their ancient race,   35
Are, as when women, wondrous fond of place.
   Behold, four Kings in majesty revered,
With hoary whiskers and a forky beard ;
And four fair Queens whose hands sustain a flower,
Th' expressive emblem of their softer power ;   40
Four Knaves in garbs succinct, a trusty band,
Caps on their heads, and halberts in their hand ;
And particoloured troops, a shining train,
Draw forth to combat on the velvet plain.
   The skilful Nymph reviews her force with care :   45
Let Spades be trumps ! she said, and trumps they were.
   Now move to war her sable Matadores,
In show like leaders of the swarthy Moors.
Spadillio first, unconquerable Lord !
Led off two captive trumps, and swept the board.   50
As many more Manillio forced to yield,
And marched a victor from the verdant field.
Him Basto followed, but his fate more hard
Gained but one trump and one Plebeian card.

   A Matadore.—From the terms used in the game of Ombre—Spadillo,
Basto, Matador, Punto, etc.—there can scarcely be a doubt that the
other nations of Western Europe derived their knowledge of it from
the Spaniards.

With his broad sabre next, a chief in years, 55
The hoary Majesty of Spades appears,
Puts forth one manly leg, to sight revealed,
The rest, his many-coloured robe concealed.
The rebel Knave, who dares his prince engage,
Proves the just victim of his royal rage. 60
Even mighty Pam, that Kings and Queens o'erthrew
And mowed down armies in the fights of Lu,
Sad chance of war ! now destitute of aid,
Falls undistinguished by the victor spade !
    Thus far both armies to Belinda yield ; 65
Now to the Baron fate inclines the field.
His warlike Amazon her host invades,
Th' imperial consort of the crown of Spades.
The Club's black Tyrant first her victim dyed,
Spite of his haughty mien, and barb'rous pride : 70
What boots the regal circle on his head,
His giant limbs, in state unwieldy spread ;
That long behind he trails his pompous robe,
And, of all monarch's, only grasps the globe ?
    The Baron now his Diamonds pours apace ; 75
Th' embroidered King who shows but half his face,
And his refulgent Queen, with powers combined
Of broken troops an easy conquest find.
Clubs, Diamonds, Hearts, in wild disorder seen,
With throngs promiscuous strow the level green. 80
Thus when dispersed a routed army runs,
Of Asia's troops, and Afric's sable sons,
With like confusion different nations fly,
Of various habit, and of various dye,
The pierced battalions dis-united fall, 85
In heaps on heaps ; one fate o'erwhelms them all.
    The Knave of Diamonds tries his wily arts,
And wins (oh shameful chance !) the Queen of Hearts.
At this, the blood the virgin's cheek forsook,
A livid paleness spreads o'er all her look ; 90
She sees, and trembles at th' approaching ill,
Just in the jaws of ruin, and Codille.

And now (as oft in some distempered State)
On one nice Trick depends the general fate.
An Ace of Hearts steps forth : The King unseen.   95
Lurked in her hand, and mourned his captive Queen :
He springs to Vengeance with an eager pace,
And falls like thunder on the prostrate Ace.
The nymph exulting fills with shouts the sky ;
The walls, the woods, and long canals reply.   100
   Oh thoughtless mortals ! ever blind to fate,
Too soon dejected, and too soon elate.
Sudden, these honours shall be snatched away,
And cursed for ever this victorious day.
   For lo ! the board with cups and spoons is crowned,
The berries crackle, and the mill turns round ;   106
On shining Altars of Japan they raise
The silver lamp ; the fiery spirits blaze :
From silver spouts the grateful liquors glide,
While China's earth receives the smoking tide :   110
At once they gratify their scent and taste,
And frequent cups prolong the rich repast.
Straight hover round the Fair her airy band ;
Some, as she sipped, the fuming liquor fanned,
Some o'er her lap their careful plumes displayed,   115
Trembling, and conscious of the rich brocade.
Coffee, (which makes the politician wise,
And see through all things with his half-shut eyes)
Sent up in vapours to the Baron's brain
New Stratagems, the radiant Lock to gain.   120
Ah cease, rash youth ! desist ere 'tis too late,
Fear the just Gods, and think of Scylla's Fate !
Changed to a bird, and sent to flit in air,
She dearly pays for Nisus' injured hair !
   But when to mischief mortals bend their will,   125
How soon they find fit instruments of ill !
Just then, Clarissa drew with tempting grace
A two-edged weapon from her shining case :
So Ladies in Romance assist their Knight,
Present the spear, and arm him for the fight.   130

He takes the gift with rev'rence, and extends
The little engine on his fingers' ends ;
This just behind Belinda's neck he spread,
As o'er the fragrant steams she bends her head.
Swift to the Lock a thousand Sprites repair,   135
A thousand wings, by turns, blow back the hair ;
And thrice they twitched the diamond in her ear ;
Thrice she looked back, and thrice the foe drew near.
Just in that instant, anxious Ariel sought
The close recesses of the Virgin's thought ;   140
As on the nosegay in her breast reclined,
He watched th' Ideas rising in her mind,
Sudden he viewed, in spite of all her art,
An earthly Lover lurking at her heart.
Amazed, confused, he found his power expired,   145
Resigned to fate, and with a sigh retired.
    The Peer now spreads the glitt'ring Forfex wide,
T' inclose the Lock ; now joins it, to divide.
Even then, before the fatal engine closed,
A wretched Sylph too fondly interposed ;   150
Fate urged the shears, and cut the Sylph in twain,
(But airy substance soon unites again)
The meeting points the sacred hair dissever
From the fair head, for ever, and for ever !
    Then flashed the living lightning from her eyes,   155
And screams of horror rend th' affrighted skies.
Not louder shrieks to pitying heaven are cast,
When husbands, or when lap-dogs breathe their last ;
Or when rich China vessels fall'n from high,
In glitt'ring dust and painted fragments lie !   160
    Let wreaths of triumph now my temples twine,
(The victor cried) the glorious Prize is mine !
While fish in streams, or birds delight in air,
Or in a coach and six the British Fair,
As long as Atalantis shall be read,   165

Atalantis.—A famous book written about that time by a woman ;
full of Court, and Party-scandal, and in a loose effeminacy of style and
sentiment which well suited the debauched taste of the better Vulgar

Or the small pillow grace a Lady's bed,
While visits shall be paid on solemn days,
When num'rous wax-lights in bright order blaze,
While nymphs take treats, or assignations give,
So long my honour, name, and praise shall live !   170
What Time would spare, from Steel receives its date,
And monuments, like men, submit to fate !
Steel could the labour of the Gods destroy,
And strike to dust th' imperial towers of Troy ;
Steel could the works of mortal pride confound,   175
And hew triumphal arches to the ground.
What wonder then, fair nymph ! thy hairs should feel,
The conq'ring force of unresisted steel ?

CANTO IV

BUT anxious cares the pensive nymph oppressed,
And secret passions laboured in her breast.
Not youthful kings in battle seized alive,
Not scornful virgins who their charms survive,
Not ardent lovers robbed of all their bliss,   5
Not ancient ladies when refused a kiss,
Not tyrants fierce that unrepenting die,
Not Cynthia when her manteau's pinned awry,
E'er felt such rage, resentment, and despair,
As thou, sad Virgin ! for thy ravished Hair.   10
    For, that sad moment, when the Sylphs withdrew
And Ariel weeping from Belinda flew,
Umbriel, a dusky, melancholy sprite,
As ever sullied the fair face of light,
Down to the central earth, his proper scene,   15
Repaired to search the gloomy Cave of Spleen.
    Swift on his sooty pinions flits the Gnome,
And in a vapour reached the dismal dome.
No cheerful breeze this sullen region knows,
The dreaded East is all the wind that blows.   20
Here in a grotto, sheltered close from air,

And screened in shades from day's detested glare,
She sighs for ever on her pensive bed,
Pain at her side, and Megrim at her head.
  Two handmaids wait the throne : alike in place,   25
But diff'ring far in figure and in face.
Here stood Ill-nature like an ancient maid,
Her wrinkled form in black and white arrayed ;
With store of prayers, for mornings, nights, and noons.
Her hand is filled ; her bosom with lampoons.   30
  There Affectation, with a sickly mien,
Shows in her cheek the roses of eighteen,
Practised to lisp, and hang the head aside,
Faints into airs, and languishes with pride,
On the rich quilt sinks with becoming woe,   35
Wrapt in a gown, for sickness, and for show.
The fair ones feel such maladies as these,
When each new night-dress gives a new disease.
  A constant Vapour o'er the palace flies ;
Strange phantoms rising as the mists arise ;   40
Dreadful, as hermit's dreams in haunted shades,
Or bright, as visions of expiring maids.
Now glaring fiends, and snakes on rolling spires,
Pale spectres, gaping tombs, and purple fires :
Now lakes of liquid gold, Elysian scenes,   45
And crystal domes, and angels in machines.
  Unnumbered throngs on every side are seen,
Of bodies changed to various forms by Spleen.
Here living Tea-pots stand, one arm held out,
One bent ; the handle this, and that the spout :   50
A Pipkin there, like Homer's Tripod walks ;
Here sighs a Jar, and there a Goose-pie talks ;
Men prove with child, as powerful fancy works,
And maids turned bottles, call aloud for corks.
  Safe past the Gnome through this fantastic band, 55
A branch of healing Spleenwort in his hand.
Then thus addressed the power : " Hail, wayward Queen !

A Goose-pie.—Alludes to a real fact, a lady of distinction imagined
herself in this condition.

Who rule the sex to fifty from fifteen :
Parent of vapours and of female wit,
Who give th' hysteric or poetic fit,   60
On various tempers act by various ways,
Make some take physic, others scribble plays ;
Who cause the proud their visits to delay,
And send the godly in a pet to pray.
A nymph there is, that all thy power disdains,   65
And thousands more in equal mirth maintains.
But oh ! if e'er thy Gnome could spoil a grace,
Or raise a pimple on a beauteous face,
Like Citron-waters matrons cheeks inflame,
Or change complexions at a losing game ;   70
If e'er with airy horns I planted heads,
Or rumpled petticoats, or tumbled beds,
Or caus'd suspicion when no soul was rude,
Or discomposed the head-dress of a Prude,
Or e'er to costive lap-dog gave disease,   75
Which not the tears of brightest eyes could ease :
Hear me, and touch Belinda with chagrin,
That single act gives half the world the spleen."
    The Goddess with a discontented air
Seems to reject him, though she grants his prayer.   80
A wondrous Bag with both her hands she binds,
Like that where once Ulysses held the winds ;
There she collects the force of female lungs,
Sighs, sobs, and passions, and the war of tongues.
A Vial next she fills with fainting fears,   85
Soft sorrows, melting griefs, and flowing tears.
The Gnome rejoicing bears her gifts away,
Spreads his black wings, and slowly mounts to day.
    Sunk in Thalestris' arms the nymph he found,
Her eyes dejected and her hair unbound.   90
Full o'er their heads the swelling bag he rent,
And all the Furies issued at the vent.
Belinda burns with more than mortal ire,
And fierce Thalestris fans the rising fire.   94
" Oh wretched maid ! " she spread her hands, and cried,

(While Hampton's echoes, " Wretched maid ! " replied)
" Was it for this you took such constant care
The bodkin, comb, and essence to prepare ?
For this your locks in paper durance bound,
For this with torturing irons wreathed around ?   100
For this with fillets strained your tender head,
And bravely bore the double loads of lead ?
Gods ! shall the ravisher display your hair,
While the Fops envy, and the Ladies stare !
Honour forbid ! at whose unrivalled shrine   105
Ease, pleasure, virtue, all our sex resign.
Methinks already I your tears survey,
Already hear the horrid things they say,
Already see you a degraded toast,
And all your honour in a whisper lost !   110
How shall I, then, your helpless fame defend ?
'Twill then be infamy to seem your friend !
And shall this prize, th' inestimable prize,
Exposed through crystal to the gazing eyes,
And heightened by the diamond's circling rays,   115
On that rapacious hand for ever blaze ?
Sooner shall grass in Hyde-park Circus grow,
And wits take lodgings in the sound of Bow ;
Sooner let earth, air, sea, to Chaos fall,
Men, monkeys, lap-dogs, parrots, perish all ! "   120
    She said ; then raging to Sir Plume repairs,
And bids her Beau demand the precious hairs :
(Sir Plume of amber snuff-box justly vain,
And the nice conduct of a clouded cane)
With earnest eyes, and round unthinking face,   125
He first the snuff-box opened, then the case,
And thus broke out—" My Lord, why, what the devil ?
Z—ds ! damn the lock ! 'fore Gad, you must be civil !
Plague on't ! 'tis past a jest—nay prithee, pox !

Sir Plume repairs.—Sir George Brown. He was the only one of
the party who took the thing seriously. He was angry that the poet
should make him talk nothing but nonsense ; and, in truth, one could
not well blame him.

Give her the hair "—he spoke, and rapped his box. 130
  " It grieves me much " (replied the Peer again)
" Who speaks so well should ever speak in vain.
But by this Lock, this sacred Lock I swear,
(Which never more shall join its parted hair ;
Which never more its honours shall renew,   135
Clipped from the lovely head where late it grew)
That while my nostrils draw the vital air,
This hand, which won it, shall for ever wear."
He spoke, and speaking, in proud triumph spread
The long-contended honours of her head.   140
  But Umbriel, hateful Gnome ! forbears not so ;
He breaks the Vial whence the sorrows flow.
Then see ! the nymph in beauteous grief appears,
Her eyes half-languishing, half-drowned in tears ;
On her heaved bosom hung her drooping head,   145
Which, with a sigh, she raised ; and thus she said.
  " For ever cursed be this detested day,
Which snatched my best, my fav'rite curl away !
Happy ! ah ten times happy had I been,
If Hampton-Court these eyes had never seen !   150
Yet am not I the first mistaken maid,
By love of Courts to numerous ills betrayed.
Oh had I rather un-admired remained
In some lone isle, or distant Northern land ;
Where the gilt Chariot never marks the way,   155
Where none learn Ombre, none e'er taste Bohea !
There kept my charms concealed from mortal eye,
Like roses, that in deserts bloom and die.
What moved my mind with youthful Lords to roam ?
Oh had I stayed, and said my prayers at home !   160
'Twas this, the morning omens seemed to tell,
Thrice from my trembling hand the patch-box fell ;
The tott'ring China shook without a wind,
Nay, Poll sat mute, and Shock was most unkind !
A Sylph too warned me of the threats of fate,   165
In mystic visions, now believed too late !
See the poor remnants of these slighted hairs !

My hands shall rend what even thy rapine spares :
These in two sable ringlets taught to break,
Once gave new beauties to the snowy neck ;   170
The sister-lock now sits uncouth, alone,
And in its fellow's fate foresees its own ;
Uncurled it hangs, the fatal shears demands,
And tempts once more, thy sacrilegious hands.
Oh hadst thou, cruel ! been content to seize   175
Hairs less in sight, or any hairs but these ! "

CANTO V

SHE said : the pitying audience melt in tears.
But Fate and Jove had stopped the Baron's ears.
In vain Thalestris with reproach assails,
For who can move when fair Belinda fails ?
Not half so fixed the Trojan could remain,   5
While Anna begged and Dido raged in vain.
Then grave Clarissa graceful waved her fan ;
Silence ensued, and thus the nymph began.
    " Say why are Beauties praised and honoured most,
The wise man's passion, and the vain man's toast ?   10
Why decked with all that land and sea afford,
Why Angels called, and Angel-like adored ?
Why round our coaches crowd the white-gloved Beaux,
Why bows the side-box from its inmost rows ;
How vain are all these glories, all our pains,   15
Unless good sense preserve what beauty gains :
That men may say, when we the front-box grace :
' Behold the first in virtue as in face ! '
Oh ! if to dance all night, and dress all day,
Charmed the small-pox, or chased old-age away ;   20
Who would not scorn what housewife's cares produce,
Or who would learn one earthly thing of use ?
To patch, nay ogle, might become a Saint,
Nor could it sure be such a sin to paint.
But since, alas ! frail beauty must decay,   25
Curled or uncurled, since Locks will turn to grey ;

Since painted, or not painted, all shall fade,
And she who scorns a man, must die a maid ;
What then remains but well our power to use,
And keep good-humour still whate'er we lose ?   30
And trust me, dear ! good-humour can prevail,
When airs, and flights, and screams, and scolding fail.
Beauties in vain their pretty eyes may roll ;
Charms strike the sight, but merit wins the soul."
    So spoke the Dame, but no applause ensued ;   35
Belinda frowned, Thalestris called her Prude.
" To arms, to arms ! " the fierce Virago cries,
And swift as lightning to the combat flies.
All side in parties, and begin th' attack ;
Fans clap, silks rustle, and tough whalebones crack ; 40
Heroes' and Heroines' shouts confus'dly rise,
And bass and treble voices strike the skies.
No common weapons in their hands are found,
Like Gods they fight, nor dread a mortal wound.
    So when bold Homer makes the Gods engage,   45
And heavenly breasts with human passions rage ;
'Gainst Pallas, Mars ; Latona, Hermes arms ;
And all Olympus rings with loud alarms :
Jove's thunder roars, heaven trembles all around,
Blue Neptune storms, the bellowing deeps resound : 50
Earth shakes her nodding towers, the ground gives way,
And the pale ghosts start at the flash of day !
    Triumphant Umbriel on a sconce's height
Clapped his glad wings, and sate to view the fight :
Propped on their bodkin spears, the Sprites survey 55
The growing combat, or assist the fray.
    While through the press enraged Thalestris flies,
And scatters death around from both her eyes,
A Beau and Witling perished in the throng,
One died in metaphor, and one in song.   60
" O cruel nymph ! a living death I bear,"
Cried Dapperwit, and sunk beside his chair.
A mournful glance Sir Fopling upwards cast,
" Those eyes are made so killing "—was his last.

Thus on Mæander's flowery margin lies   65
Th' expiring Swan, and as he sings he dies.
  When bold Sir Plume had drawn Clarissa down,
Chloe stepped in, and killed him with a frown ;
She smiled to see the doughty hero slain,
But, at her smile, the Beau revived again.   70
  Now Jove suspends his golden scales in air,
Weighs the Men's wits against the Lady's hair ;
The doubtful beam long nods from side to side ;
At length the wits mount up, the hairs subside.
  See, fierce Belinda on the Baron flies,   75
With more than usual lightning in her eyes :
Nor feared the Chief th' unequal fight to try,
Who sought no more than on his foe to die.
But this bold Lord with manly strength endued,
She with one finger and a thumb subdued :   80
Just where the breath of life his nostrils drew,
A charge of Snuff the wily virgin threw ;
The Gnomes direct, to every atom just,
The pungent grains of titillating dust.
Sudden, with starting tears each eye o'erflows,   85
And the high dome re-echoes to his nose.
  Now meet thy fate, incensed Belinda cried,
And drew a deadly bodkin from her side.
(The same, his ancient personage to deck,
Her great great grandsire wore about his neck,   90
In three seal-rings ; which after, melted down,
Formed a vast buckle for his widow's gown :
Her infant grandame's whistle next it grew,
The bells she jingled, and the whistle blew ;
Then in a bodkin graced her mother's hairs,   95
Which long she wore, and now Belinda wears.)
  " Boast not my fall " (he cried) " insulting foe !
Thou by some other shalt be laid as low,
Nor think, to die dejects my lofty mind :
All that I dread is leaving you behind !   100
Rather than so, ah let me still survive,
And burn in Cupid's flames—but burn alive."

4

" Restore the Lock ! " she cries ; and all around
" Restore the Lock ! " the vaulted roofs rebound.
Not fierce Othello in so loud a strain   105
Roared for the handkerchief that caused his pain.
But see how oft ambitious aims are crossed,
And chiefs contend 'till all the prize is lost !
The Lock, obtained with guilt, and kept with pain,
In every place is sought, but sought in vain :   110
With such a prize no mortal must be blest,
So heaven decrees ! with heaven who can contest ?
    Some thought it mounted to the Lunar sphere,
Since all things lost on earth are treasured there.
There Hero's wits are kept in pond'rous vases,   115
And beau's in snuff-boxes and tweezer-cases.
There broken vows and death-bed alms are found,
And lovers' hearts with ends of riband bound,
The courtier's promises, and sick man's prayers,
The smiles of harlots, and the tears of heirs,   120
Cages for gnats, and chains to yoke a flea,
Dried butterflies, and tomes of casuistry.
    But trust the Muse—she saw it upward rise,
Though marked by none but quick, poetic eyes :
(So Rome's great founder to the heavens withdrew, 125
To Proculus alone confessed in view)
A sudden Star, it shot through liquid air,
And drew behind a radiant trail of hair.
Not Berenice's Locks first rose so bright,
The heavens bespangling with dishevelled light.   130
The Sylphs behold it kindling as it flies,
And pleased pursue its progress through the skies.
    This the Beau monde shall from the Mall survey,
And hail with music its propitious ray.
This the blest Lover shall for Venus take,   135
And send up vows from Rosamonda's lake.
This Partridge soon shall view in cloudless skies,

This Partridge soon.—John Partridge was a ridiculous Star-gazer,
who in his Almanacks every year never failed to predict the downfall
of the Pope, and the King of France, then at war with the English.

When next he looks through Galileo's eyes ;
And hence th' egregious wizard shall foredoom
The fate of Louis, and the fall of Rome.   140
   Then cease, bright Nymph ! to mourn thy ravished
         hair,
Which adds new glory to the shining sphere !
Not all the tresses that fair head can boast,
Shall draw such envy as the Lock you lost.
For, after all the murders of your eye,   145
When, after millions slain, yourself shall die :
When those fair suns shall set, as set they must,
And all those tresses shall be laid in dust,
This Lock, the Muse shall consecrate to fame,
And 'midst the stars inscribe Belinda's name.   150

ELEGY

What beck'ning ghost, along the moon-light shade
Invites my steps, and points to yonder glade?
'Tis she!—but why that bleeding bosom gored,
Why dimly gleams the visionary sword?
Oh ever beauteous, ever friendly! tell,⠀⠀⠀⠀⠀⠀5
Is it, in heaven, a crime to love too well?
To bear too tender, or too firm a heart,
To act a Lover's or a Roman's part?
Is there no bright reversion in the sky,
For those who greatly think, or bravely die?⠀⠀⠀10
⠀⠀Why bade ye else, ye Powers! her soul aspire
Above the vulgar flight of low desire?
Ambition first sprung from your blest abodes;
The glorious fault of Angels and of Gods;
Thence to their images on earth it flows,⠀⠀⠀15
And in the breasts of Kings and Heroes glows.
Most souls, 'tis true, but peep out once an age,
Dull sullen pris'ners in the body's cage:
Dim lights of life, that burn a length of years
Useless, unseen, as lamps in sepulchres;⠀⠀⠀20
Like Eastern Kings a lazy state they keep,
And close confined to their own palace, sleep.
⠀⠀From these perhaps (ere nature bade her die)
Fate snatched her early to the pitying sky.
As into air the purer spirits flow,⠀⠀⠀⠀⠀25
And sep'rate from their kindred dregs below;
So flew the soul to its congenial place,

Unfortunate Lady.—Many attempts have been made to identify this
lady. It seems probable that the poem does not present with accuracy
the story of any specific unfortunate.

Nor left one virtue to redeem her Race.
  But thou, false guardian of a charge too good,
Thou, mean deserter of thy brother's blood! 30
See on these ruby lips the trembling breath,
These cheeks now fading at the blast of death :
Cold is that breast which warmed the world before,
And those love-darting eyes must roll no more.
Thus, if Eternal justice rules the ball, 35
Thus shall your wives, and thus your children fall ;
On all the line a sudden vengeance waits,
And frequent herses shall besiege your gates.
There passengers shall stand, and pointing say,
(While the long fun'rals blacken all the way) 40
Lo these were they, whose souls the Furies steeled,
And cursed with hearts unknowing how to yield.
Thus unlamented pass the proud away,
The gaze of fools, and pageant of a day !
So perish all, whose breast ne'er learned to glow 45
For others' good, or melt at others' woe.
  What can atone (oh ever-injured shade !)
Thy fate unpitied, and thy rites unpaid ?
No friend's complaint, no kind domestic tear
Pleased thy pale ghost, or graced thy mournful bier. 50
By foreign hands thy dying eyes were closed,
By foreign hands thy decent limbs composed,
By foreign hands thy humble grave adorned,
By strangers honoured, and by strangers mourned !
What though no friends in sable weeds appear, 55
Grieve for an hour, perhaps, then mourn a year,
And bear about the mockery of woe
To midnight dances, and the public show ?
What though no weeping Loves thy ashes grace,
Nor polished marble emulate thy face ? 60
What though no sacred earth allow thee room,
Nor hallowed dirge be muttered o'er thy tomb ?
Yet shall thy grave with rising flowers be drest,
And the green turf lie lightly on thy breast :
There shall the morn her earliest tears bestow, 65

There the first roses of the year shall blow ;
While Angels with their silver wings o'ershade
The ground, now sacred by thy reliques made.
　So peaceful rests, without a stone, a name,
What once had beauty, titles, wealth, and fame.　70
How loved, how honoured once, avails thee not,
To whom related, or by whom begot ;
A heap of dust alone remains of thee,
'Tis all thou art, and all the proud shall be !
　Poets themselves must fall, like those they sung,　75
Deaf the praised ear, and mute the tuneful tongue.
Even he, whose soul now melts in mournful lays,
Shall shortly want the gen'rous tear he pays ;
Then from his closing eyes thy form shall part,
And the last pang shall tear thee from his heart,　80
Life's idle business at one gasp be o'er,
The Muse forgot, and thou be loved no more !

ELOÏSA TO ABELARD

ARGUMENT

ABELARD and Eloïsa flourished in the twelfth Century ; they were two
of the most distinguished Persons of their age in learning and beauty,
but for nothing more famous than for their unfortunate passion.   After
a long course of calamities, they retired each to a several Convent,
and consecrated the remainder of their days to religion.   It was many
years after this separation, that a letter of Abelard's to a Friend,
which contained the history of his misfortune, fell into the hands of
Eloïsa.   This awakening all her Tenderness, occasioned those celebrated letters (out of which the following is partly extracted) which
gives so lively a picture of the struggles of grace and nature, virtue
and passion.

IN these deep solitudes and awful cells,
Where heavenly-pensive contemplation dwells,
And ever-musing melancholy reigns ;
What means this tumult in a Vestal's veins ?
Why rove my thoughts beyond this last retreat ?   **5**
Why feels my heart its long-forgotten heat ?
Yet, yet I love !—From Abelard it came,
And Eloïsa yet must kiss the name.
   Dear fatal name ! rest ever unrevealed,
Nor pass these lips in holy silence sealed :   10
Hide it, my heart, within that close disguise,
Where mixed with God's, his loved Idea lies :
O write it not my hand—the name appears
Already written—wash it out, my tears !
In vain lost Eloïsa weeps and prays,   15
Her heart still dictates, and her hand obeys.
   Relentless walls ! whose darksome round contains
Repentant sighs, and voluntary pains :
Ye rugged rocks ! which holy knees have worn ;
Ye grots and caverns shagged with horrid thorn !   20
Shrines ! where their vigils pale-eyed virgins keep,

And pitying saints, whose statues learn to weep !
Though cold like you, unmoved and silent grown,
I have not yet forgot myself to stone.*
All is not Heaven's while Abelard has part,   25
Still rebel nature holds out half my heart ;
Nor prayers nor fasts its stubborn pulse restrain,
Nor tears for ages taught to flow in vain.
    Soon as thy letters trembling I unclose,
That well-known name awakens all my woes.   30
Oh name for ever sad ! for ever dear !
Still breathed in sighs, still ushered with a tear.
I tremble too, where'er my own I find,
Some dire misfortune follows close behind.
Line after line my gushing eyes o'erflow,   35
Led through a sad variety of woe :
Now warm in love, now with'ring in my bloom,
Lost in a convent's solitary gloom !
There stern Religion quenched th' unwilling flame,
There died the best of passions, Love and Fame.   40
    Yet write, oh write me all, that I may join
Griefs to thy griefs, and echo sighs to thine.
Nor foes nor fortune take this power away ;
And is my Abelard less kind than they ?
Tears still are mine, and those I need not spare,   45
Love but demands what else were shed in prayer ;
No happier task these faded eyes pursue ;
To read and weep is all they now can do.
    Then share thy pain, allow that sad relief ;
Ah, more than share it, give me all thy grief.   50
Heaven first taught letters for some wretch's aid,
Some banished lover, or some captive maid ;
They live, they speak, they breathe what love inspires,
Warm from the soul, and faithful to its fires,
The virgin's wish without her fears impart,   55

---

* " Forget thyself to marble," Milton, *Il Penseroso*. The expression
" caverns shagged with horrid thorn," and the epithets " pale-eyed,"
" twilight," " low-thoughted care," and others, are first used in the
smaller poems of Milton, which Pope seems to have been just reading.

Excuse the blush, and pour out all the heart,
Speed the soft intercourse from soul to soul,
And waft a sigh from Indus to the Pole.
 Thou know'st how guiltless first I met thy flame.
When Love approached me under Friendship's name ;
My fancy formed thee of angelic kind,   61
Some emanation of th' all-beauteous Mind.
Those smiling eyes, attemp'ring every ray,
Shone sweetly lambent with celestial day.
Guiltless I gazed ; heaven listened while you sung ; 65
And truths divine came mended from that tongue.
From lips like those what precept failed to move ?
Too soon they taught me 'twas no sin to love :
Back through the paths of pleasing sense I ran,
Nor wished an Angel whom I loved a Man.   70
Dim and remote the joys of saints I see ;
Nor envy them that heaven I lose for thee.
 How oft, when pressed to marriage, have I said,
Curse on all laws but those which love has made ?
Love, free as air, at sight of human ties,   75
Spreads his light wings, and in a moment flies.
Let wealth, let honour, wait the wedded dame,
August her deed, and sacred be her fame ;
Before true passion all those views remove,
Fame, wealth, and honour ! what are you to Love ? 80
The jealous God, when we profane his fires,
Those restless passions in revenge inspires,
And bids them make mistaken mortals groan,
Who seek in love for aught but love alone.
Should at my feet the world's great master fall,   85
Himself, his throne, his world, I'd scorn 'em all :
Not Cæsar's empress would I deign to prove ;
No, make me mistress to the man I love ;
If there be yet another name more free,
More fond than mistress, make me that to thee !   90

 Another name more free.—These lines cannot be justified by anything in the letters of Eloïsa, where she merely prays Abelard to write
to her.

             4 *a*

Oh ! happy state ! when souls each other draw,
When love is liberty, and nature law :
All then is full, possessing, and possessed,
No craving void left aking in the breast :   94
Even thought meets thought, ere from the lips it part,
And each warm wish springs mutual from the heart.
This sure is bliss (if bliss on earth there be)
And once the lot of Abelard and me.

    Alas, how changed ! what sudden horrors rise !
A naked Lover bound and bleeding lies !   100
Where, where was Eloïse ? her voice, her hand,
Her poniard, had opposed the dire command.
Barbarian, stay ! that bloody stroke restrain ;
The crime was common, common be the pain.
I can no more ; by shame, by rage suppressed,   105
Let tears, and burning blushes speak the rest.

    Canst thou forget that sad, that solemn day,
When victims at yon altar's foot we lay ?
Canst thou forget what tears that moment fell,
When, warm in youth, I bade the world farewell ?   110
As with cold lips I kissed the sacred veil,
The shrines all trembled, and the lamps grew pale :
Heaven scarce believed the Conquest it surveyed,
And Saints with wonder heard the vows I made.
Yet then, to those dread altars as I drew,   115
Not on the Cross my eyes were fixed, but you :
Not grace, or zeal, love only was my call,
And if I lose thy love, I lose my all.
Come ! with thy looks, thy words, relieve my woe ;
Those still at least are left thee to bestow.   120
Still on that breast enamoured let me lie,
Still drink delicious poison from thy eye,
Pant on thy lip, and to thy heart be pressed ;
Give all thou canst—and let me dream the rest.
Ah no ! instruct me other joys to prize,   125
With other beauties charm my partial eyes,
Full in my view set all the bright abode,
And make my soul quit Abelard for God.

Ah, think at least thy flock deserves thy care,
Plants of thy hand, and children of thy prayer.　130
From the false world in early youth they fled,
By thee to mountains, wilds, and deserts led.
You raised these hallowed walls ; the desert smiled,
And Paradise was opened in the Wild.
No weeping orphan saw his father's stores　135
Our shrines irradiate, or emblaze the floors ;
No silver saints, by dying misers given,
Here bribed the rage of ill-requited heaven :
But such plain roofs as Piety could raise,
And only vocal with the Maker's praise.　140
In these lone walls (their days eternal bound)
These moss-grown domes with spiry turrets crowned,
Where awful arches make a noon-day night,
And the dim windows shed a solemn light ;
Thy eyes diffused a reconciling ray,　145
And gleams of glory brightened all the day.
But now no face divine contentment wears,
'Tis all blank sadness, or continual tears.
See how the force of others' prayers I try,
(O pious fraud of am'rous charity !)　150
But why should I on others' prayers depend ?
Come thou, my father, brother, husband, friend !
Ah let thy handmaid, sister, daughter move,
And all those tender names in one, thy love !
The darksome pines that o'er yon rocks reclined　155
Wave high, and murmur to the hollow wind,
The wandering streams that shine between the hills,
The grots that echo to the tinkling rills,
The dying gales that pant upon the trees,
The lakes that quiver to the curling breeze ;　160
No more these scenes my meditation aid,
Or lull to rest the visionary maid.
But o'er the twilight groves and dusky caves,
Long-sounding aisles, and intermingled graves,

You raised these hallowed walls.—He founded the Monastery.

Black Melancholy sits, and round her throws   163
A death-like silence, and a dead repose :
Her gloomy presence saddens all the scene,
Shades every flower, and darkens every green,
Deepens the murmur of the falling floods,
And breathes a browner horror on the woods.   170
    Yet here for ever, ever must I stay ;
Sad proof how well a lover can obey !
Death, only death, can break the lasting chain :
And here, even then, shall my cold dust remain,
Here all its frailties, all its flames resign,   175
And wait till 'tis no sin to mix with thine.
    Ah wretch ! believed the spouse of God in vain,
Confessed within the slave of love and man.
Assist me, heaven ! but whence arose that prayer ?
Sprung it from piety, or from despair ?   180
Even here, where frozen chastity retires,
Love finds an altar for forbidden fires.
I ought to grieve, but cannot what I ought ;
I mourn the lover, not lament the fault ;
I view my crime, but kindle at the view,   185
Repent old pleasures, and solicit new ;
Now turned to heaven, I weep my past offence,
Now think of thee, and curse my innocence.
Of all affliction taught a lover yet,
'Tis sure the hardest science to forget !   190
How shall I lose the sin, yet keep the sense,
And love th' offender, yet detest th' offence ?
How the dear object from the crime remove,
Or how distinguish penitence from love ?
Unequal task ! a passion to resign,   195
For hearts so touched, so pierced, so lost as mine.
Ere such a soul regains its peaceful state,
How often must it love, how often hate !
How often hope, despair, resent, regret,
Conceal, disdain,—do all things but forget.   200
But let heaven seize it, all at once 'tis fired :
Not touched, but rapt ; not wakened, but inspired !

Oh come ! oh teach me nature to subdue,
Renounce my love, my life, myself—and you.
Fill my fond heart with God alone, for he   205
Alone can rival, can succeed to thee.
   How happy is the blameless Vestal's lot !
The world forgetting, by the world forgot :
Eternal sunshine of the spotless mind !
Each prayer accepted, and each wish resigned ;   210
Labour and rest, that equal periods keep ;
" Obedient slumbers that can wake and weep ; "
Desires composed, affections ever even ;
Tears that delight, and sighs that waft to heaven.
Grace shines around her with serenest beams,   215
And whisp'ring Angels prompt her golden dreams.
For her th' unfading rose of Eden blooms,
And wings of Seraphs shed divine perfumes,
For her the Spouse prepares the bridal ring,
For her white virgins Hymenæals sing,   220
To sounds of heavenly harps she dies away,
And melts in visions of eternal day.
   Far other dreams my erring soul employ,
Far other raptures, of unholy joy :
When at the close of each sad, sorrowing day,   225
Fancy restores what vengeance snatched away,
Then conscience sleeps, and leaving nature free,
All my loose soul unbounded springs to thee.
Oh curst, dear horrors of all-conscious night ;
How glowing guilt exalts the keen delight !   230
Provoking Dæmons all restraint remove,
And stir within me every source of love.
I hear thee, view thee, gaze o'er all thy charms,
And round thy phantom glue my clasping arms.
I wake :—no more I hear, no more I view,   235
The phantom flies me, as unkind as you.
I call aloud ; it hears not what I say :
I stretch my empty arms ; it glides away.
To dream once more I close my willing eyes ;
Ye soft illusions, dear deceits, arise !   240

Alas, no more ! methinks we wand'ring go
Through dreary wastes, and weep each other's woe,
Where round some mould'ring tower pale ivy creeps,
And low-browed rocks hang nodding o'er the deeps.
Sudden you mount, you beckon from the skies ;   245
Clouds interpose, waves roar, and winds arise.
I shriek, start up, the same sad prospect find,
And wake to all the griefs I left behind.
   For thee the fates, severely kind, ordain
A cool suspense from pleasure and from pain ;   250
Thy life a long dead calm of fixed repose ;
No pulse that riots, and no blood that glows.
Still as the sea, ere winds were taught to blow,
Or moving spirit bade the waters flow ;
Soft as the slumbers of a saint forgiven,   255
And mild as opening gleams of promised heaven.
   Come, Abelard ! for what hast thou to dread ?
The torch of Venus burns not for the dead.
Nature stands checked ; Religion disapproves ;
Even thou art cold—yet Eloïsa loves.   260
Ah hopeless, lasting flames ! like those that burn
To light the dead, and warm th' unfruitful urn.
   What scenes appear where'er I turn my view ?
The dear Ideas, where I fly, pursue,
Rise in the grove, before the altar rise,   265
Stain all my soul, and wanton in my eyes.
I waste the Matin lamp in sighs for thee,
Thy image steals between my God and me,
Thy voice I seem in every hymn to hear,
With every bead I drop too soft a tear.   270
When from the censer clouds of fragrance roll,
And swelling organs lift the rising soul,
One thought of thee puts all the pomp to flight,
Priests, tapers, temples, swim before my sight :
In seas of flame my plunging soul is drowned,   275
While Altars blaze, and Angels tremble round.
   While prostrate here in humble grief I lie,
Kind, virtuous drops just gath'ring in my eye,

While praying, trembling, in the dust I roll,
And dawning grace is opening on my soul : 280
Come, if thou dar'st, all charming as thou art !
Oppose thyself to heaven ; dispute my heart ;
Come, with one glance of those deluding eyes
Blot out each bright Idea of the skies ;
Take back that grace, those sorrows, and those tears ;
Take back my fruitless penitence and prayers ; 286
Snatch me, just mounting, from the blest abode ;
Assist the fiends, and tear me from my God !
  No, fly me, fly me, far as Pole from Pole ;
Rise Alps between us ! and whole oceans roll ! 290
Ah, come not, write not, think not once of me,
Nor share one pang of all I felt for thee.
Thy oaths I quit, thy memory resign ;
Forget, renounce me, hate whate'er was mine.
Fair eyes, and tempting looks (which yet I view !) 295
Long loved, adored ideas, all adieu !
Oh Grace serene ! oh virtue heavenly fair !
Divine oblivion of low-thoughted care !
Fresh blooming Hope, gay daughter of the sky !
And Faith, our early immortality ! 300
Enter, each mild, each amicable guest ;
Receive, and wrap me in eternal rest !
  See in her cell sad Eloïsa spread,
Propt on some tomb, a neighbour of the dead.
In each low wind methinks a Spirit calls, 305
And more than Echoes talk along the walls.
Here, as I watched the dying lamps around,
From yonder shrine I heard a hollow sound.
"Come, sister, come !" (it said, or seemed to say)
"Thy place is here, sad sister, come away ! 310
Once like thyself, I trembled, wept, and prayed,
Love's victim then, though now a sainted maid :
But all is calm in this eternal sleep ;
Here grief forgets to groan, and love to weep,
Even superstition loses every fear : 315
For God, not man, absolves our frailties here."

I come, I come ! prepare your roseate bowers,
Celestial palms, and ever-blooming flowers.
Thither, where sinners may have rest, I go,
Where flames refined in breasts seraphic glow :   320
Thou, Abelard ! the last sad office pay,
And smooth my passage to the realms of day ;
See my lips tremble, and my eye-balls roll,
Suck my last breath, and catch my flying soul !
Ah no—in sacred vestments may'st thou stand,   325
The hallowed taper trembling in thy hand,
Present the Cross before my lifted eye,
Teach me at once, and learn of me to die.
Ah then, thy once-loved Eloïsa see !
It will be then no crime to gaze on me.   330
See from my cheek the transient roses fly !
See the last sparkle languish in my eye !
'Til every motion, pulse, and breath be o'er ;
And even my Abelard be loved no more.
O Death all-eloquent ! you only prove   335
What dust we dote on, when 'tis man we love.
    Then too, when fate shall thy fair frame destroy,
(That cause of all my guilt, and all my joy)
In trance ecstatic may thy pangs be drowned,
Bright clouds descend, and Angels watch thee round,
From opening skies may streaming glories shine,   341
And saints embrace thee with a love like mine.
    May one kind grave unite each hapless name,
And graft my love immortal on thy fame !
Then, ages hence, when all my woes are o'er,   345
When this rebellious heart shall beat no more ;
If ever chance two wand'ring lovers brings
To Paraclete's white walls and silver springs,
O'er the pale marble shall they join their heads,
And drink the falling tears each other sheds ;   350
Then sadly say, with mutual pity moved,

    May one kind grave, etc.—Abelard and Eloïsa were interred in the
same grave, or in monuments adjoining, in the Monastery of the
Paraclete ; he died in the year 1142, she in 1163.

" Oh may we never love as these have loved ! "
From the full choir when loud Hosannas rise,
And swell the pomp of dreadful sacrifice,
Amid that scene if some relenting eye   355
Glance on the stone where our cold relics lie,
Devotion's self shall steal a thought from heaven,
One human tear shall drop and be forgiven.
And sure, if fate some future bard shall join
In sad similitude of griefs to mine,   360
Condemned whole years in absence to deplore,
And image charms he must behold no more ;
Such if there be, who loves so long, so well ;
Let him our sad, our tender story tell ;
The well-sung woes will soothe my pensive ghost ;   365
He best can paint 'em who shall feel 'em most.

AN ESSAY ON MAN

To Henry St. John Lord Bolingbroke

THE DESIGN

HAVING proposed to write some pieces on Human Life and Manners, such as (to use my Lord Bacon's expression) *come home to Men's Business and Bosoms*, I thought it more satisfactory to begin with considering *Man* in the abstract, his *Nature* and his *State ;* since, to prove any moral duty, to enforce any moral precept, or to examine the perfection or imperfection of any creature whatsoever, it is necessary first to know what *condition* and *relation* it is placed in, and what is the proper *end* and *purpose* of its *being*.

The science of Human Nature is, like all other sciences, reduced to a *few clear points :* There are not *many certain truths* in this world. It is therefore in the Anatomy of the mind as in that of the Body ; more good will accrue to mankind by attending to the large, open, and perceptible parts, than by studying too much such finer nerves and vessels, the conformations and uses of which will for ever escape our observation. The *disputes* are all upon these last, and, I will venture to say, they have less sharpened the *wits* than the *hearts* of men against each other, and have diminished the practice, more than advanced the theory of Morality. If I could flatter myself that this Essay has any merit, it is in steering betwixt the extremes of doctrines seemingly opposite, in passing over terms utterly unintelligible, and in forming a *temperate* yet not *inconsistent*, and a *short* yet not *imperfect* system of Ethics.

114

This I might have done in prose, but I chose verse, and even rhyme, for two reasons. The one will appear obvious ; that principles, maxims, or precepts so written, both strike the reader more strongly at first, and are more easily retained by him afterwards : The other may seem odd, but is true, I found I could express them more *shortly* this way than in prose itself ; and nothing is more certain, than that much of the *force* as well as *grace* of arguments or instructions, depends on their *conciseness*. I was unable to treat this part of my subject more in *detail*, without becoming dry and tedious ; or more *poetically*, without sacrificing perspicuity to ornament, without wandering from the precision, or breaking the chain of reasoning : If any man can unite all these without diminution of any of them, I freely confess he will compass a thing above my capacity.

What is now published, is only to be considered as a *general Map* of MAN, marking out no more than the *greater parts*, their *extent*, their *limits*, and their *connection*, and leaving the particular to be more fully delineated in the charts which are to follow. Consequently, these Epistles in their progress (if I have health and leisure to make any progress) will be less dry, and more susceptible of poetical ornament. I am here only opening the *fountains*, and clearing the passage. To deduce the *rivers*, to follow them in their course, and to observe their effects, may be a task more agreeable.

AN ESSAY ON MAN

ARGUMENT OF EPISTLE I

Of the Nature and State of Man, with respect to the UNIVERSE

OF *Man* in the abstract.   I. That we can judge only with regard to our *own system*, being ignorant of the *relations* of systems and things. II. That Man is not to be deemed *imperfect*, but a Being suited to his *place* and *rank* in the creation, agreeable to the *general Order* of things, and conformable to *Ends* and *Relations* to him unknown.   III. That it is partly upon his *ignorance* of *future* events, and partly upon the *hope* of a *future* state, that all his happiness in the present depends. IV. The *pride* of aiming at more knowledge, and pretending to more Perfection, the cause of Man's error and misery.   The *impiety* of putting himself in the place of *God*, and judging of the fitness or unfitness, perfection or imperfection, justice or injustice of his dispensations.   V. The *absurdity* of conceiting himself the *final cause* of the creation, or expecting that perfection in the *moral* world, which is not in the *natural*.   VI. The *unreasonableness* of his complaints against *Providence*, while on the one hand he demands the Perfections of the Angels, and on the other the bodily qualifications of the Brutes ; though, to possess any of the *sensitive faculties* in a higher degree, would render him miserable.   VII. That throughout the whole visible world, an universal *order* and *gradation* in the sensual and mental faculties is observed, which causes a *subordination* of creature to creature, and of all creatures to Man.   The gradations of *sense, instinct, thought, reflection, reason;* that Reason alone countervails all the other faculties.   VIII. How much further this *order* and *subordination* of living creatures may extend, above and below us ; were any part of which broken, not that part only, but the whole connected *creation* must be destroyed.   IX. The *extravagance, madness,* and *pride* of such a desire.   X. The consequence of all, the *absolute submission* due to Providence, both as to our *present* and *future* state.

EPISTLE I

AWAKE, my ST. JOHN ! leave all meaner things
To low ambition, and the pride of Kings.
Let us (since Life can little more supply
Than just to look about us and to die)
Expatiate free o'er all this scene of Man ;   5
A mighty maze ! but not without a plan ;

A Wild, where weeds and flowers promiscuous shoot ;
Or Garden, tempting with forbidden fruit.
Together let us beat this ample field,
Try what the open, what the covert yield ;   10
The latent tracts, the giddy heights, explore
Of all who blindly creep, or sightless soar ;
Eye Nature's walks, shoot Folly as it flies,
And catch the Manners living as they rise ;
Laugh where we must, be candid where we can ;   15
But vindicate the ways of God to Man.
    I.   Say first, of God above, or Man below,
What can we reason, but from what we know ?
Of Man, what see we but his station here,
From which to reason, or to which refer ?   20
Through worlds unnumbered though the God be known,
'Tis ours to trace him only in our own.
He, who through vast immensity can pierce,
See worlds on worlds compose one universe,
Observe how system into system runs,   25
What other planets circle other suns,
What varied Being peoples every star,
May tell why Heaven has made us as we are.
But of this frame the bearings, and the ties,
The strong connexions, nice dependencies,   30
Gradations just, has thy pervading soul
Looked through ? or can a part contain the whole ?
   Is the great chain, that draws all to agree,
And drawn supports, upheld by God, or thee ?
    II.   Presumptuous Man ! the reason wouldst thou find,
Why formed so weak, so little, and so blind ?   36
First, if thou canst, the harder reason guess,
Why formed no weaker, blinder, and no less ?
Ask of thy mother earth, why oaks are made
Taller or stronger than the weeds they shade ?   40
Or ask of yonder argent fields above,
Why JOVE's satellites are less than JOVE ?
   Of Systems possible, if 'tis confest
That Wisdom infinite must form the best,

Where all must full or not coherent be,   45
And all that rises, rise in due degree ;
Then, in the scale of reas'ning life, 'tis plain,
There must be, somewhere, such a rank as Man :
And all the question (wrangle e'er so long)
Is only this, if God has placed him wrong ?   50
    Respecting Man, whatever wrong we call,
May, must be right, as relative to all.
In human works, though laboured on with pain,
A thousand movements scarce one purpose gain ;
In God's, one single can its end produce ;   55
Yet serves to second too some other use.
So Man, who here seems principal alone,
Perhaps acts second to some sphere unknown,
Touches some wheel, or verges to some goal ;
'Tis but a part we see, and not a whole.   60
    When the proud steed shall know why Man restrains
His fiery course, or drives him o'er the plains :
When the dull Ox, why now he breaks the clod,
Is now a victim, and now Ægypt's God :
Then shall Man's pride and dulness comprehend   65
His actions', passions', being's, use and end ;
Why doing, suffering, checked, impelled ; and why
This hour a slave, the next a deity.
    Then say not Man's imperfect, Heaven in fault ;
Say rather, Man's as perfect as he ought :   70
His knowledge measured to his state and place ;
His time a moment, and a point his space.
If to be perfect in a certain sphere,
What matter, soon or late, or here or there ?
The blest to day is as completely so,   75
As who began a thousand years ago.
    III.   Heaven from all creatures hides the book of Fate,
All but the page prescribed, their present state :
From brutes what men, from men what spirits know :
Or who could suffer Being here below ?   80
The lamb thy riot dooms to bleed to-day,
Had he thy Reason, would he skip and play ?

Pleased to the last, he crops the flowery food,
And licks the hand just raised to shed his blood.
Oh blindness to the future ! kindly given,   85
That each may fill the circle marked by Heaven :
Who sees with equal eye, as God of all,
A hero perish, or a sparrow fall,
Atoms or systems into ruin hurled,
And now a bubble burst, and now a world.   90
   Hope humbly then ; with trembling pinions soar ;
Wait the great teacher Death ; and God adore.
What future bliss, he gives not thee to know,
But gives that Hope to be thy blessing now.
Hope springs eternal in the human breast :   95
Man never Is, but always To be blest :
The soul, uneasy and confined from home,
Rests and expatiates in a life to come.
   Lo, the poor Indian ! whose untutored mind
Sees God in clouds, or hears him in the wind ;   100
His soul, proud Science never taught to stray
Far as the solar walk, or milky way ;
Yet simple Nature to his hope has given,
Behind the cloud-topt hill, an humbler heaven ;
Some safer world in depth of woods embraced,   105
Some happier island in the watery waste,
Where slaves once more their native land behold,
No fiends torment, no Christians thirst for gold.
To Be, contents his natural desire,
He asks no Angel's wing, no Seraph's fire ;   110
But thinks, admitted to that equal sky,
His faithful dog shall bear him company.
   IV. Go, wiser thou ! and, in thy scale of sense,
Weigh thy Opinion against Providence ;
Call imperfection what thou fanciest such,   115
Say, here he gives too little, there too much :
Destroy all Creatures for thy sport or gust,
Yet cry, If Man's unhappy, God's unjust ;
If Man alone engross not Heaven's high care,
Alone made perfect here, immortal there :   120

Snatch from his hand the balance and the rod,
Re-judge his justice, be the GOD of GOD.
In Pride, in reas'ning Pride, our error lies ;
All quit their sphere, and rush into the skies.
Pride still is aiming at the blest abodes,   125
Men would be Angels, Angels would be Gods.
Aspiring to be Gods, if Angels fell,
Aspiring to be Angels, Men rebel :
And who but wishes to invert the laws
Of ORDER, sins against th' Eternal Cause.   130

V.   Ask for what end the heavenly bodies shine,
Earth for whose use ? Pride answers, " 'Tis for mine :
For me kind Nature wakes her genial Power,
Suckles each herb, and spreads out every flower ;
Annual for me, the grape, the rose renew   135
The juice nectareous, and the balmy dew ;
For me, the mine a thousand treasures brings ;
For me, health gushes from a thousand springs ;
Seas roll to waft me, suns to light me rise ;
My foot-stool earth, my canopy the skies."   140

But errs not Nature from this gracious end,
From burning suns when livid deaths descend,
When earthquakes swallow, or when tempests sweep
Towns to one grave, whole nations to the deep ?
" No, ('tis replied) the first Almighty Cause   145
Acts not by partial, but by gen'ral laws ;
Th' exceptions few ; some change since all began :
And what created perfect ? "—Why then Man ?
If the great end be human Happiness,
Then Nature deviates ; and can Man do less ?   150
As much that end a constant course requires
Of showers and sun-shine, as of Man's desires ;

Then Nature deviates, etc.—" While comets move in very eccentric
orbs, in all manner of positions, blind fate could never make all the
planets move one and the same way in orbs concentric ; some inconsiderable irregularities excepted, which may have risen from mutual
actions of comets and planets upon one another, and which will be apt
to increase, till this system wants a reformation."—*Sir Isaac Newton's*
" Optics," Quest. ult.

As much eternal springs and cloudless skies,
As Men for ever temp'rate, calm, and wise.
If plagues or earthquakes break not Heaven's design,
Why then a Borgia, or a Catiline ?   156
Who knows but he, whose hand the lightning forms,
Who heaves old Ocean, and who wings the storms ;
Pours fierce Ambition in a Cæsar's mind,
Or turns young Ammon loose to scourge mankind ? 160
From pride, from pride, our very reasoning springs ;
Account for moral, as for natural things :
Why charge we Heaven in those, in these acquit ?
In both, to reason right is to submit.

Better for Us, perhaps, it might appear,   165
Were there all harmony, all virtue here ;
That never air or ocean felt the wind ;
That never passion discomposed the mind.
But ALL subsists by elemental strife ;
And Passions are the elements of Life.   170
The gen'ral ORDER, since the whole began,
Is kept in Nature, and is kept in Man.

VI.   What would this Man ? Now upward will he soar,
And little less than Angel, would be more ;
Now looking downwards, just as grieved appears   175
To want the strength of bulls, the fur of bears.
Made for his use all creatures if he call,
Say what their use, had he the powers of all ?
Nature to these, without profusion, kind,
The proper organs, proper powers assigned ;   180
Each seeming want compensated of course,
Here with degrees of swiftness, there of force ;
All in exact proportion to the state ;
Nothing to add, and nothing to abate.
Each beast, each insect, happy in its own :   185
Is heaven unkind to Man, and Man alone ?

Here with degrees of swiftness, etc.—It is a certain axiom in the
anatomy of creatures, that in proportion as they are formed for strength,
their swiftness is lessened ; or as they are formed for swiftness, their
strength is abated.

Shall he alone, whom rational we call,
Be pleased with nothing, if not blessed with all ?
　The bliss of Man (could Pride that blessing find)
Is not to act or think beyond mankind ;　　　　　190
No powers of body or of soul to share,
But what his nature and his state can bear.
Why has not Man a microscopic eye ?
For this plain reason, Man is not a Fly.
Say what the use, were finer optics given,　　　195
T' inspect a mite, not comprehend the heaven ?
Or touch, if tremblingly alive all o'er,
To smart and agonize at every pore ?
Or quick effluvia darting through the brain,
Die of a rose in aromatic pain ?　　　　　　　200
If nature thundered in his opening ears,
And stunned him with the music of the spheres,
How would he wish that Heaven had left him still
The whisp'ring Zephyr, and the purling rill ?
Who finds not Providence all good and wise,　205
Alike in what *it* gives, and what denies ?
　VII.　Far as Creation's ample range extends,
The scale of sensual, mental powers ascends :
Mark how it mounts, to Man's imperial race,
From the green myriads in the peopled grass :　210
What modes of sight betwixt each wide extreme,
The mole's dim curtain, and the lynx's beam :
Of smell, the headlong lioness between,
And hound sagacious on the tainted green :
Of hearing, from the life that fills the Flood,　215
To that which warbles through the vernal wood :
The spider's touch, how exquisitely fine !

　A microscopic eye.—That particular expression, and the whole
reasoning of this astonishing piece of poetry, is taken from Locke's
Essay on the Human Understanding, Bk. II. chap. 3, sec. 12.
　The headlong lioness.—The manner of the lions hunting their prey
in the deserts of Africa is this : At their first going out in the night-
time they set up a loud roar, and then listen to the noise made by the
beasts in their flight, pursuing them by the ear, and not by the nostril.
It is probable the story of the jackal's hunting for the lion was occasioned by observation of this defect of scent in that terrible animal.

Feels at each thread, and lives along the line :
In the nice bee, what sense so subtly true
From pois'nous herbs extracts the healing dew ?   220
How Instinct varies in the grov'lling swine,
Compared, half-reas'ning elephant, with thine !
'Twixt that, and Reason, what a nice barrier,
For ever sep'rate, yet for ever near !
Remembrance and Reflection how allied ;   225
What thin partitions Sense from Thought divide :
And Middle natures, how they long to join,
Yet never pass th' insuperable line !
Without this just gradation, could they be
Subjected, these to those, or all to thee ?   230
The powers of all subdued by thee alone,
Is not thy Reason all these powers in one ?
    VIII.   See, through this air, this ocean, and this earth,
All matter quick, and bursting into birth.
Above, how high, progressive life may go !   235
Around, how wide ! how deep extend below !
Vast chain of Being ! which from God began,
Natures ethereal, human, angel, man,
Beast, bird, fish, insect, what no eye can see,
No glass can reach ; from Infinite to thee,   240
From thee to Nothing.—On superior powers
Were we to press, inferior might on ours :
Or in the full creation leave a void,
Where, one step broken, the great scale's destroyed :
From Nature's chain whatever link you strike,   245
Tenth or ten thousandth, breaks the chain alike.
    And, if each system in gradation roll
Alike essential to th' amazing Whole,
The least confusion but in one, not all
That system only, but the Whole must fall.   250
Let Earth unbalanced from her orbit fly,
Planets and Suns run lawless through the sky ;

What thin partitions, *etc.*—So *thin*, that the Atheistic philosophers,
as Protagoras, held that *thought was only sense ;* and from thence
concluded that *every imagination or opinion of every man was true.*

Let ruling Angels from their spheres be hurled,
Being on Being wrecked, and world on world ;
Heaven's whole foundations to their centre nod,   255
And Nature tremble to the throne of God.
All this dread ORDER break—for whom ? for thee ?
Vile worm !—Oh Madness ! Pride ! Impiety !

IX.   What if the foot, ordained the dust to tread,
Or hand, to toil, aspired to be the head ?   260
What if the head, the eye, or ear repined
To serve mere engines to the ruling Mind ?
Just as absurd for any part to claim
To be another, in this gen'ral frame :
Just as absurd, to mourn the tasks or pains,   265
The great directing MIND of ALL ordains.

All are but parts of one stupendous whole,
Whose body Nature is, and God the soul ;
That, changed through all, and yet in all the same ;
Great in the earth, as in th' ethereal frame ;   270
Warms in the sun, refreshes in the breeze,
Glows in the stars, and blossoms in the trees,
Lives through all life, extends through all extent,
Spreads undivided, operates unspent ;
Breathes in our soul, informs our mortal part,   275
As full, as perfect, in a hair as heart :
As full, as perfect, in vile Man that mourns,
As the rapt Seraph that adores and burns :
To him no high, no low, no great, no small ;
He fills, he bounds, connects, and equals all.   280

X.   Cease then, nor ORDER Imperfection name :
Our proper bliss depends on what we blame.
Know thy own point : This kind, this due degree
Of blindness, weakness, Heaven bestows on thee.
Submit.—In this, or any other sphere,   285
Secure to be as blest as thou canst bear :
Safe in the hand of one disposing Power,
Or in the natal, or the mortal hour.

As the rapt Seraph, etc.—Alluding to the name *Seraphim*, signifying
burners.

All Nature is but Art, unknown to thee ;
All Chance, Direction, which thou canst not see ; 290
All Discord, Harmony not understood ;
All partial Evil, universal Good :
And, spite of Pride, in erring Reason's spite,
One truth is clear, WHATEVER IS, IS RIGHT.

ARGUMENT OF EPISTLE II

Of the Nature and State of Man with respect to HIMSELF, as an Individual

I. *The* business of Man not to pry into *God*, but to study *himself*. His *Middle Nature ;* his Powers and Frailties. The Limits of his *Capacity.* II. The two Principles of Man, *Self-love* and *Reason*, both necessary. *Self-love* the stronger, and why. Their end the same. III. The *Passions* and their use. The *predominant Passion*, and its force. Its Necessity, in directing Men to different purposes. Its providential Use, in fixing our Principle, and ascertaining our Virtue. IV. *Virtue* and *Vice* joined in our *mixed Nature ;* the limits near, yet the things *separate* and *evident :* What is the Office of *Reason.* V. How odious *Vice* in itself, and how we deceive ourselves into it. VI. That, however, the *Ends of Providence* and *general Good* are answered in our Passions and Imperfections. How usefully these are distributed to all *Orders of Men.* How useful they are to *Society.* And to the *Individuals.* In every *state*, and every *age* of life.

EPISTLE II

I. KNOW then thyself, presume not God to scan ;
The proper study of Mankind is Man.
Placed on this isthmus of a middle state,
A Being darkly wise, and rudely great :
With too much knowledge for the Sceptic side, 5
With too much weakness for the Stoic's pride,
He hangs between ; in doubt to act, or rest ;
In doubt to deem himself a God, or Beast ;
In doubt his Mind or Body to prefer ;
Born but to die, and reas'ning but to err ; 10
Alike in ignorance, his reason such,
Whether he thinks too little, or too much :

Chaos of Thought and Passion, all confused ;
Still by himself abused, or disabused ;
Created half to rise, and half to fall ;　　　　　　15
Great lord of all things, yet a prey to all ;
Sole judge of Truth, in endless Error hurled :
The glory, jest, and riddle of the world !
　Go, wondrous creature ! mount where Science guides,
Go, measure earth, weigh air, and state the tides ;　20
Instruct the planets in what orbs to run,
Correct old Time, and regulate the Sun ;
Go, soar with Plato to th' empyreal sphere,
To the first good, first perfect, and first fair ;
Or tread the mazy round his follow'rs trod,　　　25
And quitting sense call imitating God ;
As Eastern priests in giddy circles run,
And turn their heads to imitate the Sun.
Go, teach Eternal Wisdom how to rule—
Then drop into thyself, and be a fool !　　　　　30
　Superior beings when of late they saw
A mortal Man unfold all Nature's law,
Admired such wisdom in an earthly shape,
And shewed a NEWTON as we shew an Ape.
　Could he, whose rules the rapid Comet bind,　35
Describe or fix one movement of his Mind ?
Who saw its fires here rise, and there descend,
Explain his own beginning, or his end ?
Alas what wonder ! Man's superior part
Unchecked may rise, and climb from art to art ;　40
But when his own great work is but begun,
What Reason weaves, by Passion is undone.

　In endless Error hurled.—To *hurl* signifies, not simply to *cast*, but to
cast *backward and forward*, and is taken from the rural game called
hurling.　[Scoticè : curling.]
　Correct old Time.—This alludes to Sir Isaac Newton's Grecian
Chronology, which he reformed on those two sublime conceptions, the
difference between the reigns of kings and the generations of men ;
and the position of the colures of the equinoxes and solstices at the
time of the Argonautic expedition.
　Go, teach Eternal Wisdom, etc.—These two lines are a conclusion from
all that had been said.

Trace Science then, with Modesty thy guide ;
First strip off all her equipage of Pride ;
Deduct what is but Vanity, or Dress,   45
Or Learning's Luxury, or Idleness ;
Or tricks to shew the stretch of human brain,
Mere curious pleasure, or ingenious pain ;
Expunge the whole, or lop th' excrescent parts
Of all our Vices have created Arts ;   50
Then see how little the remaining sum,
Which served the past, and must the times to come !
    II. Two Principles in human nature reign ;
Self-love, to urge, and Reason, to restrain ;
Nor this a good, nor that a bad we call,   55
Each works its end, to move or govern all :
And to their proper operation still,
Ascribe all Good ; to their improper, Ill.
    Self-love, the spring of motion, acts the soul ;
Reason's comparing balance rules the whole.   60
Man, but for that, no action could attend,
And but for this, were active to no end :
Fixed like a plant on his peculiar spot,
To draw nutrition, propagate, and rot ;
Or, meteor-like, flame lawless through the void,   65
Destroying others, by himself destroyed.
    Most strength the moving principle requires ;
Active its task, it prompts, impels, inspires.
Sedate and quiet the comparing lies,
Formed but to check, delib'rate, and advise.   70
Self-love still stronger, as its objects nigh ;
Reason's at distance, and in prospect lie :
That sees immediate good by present sense ;
Reason, the future and the consequence.
Thicker than arguments, temptations throng,   75
At best more watchful this, but that more strong.
The action of the stronger to suspend,
Reason still use, to Reason still attend.
Attention, habit and experience gains ;
Each strengthens Reason, and Self-love restrains.   80

Let subtle schoolmen teach these friends to fight,
More studious to divide than to unite ;
And Grace and Virtue, Sense and Reason split,
With all the rash dexterity of wit.
Wits, just like Fools, at war about a name,   85
Have full as oft no meaning, or the same.
Self-love and Reason to one end aspire,
Pain their aversion, Pleasure their desire ;
But greedy That, its object would devour,
This taste the honey, and not wound the flower :   90
Pleasure, or wrong or rightly understood,
Our greatest evil, or our greatest good.
   III. Modes of Self-love the Passions we may call :
'Tis real good, or seeming, moves them all :
But since not every good we can divide,   95
And Reason bids us for our own provide ;
Passions, though selfish, if their means be fair,
List under Reason, and deserve her care ;
Those, that imparted, court a nobler aim,
Exalt their kind, and take some Virtue's name.   100
   In lazy Apathy let Stoics boast
Their Virtue fixed ; 'tis fixed as in a frost ;
Contracted all, retiring to the breast ;
But strength of mind is Exercise, not Rest :

Let subtle schoolmen, etc.—From this description of Self-love and Reason it follows, as the poet observes, that both conspire to one end, namely, human happiness, though they be not equally expert in the choice of the means ; the difference being this, that the first hastily seizes every thing which hath the appearance of good : the other weighs and examines whether it *be indeed* what it appears.

This shews, as he next observes, the folly of the schoolmen, who consider them as two opposite principles, the one good and the other evil. The observation is seasonable and judicious ; for this dangerous school-opinion gives great support to the Manichean or Zoroastrian error, the confutation of which was one of the author's chief ends in writing. For if there be *two principles* in Man, a *good* and a *bad*, it is natural to think him the joint product of the two Manichean deities (the first of which contributed to his *Reason*, the other to his *Passions*) rather than the creature of one Individual Cause. This was Plutarch's notion, and, as we may see in him, of the more ancient Manicheans.

The rising tempest puts in act the soul,   105
Parts it may ravage, but preserves the whole.
On life's vast ocean diversely we sail,
Reason the card, but Passion is the gale ;
Nor God alone in the still calm we find,
He mounts the storm, and walks upon the wind.   110
  Passions, like Elements, though born to fight,
Yet, mixed and softened, in his work unite :
These 'tis enough to temper and employ ;
But what composes Man, can Man destroy ?
Suffice that Reason keep to Nature's road,   115
Subject, compound them, follow her and God.
Love, Hope, and Joy, fair pleasure's smiling train,
Hate, Fear, and Grief, the family of pain,
These mixed with art, and to due bounds confined,
Make and maintain the balance of the mind :   120
The lights and shades, whose well accorded strife
Gives all the strength and colour of our life.
  Pleasures are ever in our hands or eyes ;
And when in act they cease, in prospect rise :
Present to grasp, and future still to find,   125
The whole employ of body and of mind.
All spread their charms, but charm not all alike ;
On diff'rent senses diff'rent objects strike ;
Hence diff'rent Passions more or less inflame,
As strong or weak, the organs of the frame ;   130
And hence one MASTER PASSION in the breast,
Like Aaron's serpent, swallows up the rest.
  As Man, perhaps, the moment of his breath,
Receives the lurking principle of death ;
The young disease, that must subdue at length,   135
Grows with his growth,and strengthens with his strength :
So, cast and mingled with his very frame,
The Mind's disease, its RULING PASSION came ;
Each vital humour which should feed the whole,
Soon flows to this, in body and in soul :   140
Whatever warms the heart, or fills the head,
As the mind opens, and its functions spread,

Imagination plies her dang'rous art,
And pours it all upon the peccant part.
    Nature its mother, Habit is its nurse ;   145
Wit, Spirit, Faculties, but make it worse ;
Reason itself but gives it edge and power ;
As Heaven's blest beam turns vinegar more sour.
    We, wretched subjects, though to lawful sway,
In this weak queen some fav'rite still obey :   150
Ah ! if she lend not arms, as well as rules,
What can she more than tell us we are fools ?
Teach us to mourn our Nature, not to mend,
A sharp accuser, but a helpless friend !
Or from a judge turn pleader, to persuade   155
The choice we make, or justify it made ;
Proud of an easy conquest all along,
She but removes weak passions for the strong :
So, when small humours gather to a gout,
The doctor fancies he has driven them out.   160
    Yes, Nature's road must ever be preferred ;
Reason is here no guide, but still a guard :
'Tis hers to rectify, not overthrow,
And treat this passion more as friend than foe :
A mightier Power the strong direction sends,   165
And several Men impels to several ends :
Like varying winds, by other passions tost,
This drives them constant to a certain coast.
Let power or knowledge, gold or glory, please,
Or (oft more strong than all) the love of ease ;   170
Through life 'tis followed, even at life's expense ;
The merchant's toil, the sage's indolence,
The monk's humility, the hero's pride,
All, all alike, find Reason on their side.
    Th' Eternal Art educing good from ill,   175
Grafts on this Passion our best principle :
'Tis thus the Mercury of Man is fixed,
Strong grows the Virtue with his nature mixed ;
The dross cements what else were too refined,
And in one interest body acts with mind.   180

As fruits, ungrateful to the planter's care,
On savage stocks inserted, learn to bear ;
The surest Virtues thus from Passions shoot,
Wild Nature's vigor working at the root.
What crops of wit and honesty appear   185
From spleen, from obstinacy, hate, or fear !
See anger, zeal and fortitude supply ;
Even av'rice, prudence ; sloth, philosophy ;
Lust, through some certain strainers well refined,
Is gentle love, and charms all womankind ;   190
Envy, to which th' ignoble mind's a slave,
Is emulation in the learned or brave ;
Nor Virtue, male or female, can we name,
But what will grow on Pride, or grow on Shame.
   Thus Nature gives us (let it check our pride)   195
The virtue nearest to our vice allied :
Reason the bias turns to good from ill,
And Nero reigns a Titus, if he will.
The fiery soul abhorred in Catiline,
In Decius charms, in Curtius is divine :   200
The same ambition can destroy or save,
And makes a patriot as it makes a knave.
   IV.   This light and darkness in our chaos joined,
What shall divide ?   The God within the mind :
   Extremes in Nature equal ends produce,   205
In Man they join to some mysterious use ;
Though each by turns the other's bound invade,
As, in some well-wrought picture, light and shade,
And oft so mix, the diff'rence is too nice
Where ends the Virtue, or begins the Vice.   210
   Fools ! who from hence into the notion fall,
That Vice or Virtue there is none at all.
If white and black blend, soften, and unite
A thousand ways, is there no black or white ?
Ask your own heart, and nothing is so plain ;   215
'Tis to mistake them, costs the time and pain.
   V.   Vice is a monster of so frightful mien,
As, to be hated, needs but to be seen ;

Yet seen too oft, familiar with her face,
We first endure, then pity, then embrace.   220
But where th' Extreme of Vice, was ne'er agreed :
Ask where's the North ? at York, 'tis on the Tweed ;
In Scotland, at the Orcades ; and there,
At Greenland, Zembla, or the Lord knows where.
No creature owns it in the first degree,   225
But thinks his neighbour further gone than he ;
Even those who dwell beneath its very zone,
Or never feel the rage, or never own ;
What happier natures shrink at with affright,
The hard inhabitant contends is right.   230
    VI.   Virtuous and vicious every Man must be,
Few in th' extreme, but all in the degree ;
The rogue and fool by fits is fair and wise ;
And even the best, by fits, what they despise.
'Tis but by parts we follow good or ill ;   235
For, Vice or Virtue, Self directs it still ;
Each individual seeks a sev'ral goal ;
But HEAVEN'S great view is One, and that the Whole.
That counter-works each folly and caprice ;
That disappoints th' effect of every vice ;   240
That, happy frailties to all ranks applied,
Shame to the virgin, to the matron pride,
Fear to the statesman, rashness to the chief,
To kings presumption, and to crowds belief :
That, Virtue's ends from Vanity can raise,   245
Which seeks no int'rest, no reward but praise ;
And build on wants, and on defects of mind,
The joy, the peace, the glory of Mankind.
    Heaven forming each on other to depend,
A master, or a servant, or a friend,   250
Bids each on other for assistance call,
Till one Man's weakness grows the strength of all.
Wants, frailties, passions, closer still ally
The common int'rest, or endear the tie.
To these we owe true friendship, love sincere,   255
Each home-felt joy that life inherits here ;

Yet from the same we learn, in its decline,
Those joys, those loves, those int'rests to resign ;
Taught half by Reason, half by mere decay,
To welcome death, and calmly pass away. 260
    Whate'er the Passion, knowledge, fame, or pelf,
Not one will change his neighbour with himself.
The learned is happy nature to explore,
The fool is happy that he knows no more ;
The rich is happy in the plenty given, 265
The poor contents him with the care of Heaven.
See the blind beggar dance, the cripple sing,
The sot a hero, lunatic a king ;
The starving chemist in his golden views
Supremely blest, the poet in his Muse. 270
    See some strange comfort every state attend,
And Pride bestowed on all, a common friend ;
See some fit Passion every age supply,
Hope travels through, nor quits us when we die.
    Behold the child, by Nature's kindly law, 275
Pleased with a rattle, tickled with a straw :
Some livelier play-thing gives his youth delight,
A little louder, but as empty quite :
Scarfs, garters, gold, amuse his riper stage,
And beads and prayer-books are the toys of age : 280
Pleased with this bauble still, as that before ;
'Til tired he sleeps, and Life's poor play is o'er.
    Meanwhile Opinion gilds with varying rays
Those painted clouds that beautify our days ;
Each want of happiness by hope supplied, 285
And each vacuity of sense by Pride :
These build as fast as knowledge can destroy ;
In Folly's cup still laughs the bubble, joy :
One prospect lost, another still we gain ;
And not a vanity is given in vain ; 290
Even mean Self-love becomes, by force divine,
The scale to measure others' wants by thine.
See ! and confess, one comfort still must rise,
'Tis this, Though Man's a fool, yet GOD IS WISE.

ARGUMENT OF EPISTLE III

Of the Nature and State of Man with respect to SOCIETY

I. The whole Universe one system of Society. Nothing made wholly for *itself*, nor yet wholly for *another*. The happiness of *Animals* mutual. II. *Reason* or *Instinct* operate alike to the good of each Individual. *Reason* or *Instinct* operate also to Society, in all animals. III. How far *Society* carried by Instinct. How much farther by Reason. IV. Of that which is called the *State of Nature*. Reason instructed by Instinct in the invention of *Arts*, and in the Forms of *Society*. V. Origin of Political Societies. Origin of Monarchy. Patriarchal government. VI. Origin of true Religion and Government, from the same principle, of Love. Origin of Superstition and Tyranny, from the same principle, of Fear. The Influence of Self-love operating to the *social* and *public* Good. Restoration of true Religion and Government on their first principle. Mixed Government. Various Forms of each, and the true end of all.

EPISTLE III

HERE then we rest : " The Universal Cause
Acts to one end, but acts by various laws."
In all the madness of superfluous health,
The trim of pride, the impudence of wealth,
Let this great truth be present night and day ;   5
But most be present, if we preach or pray.
   I.   Look round our World ; behold the chain of Love
Combining all below and all above.
See plastic Nature working to this end,
The single atoms each to other tend,   10
Attract, attracted to, the next in place
Formed and impelled its neighbour to embrace.
See Matter next, with various life endued,
Press to one centre still, the gen'ral Good.
See dying vegetables life sustain,   15
See life dissolving vegetate again :
All forms that perish other forms supply,
(By turns we catch the vital breath, and die,)

Like bubbles on the sea of Matter born,
They rise, they break, and to that sea return.   20
Nothing is foreign : Parts relate to whole ;
One all-extending, all-preserving Soul
Connects each being, greatest with the least ;
Made Beast in aid of Man, and Man of Beast ;
All served, all serving : nothing stands alone ;   25
The chain holds on, and where it ends, unknown.
   Has God, thou fool ! worked solely for thy good,
Thy joy, thy pastime, thy attire, thy food ?
Who for thy table feeds the wanton fawn,
For him as kindly spread the flowery lawn :   30
Is it for thee the lark ascends and sings ?
Joy tunes his voice, joy elevates his wings.
Is it for thee the linnet pours his throat ?
Loves of his own and raptures swell the note.
The bounding steed you pompously bestride,   35
Shares with his lord the pleasure and the pride.
Is thine alone the seed that strews the plain ?
The birds of heaven shall vindicate their grain.
Thine the full harvest of the golden year ?
Part pays, and justly, the deserving steer :   40
The hog, that ploughs not nor obeys thy call,
Lives on the labours of this lord of all.
   Know, Nature's children all divide her care ;
The fur that warms a monarch, warmed a bear.
While Man exclaims, " See all things for my use ! "   45
" See man for mine ! " replies a pampered goose :
And just as short of reason he must fall,
Who thinks all made for one, not one for all.
   Grant that the powerful still the weak controul ;
Be Man the Wit and Tyrant of the whole :   50
Nature that Tyrant checks ; he only knows,
And helps, another creature's wants and woes.
Say, will the falcon, stooping from above,
Smit with her varying plumage, spare the dove ?
Admires the jay the insect's gilded wings ?   55
Or hears the hawk when Philomela sings ?

Man cares for all : to birds he gives his woods,
To beasts his pastures, and to fish his floods ;
For some his Interest prompts him to provide,
For more his pleasure, yet for more his pride :   60
All feed on one vain Patron, and enjoy
Th' extensive blessing of his luxury.
That very life his learnèd hunger craves,
He saves from famine, from the savage saves ;
Nay, feasts the animal he dooms his feast,   65
And, 'til he ends the being, makes it blest ;
Which sees no more the stroke, or feels the pain,
Than favoured Man by touch ethereal slain.
The creature had his feast of life before ;
Thou too must perish, when thy feast is o'er !   70
   To each unthinking being Heaven, a friend,
Gives not the useless knowledge of its end :
To Man imparts it ; but with such a view
As, while he dreads it, makes him hope it too :
The hour concealed, and so remote the fear,   75
Death still draws nearer, never seeming near.
Great standing miracle ! that Heaven assigned
Its only thinking thing this turn of mind.
   II.   Whether with Reason, or with Instinct blest,
Know, all enjoy that power which suits them best ;   80
To bliss alike by that direction tend,
And find the means proportioned to their end.
Say, where full Instinct is th' unerring guide,
What Pope or Council can they need beside ?
Reason, however able, cool at best,   85
Cares not for service, or but serves when prest,
Stays 'til we call, and then not often near ;
But honest Instinct comes a volunteer,
Sure never to o'er-shoot, but just to hit ;
While still too wide or short is human Wit ;   90
Sure by quick Nature happiness to gain,

Than favoured Man, etc.—Several of the ancients, and many of the Orientals since, esteemed those who were struck by lightning as sacred persons, and the particular favourites of Heaven.

Which heavier Reason labours at in vain,
This too serves always, Reason never long ;
One must go right, the other may go wrong.
See then the acting and comparing powers   95
One in their nature, which are two in ours ;
And Reason raise o'er Instinct as you can,
In this 'tis God directs, in that 'tis Man.
    Who taught the nations of the field and wood
To shun their poison, and to choose their food ?   100
Prescient, the tides or tempests to withstand,
Build on the wave, or arch beneath the sand ?
Who made the spider parallels design,
Sure as Demoivre, without rule or line ?
Who did the stork, Columbus-like, explore   105
Heavens not his own, and worlds unknown before ?
Who calls the council, states the certain day,
Who forms the phalanx, and who points the way ?
    III.   God in the nature of each being founds
Its proper bliss, and sets its proper bounds :   110
But as he framed a Whole, the Whole to bless,
On mutual Wants built mutual Happiness :
So from the first, eternal ORDER ran,
And creature linked to creature, man to man.
Whate'er of life all-quickening æther keeps,   115
Or breathes through air, or shoots beneath the deeps,
Or pours profuse on earth, one nature feeds
The vital flame, and swells the genial seeds.
Not Man alone, but all that roam the wood,
Or wing the sky, or roll along the flood,   120
Each loves itself, but not itself alone,
Each sex desires alike, 'til two are one.
Nor ends the pleasure with the fierce embrace ;
They love themselves, a third time, in their race.
Thus beast and bird their common charge attend,   125
The mothers nurse it, and the sires defend ;
The young dismissed to wander earth or air,
There stops the Instinct, and there ends the care ;
The link dissolves, each seeks a fresh embrace,

Another love succeeds, another race. 130
A longer care Man's helpless kind demands ;
That longer care contracts more lasting bands :
Reflection, Reason, still the ties improve,
At once extend the int'rest, and the love ;
With choice we fix, with sympathy we burn ; 135
Each Virtue in each Passion takes its turn ;
And still new needs, new helps, new habits rise,
That graft benevolence on charities.
Still as one brood, and as another rose,
These nat'ral love maintained, habitual those : 140
The last, scarce ripened into perfect Man,
Saw helpless him from whom their life began :
Mem'ry and fore-cast just returns engage,
That pointed back to youth, this on to age ;
While pleasure, gratitude, and hope, combined, 145
Still spread the int'rest, and preserved the kind.
  IV.   Nor think, in NATURE'S STATE they blindly trod ;
The state of Nature was the reign of God :
Self-love and Social at her birth began,
Union the bond of all things, and of Man. 150
Pride then was not ; nor Arts, that Pride to aid ;
Man walked with beast, joint tenant of the shade ;
The same his table, and the same his bed ;
No murder clothed him, and no murder fed.
In the same temple, the resounding wood, 155
All vocal beings hymned their equal God :
The shrine with gore unstained, with gold undrest,
Unbribed, unbloody, stood the blameless priest :
Heaven's attribute was Universal Care,
And Man's perogative to rule, but spare. 160
Ah ! how unlike the man of times to come !
Of half that live the butcher and the tomb ;
Who, foe to Nature, hears the gen'ral groan,
Murders their species, and betrays his own.
But just disease to luxury succeeds, 165
And every death its own avenger breeds ;
The Fury-passions from that blood began,

And turned on Man a fiercer savage, Man.
  See him from Nature rising slow to Art !
To copy Instinct then was Reason's part ;   170
Thus then to Man the voice of Nature spake—
" Go, from the Creatures thy instructions take :
Learn from the birds what food the thickets yield ;
Learn from the beasts the physic of the field ;
Thy arts of building from the bee receive ;   175
Learn of the mole to plough, the worm to weave ;
Learn of the little Nautilus to sail,
Spread the thin oar, and catch the driving gale.
Here too all forms of social union find,
And hence let Reason, late, instruct Mankind :   180
Here subterranean works and cities see ;
There towns aerial on the waving tree.
Learn each small People's genius, policies,
The Ant's republic, and the realm of Bees ;
How those in common all their wealth bestow,   185
And Anarchy without confusion know ;
And these for ever, though a Monarch reign,
Their sep'rate cells and properties maintain.
Mark what unvaried laws preserve each state,
Laws wise as Nature, and as fixed as Fate.   190
In vain thy Reason finer webs shall draw,
Entangle Justice in her net of Law,
And right, too rigid, harden into wrong ;
Still for the strong too weak, the weak too strong.
Yet go ! and thus o'er all the creatures sway,   195
Thus let the wiser make the rest obey ;
And, for those Arts mere Instinct could afford,

Learn from the beasts, etc.—See Pliny's *Natural History*, Lib. viii.
c. 27, where several instances are given of animals discovering the
medicinal efficacy of herbs by their own use of them ; and pointing
out to some operations in the art of healing by their own practice.
  Learn of the little Nautilus.—Oppian. *Halieut.* Lib. i. describes this
fish in the following manner : " They swim on the surface of the sea,
on the back of their shells, which exactly resemble the hulk of a ship ;
they raise two feet like masts, and extend a membrane between,
which serves as a sail ; the other two feet they employ as oars at the
side. They are usually seen in the Mediterranean."

Be crowned as Monarchs, or as Gods adored."
    V.   Great Nature spoke ; observant Men obeyed ;
Cities were built, Societies were made :   200
Here rose one little state ; another near
Grew by like means, and joined, through love or fear.
Did here the trees with ruddier burdens bend,
And there the streams in purer rills descend ?
What War could ravish, Commerce could bestow,   205
And he returned a friend, who came a foe.
Converse and Love mankind might strongly draw,
When Love was Liberty, and Nature Law.
Thus States were formed ; the name of King unknown,
'Til common int'rest placed the sway in one.   210
'Twas VIRTUE ONLY (or in arts or arms,
Diffusing blessings, or averting harms)
The same which in a Sire the Sons obeyed,
A Prince the Father of a People made.
    VI.   'Til then, by Nature crowned, each Patriarch sate,
King, priest, and parent of his growing state ;   216
On him, their second Providence, they hung,
Their law his eye, their oracle his tongue.
He from the wond'ring furrow called the food,
Taught to command the fire, control the flood,   220
Draw forth the monsters of th' abyss profound,
Or fetch th' aerial eagle to the ground.
'Til drooping, sick'ning, dying they began
Whom they revered as God to mourn as Man :
Then, looking up from sire to sire, explored   225
One great first father, and that first adored.
Or plain tradition that this All begun,
Conveyed unbroken faith from sire to son ;
The worker from the work distinct was known,
And simple Reason never sought but one :   230
Ere Wit oblique had broke that steady light,
Man, like his Maker, saw that all was right ;
To Virtue, in the paths of Pleasure, trod,
And owned a Father when he owned a God.
LOVE all the faith, and all th' allegiance then ;   235

For Nature knew no right divine in Men,
No ill could fear in God ; and understood
A sov'reign being but a sov'reign good.
True faith, true policy, united ran,
This was but love of God, and this of Man.   240
    Who first taught souls enslaved, and realms undone,
Th' enormous faith of many made for one ;
That proud exception to all Nature's laws,
T' invert the world, and counter-work its Cause ?
Force first made Conquest, and that conquest, Law ;
'Til Superstition taught the tyrant awe,   246
Then shared the Tyranny, then lent it aid,
And Gods of Conq'rors, Slaves of Subjects made :
She 'midst the lightning's blaze, and thunder's sound,
When rocked the mountains, and when groaned the
        ground,   250
She taught the weak to bend, the proud to pray,
To Power unseen, and mightier far than they :
She, from the rending earth and bursting skies,
Saw Gods descend, and fiends infernal rise :
Here fixed the dreadful, there the blest abodes ;   255
Fear made her Devils, and weak Hope her Gods ;
Gods partial, changeful, passionate, unjust,
Whose attributes were Rage, Revenge, or Lust ;
Such as the souls of cowards might conceive,
And, formed like tyrants, tyrants would believe.   260
Zeal then, not charity, became the guide ;
And hell was built on spite, and heaven on pride,
Then sacred seemed th' ethereal vault no more ;
Altars grew marble then, and reeked with gore :
Then first the Flamen tasted living food ;   265
Next his grim idol smeared with human blood ;
With Heaven's own thunders shook the world below,
And played the God an engine on his foe.

Th' enormous faith, etc.—In this Aristotle placeth the difference
between a King and a Tyrant, that the first supposeth himself made
for the People ; the other, that the People are made for him. *Pol.*
Lib. v. cap. 10.

So drives Self-love, through just and through unjust,
To one Man's power, ambition, lucre, lust : 270
The same Self-love, in all, becomes the cause
Of what restrains him, Government and Laws.
For, what one likes if others like as well,
What serves one will, when many wills rebel ?
How shall he keep, what, sleeping or awake, 275
A weaker may surprise, a stronger take ?
His safety must his liberty restrain :
All join to guard what each desires to gain.
Forced into virtue thus by Self-defence,
Even Kings learned justice and benevolence : 280
Self-love forsook the path it first pursued,
And found the private in the public good.
    'Twas then, the studious head or gen'rous mind,
Follower of God or friend of human-kind,
Poet or Patriot, rose but to restore 285
The Faith and Moral Nature gave before ;
Re-lumed her ancient light, not kindled new ;
If not God's image, yet his shadow drew :
Taught Power's due use to People and to Kings,
Taught nor to slack, nor strain its tender strings, 290
The less, or greater, set so justly true,
That touching one must strike the other too ;
'Til jarring int'rests, of themselves create
Th' according music of a well-mixed State.
Such is the World's great harmony, that springs 295
From Order, Union, full Consent of things :
Where small and great, where weak and mighty, made
To serve, not suffer, strengthen, not invade ;
More powerful each as needful to the rest,
And, in proportion as it blesses, blest ; 300
Draw to one point, and to one centre bring
Beast, Man, or Angel, Servant, Lord, or King.
    For Forms of Government let fools contest ;
Whate'er is best administered is best :
For Modes of Faith let graceless zealots fight ; 305
His can't be wrong whose life is in the right :

In Faith and Hope the world will disagree,
But all Mankind's concern is Charity :
All must be false that thwart this One great End ;
And all of God, that bless Mankind or mend.   310
   Man, like the gen'rous vine, supported lives ;
The strength he gains is from th' embrace he gives.
On their own Axis as the Planets run,
Yet make at once their circle round the Sun ;
So two consistent motions act the Soul ;   315
And one regards Itself, and one the Whole.
   Thus God and Nature linked the gen'ral frame,
And bade Self-love and Social be the same.

ARGUMENT OF EPISTLE IV

Of the Nature and State of Man with respect to HAPPINESS

I. False Notions of Happiness, Philosophical and Popular, answered.
II. It is the End of all Men, and attainable by all. God intends
Happiness to be *equal ;* and to be so, it must be *social,* since all
particular happiness depends on general, and since he governs by
general, not *particular Laws.* As it is necessary for *Order,* and the
peace and welfare of *Society,* that *external goods* should be *unequal,*
Happiness is not made to consist in these. But, notwithstanding that
inequality, the *balance* of Happiness among Mankind is kept even by
Providence, by the two Passions of *Hope* and *Fear.* **III.** What the
Happiness of *Individuals* is, as far as is consistent with the constitution
of this world ; and that the *good Man* has here the advantage. The
error of imputing to *Virtue* what are only the calamities of *Nature,*
or of *Fortune.* **IV.** The folly of expecting that God should alter his
general Laws in favour of particulars. **V.** That we are not judges
who are good ; but that, whoever they are, they must be happiest.
VI. That *external goods* are not the proper rewards, but often inconsistent with, or destructive of Virtue. That even these can make
no Man happy without Virtue : Instanced in *Riches ; Honours ;
Nobility ; Greatness ; Fame ; Superior Talents.* With pictures of
human Infelicity in Men possessed of them all. **VII.** That *Virtue
only* constitutes a Happiness, whose object is *universal,* and whose
prospect *eternal.* That the *perfection* of *Virtue* and *Happiness* consists
in a *conformity* to the ORDER of PROVIDENCE here, and a *Resignation*
to it here and hereafter.

EPISTLE IV

OH HAPPINESS ! our being's end and aim !
Good, Pleasure, Ease, Content ! whate'er thy name :

That something still which prompts th' eternal sigh,
For which we bear to live, or dare to die,
Which still so near us, yet beyond us lies,　　　　5
O'er-looked, seen double, by the fool, and wise.
Plant of celestial seed ! if dropt below,
Say, in what mortal soil thou deign'st to grow ?
Fair opening to some Court's propitious shine,
Or deep with diamonds in the flaming mine ?　　　10
Twined with the wreaths Parnassian laurels yield,
Or reaped in iron harvests of the field ?
Where grows ?—where grows it not ?　If vain our toil,
We ought to blame the culture, not the soil :
Fixed to no spot is Happiness sincere,　　　　　15
'Tis nowhere to be found, or everywhere ;
'Tis never to be bought, but always free,
And fled from monarchs, St. John ! dwells with thee.
　I. Ask of the Learned the way ? The Learned are blind;
This bids to serve, and that to shun mankind ;　　20
Some place the bliss in action, some in ease,
Those call it Pleasure, and Contentment these ;
Some sunk to Beasts, find pleasure end in pain ;
Some swelled to Gods, confess even Virtue vain ;
Or indolent, to each extreme they fall,　　　　25
To trust in every thing, or doubt of all.
　Who thus define it, say they more or less
Than this, that Happiness is Happiness ?
　II.　Take Nature's path, and mad Opinion's leave;
All states can reach it, and all heads conceive ;　　30
Obvious her goods, in no extreme they dwell ;
There needs but thinking right, and meaning well ;
And mourn our various portions as we please,
Equal is Common Sense, and Common Ease.
　Remember, Man, " the Universal Cause　　　35
Acts not by partial, but by gen'ral laws ; "
And makes what Happiness we justly call
Subsist not in the good of one, but all.
There's not a blessing Individuals find,
But some way leans and hearkens to the kind :　　40

No Bandit fierce, no Tyrant mad with pride,
No caverned Hermit, rests self-satisfied :
Who most to shun or hate Mankind pretend,
Seek an admirer, or would fix a friend :
Abstract what others feel, what others think,   45
All pleasures sicken, and all glories sink :
Each has his share ; and who would more obtain,
Shall find, the pleasure pays not half the pain.

  ORDER is Heaven's first law ; and this confest,
Some are, and must be, greater than the rest,   50
More rich, more wise ; but who infers from hence
That such are happier, shocks all common sense.
Heaven to Mankind impartial we confess,
If all are equal in their Happiness :
But mutual wants this Happiness increase ;   55
All Nature's diff'rence keeps all Nature's peace.
Condition, circumstance is not the thing ;
Bliss is the same in subject or in king,
In who obtain defence, or who defend,
In him who is, or him who finds a friend :   60
Heaven breathes through every member of the whole
One common blessing, as one common soul.
But Fortune's gifts if each alike possest,
And each were equal, must not all contest ?
If then to all Men Happiness was meant,   65
God in Externals could not place Content.

  Fortune her gifts may variously dispose,
And these be happy called, unhappy those ;
But Heaven's just balance equal will appear,
While those are placed in Hope, and these in Fear :   70
Nor present good or ill, the joy or curse,
But future views of better, or of worse.

  Oh sons of earth ! attempt ye still to rise,
By mountains piled on mountains, to the skies ?
Heaven still with laughter the vain toil surveys,   75
And buries madmen in the heaps they raise.

  III.   Know, all the good that individuals find,
Or God and Nature meant to mere Mankind,

Reason's whole pleasure, all the joys of Sense,
Lie in three words, Health, Peace, and Competence. 80
But Health consists with Temperance alone ;
And Peace, oh Virtue ! Peace is all thy own.
The good or bad the gifts of Fortune gain ;
But these less taste them, as they worse obtain.
Say, in pursuit of profit or delight, 85
Who risk the most, that take wrong means, or
   right ?
Of Vice or Virtue, whether blest or curst,
Which meets contempt, or which compassion first ?
Count all th' advantage prosp'rous Vice attains,
'Tis but what Virtue flies from and disdains : 90
And grant the bad what happiness they would,
One they must want, which is, to pass for good.
   Oh blind to truth, and God's whole scheme below,
Who fancy Bliss to Vice, to Virtue Woe !
Who sees and follows that great scheme the best, 95
Best knows the blessing, and will most be blest.
But fools the Good alone unhappy call,
For ills or accidents that chance to all.
See FALKLAND dies, the virtuous and the just !
See god-like TURENNE prostrate on the dust ! 100
See SIDNEY bleeds amid the martial strife !
Was this their Virtue, or Contempt of Life ?
Say, was it Virtue, more though Heaven ne'er gave,
Lamented DIGBY ! sunk thee to the grave ?
Tell me, if Virtue made the Son expire, 105
Why, full of days and honour, lives the Sire ?
Why drew Marseille's good bishop purer breath,
When Nature sickened, and each gale was death ?
Or why so long (in life if long can be)
Lent Heaven a parent to the poor and me ? 110

Marseille's good bishop.—M. de Belsance was made bishop of Mar-
seilles in 1709. In the plague of that city, in the year 1720, he distinguished himself by his zeal and activity, being the pastor, the
physician, and the magistrate of his flock, whilst that horrid calamity
prevailed. He died in the year 1755.

What makes all physical or moral ill ?
There deviates Nature, and here wanders Will.
God sends not ill ; if rightly understood,
Or partial Ill is universal Good,
Or Change admits, or Nature lets it fail ;   115
Short, and but rare, till Man improved it all.
We just as wisely might of Heaven complain
That righteous Abel was destroyed by Cain,
As that the virtuous son is ill at ease
When his lewd father gave the dire disease.   120
Think we, like some weak Prince, th' Eternal Cause
Prone for his fav'rites to reverse his laws ?
   IV.   Shall burning Ætna, if a sage requires,
Forget to thunder, and recall her fires ?
On air or sea new motions be imprest,   125
Oh blameless Bethel ! to relieve thy breast ?
When the loose mountain trembles from on high,
Shall gravitation cease, if you go by ?
Or some old temple, nodding to its fall,
For Chartres' head reserve the hanging wall ?   130
   V.   But still this world (so fitted for the knave)
Contents us not.   A better shall we have ?
A kingdom of the Just then let it be :
But first consider how those Just agree.
The good must merit God's peculiar care ;   135

A parent to, etc.—The mother of the author, a person of great piety and charity, died the year this poem was finished, viz. 1733.

Shall burning Ætna, etc.—Alluding to the fate of those two great Naturalists, Empedocles and Pliny, who both perished by too near an approach to Ætna and Vesuvius, while they were exploring the cause of their eruptions.

Blameless Bethel.—Pope seems to hint at this passage in a letter written to Mr. Bethel soon after the death of his mother : " I have now too much melancholy leisure, and no other care but to finish my *Essay on Man*. There will be in it but one line that will offend you (I fear), and yet I will not alter it or omit it, unless you come to town and prevent it. It is all a poor Poet can do, to bear testimony to the virtue he cannot reach."—*Ruffhead*.

The hanging wall.—Eusebius is weak enough to relate, from the testimonies of Irenæus and Polycarp, that the roof of the building under which Cerinthus the heretic was bathing, providentially fell down and crushed him to death.—Lib. III. cap. 29.—*Warton*.

But who, but God, can tell us who they are ?
One thinks on Calvin Heaven's own spirit fell ;
Another deems him instrument of hell ;
If Calvin feel Heaven's blessing, or its rod,
This cries there is, and that, there is no God.   140
What shocks one part will edify the rest,
Nor with one system can they all be blest.
The very best will variously incline,
And what rewards your Virtue, punish mine.
WHATEVER IS, IS RIGHT.—This world, 'tis true,   145
Was made for Cæsar—but for Titus too :
And which more blest ? who chained his country, say,
Or he whose Virtue sighed to lose a day ?
   " But sometimes Virtue starves, while Vice is fed."
What then ? Is the reward of Virtue bread ?   150
That, Vice may merit, 'tis the price of toil ;
The knave deserves it, when he tills the soil,
The knave deserves it, when he tempts the main,
Where Folly fights for kings, or dives for gain.
The good man may be weak, be indolent ;   155
Nor is his claim to plenty, but content.
But grant him Riches, your demand is o'er ?
"No—shall the good want Health, the good want Power?"
Add Health, and Power, and every earthly thing,
" Why bounded Power ? why private ? why no king ? "
Nay, why external for internal given ?   161
Why is not Man a God, and Earth a Heaven ?
Who ask and reason thus, will scarce conceive
God gives enough, while he has more to give :
Immense the power, immense were the demand ;   165
Say, at what part of nature will they stand ?
   VI. What nothing earthly gives, or can destroy,
The soul's calm sunshine, and the heart-felt joy,
Is Virtue's prize : A better would you fix ?
Then give humility a coach and six,   170
Justice a Conq'ror's sword, or Truth a gown,
Or Public Spirit its great cure, a Crown.
Weak, foolish man ! will Heaven reward us there

With the same trash mad mortals wish for here ?
The Boy and Man an individual makes,   175
Yet sigh'st thou now for apples and for cakes ?
Go, like the Indian, in another life
Expect thy dog, thy bottle, and thy wife :
As well as dream such trifles are assigned,
As toys and empires, for a god-like mind.   180
Rewards, that either would to Virtue bring
No joy, or be destructive of the thing :
How oft by these at sixty are undone
The Virtues of a saint at twenty-one !
To whom can Riches give Repute, or Trust,   185
Content, or Pleasure, but the Good and Just ?
Judges and Senates have been bought for gold,
Esteem and Love were never to be sold.
Oh fool ! to think God hates the worthy mind,
The lover and the love of human-kind,   190
Whose life is healthful, and whose conscience clear,
Because he wants a thousand pounds a year.
   Honour and shame from no Condition rise ;
Act well your part, there all the honour lies.
Fortune in Men has some small diff'rence made,   195
One flaunts in rags, one flutters in brocade ;
The cobbler aproned, and the parson gowned,
The friar hooded, and the monarch crowned.
" What differ more (you cry) than crown and cowl ? "
I'll tell you, friend ! a wise man and a Fool.   200
You'll find, if once the monarch acts the monk,
Or, cobbler-like, the parson will be drunk,
Worth makes the man, and want of it the fellow ;
The rest is all but leather or prunella.
   Stuck o'er with titles and hung round with strings,
That thou mayst be by kings, or whores of kings.   206
Boast the pure blood of an illustrious race,
In quiet flow from Lucrece to Lucrece :
But by your fathers' worth if yours you rate,
Count me those only who were good and great.   210

  Prunella.—Clergymen's gowns were often made of this material.

Go ! if your ancient, but ignoble blood
Has crept through scoundrels ever since the flood,
Go ! and pretend your family is young ;
Nor own, your fathers have been fools so long.
What can ennoble sots, or slaves, or cowards ?   215
Alas ! not all the blood of all the HOWARDS.

    Look next on Greatness ; say where Greatness lies ?
" Where, but among the Heroes and the wise ? "
Heroes are much the same, the point's agreed,
From Macedonia's madman to the Swede ;   220
The whole strange purpose of their lives, to find
Or make, an enemy of all mankind !
Not one looks backward, onward still he goes,
Yet ne'er looks forward farther than his nose.
No less alike the Politic and Wise ;   225
All sly slow things, with circumspective eyes :
Men in their loose unguarded hours they take,
Not that themselves are wise, but others weak.
But grant that those can conquer, these can cheat ;
'Tis phrase absurd to call a Villain Great :   230
Who wickedly is wise, or madly brave,
Is but the more a fool, the more a knave.
Who noble ends by noble means obtains,
Or failing, smiles in exile or in chains,
Like good Aurelius let him reign, or bleed   235
Like Socrates, that Man is great indeed.

    What's Fame ? a fancied life in others' breath,
A thing beyond us, even before our death.
Just what you hear, you have, and what's unknown
The same (my Lord) if Tully's, or your own.   240
All that we feel of it begins and ends
In the small circle of our foes or friends ;
To all beside as much an empty shade
An Eugene living, as a Cæsar dead ;
Alike or when, or where, they shone, or shine,   245
Or on the Rubicon, or on the Rhine.

   Like Socrates.—Considering the manner in which Socrates was put
to death, the word " bleed " seems to be improperly used.

A Wit's a feather, and a Chief a rod ;
An honest Man's the noblest work of God.
Fame but from death a villain's name can save,
As Justice tears his body from the grave ;   250
When what t' oblivion better was resigned,
Is hung on high, to poison half mankind.
All fame is foreign, but of true desert ;
Plays round the head, but comes not to the heart :
One self-approving hour whole years out-weighs   255
Of stupid starers, and of loud huzzas ;
And more true joy Marcellus exiled feels,
Than Cæsar with a senate at his heels.
   In Parts superior what advantage lies ?
Tell (for You can) what is it to be wise ?   260
'Tis but to know how little can be known ;
To see all others' faults, and feel our own :
Condemned in business or in arts to drudge,
Without a second, or without a judge :
Truths would you teach, or save a sinking land   265
All fear, none aid you, and few understand.
Painful pre-eminence ! yourself to view
Above life's weakness, and its comforts too.
   Bring then these blessings to a strict account ;
Make fair deductions ; see to what they mount :   270
How much of other each is sure to cost ;
How each for other oft is wholly lost ;
How inconsistent greater goods with these ;
How sometimes life is risked, and always ease :
Think, and if still the things thy envy call,   275
Say, wouldst thou be the Man to whom they fall ?
To sigh for ribbands if thou art so silly,
Mark how they grace Lord Umbra, or Sir Billy :
Is yellow dirt the passion of thy life ?
Look but on Gripus, or on Gripus' wife :   280
If Parts allure thee, think how Bacon shined,
The wisest, brightest, meanest of mankind :
Or ravished with the whistling of a Name,
See Cromwell, damned to everlasting fame !

If all, united, thy ambition call,   285
From ancient story learn to scorn them all.
There, in the rich, the honoured, famed, and great,
See the false scale of Happiness complete !
In hearts of Kings, or arms of Queens who lay,
How happy ! those to ruin, these betray.   290
Mark by what wretched steps their glory grows,
From dirt and sea-weed as proud Venice rose ;
In each how guilt and greatness equal ran,
And all that raised the Hero. sunk the Man :
Now Europe's laurels on their brows behold,   295
But stained with blood, or ill exchanged for gold :
Then see them broke with toils, or sunk in ease,
Or infamous for plundered provinces.
Oh wealth ill-fated ! which no act of fame
E'er taught to shine, or sanctified from shame !   300
What greater bliss attends their close of life ?
Some greedy minion, or imperious wife.
The trophied arches, storied halls invade
And haunt their slumbers in the pompous shade.
Alas ! not dazzled with their noon-tide ray,   305
Compute the morn and evening to the day ;
The whole amount of that enormous fame,
A Tale, that blends their glory with their shame !
   VII.   Know then this truth (enough for Man to know)
" Virtue alone is Happiness below."   310
The only point where human bliss stands still,
And tastes the good without the fall to ill ;
Where only Merit constant pay receives,
Is blest in what it takes, and what it gives ;
The joy unequalled, if its end it gain,   315
And if it lose, attended with no pain :
Without satiety, though e'er so blessed,
And but more relished as the more distressed :
The broadest mirth unfeeling Folly wears,
Less pleasing far than Virtue's very tears :   320
Good, from each object, from each place acquired,
For ever exercised, yet never tired :

Never elated, while one man's oppressed ;
Never dejected, while another's blessed ;
And where no wants, no wishes can remain,　325
Since be to wish more Virtue, is to gain.
　　See the sole bliss Heaven could on all bestow !
Which who but feels can taste, but thinks can know :
Yet poor with fortune, and with learning blind,
The bad must miss ; the good, untaught, will find ;　330
Slave to no sect, who takes no private road,
But looks through Nature up to Nature's God ;
Pursues that Chain which links the immense design,
Joins heaven and earth, and mortal and divine ;
Sees, that no Being any bliss can know,　335
But touches some above, and some below ;
Learns, from this union of the rising Whole,
The first, last purpose of the human soul ;
And knows, where Faith, Law, Morals, all began,
All end, in LOVE OF GOD, and LOVE OF MAN.　340
　　For him alone, Hope leads from goal to goal,
And opens still, and opens on his soul ;
'Til lengthened on to Faith, and unconfined,
It pours the bliss that fills up all the mind.
He sees, why Nature plants in Man alone　345
Hope of known bliss, and Faith in bliss unknown :
(Nature, whose dictates to no other kind
Are given in vain, but what they seek they find)
Wise is her present ; she connects in this
His greatest Virtue with his greatest Bliss ;　350
At once his own bright prospect to be blest,
And strongest motive to assist the rest.
　　Self-love thus pushed to social, to divine,
Gives thee to make thy neighbour's blessing thine.
Is this too little for the boundless heart ?　355
Extend it, let thy enemies have part :
Grasp the whole worlds of Reason, Life, and Sense,
In one close system of Benevolence :
Happier as kinder, in whate'er degree,
And height of Bliss but height of Charity.　360

God loves from Whole to Parts : but human soul
Must rise from Individual to the Whole.
Self-love but serves the virtuous mind to wake,
As the small pebble stirs the peaceful lake ;
The centre moved, a circle straight succeeds,   365
Another still, and still another spreads ;
Friend, parent, neighbour, first it will embrace ;
His country next ; and next all human race ;
Wide and more wide, th' o'erflowings of the mind
Take every creature in, of every kind ;   370
Earth smiles around, with boundless bounty blest,
And Heaven beholds its image in his breast.
    Come then, my Friend ! my Genius ! come along ;
Oh master of the poet, and the song !
And while the Muse now stoops, or now ascends,   375
To Man's low passions, or their glorious ends,
Teach me, like thee, in various nature wise,
To fall with dignity, with temper rise ;
Formed by thy converse, happily to steer
From grave to gay, from lively to severe ;   380
Correct with spirit, eloquent with ease,
Intent to reason, or polite to please.
Oh ! while along the stream of Time thy name
Expanded flies, and gathers all its fame,
Say, shall my little bark attendant sail,   385
Pursue the triumph, and partake the gale ?
When statesmen, heroes, kings, in dust repose,
Whose sons shall blush their fathers were thy foes,
Shall then this verse to future age pretend
Thou wert my guide, philosopher, and friend ?   390
That urged by thee, I turned the tuneful art
From sounds to things, from fancy to the heart ;
For Wit's false mirror held up Nature's light ;
Shewed erring Pride, WHATEVER IS, IS RIGHT ;
That REASON, PASSION, answer one great aim ;   395
That true SELF-LOVE and SOCIAL are the same ;
That VIRTUE only makes our Bliss below ;
And all our Knowledge is, OURSELVES TO KNOW.

THE UNIVERSAL PRAYER

DEO OPT. MAX

FATHER of All ! in every Age,
  In every Clime adored,
By Saint, by Savage, and by Sage,
  Jehovah, Jove, or Lord !

Thou Great First Cause, least understood : 5
  Who all my Sense confined
To know but this, that Thou art Good,
  And that myself am blind ;

Yet gave me, in this dark Estate,
  To see the Good from Ill ; 10
And binding Nature fast in Fate,
  Left free the Human Will.

What Conscience dictates to be done,
  Or warns me not to do,
This, teach me more than Hell to shun, 15
  That, more than Heaven pursue.

What Blessings thy free Bounty gives,
  Let me not cast away ;
For God is pay'd when Man receives,
  T' enjoy is to obey. 20

Universal Prayer.—Concerning this poem, it may be proper to observe that some passages, in the preceding *Essay*, having been unjustly suspected of a tendency towards Fate and *Naturalism*, the author composed this Prayer as the sum of all, to shew that his system was founded in *free-will*, and terminated in piety ; that the First Cause was as well the Lord and Governor of the Universe as the Creator of it ; and that, by submission to his will (the great Principle enforced throughout the *Essay*) was not meant the suffering ourselves to be carried along with a blind determination ; but a religious acquiescence, and confidence full of *Hope* and Immortality. To give all this the greater weight and reality, the poet chose for his model the LORD'S PRAYER, which, of all others, best deserves the title prefixed to this Paraphrase.

Yet not to Earth's contracted Span
    Thy Goodness let me bound,
Or think Thee Lord alone of Man,
    When thousand Worlds are round:

Let not this weak, unknowing hand   25
    Presume thy bolts to throw,
And deal damnation round the land,
    On each I judge thy Foe.

If I am right, thy grace impart,
    Still in the right to stay ;   30
If I am wrong, oh teach my heart
    To find that better way.

Save me alike from foolish Pride,
    Or impious Discontent,
At aught thy Wisdom has denied,   35
    Or aught thy Goodness lent.

Teach me to feel another's Woe,
    To hide the Fault I see ;
That Mercy I to others shew,
    That Mercy shew to me.   40

Mean though I am, not wholly so,
    Since quickened by thy Breath ;
Oh lead me wheresoe'er I go,
    Through this day's Life or Death.

This day, be Bread and Peace my Lot :   45
    All else beneath the Sun,
Thou know'st if best bestowed or not ;
    And let Thy Will be done.

To thee, whose Temple is all Space,
    Whose Altar Earth, Sea, Skies,
One Chorus let all Being raise,   50
    All Nature's Incense rise !

MORAL ESSAYS

EPISTLES TO SEVERAL PERSONS

Est brevitate opus, ut currat sententia, neu se
Impediat verbis lassis onerantibus aures :
Et sermone opus est modo tristi, sæpe jocoso,
Defendente vicem modo Rhetoris atque Poetæ,
Interdum urbani, parcentis viribus, atque
Extenuantis eas consultò.—Hor. *Sat.* I. x. 17–22.

ARGUMENT OF EPISTLE I

Of the Knowledge and Characters of Men

That it is not sufficient for this knowledge to consider Man in the
Abstract : Books will not serve the purpose, nor yet our own *Experience* singly. General maxims, unless they be formed upon *both,*
will be but notional. Some Peculiarity in every man, characteristic
to himself, yet varying from himself. Difficulties arising from our own
Passions, Fancies, Faculties, etc. The shortness of Life, to observe
in, and the uncertainty of the *Principles of Action* in men, to observe
by. Our *own* Principle of action often hid from ourselves. Some
few characters plain, but in general confounded, dissembled, or inconsistent. The same man utterly different in different places and
seasons. Unimaginable weaknesses in the greatest. Nothing constant and certain but *God* and *Nature.* No judging of the *Motives*
from the actions ; the same actions proceeding from contrary Motives,
and the same Motives influencing contrary actions. Yet to form
Characters, we can only take the *strongest actions* of a man's life, and
try to make them *agree :* The utter uncertainty of this, from *Nature*
itself, and from *Policy. Characters* given according to the *rank* of
men of the world. And some reason for it. *Education* alters the
Nature, or at least *Character* of many. *Actions, Passions, Opinions,
Manners, Humours,* or *Principles* all subject to change. No judging
by *Nature.* It only remains to find (if we can) his Ruling Passion :
That will certainly influence all the rest, and can reconcile the seeming
or real inconsistency of all his actions. Instanced in the extraordinary
character of *Clodio.* A caution against mistaking *second qualities* for
first, which will destroy all possibility of the knowledge of mankind.
Examples of the strength of the *Ruling Passion,* and its continuation
to the last breath.

EPISTLE I

To Sir Richard Temple, Lord Cobham

I. Yes, you despise the man to Books confined,
Who from his study rails at human kind ;
Though what he learns he speaks, and may advance
Some general maxims, or be right by chance.
The coxcomb bird, so talkative and grave,   5
That from his cage cries Cuckold, Whore, and Knave,
Though many a passenger he rightly call,
You hold him no Philosopher at all.
    And yet the fate of all extremes is such,
Men may be read as well as Books, too much.   10
To observations which ourselves we make,
We grow more partial for the Observer's sake :
To written Wisdom, as another's, less :
Maxims are drawn from Notions, those from Guess.
There's some Peculiar in each leaf and grain,   15
Some unmarked fibre, or some varying vein :
Shall only Man be taken in the gross ?
Grant but as many sorts of Mind as Moss.
    That each from other differs, first confess ;
Next, that he varies from himself no less ;   20
Add Nature's, Custom's, Reason's, Passion's strife,
And all Opinion's colours cast on life.
    Our depths who fathoms, or our shallows finds,
Quick whirls, and shifting eddies, of our minds ?
On human actions reason though you can,   25
It may be Reason, but it is not Man :
His Principle of action once explore,
That instant 'tis his Principle no more.
Like following life through creatures you dissect,
You lose it in the moment you detect.   30
    Yet more ; the difference is as great between
The optics seeing, as the object seen.
All Manners take a tincture from our own ;

Or come discoloured through our Passions shown.
Or Fancy's beam enlarges, multiplies,   35
Contracts, inverts, and gives ten thousand dyes.
   Nor will Life's stream for Observation stay,
It hurries all too fast to mark their way :
In vain sedate reflections we would make,
When half our knowledge we must snatch, not take. 40
Oft, in the Passions' wild rotation tost,
Our spring of action to ourselves is lost :
Tired, not determined, to the last we yield,
And what comes then is master of the field.
As the last image of that troubled heap,   45
When Sense subsides, and Fancy sports in sleep,
(Though past the recollection of the thought,)
Becomes the stuff of which our dream is wrought :
Something as dim to our internal view,
Is thus, perhaps, the cause of most we do.   50
   True, some are open, and to all men known ;
Others so very close, they're hid from none ;
(So Darkness strikes the sense no less than Light)
Thus gracious CHANDOS is beloved at sight ;
And every child hates Shylock, though his soul   55
Still sits at squat, and peeps not from its hole.
At half mankind when gen'rous Manly raves,
All know 'tis Virtue, for he thinks them knaves :
When universal homage Umbra pays,
All see 'tis Vice, and itch of vulgar praise.   60
When Flattery glares, all hate it in a Queen,
While one there is who charms us with his Spleen.
   But these plain Characters we rarely find ;
Though strong the bent, yet quick the turns of mind :
Or puzzling Contraries confound the whole ;   65
Or Affectations quite reverse the soul.
The Dull, flat Falsehood serves for policy ;
And in the Cunning, Truth itself's a lie :
Unthought-of Frailties cheat us in the Wise ;
The Fool lies hid in inconsistencies.   70
   See the same man, in vigour, in the gout :

Alone, in company ; in place, or out ;
Early at Business, and at Hazard late ;
Mad at a Fox-chase, wise at a Debate ;
Drunk at a Borough, civil at a Ball ;   75
Friendly at Hackney, faithless at Whitehall.

　　Catius is ever moral, ever grave,
Thinks who endures a knave, is next a knave,
Save just at dinner—then, prefers, no doubt,
A Rogue with Ven'son to a Saint without.   80

　　Who would not praise Patritio's high desert,
His hand unstained, his uncorrupted heart,
His comprehensive head ! all Int'rests weighed,
All Europe saved, yet Britain not betrayed.
He thanks you not, his pride is in Piquet,   85
New-market-fame, and judgment at a Bet.

　　What made (say Montagne, or more sage Charron !)
Otho a warrior, Cromwell a buffoon ?
A perjured Prince a leaden Saint revere,
A godless Regent tremble at a Star ?   90
The throne a Bigot keep, a Genius quit,
Faithless through Piety, and duped through Wit ?
Europe a Woman, Child, or Dotard rule,
And just her wisest monarch made a fool ?

　　Know, GOD and NATURE only are the same :   95
In Man, the judgment shoots at flying game,
A bird of passage ! gone as soon as found,
Now in the Moon perhaps, now under ground.

　　In vain the Sage, with retrospective eye,
Would from th' apparent What conclude the Why,
Infer the Motive from the Deed, and shew,   101

A perjured Prince.—Louis XI. of France wore in his hat a leaden
image of the Virgin Mary, which when he swore by, he feared to break
his oath.

A godless Regent tremble at a Star.—Philip Duke of Orleans, Regent
of France in the minority of Louis XV., superstitious in judicial
astrology, though an unbeliever in all religion.

The throne a Bigot keep, a Genius quit.—Philip V. of Spain, who,
after renouncing the throne for religion, resumed it to gratify his
Queen ; and Victor Amadeus II., King of Sardinia, who resigned the
Crown, and trying to reassume it, was imprisoned till his death.

That what we chanced was what we meant to do.
Behold ! If Fortune or a Mistress frowns,
Some plunge in business, others shave their crowns :
To ease the Soul of one oppressive weight,   105
This quits an Empire, that embroils a State :
The same adust complexion has impelled
Charles to the Convent, Philip to the Field.

  Not always Actions shew the man : we find
Who does a kindness, is not therefore kind ;   110
Perhaps Prosperity becalmed his breast,
Perhaps the Wind just shifted from the east :
Not therefore humble he who seeks retreat,
Pride guides his steps, and bids him shun the great :
Who combats bravely is not therefore brave,   115
He dreads a death-bed like the meanest slave :
Who reasons wisely is not therefore wise,
His pride in Reasoning not in Acting lies.

  II. But grant that Actions best discover man ;
Take the most strong, and sort them as you can. 120
The few that glare each character must mark,
You balance not the many in the dark.
What will you do with such as disagree ?
Suppress them, or miscall them Policy ?
Must then at once (the character to save)   125
The plain rough Hero turn a crafty Knave ?
Alas ! in truth the man but changed his mind,
Perhaps was sick, in love, or had not dined.
Ask why from Britain Cæsar would retreat ?
Cæsar himself might whisper he was beat.   130
Why risk the world's great empire for a Punk ?
Cæsar perhaps might answer he was drunk.
But, sage historians ! 'tis your task to prove
One action Conduct ; one, heroic Love.

  'Tis from high Life high Characters are drawn ; 135
A Saint in Crape is twice a Saint in Lawn ;
A Judge is just, a Chancellor juster still ;
A Gownman, learned : a Bishop, what you will ;

6

Wise, if a Minister ; but, if a King,
More wise, more learned, more just, more everything.
Court-virtues bear, like Gems, the highest rate,   141
Born where Heaven's influence scarce can penetrate :
In life's low vale, the soil the Virtues like,
They please as beauties, here as wonders strike.
Though the same Sun with all-diffusive rays   145
Blush in the Rose, and in the Diamond blaze,
We prize the stronger effort of his power,
And justly set the Gem above the Flower.
'Tis Education forms the common mind,
Just as the Twig is bent, the Tree's inclined.   150
Boastful and rough, your first Son is a Squire ;
The next a Tradesman, meek, and much a liar ;
Tom struts a Soldier, open, bold, and brave ;
Will sneaks a Scrivener, an exceeding knave :
Is he a Churchman ? then he's fond of power :   155
A Quaker ? sly : A Presbyterian ? sour :
A smart Free-thinker ? all things in an hour.
　Ask men's Opinions : Scoto now shall tell
How Trade increases, and the World goes well ;
Strike off his Pension, by the setting sun,   160
And Britain, if not Europe, is undone.
　That gay Free-thinker, a fine talker once,
What turns him now a stupid silent dunce ?
Some God, or Spirit he has lately found :
Or chanced to meet a Minister that frowned.   165
　Judge we by Nature ? Habit can efface,
Interest o'ercome, or Policy take place :
By Actions ? those Uncertainty divides :
By Passions ? these Dissimulation hides :
Opinions ? they still take a wider range :   170
Find, if you can, in what you cannot change.
　Manners with Fortunes, Humours turn with Climes,
Tenets with Books, and Principles with Times.

Scoto now shall tell.—In the first edition : " J—n now shall tell ; "
meaning perhaps Johnston, the Scottish Secretary, a neighbour of
Pope's at Twickenham.

III.   Search then the RULING PASSION : there, alone,

The Wild are constant, and the Cunning known ;   175
The Fool consistent, and the False sincere ;
Priests, Princes, Women, no dissemblers here.
This clue once found, unravels all the rest,
The prospect clears, and Wharton stands confest.
Wharton, the scorn and wonder of our days,   180
Whose ruling Passion was the Lust of Praise :
Born with whate'er could win it from the Wise,
Women and Fools must like him or he dies ;
Though wond'ring Senates hung on all he spoke,
The Club must hail him master of the joke.   185
Shall parts so various aim at nothing new ?
He'll shine a Tully and a Wilmot too.
Then turns repentant, and his God adores
With the same spirit that he drinks and whores ;
Enough if all around him but admire,   190
And now the Punk applaud, and now the Friar.
Thus with each gift of nature and of art,
And wanting nothing but an honest heart ;
Grown all to all, from no one vice exempt ;
And most contemptible, to shun contempt :   195
His Passion still, to covet general praise,
His Life, to forfeit it a thousand ways ;
A constant Bounty which no friend has made ;
An angel Tongue, which no man can persuade ;
A Fool, with more of Wit than half mankind,   200
Too rash for Thought, for Action too refined :
A Tyrant to the wife his heart approves ;
A Rebel to the very king he loves ;
He dies, sad outcast of each church and state,
And, harder still ! flagitious, yet not great.   205
Ask you why Wharton broke through every rule ?
'Twas all for fear the Knaves should call him Fool.
   Nature well known, no prodigies remain,

Wilmot.—John Wilmot, E. of Rochester, famous for his Wit and Extravagancies in the time of Charles the Second.

Comets are regular, and Wharton plain.
    Yet, in this search, the wisest may mistake,   210
If second qualities for first they take.
When Catiline by rapine swelled his store ;
When Cæsar made a noble dame a whore ;
In this the Lust, in that the Avarice
Were means, not ends ; Ambition was the vice.   215
That very Cæsar, born in Scipio's days,
Had aimed, like him, by Chastity at praise.
Lucullus, when Frugality could charm,
Had roasted turnips in the Sabine farm.
    In vain th' observer eyes the builder's toil,   220
But quite mistakes the scaffold for the pile.
In this one Passion man can strength enjoy,
As Fits give vigour, just when they destroy.
Time, that on all things lays his lenient hand,
Yet tames not this ; it sticks to our last sand.   225
Consistent in our follies and our sins,
Here honest Nature ends as she begins.
Old Politicians chew on wisdom past,
And totter on in business to the last ;
As weak, as earnest ; and as gravely out,   230
As sober Lanesb'row dancing in the gout.
    Behold a rev'rend sire, whom want of grace
Has made the father of a nameless race,
Shoved from the wall perhaps, or rudely pressed
By his own son, that passes by unblessed :   235
Still to his wench he crawls on knocking knees,
And envies every sparrow that he sees.
    A salmon's belly, Helluo, was thy fate ;
The doctor called, declares all help too late :
" Mercy ! " cries Helluo, " mercy on my soul ! "   240
" Is there no hope ?—Alas !—then bring the jowl."
    The frugal Crone, whom praying priests attend,

Lanesb'row.—An ancient Nobleman, who continued this practice
long after his legs were disabled by the gout. Upon the death of Prince
George of Denmark, he demanded an audience of the Queen, to advise
her to preserve her health and dispel her grief by *Dancing.*

Still tries to save the hallowed taper's end,
Collects her breath, as ebbing life retires,
For one puff more, and in that puff expires.   245
   " Odious ! in woollen ! 'twould a Saint provoke,"
(Were the last words that poor Narcissa spoke)
" No, let a charming Chintz, and Brussels lace
Wrap my cold limbs, and shade my lifeless face :
One would not, sure, be frightful when one's dead—
And—Betty—give this Cheek a little Red."   251
   The Courtier smooth, who forty years had shined
An humble servant to all human kind,
Just brought out this, when scarce his tongue could stir,
" If—where I'm going—I could serve you, Sir ? "   255
   " I give and I devise (old Euclio said,
And sighed) " my lands and tenements to Ned."
" Your money, Sir ; " " My money, Sir, what all ?
Why,—if I must—(then wept) I give it Paul."
" The Manor, Sir ? "—" The Manor ! hold," he cried,
" Not that,—I cannot part with that "—and died.   261
   And you ! brave COBHAM, to the latest breath
Shall feel your ruling passion strong in death :
Such in those moments as in all the past,
" Oh, save my Country, Heaven ! " shall be your last.

EPISTLE II

TO A LADY

Of the Characters of WOMEN

NOTHING so true as what you once let fall,
" Most Women have no Characters at all."

   In that puff expires.—A fact told him by Lady Bolingbroke of an
old Countess at Paris.
   The last words that poor Narcissa spoke.—This story, as well as the
others, is founded on fact, though the author had the goodness not
to mention the names. Several attribute this in particular to a very
celebrated Actress, who, in detestation of the thought of being buried
in woollen, gave these her last orders with her dying breath. Mrs.
Oldfield was said to be this actress. To stimulate the woollen trade the
laws required all shrouds to be made of wool.

Matter too soft a lasting mark to bear,
And best distinguished by black, brown, or **fair.**
 How many pictures of one Nymph we view, 5
All how unlike each other, all how true !
Arcadia's Countess, here, in ermined pride,
Is, there, Pastora by a fountain side.
Here Fannia, leering on her own good man,
And there, a naked Leda with a Swan. 10
Let then the Fair one beautifully cry,
In Magdalen's loose hair, and lifted eye,
Or drest in smiles of sweet Cecilia shine,
With simp'ring Angels, Palms, and Harps divine ;
Whether the Charmer sinner it, or saint it, 15
If Folly grow romantic, I must paint it.
 Come then, the colours and the ground prepare !
Dip in the Rainbow, trick her off in Air ;
Choose a firm Cloud, before it fall, and in it
Catch, ere she change, the Cynthia of this minute. 20
 Rufa, whose eye quick-glancing o'er the Park,
Attracts each light gay meteor of a Spark,
Agrees as ill with Rufa studying Locke,
As Sappho's diamonds with her dirty smock ;
Or Sappho at her toilet's greasy task, 25
With Sappho fragrant at an evening Masque :
So morning Insects that in muck begun,
Shine, buzz, and fly-blow in the setting-sun.
 How soft is Silia ! fearful to offend ;
The Frail one's advocate, the Weak one's friend : 30
To her, Calista proved her conduct nice ;
And good Simplicius asks of her advice.
Sudden, she storms ! she raves ! You tip the wink,
But spare your censure ; Silia does not drink.
All eyes may see from what the change arose, 35

Arcadia's Countess,—Pastora by a fountain—Leda with a swan—
Magdalen—Cecilia.—Attitudes in which several ladies affected to be
drawn, and sometimes one lady in them all. The poet's politeness
and complaisance to the sex is observable in this instance, amongst
others, that, where, as in the *Characters of Men* he has sometimes made
use of real names, in the *Characters of Women* always fictitious.

All eyes may see—a Pimple on her nose.
  Papillia, wedded to her am'rous spark,
Sighs for the shades—" How charming is a Park ! "
A Park is purchased, but the Fair he sees
All bathed in tears—" Oh, odious, odious Trees ! " 40
  Ladies, like variegated Tulips, show ;
'Tis to their Changes half their charms we owe ;
Fine by defect, and delicately weak,
Their happy Spots the nice admirer take,
'Twas thus Calypso once each heart alarmed,   45
Awed without Virtue, without Beauty charmed ;
Her tongue bewitched as oddly as her Eyes,
Less Wit than Mimic, more a Wit than wise ;
Strange graces still, and stranger flights she had,
Was just not ugly, and was just not mad ;   50
Yet ne'er so sure our passion to create,
As when she touched the brink of all we hate.
  Narcissa's nature, tolerably mild,
To make a wash, would hardly stew a child ;
Has even been proved to grant a Lover's prayer,   55
And paid a Tradesman once to make him stare ;
Gave alms at Easter, in a Christian trim,
And made a Widow happy, for a whim.
Why then declare Good-nature is her scorn,
When 'tis by that alone she can be borne ?   60
Why pique all mortals, yet affect a name ?
A fool to Pleasure, yet a slave to Fame :
Now deep in Taylor and the Book of Martyrs,
Now drinking citron with his Grace and Chartres :
Now Conscience chills her, and now Passion burns ;
And Atheism and Religion take their turns ;   66
A very Heathen in the carnal part,
Yet still a sad, good Christian at her heart.
  See Sin in State, majestically drunk ;
Proud as a Peeress, prouder as a Punk ;   70
Chaste to her Husband, frank to all beside,
A teeming Mistress, but a barren Bride.
What then ? let Blood and Body bear the fault,

Her Head's untouched, that noble Seat of Thought :
Such this day's doctrine—in another fit   75
She sins with Poets through pure Love of Wit.
What has not fired her bosom or her brain ?
Cæsar and Tall-boy, Charles and Charlemagne.
As Helluo, late Dictator of the Feast,
The Nose of Hautgout, and the Tip of Taste,   80
Critiqued your wine, and analysed your meat,
Yet on plain Pudding deigned at home to eat ;
So Philomedé, lect'ring all mankind
On the soft Passion, and the Taste refined,
Th' Address, the Delicacy—stoops at once,   85
And makes her hearty meal upon a Dunce.

Flavia's a Wit, has too much sense to Pray ;
To Toast our wants and wishes, is her way ;
Nor asks of God, but of her Stars, to give
The mighty blessing, " while we live, to live."   90
Then all for Death, that Opiate of the soul !
Lucretia's dagger, Rosamonda's bowl.
Say, what can cause such impotence of mind ?
A spark too fickle, or a Spouse too kind.
Wise Wretch ! with Pleasures too refined to please ;   95
With too much Spirit to be e'er at ease ;
With too much Quickness ever to be taught ;
With too much Thinking to have common Thought :
You purchase Pain with all that Joy can give,
And die of nothing but a Rage to live.   100

Turn then from Wits ; and look on Simo's Mate,
No Ass so meek, no Ass so obstinate.
Or her, that owns her Faults, but never mends,
Because she's honest, and the best of Friends.
Or her, whose life the Church and Scandal share,   105
For ever in a Passion, or a Prayer.
Or her, who laughs at Hell, but (like her Grace)
Cries, " Ah ! how charming, if there's no such place ! "
Or who in sweet vicissitude appears
Of Mirth and Opium, Ratafie and Tears,   110
The daily Anodyne, and nightly Draught,

To kill those foes to Fair ones, Time and Thought.
Woman and Fool are two hard things to hit ;
For true No-meaning puzzles more than Wit.
   But what are these to great Atossa's mind ?   115
Scarce once herself, by turns all Womankind !
Who, with herself, or others, from her birth
Finds all her life one warfare upon earth :
Shines in exposing Knaves, and painting Fools,
Yet is, whate'er she hates and ridicules.   120
No Thought advances, but her Eddy Brain
Whisks it about, and down it goes again.
Full sixty years the World has been her Trade,
The wisest Fool much Time has ever made.
From loveless youth to unrespected age,   125
No passion gratified except her Rage.
So much the Fury still out-ran the Wit,
The Pleasure missed her, and the Scandal hit.
Who breaks with her, provokes Revenge from Hell,
But he's a bolder man who dares be well.   130
Her every turn with Violence pursued,
Nor more a storm her Hate than Gratitude :
To that each Passion turns, or soon or late ;
Love, if it makes her yield, must make her hate :
Superiors ? death ! and Equals ? what a curse !   135
But an Inferior not dependant ? worse.
Offend her, and she knows not to forgive ;
Oblige her, and she'll hate you while you live :
But die, and she'll adore you—Then the Bust
And Temple rise—then fall again to dust.   140
Last night, her Lord was all that's good and great ;
A Knave this morning, and his Will a Cheat.
Strange ! by the Means defeated of the Ends,
By Spirit robbed of Power, by Warmth of Friends,
By Wealth of Followers ! without one distress   145
Sick of herself through very selfishness !
Atossa, cursed with every granted prayer,
Childless with all her Children, wants an Heir.
To Heirs unknown descends th' unguarded store,

Or wanders, Heaven-directed, to the Poor.   150
 Pictures like these, dear Madam, to design,
Asks no firm hand, and no unerring line ;
Some wand'ring touches, some reflected light,
Some flying stroke alone can hit 'em right :
For how should equal Colours do the knack ?   155
Chameleons who can paint in white and black ?
 " Yet Chloe sure was formed without a spot "—
Nature in her then erred not, but forgot.
" With every pleasing, every prudent part,
Say, what can Chloe want ? "—She wants a Heart.
She speaks, behaves, and acts just as she ought ;   161
But never, never, reached one gen'rous Thought.
Virtue she finds too painful an endeavour,
Content to dwell in Decencies for ever.
So very reasonable, so unmoved,   165
As never yet to love, or to be loved.
She, while her Lover pants upon her breast,
Can mark the figures on an Indian chest ;
And when she sees her Friend in deep despair,
Observes how much a Chintz exceeds Mohair.   170
Forbid it Heaven, a Favour or a Debt
She e'er should cancel—but she may forget.
Safe is your Secret still in Chloe's ear ;
But none of Chloe's shall you ever hear.
Of all her Dears she never slandered one,   175
But cares not if a thousand are undone.
Would Chloe know if you're alive or dead ?
She bids her Footman put it in her head.
Chloe is prudent—Would you too be wise ?
Then never break your heart when Chloe dies.   180
 One certain Portrait may (I grant) be seen,
Which Heaven has varnished out, and made a *Queen*:
THE SAME FOR EVER ! and described by all
With Truth and Goodness, as with Crown and Ball.
Poets heap Virtues, Painters Gems at will,   185
And shew their zeal, and hide their want of skill.
'Tis well—but, Artists ! who can paint or write,

To draw the Naked is your true delight.
That robe of Quality so struts and swells,
None see what Parts of Nature it conceals : 190
Th' exactest traits of Body or of Mind,
We owe to models of an humble kind.
If QUEENSBURY to strip there's no compelling,
'Tis from a Handmaid we must take a Helen,
From Peer or Bishop 'tis no easy thing 195
To draw the man who loves his God, or King :
Alas ! I copy (or my draught would fail)
From honest Mah'met, or plain Parson Hale.
    But grant, in Public Men sometimes are shown,
A Woman's seen in Private life alone : 200
Our bolder Talents in full light displayed ;
Your virtues open fairest in the shade.
Bred to disguise, in Public 'tis you hide ;
There, none distinguish 'twixt your Shame or Pride,
Weakness or Delicacy ; all so nice, 205
That each may seem a Virtue, or a Vice.
    In Men, we various Ruling Passions find ;
In Women, two almost divide the kind ;
Those, only fixed, they first or last obey,
The Love of Pleasure, and the Love of Sway. 210
    That, Nature gives ; and where the lesson taught
Is but to please, can Pleasure seem a fault ?
Experience, this ; by Man's oppression curst,
They seek the second not to lose the first.
    Men, some to Business, some to Pleasure take ; 215
But every Woman is at heart a Rake :
Men, some to Quiet, some to public Strife ;
But every Lady would be Queen for life.
    Yet mark the fate of a whole Sex of Queens !
Power all their end, but Beauty all the means : 220
In Youth they conquer, with so wild a rage,
As leaves them scarce a subject in their Age :
For foreign glory, foreign joy, they roam ;
No thought of peace or happiness at home.
But Wisdom's triumph is well-timed Retreat, 225

As hard a science to the Fair as Great !
Beauties, like Tyrants, old and friendless grown,
Yet hate repose, and dread to be alone,
Worn out in public, weary every eye,
Nor leave one sigh behind them when they die.   230
    Pleasures the sex, as children Birds, pursue,
Still out of reach, yet never out of view ;
Sure, if they catch, to spoil the Toy at most,
To covet flying, and regret when lost :
At last, to follies Youth could scarce defend,   235
It grows their Age's prudence to pretend ;
Ashamed to own they gave delight before,
Reduced to feign it, when they give no more :
As Hags hold Sabbaths, less for joy than spite,
So these their merry, miserable Night ;   240
Still round and round the Ghosts of Beauty glide,
And haunt the places where their Honour died.
    See how the World its Veterans rewards !
A Youth of Frolics, an old Age of Cards ;
Fair to no purpose, artful to no end,   245
Young without Lovers, old without a Friend ;
A Fop their Passion, but their Prize a Sot ;
Alive, ridiculous, and dead, forgot !
    Ah ! Friend ! to dazzle let the Vain design ;   249
To raise the Thought, and touch the Heart be thine !
That Charm shall grow, while what fatigues the Ring,
Flaunts and goes down, an unregarded thing :
So when the Sun's broad beam has tired the sight,
All mild ascends the Moon's more sober light,
Serene in Virgin Modesty she shines,   255
And unobserved the glaring Orb declines.
    Oh ! blest with Temper, whose unclouded ray
Can make to-morrow cheerful as to-day ;
She, who can love a Sister's charms, or hear
Sighs for a daughter with unwounded ear ;   260
She, who ne'er answers till a Husband cools,
Or, if she rules him, never shews she rules ;
Charms by accepting, by submitting sways,

Yet has her humour most, when she obeys ;
Let Fops or Fortune fly which way they will ; 265
Disdains all loss of Tickets, or Codille :
Spleen, Vapours, or Small-pox, above them all,
And Mistress of herself, though China fall.
    And yet, believe me, good as well as ill,
Woman's at best a Contradiction still. 270
Heaven, when it strives to polish all it can
Its last best work, but forms a softer Man ;
Picks from each sex, to make the Fav'rite blest,
Your love of Pleasure, or desire of Rest :
Blends, in exception to all general rules, 275
Your Taste of Follies, with our Scorn of Fools :
Reserve with Frankness, Art with Truth allied,
Courage with Softness, Modesty with Pride ;
Fixed Principles, with Fancy ever new ;
Shakes all together, and produces—You. 280
    Be this a Woman's Fame : with this unblest,
Toasts live a scorn, and Queens may die a jest.
This Phœbus promised (I forget the year)
When those blue eyes first opened on the sphere ;
Ascendant Phœbus watched that hour with care, 285
Averted half your Parents' simple Prayer ;
And gave you Beauty, but denied the Pelf
That buys your sex a Tyrant o'er itself.
The gen'rous God, who Wit and Gold refines,
And ripens Spirits as he ripens Mines, 290
Kept Dross for Duchesses, the world shall know it,
To you gave Sense, Good-humour, and a Poet.

EPISTLE III

Epistle.—This Epistle was written after a violent outcry against our Author, on a supposition that he had ridiculed a worthy nobleman merely for his wrong taste.   He justified himself upon that article in a letter to the Earl of Burlington ; at the end of which are these words : " I have learnt that there are some who would rather be wicked than ridiculous : and therefore it may be safer to attack vices than follies. I will therefore leave my betters in the quiet possession of their idols, their groves, and their high places'; and change my subject from their pride to their meanness, from their vanities to their miseries ; and as the only certain way to avoid misconstructions, to lessen offence, and not to multiply ill-natured applications, I may probably, in my next, make use of real names instead of fictitious ones."

To Allen Lord Bathurst

ARGUMENT

Of the Use of Riches

That it is known to few, most falling into one of the extremes, *Avarice* or *Profusion*. The point discussed, whether the invention of Money has been more commodious or pernicious to Mankind. That Riches, either to the *Avaricious* or the *Prodigal*, cannot afford Happiness, scarcely Necessaries. That Avarice is an absolute Frenzy, without an End or Purpose. Conjectures about the Motives of Avaricious men. That the conduct of men, with respect to Riches, can only be accounted for by the Order of Providence, which works the general Good out of Extremes, and brings all to its great End by perpetual Revolutions. How a *Miser* acts upon Principles which appear to him reasonable. How a *Prodigal* does the same. The due Medium, and true use of Riches. The *Man* of *Ross*. The fate of the *Profuse* and the *Covetous*, in two examples ; both miserable in Life and in Death. The story of Sir *Balaam.*

P.   Who shall decide, when Doctors disagree,
And soundest Casuists doubt, like you and me ?
You hold the word, from Jove to Momus given
That Man was made the standing jest of Heaven ;
And Gold but sent to keep the fools in play,   5
For some to heap, and some to throw away.
    But I, who think more highly of our kind,
(And surely, Heaven and I are of a mind)
Opine, that Nature, as in duty bound,

Deep hid the shining mischief under ground :   10
But when by Man's audacious labour won,
Flamed forth this rival to its Sire, the Sun,
Then careful Heaven supplied two sorts of Men,
To squander These, and Those to hide again.

Like Doctors thus, when much dispute has past,
We find our tenets just the same at last.   16
Both fairly owning Riches, in effect,
No grace of Heaven or token of th' Elect ;
Given to the Fool, the Mad, the Vain, the Evil,
To Ward, to Waters, Chartres, and the Devil.   20

To Ward.—John Ward, of Hackney, Esq. ; Member of Parliament, being prosecuted by the Duchess of Buckingham, and convicted of Forgery, was first expelled the House, and then stood in the Pillory on March 17, 1727. He was suspected of joining in a conveyance with Sir John Blunt, to secrete fifty thousand pounds of that Director's Estate, forfeited to the South-Sea Company by Act of Parliament. The company recovered the fifty thousand pounds against Ward ; but he set up prior conveyances of his real estate to his brother and son, and concealed all his personal, which was computed to be one hundred and fifty thousand pounds. These conveyances being also set aside by a bill in Chancery, Ward was imprisoned, and hazarded the forfeiture of his life, by not giving in his effects till the last day, which was that of his examination. During his confinement, his amusement was to give poison to dogs and cats, and to see them expire by slower or quicker torments. To sum up the *worth* of this gentleman, at the several æras of his life : At his standing in the Pillory he was *worth above two hundred thousand pounds ;* at his commitment to Prison, he was *worth one hundred and fifty thousand ;* but has been since so far diminished in his reputation, as to be thought a *worse man* by *fifty or sixty thousand.*

Mr. Waters.—The second of these worthies was a man no way resembling the former in his military, but extremely so in his civil capacity ; his great fortune having been raised by the like diligent attendance on the necessities of others. But this gentleman's history must be deferred till his death, when his *worth* may be known more certainly.

Fr. Chartres.—A man infamous for all manner of vices. When he was an ensign in the army, he was drummed out of the regiment for a cheat ; he was next banished Brussels, and drummed out of Ghent on the same account. After a hundred tricks at the gaming tables, he took to lending of money at exorbitant interest and on great penalties accumulating premium, interest, and capital into a new capital, and seizing to a minute when the payments became due ; in a word, by a constant attention to the vices, wants, and follies of mankind, he acquired an immense fortune. His house was a perpetual bawdy-house. He was twice condemned for rapes, and pardoned : but the last time not without imprisonment in Newgate, and large confiscations.

B. What nature wants, commodious Gold bestows,
'Tis thus we eat the bread another sows.
P. But how unequal it bestows, observe,
'Tis thus we riot, while, who sow it, starve :

He died in Scotland in 1731, aged 62. The populace at his funeral raised a great riot, almost tore the body out of the coffin, and cast dead dogs, etc., into the grave along with it. The following Epitaph contains his character very justly drawn by Dr. Arbuthnot :—

HERE continueth to rot
The Body of FRANCIS CHARTRES,
Who with an INFLEXIBLE CONSTANCY,
and INIMITABLE UNIFORMITY of Life,
PERSISTED,
In spite of AGE and INFIRMITIES,
In the Practice of EVERY HUMAN VICE ;
Excepting PRODIGALITY and HYPOCRISY :
His insatiable AVARICE exempted him from the first,
His matchless IMPUDENCE from the second.
Nor was he more singular
in the undeviating *Pravity* of his *Manners*
Than successful
in *Accumulating* WEALTH.
For, without TRADE or PROFESSION,
Without TRUST of PUBLIC MONEY,
And without BRIBE-WORTHY Service,
He acquired, or more properly created,
A MINISTERIAL ESTATE.
He was the only Person of his Time,
Who could CHEAT without the Mask of HONESTY,
Retain his Primeval MEANNESS
When possessed of TEN THOUSAND a YEAR,
And having daily deserved the GIBBET for what he *did*
Was at last condemned to it for what he *could* not *do*.
Oh, Indignant Reader !
Think not his Life useless to Mankind !
PROVIDENCE connived at his execrable Designs,
To give to After-ages
A conspicuous PROOF and EXAMPLE,
Of how small Estimation is EXORBITANT WEALTH
in the Sight of GOD,
By his bestowing it on the most UNWORTHY of
ALL MORTALS.

This Gentleman was *worth seven thousand pounds a year* estate in Land, and about *one hundred thousand* in Money.

And the Devil.—Alluding to the vulgar opinion, that all mines of metal and subterraneous treasure are in the guard of the Devil : which seems to have taken its rise from the pagan fable of Plutus the God of Riches.

What Nature wants (a phrase I much distrust) 25
Extends to Luxury, extends to Lust :
Useful, I grant, it serves what life requires,
But, dreadful too, the dark Assassin hires :
B.   Trade it may help, Society extend.
P.   But lures the Pirate, and corrupts the Friend. 30
B.   It raises Armies in a Nation's aid.
P.   But bribes a Senate, and the Land's betrayed.
In vain may Heroes fight, and Patriots rave ;
If secret Gold sap on from knave to knave.
Once, we confess, beneath the Patriot's cloak, 35
From the cracked bag the dropping Guinea spoke,
And jingling down the back-stairs, told the crew,
" Old Cato is as great a Rogue as you."
Blest paper-credit ! last and best supply !
That lends Corruption lighter wings to fly ! 40
Gold imp'd by thee, can compass hardest things,
Can pocket States, can fetch or carry Kings ;
A single leaf shall waft an Army o'er,
Or ship off Senates to a distant Shore ;
A leaf, like Sibyl's, scatter to and fro 45
Our fates and fortunes, as the winds shall blow :

If secret Gold sap on from knave to knave.—The expression is fine,
and gives us the image of a place invested, where the approaches are
made by communications which support each other ; as the connections amongst knaves, after they have been taken in by a state
engineer, serve to screen and encourage one another's private corrup-
tions.

Beneath the Patriot's cloak.—This is a true story, which happened
in the reign of William III. to an unsuspected old Patriot, who coming
out at the back-door from having been closeted by the King, where
he had received a large bag of Guineas, the bursting of the bag discovered his business there.

Fetch or carry Kings.—In our author's time, many Princes had
been sent about the world, and great changes of Kings projected in
Europe. The partition-treaty had disposed of Spain ; France had
set up a King for England, who was sent to Scotland, and back again ;
King Stanislaus was sent to Poland, and back again ; the Duke of
Anjou was sent to Spain, and Don Carlos to Italy.

Or ship off Senates to a distant Shore.—Alludes to several Ministers,
Counsellors, and Patriots banished in our times to Siberia, and to
that MORE GLORIOUS FATE of the PARLIAMENT OF PARIS, banished
to Pontoise in the year 1720.

Pregnant with thousands flits the Scrap unseen,
And silent sells a King, or buys a Queen.
   Oh ! that such bulky Bribes as all might see,
Still, as of old, encumbered Villainy !   50
Could France or Rome divert our brave designs,
With all their brandies or with all their wines ?
What could they more than Knights and Squires con-
     found,
Or water all the Quorum ten miles round ?
A Statesman's slumbers how this speech would spoil !
" Sir, Spain has sent a thousand jars of oil ;   56
Huge bales of British cloth blockade the door ;
A hundred oxen at your levee roar."
   Poor Avarice one torment more would find ;
Nor could Profusion squander all in kind.   60
Astride his cheese Sir Morgan might we meet ;
And Worldly crying coals from street to street,
Whom with a wig so wild, and mien so mazed,
Pity mistakes for some poor tradesman crazed.
Had Colepepper's whole wealth been hops and hogs, 65
Could he himself have sent it to the dogs ?
His Grace will game : to White's a Bull be led,
With spurning heels and with a butting head.
To White's be carried, as to ancient games,
Fair Coursers, Vases, and alluring Dames,   70
Shall then Uxorio, if the stakes he sweep,
Bear home six Whores, and make his Lady weep ?
Or soft Adonis, so perfumed and fine,
Drive to St. James's a whole herd of swine ?

   From street to street.—Some misers of great wealth, proprietors of
the coal-mines, had entered at this time into an association to keep
up coals to an extravagant price, whereby the poor were reduced
almost to starve, till one of them taking the advantage of underselling
the rest, defeated the design. One of these Misers was *worth ten
thousand*, another *seven thousand* a year.
   Colepepper.—Sir William Colepepper, Bart., a person of an ancient
family and ample fortune, without one other quality of a Gentleman,
who, after ruining himself at the Gaming-table, passed the rest of his
days in sitting there to see the ruin of others ; preferring to subsist
upon borrowing and begging, rather than to enter into any reputable
method of life, and refusing a post in the army which was offered him.

Oh filthy check on all industrious skill,   75
To spoil the nation's last great trade, Quadrille !
Since then, my Lord, on such a World we fall,
What say you ?   B.   Say ?   Why take it, Gold and
    all.
P.   What Riches give us let us then enquire :
Meat, Fire and Clothes.   B.   What more ?   P.   Meat,
    Clothes, and Fire.   80
Is this too little ?   would you more than live ?
Alas ! 'tis more than Turner finds they give.
Alas ! 'tis more than (all his Visions past)
Unhappy Wharton, waking, found at last !
What can they give ?   to dying Hopkins, Heirs ;   85
To Chartres, Vigour ; Japhet, Nose and Ears ?
Can they, in gems bid pallid Hippia glow,
In Fulvia's buckle ease the throbs below ;
Or heal, old Narses, thy obscener ail,

Turner.—One who, being possessed of three hundred thousand
pounds, laid down his Coach, because Interest was reduced from five
to four *per cent.*, and then put seventy thousand into the Charitable
Corporation for better interest ; which sum having lost, he took it
so much to heart, that he kept his chamber ever after.   It is thought
he would not have outlived it, but that he was heir to another considerable estate, which he daily expected, and that by this course
of life he saved both cloaths and all other expences.

Unhappy Wharton.—A Nobleman of great qualities, but as unfortunate in the application of them, as if they had been vices and follies.
See his Character in the first Epistle.

Hopkins.—A Citizen whose rapacity obtained him the name of
Vulture Hopkins.   He lived worthless, but died *worth three hundred
thousand pounds,* which he would give to no person living, but left it
so as not to be inherited till after the second generation.   His counsel
representing to him how many years it must be before this could
take effect, and that his money could only lie at interest all that time,
he expressed great joy thereat, and said, " They would then be as long
in spending as he had been in getting it."   But the Chancery afterwards set aside the will, and gave it to the heir-at-law.

Japhet, Nose, and Ears.—Japhet Crook, alias Sir *Peter Stranger,*
was punished with the loss of those parts for having forged a conveyance of an Estate to himself, upon which he took up several thousand pounds.   He was at the same time sued in Chancery for having
fraudulently obtained a Will, by which he possessed another considerable Estate, in wrong of the brother of the deceased.   By these means
he was *worth* a great sum, which (in reward for the small loss of his
ears) he enjoyed in prison till his death, and quietly left to his executor.

With all th' embroidery plaistered at thy tail ?   90
They might (were Harpax not too wise to spend)
Give Harpax' self the blessing of a friend ;
Or find some Doctor that would save the life
Of wretched Shylock, spite of Shylock's Wife :
But thousands die, without or this or that,   95
Die, and endow a College, or a Cat.
To some indeed, Heaven grants the happier fate,
T' enrich a Bastard, or a Son they hate.
  Perhaps you think the Poor might have their part ?
Bond damns the Poor and hates them from **his**
          heart :   100
The grave Sir Gilbert holds it for a rule,
That " every man in want is knave or fool :
God cannot love (says Blunt, with tearless eyes)
The wretch he starves "—and piously denies :
But the good Bishop, with a meeker air,   105
Admits, and leaves them, Providence's care.
  Yet, to be just to these poor men of pelf,
Each does but hate his neighbour as himself :
Damned to the Mines, an equal fate betides
The Slave that digs it, and the Slave that hides.   110
B.   Who suffer thus, mere Charity should own,
Must act on motives powerful, though unknown.
P.   Some War, some Plague, or Famine they foresee,
Some Revelation hid from you and me.

  Die, and endow a College, or a Cat.—A famous Duchess of Richmond
in her last will left considerable legacies and annuities to her Cats.
  Bond damns the Poor, etc.—This epistle was written in the year
1730, when a corporation was established to lend money to the poor
upon pledges, by the name of the *Charitable Corporation ;* but the whole
was turned only to an iniquitous method of enriching particular people,
to the ruin of such numbers, that it became a parliamentary concern
to endeavour the relief of those unhappy sufferers, and three of the
managers, who were members of the House, were expelled. By the
report of the committee, appointed to inquire into that iniquitous
affair, it appears, that when it was objected to the intended removal
of the office, that the Poor, for whose use it was erected, would be hurt
by it, Bond, one of the Directors, replied, *Damn the Poor.* That
" God hates the poor," and, " That every man in want is knave or
fool," etc., were the genuine apothegms of some of the persons here
mentioned.

Why Shylock wants a meal, the cause is found,   115
He thinks a Loaf will rise to fifty pound.
What made Directors cheat in South-Sea year?
To live on Ven'son when it sold so dear.
Ask you why Phryne the whole Auction buys?
Phryne foresees a general Excise.   120
Why she and Sappho raise that monstrous sum?
Alas! they fear a man will cost a plum.
   Wise Peter sees the World's respect for Gold,
And therefore hopes this Nation may be sold:
Glorious Ambition! Peter, swell thy store,   125
And be what Rome's great Didius was before.
   The Crown of Poland, venal twice an age,
To just three millions stinted modest Gage.
But nobler scenes Maria's dreams unfold,
Hereditary Realms, and worlds of Gold.   130
Congenial souls! whose life one Av'rice joins,
And one fate buries th' Asturian Mines.

To live on Ven'son.—In the extravagance and luxury of the South-Sea year the price of a haunch of Venison was from three to five pounds.

General Excise.—Many people about the year 1733 had a conceit that such a thing was intended, of which it is not improbable this lady might have some intimation.

Wise Peter.—Peter Walter, a person not only eminent in the wisdom of his profession, as a dextrous attorney, but allowed to be a good, if not a safe conveyancer; extremely respected by the Nobility of this land, though free from all manner of luxury and ostentation: his Wealth was never seen, and his bounty never heard of, except to his own son, for whom he procured an employment of considerable profit, of which he gave him as much as was *necessary*. Therefore the taxing this gentleman with any Ambition is certainly a great wrong to him.

Rome's great Didius.—A Roman Lawyer, so rich as to purchase the Empire when it was set to sale upon the death of Pertinax.

The Crown of Poland, etc.—The two persons here mentioned were of Quality, each of whom in the Mississippi despised to realize above *three hundred thousand pounds;* the Gentleman with a view to the purchase of the Crown of Poland, the Lady on a vision of the like royal nature. They since retired into Spain, where they are still in search of gold in the mines of the Asturies.

Modest Gage.—A Mr. Gage, of the ancient Suffolk Catholic family of that name; and Lady Mary Herbert, daughter of the Marquess of Powis and of a natural daughter of James II.; whence the phrase "*hereditary* realms."

Much injured Blunt ! why bears he Britain's hate ?
A wizard told him in these words our fate :
" At length Corruption, like a general flood,   135
(So long by watchful Ministers withstood)
Shall deluge all ; and Av'rice, creeping on,
Spread like a low-born mist, and blot the Sun ;
Statesman and Patriot ply alike the stocks,
Peeress and Butler share alike the Box,   140
And Judges job, and Bishops bite the town,
And mighty Dukes pack Cards for half a crown.
See Britain sunk in lucre's sordid charms,
And France revenged of ANNE's and EDWARD's arms ? "
'Twas no Court-badge, great Scrivener ! fired thy brain,
Nor lordly Luxury, nor City Gain :   146
No, 'twas thy righteous end, ashamed to see
Senates degenerate, Patriots disagree,
And, nobly wishing Party-rage to cease,
To buy both sides, and give thy Country peace.   150
" All this is madness," cries a sober sage :
But who, my friend, has reason in his rage ?
" The ruling Passion, be it what it will,
The ruling Passion conquers Reason still."
Less mad the wildest whimsey we can frame,   155
That even that Passion, if it has no Aim ;
For though such motives Folly you may call,
The Folly's greater to have none at all.
Hear then the truth : " 'Tis Heaven each Passion
          sends,
And different men directs to different ends.   160

Much injured Blunt !—Sir John Blunt, originally a scrivener, was
one of the first projectors of the South-Sea Company, and afterwards
one of the directors and chief managers of the famous scheme in 1720.
He was also one of those who suffered most severely by the bill of
pains and penalties on the said directors. He was a Dissenter of a
most religious deportment, and professed to be a greater believer.
Whether he did really credit the prophecy here mentioned is not
certain, but it was constantly in this very style he declaimed against
the corruption and luxury of the age, the partiality of Parliaments,
and the misery of party-spirit. He was particularly eloquent against
Avarice in great and noble persons, of which he had indeed lived to see
many miserable examples. He died in the year 1732.

Extremes in Nature equal good produce,
Extremes in Man concur to general use."
Ask we what makes one keep, and one bestow?
That POWER who bids the Ocean ebb and flow,
Bids seed-time, harvest, equal course maintain,   165
Through reconciled extremes of drought and rain,
Builds life on Death, on Change Duration founds,
And gives th' eternal wheels to know their rounds.

Riches, like insects, when concealed they lie,
Wait but for Wings, and in their season fly.   170
Who sees pale Mammon pine amidst his store,
Sees but a backward steward for the Poor ;
This year a Reservoir, to keep and spare ;
The next, a Fountain, spouting through his Heir,
In lavish streams to quench a Country's thirst,   175
And men and dogs shall drink him till they burst.

Old Cotta shamed his fortune and his birth,
Yet was not Cotta void of wit or worth :
What though (the use of barb'rous spits forgot)
His kitchen vied in coolness with his grot ?   180
His court with nettles, moats with cresses stored,
With soups unbought and salads blessed his board ?
If Cotta lived on pulse, it was no more
Than Brahmins, Saints, and Sagas did before ;
To cram the Rich was prodigal expense,   185
And who would take the Poor from Providence ?
Like some lone Chartreux stands the good old Hall,
Silence without, and Fasts within the wall ;
No raftered roofs with dance and tabor sound,
No noontide-bell invites the country round ;   190
Tenants with sighs the smokeless towers survey,
And turn th' unwilling steeds another way ;
Benighted wanderers, the forest o'er,
Curse the saved candle, and unopening door ;
While the gaunt mastiff growling at the gate,   195
Affrights the beggar whom he longs to eat.

Not so his Son ; he marked this oversight,
And then mistook reverse of wrong for right.

(For what to shun will no great knowledge need ;
But what to follow, is a task indeed.)   200
Yet sure, of qualities deserving praise,
More go to ruin Fortunes, than to raise.
What slaughtered hecatombs, what floods of wine,
Fill the capacious Squire, and deep Divine !
Yet no mean motive this profusion draws,   205
His oxen perish in his country's cause ;
'Tis GEORGE and LIBERTY that crowns the cup,
And Zeal for that great House which eats him up.
The woods recede around the naked seat ;
The Sylvans groan—no matter—for the Fleet ;   210
Next goes his Wool—to clothe our valiant bands ;
Last, for his Country's love, he sells his Lands.
To town he comes, completes the nation's hope,
And heads the bold Train-bands, and burns a Pope.
And shall not Britain now reward his toils,   215
Britain, that pays her Patriots with her Spoils ?
In vain at Court the Bankrupt pleads his cause,
His thankless Country leaves him to her Laws.
    The Sense to value Riches, with the Art
T' enjoy them, and the Virtue to impart,   220
Not meanly, nor ambitiously pursued,
Not sunk by sloth, nor raised by servitude ;
To balance Fortune by a just expense,
Join with Economy, Magnificence ;
With Splendour, Charity ; with Plenty, Health ;   225
O teach us, BATHURST ! yet unspoiled by wealth !
That secret rare, between th' extremes to move
Of mad Good-nature, and of mean Self-love.
    B.   To Worth or Want well-weighed, be Bounty given,
And ease, or emulate, the care of Heaven ;   230
(Whose measure full o'erflows on human race)
Mend Fortune's fault, and justify her grace.
Wealth in the gross is death, but life diffused ;
As Poison heals, in just proportion used :
In heaps, like Ambergrise, a stink it lies,   235
But well-dispersed, is Incense to the Skies.

P.   Who starves by Nobles, or with Nobles eats?
The Wretch that trusts them, and the Rogue that cheats.
Is there a Lord, who knows a cheerful noon
Without a Fiddler, Flatt'rer, or Buffoon?   240
Whose table, Wit, or modest Merit share,
Unelbowed by a Gamester, Pimp, or Player?
Who copies Yours or OXFORD's better part,
To ease th' oppressed, and raise the sinking heart?
Where-e'er he shines, oh Fortune, gild the scene,   245
And Angels guard him in the golden Mean!
There, English Bounty yet awhile may stand,
And Honour linger ere it leaves the land.
      But all our praises why should Lords engross?
Rise, honest Muse! and sing the MAN of ROSS: 250
Pleased Vaga echoes through her winding bounds,
And rapid Severn hoarse applause resounds.
Who hung with woods yon mountain's sultry brow?
From the dry rock who bade the waters flow?
Not to the skies in useless columns tost,   255
Or in proud falls magnificently lost,
But clear and artless, pouring through the plain
Health to the sick, and solace to the swain.
Whose Cause-way parts the vale with shady rows?
Whose Seats the weary Traveller repose?   260
Who taught that heaven-directed spire to rise?
"The MAN of ROSS," each lisping babe replies.
Behold the Market-place with poor o'erspread!
The MAN of Ross divides the weekly bread;
He feeds yon Alms-house, neat, but void of state,   265

Oxford's better part.—Edward Harley, Earl of Oxford. The son of Robert, created Earl of Oxford and Earl Mortimer by Queen Anne. This Nobleman died regretted by all men of letters, great numbers of whom had experienced his benefits. He left behind him one of the most noble Libraries in Europe.

The Man of Ross.—The person here celebrated, who with a small Estate actually performed all these good works, and whose true name was almost lost (partly by the title of the *Man of Ross* given him by way of eminence, and partly by being buried without so much as an inscription) was called Mr. John Kyrle. He died in the year 1724, aged 90, and lies interred in the chancel of the church of Ross in Herefordshire.

Where Age and Want sit smiling at the gate ;
Him portioned maids, apprenticed orphans blest,
The young who labour, and the old who rest.
Is any sick ? the MAN of Ross relieves,
Prescribes, attends, the med'cine makes, and gives. 270
Is there a variance ? enter but his door,
Balked are the Courts, and contest is no more.
Despairing Quacks with curses fled the place,
And vile Attorneys, now an useless race.
　　B.   Thrice happy man ! enabled to pursue   275
What all so wish, but want the power to do !
Oh say, what sums that gen'rous hand supply ?
What mines, to swell that boundless charity ?
　　P.   Of Debts, and Taxes, Wife and Children clear,
This man possest—five hundred pounds a year.   280
Blush, Grandeur, blush ! proud Courts, withdraw your
　　　　blaze !
Ye little Stars ! hide your diminished rays.
　　B.   And what ? no monument, inscription, stone ?
His race, his form, his name almost unknown ?
P.   Who builds a Church to God, and not to Fame, 285
Will never mark the marble with his Name :
Go, search it there, where to be born and die,
Of rich and poor makes all the history ;
Enough, that Virtue filled the space between ;
Proved, by the ends of being, to have been.   290
When Hopkins dies, a thousand lights attend
The wretch, who living saved a candle's end :
Should'ring God's altar a vile image stands,
Belies his features, nay extends his hands ;
That live-long wig which Gorgon's self might own,   295
Eternal buckle takes in Parian stone.

　　Go, search it there.—The Parish-register.
　　When Hopkins dies.—Edmund Boulter, Esq., executor to Vulture
Hopkins, made so splendid a funeral for him, that the expenses
amounted to £7,666.
　　Eternal buckle takes in Parian stone.—The poet ridicules the wretched
taste of carving large perriwigs on bustos, of which there are several
vile examples in the tombs at Westminster and elsewhere.

Behold what blessings Wealth to life can lend !
And see, what comfort it affords our end.

   In the worst inn's worst room, with mat half-hung,
The floors of plaister, and the walls of dung,   300
On once a flock-bed, but repaired with straw,
With tape-tied curtains, never meant to draw,
The George and Garter dangling from that bed
Where tawdry yellow strove with dirty red,
Great Villiers lies—alas ! how changed from him,   305
That life of pleasure, and that soul of whim !
Gallant and gay, in Cliveden's proud alcove,
The bower of wanton Shrewsbury and love ;
Or just as gay, at Council, in a ring
Of mimicked Statesmen, and their merry King.   310
No Wit to flatter left of all his store !
No Fool to laugh at, which he valued more.
There, Victor of his health, of fortune, friends,
And fame, this lord of useless thousands ends.

   His Grace's fate sage Cutler could foresee,
And well (he thought) advised him, " Live like me." 315
As well his Grace replied, " Like you, Sir John ?
That I can do, when all I have is gone."
Resolve me, Reason, which of these is worse,
Want with a full, or with an empty purse ?   320
Thy life more wretched, Cutler, was confessed,
Arise, and tell me, was thy death more blessed ?
Cutler saw tenants break, and houses fall,
For very want ; he could not build a wall.
His only daughter in a stranger's power,   325

   Great Villiers lies.—This Lord, yet more famous for his vices than
his misfortunes, after having been possessed of about £50,000 a year,
and passed through many of the highest posts in the kingdom, died
in the year 1687, in a remote inn in Yorkshire, reduced to the utmost
misery.

   Cliveden.—A delightful palace, on the banks of the Thames, built
by the Duke of Buckingham.

   Shrewsbury.—The Countess of Shrewsbury, a woman abandoned to
gallantries. The Earl, her husband, was killed by the Duke of Buckingham in a duel ; and it has been said that during the combat she held
the Duke's horses in the habit of a page.

For very want ; he could not pay a dower.
A few grey hairs his rev'rend temples crowned,
'Twas very want that sold them for two pound.
What even denied a cordial at his end,
Banished the doctor, and expelled the friend ? 330
What but a want, which you perhaps think mad,
Yet numbers feel the want of what he had !
Cutler and Brutus, dying both exclaim,
" Virtue ! and Wealth ! what are ye but a name ! "
Say, for such worth are other worlds prepared ? 335
Or are they both, in this their own reward ?
A knotty point ! to which we now proceed.
But you are tired—I'll tell a tale— B. Agreed.
P. Where London's column, pointing at the skies,
Like a tall bully, lifts the head and lies ; 340
There dwelt a Citizen of sober fame,
A plain good man, and Balaam was his name ;
Religious, punctual, frugal, and so forth ;
His word would pass for more than he was worth.
One solid dish his week-day meal affords, 345
An added pudding solemnized the Lord's :
Constant at Church, and Change ; his gains were sure,
His givings rare, save farthings to the poor.
The Dev'l was piqued such saintship to behold,
And longed to tempt him like good Job of old : 350
But Satan now is wiser than of yore,
And tempts by making rich, not making poor.
Roused by the Prince of Air, the whirlwinds sweep
The surge, and plunge his Father in the deep ;
Then full against his Cornish lands they roar, 355

Where London's column.—The Monument, on Fish Street Hill, built
in memory of the fire of London of 1666, with an inscription, import-
ing that city to have been burnt by the Papists.
   Cornish.—The author has placed the scene of these shipwrecks in
Cornwall, not only from their frequency on that coast, but from the
inhumanity of the inhabitants to those to whom that misfortune
arrives. When a ship happens to be stranded there, they have been
known to bore holes in it, to prevent its getting off ; to plunder,
and sometimes even to massacre the People : nor has the Parliament
of England been yet able wholly to suppress these barbarities.

And two rich ship-wrecks bless the lucky shore.
 Sir Balaam now, he lives like other folks,
He takes his chirping pint, and cracks his jokes :
" Live like yourself," was soon my Lady's word ;
And lo ! two puddings smoked upon the board. 360
 Asleep and naked as an Indian lay,
An honest factor stole a Gem away :
He pledged it to the knight ; the knight had wit,
So kept the Diamond, and the rogue was bit.
Some scruple rose, but thus he eased his thought, 365
" I'll now give six-pence where I gave a groat ;
Where once I went to Church, I'll now go twice—
And am so clear too of all other vice."
 The Tempter saw his time ; the work he plied ;
Stocks and Subscriptions pour on every side, 370
'Til all the Demon makes his full descent
In one abundant shower of Cent per Cent,
Sinks deep within him, and possesses whole,
Then dubs Director, and secures his soul.
 Behold Sir Balaam, now a man of spirit, 375
Ascribes his gettings to his parts and merit ;
What late he called a Blessing, now was Wit,
And God's good Providence, a lucky Hit.
Things change their titles, as our manners turn :
His Counting-house employed the Sunday-morn ; 380
Seldom at Church ('twas such a busy life)
But duly sent his family and wife.
There (so the Dev'l ordained) one Christmas-tide
My good old Lady catched a cold, and died.
 A Nymph of Quality admires our Knight ; 385
He marries, bows at Court, and grows polite :
Leaves the dull Cits, and joins (to please the fair)
The well-bred cuckolds in St. James's air :
First, for his Son a gay commission buys,

Gem.—Pope was supposed to allude here to the Pitt diamond
brought to England by Thomas Pitt, Governor of Madras, about
1700, and sold to the King of France for £20,000. Thomas Pitt was
grandfather of the first Earl of Chatham.

Who drinks, whores, fights, and in a duel dies :   390
His daughter flaunts a Viscount's tawdry wife ;
She bears a Coronet and P—x for life.
In Britain's Senate he a seat obtains,
And one more Pensioner St. Stephen gains.
My Lady falls to play ; so bad her chance,   395
He must repair it ; takes a bribe from France ;
The House impeach him ; Coningsby harangues ;
The Court forsake him, and Sir Balaam hangs :
Wife, son, and daughter, Satan ! are thy own,
His wealth, yet dearer, forfeit to the Crown :   400
The Devil and the King divide the prize,
And sad Sir Balaam curses God and dies.

EPISTLE IV

To Richard Boyle, Earl of Burlington

ARGUMENT

Of the Use of Riches

The Vanity of Expense in People of Wealth and Quality.   The abuse
of the word *Taste*.   That the first principle and foundation, in this
as in every thing else, is *Good Sense*.   The chief proof of it is to *follow
Nature* even in works of mere Luxury and Elegance.   Instanced in
Architecture and *Gardening*, where all must be adapted to the Genius
and *Use* of the Place, and the Beauties not forced into it, but resulting
from it.   How men are disappointed in their most expensive under-
takings, for want of this true Foundation, without which nothing can
please *long*, if *at all ;* and the best *Examples* and *Rules* will but be
perverted into something *burdensome* or ridiculous.   A description
of the *false Taste* of *Magnificence ;* the first grand Error of which is to
imagine that *Greatness* consists in the *Size* and *Dimension*, instead of
the *Proportion* and *Harmony* of the *whole*, and the second, either in
joining together *Parts incoherent*, or too *minutely resembling*, or in
the *Repetition* of the *same* too frequently.   A word or two of false
Taste in *Books*, in *Music*, in *Painting*, even in *Preaching* and *Prayer*,
and lastly in *Entertainments*.   Yet Providence is justified in giving
Wealth to be squandered in this manner, since it is dispersed to the
Poor and Laborious part of mankind [recurring to what is laid down
in the first book, Ep. ii. and in the Epistle preceding this].   What
are the *proper Objects* of Magnificence, and a proper field for the Expense
of *Great Men*, and finally, the Great and Public Works which become
a *Prince*.

'TIS strange, the Miser should his Cares employ
To gain those Riches he can ne'er enjoy :
Is it less strange, the Prodigal should waste
His wealth, to purchase what he ne'er can taste ?
Not for himself he sees, or hears, or eats ;   5
Artists must choose his Pictures, Music, Meats :
He buys for Topham, Drawings and Designs,
For Pembroke, Statues, dirty Gods, and Coins ;
Rare monkish Manuscripts for Hearne alone,
And Books for Mead, and Butterflies for Sloane.   10
Think we all these are for himself ? no more
Than his fine Wife, alas ! or finer Whore.
   For what has Virro painted, built, and planted ?
Only to shew, how many Tastes he wanted.
What brought Sir Visto's ill got wealth to waste ?   15
Some Dæmon whispered, " Visto ! have a Taste."
Heaven visits with a Taste the wealthy fool,
And needs no Rod but Ripley with a Rule.
See ! sportive fate, to punish awkward pride,
Bids Bubo build, and sends him such a Guide :   20
A standing sermon, at each year's expense,
That never Coxcomb reached Magnificence !
   You shew us, Rome was glorious, not profuse,
And pompous buildings once were things of Use.
Yet shall, my Lord, your just, your noble rules   25
Fill half the land with Imitating-Fools ;
Who random drawings from your sheets shall take,
And of one beauty many blunders make ;
Load some vain Church with old Theatric state,

Topham.—A Gentleman famous for a judicious collection of Drawings.
And Books for Mead, and Butterflies for Sloane.—Two eminent
Physicians ; the one had an excellent Library, the other the finest
collection in Europe of natural curiosities ; both men of great learning
and humanity.
   Ripley.—This man was a carpenter, employed by a first Minister,
who raised him to an Architect, without any genius in the art ; and
after some wretched proofs of his insufficiency in public Buildings, made
him Comptroller of the Board of Works.
   Not profuse.—The Earl of Burlington was then publishing the
Designs of Inigo Jones, and the *Antiquities of Rome* by Palladio.

Turn Arcs of triumph to a Garden-gate ;   30
Reverse your Ornaments, and hang them all
On some patched dog-hole eked with ends of wall ;
Then clap four slices of Pilaster on't,
That, laced with bits of rustic, makes a Front.
Shall call the winds through long arcades to roar,   35
Proud to catch cold at a Venetian door ;
Conscious they act a true Palladian part,
And, if they starve, they starve by rules of art.
    Oft have you hinted to your brother Peer
A certain truth, which many buy too dear :   40
Something there is more needful than Expense,
And something previous even to Taste—'tis Sense :
Good Sense, which only is the gift of Heaven,
And though no Science, fairly worth the seven :
A Light, which in yourself you must perceive ;   45
Jones and Le Nôtre have it not to give.
    To build, to plant, whatever you intend,
To rear the Column, or the Arch to bend,
To swell the Terrace, or to sink the Grot ;
In all, let Nature never be forgot.   50
But treat the Goddess like a modest fair,
Nor over-dress, nor leave her wholly bare ;
Let not each beauty everywhere be spied,
Where half the skill is decently to hide.
He gains all points, who pleasingly confounds,   55
Surprises, varies, and conceals the Bounds.
    Consult the Genius of the Place in all ;
That tells the Waters or to rise, or fall ;
Or helps th' ambitious Hill the heavens to scale,
Or scoops in circling theatres the Vale ;   60
Calls in the Country, catches op'ning glades,
Joins willing woods, and varies shades from shades ;
Now breaks, or now directs, th' intending Lines ;

Venetian door.—A door or window so called, from being much practised at Venice by alladio and others.
Jones and Le Nôtre.—Inigo Jones, the celebrated Architect, and M. Le Nôtre, the designer of the best gardens of France.

Paints as you plant, and, as you work, designs.
  Still follow Sense, of every Art the Soul, 65
Parts answ'ring parts shall slide into a whole,
Spontaneous beauties all around advance,
Start even from Difficulty, strike from Chance ;
Nature shall join you ; Time shall make it grow
A Work to wonder at—perhaps a STOWE. 70
  Without it, proud Versailles ! thy glory falls ;
And Nero's Terraces desert their walls :
The vast Parterres a thousand hands shall make,
Lo ! COBHAM comes, and floats them with a Lake :
Or cut wide views through Mountains to the Plain, 75
You'll wish your hill or sheltered seat again.
Even in an ornament its place remark,
Nor in an Hermitage set Dr. Clarke.
  Behold Villario's ten years' toil complete ;
His Quincunx darkens, his Espaliers meet ; 80
The Wood supports the Plain, the parts unite,
And strength of Shade contends with strength of Light ;
A waving Glow the bloomy beds display,
Blushing in bright diversities of day,
With silver-quiv'ring rills mæandered o'er— 85
Enjoy them, you ! Villario can no more ;
Tired of the scene Parterres and Fountains yield,
He finds at last he better likes a Field.
  Through his young Woods how pleased Sabinus
    strayed,
Or sat delighted in the thick'ning shade,
With annual joy the redd'ning shoots to greet, 90
Or see the stretching branches long to meet !

Stowe.—The seat and gardens of the Lord Viscount Cobham **in**
Buckinghamshire.
  *Or cut wide views through Mountains to the Plain, You'll wish your
hill or sheltered seat again.*—This was done in Hertfordshire, by **a**
wealthy citizen, at the expense of above £5,000, by which means
(merely to overlook a dead plain) he let in the north wind upon his house
and parterre, which were before adorned and defended by beautiful
woods.
  Set Dr. Clarke.—Dr. S. Clarke's busto placed by the Queen in the
Hermitage, while the doctor duly frequented the Court.

7

His Son's fine Taste an op'ner Vista loves,
Foe to the Dryads of his Father's groves ;
One boundless Green, or flourished Carpet views,   95
With all the mournful family of Yews ;
The thriving plants ignoble broomsticks made,
Now sweep those Alleys they were born to shade.

    At Timon's Villa let us pass a day,
Where all cry out, " What sums are thrown away ! "
So proud, so grand ; of that stupendous air,   101
Soft and Agreeable come never there.
Greatness, with Timon, dwells in such a draught
As brings all Brobdignag before your thought.
To compass this, his building is a Town,   105
His pond an Ocean, his parterre a Down :
Who but must laugh, the Master when he sees,
A puny insect, shivering at a breeze !
Lo, what huge heaps of littleness around !
The whole, a laboured Quarry above ground ;   110
Two Cupids squirt before ; a Lake behind
Improves the keenness of the Northern wind.
His Gardens next your admiration call,
On every side you look, behold the Wall !
No pleasing Intricacies intervene,   115
No artful wildness to perplex the scene ;

    Carpet views.—The two extremes in parterres, which are equally faulty; a *boundless Green*, large and naked as a field, or a *flourished Carpet*, where the greatness and nobleness of the piece is lessened by being divided into too many parts, with scrolled works and beds, of which the examples are frequent.
    Mournful family of Yews.—Touches upon the ill taste of those who are so fond of Evergreens (particularly Yews, which are the most tonsile) as to destroy the nobler Forest-trees, to make way for such little ornaments as Pyramids of dark-green continually repeated, not unlike a Funeral procession.
    At Timon's Villa.—This description is intended to comprise the principles of a false Taste of Magnificence, and to exemplify what was said before, that nothing but Good Sense can attain it.
    Lo, what huge heaps of littleness around !—*Grandeur* in building, as in the human frame, takes not its denomination from the *body*, but the *soul* of the work : when the soul therefore is lost or encumbered in its envelope, the unanimated parts, how *huge* soever, are not members of grandeur, but mere *heaps of littleness.*

Grove nods at grove, each Alley has a brother,
And half the platform just reflects the other.
The suff'ring eye inverted Nature sees,
Trees cut to Statues, Statues thick as trees ;   120
With here a Fountain, never to be played ;
And there a Summer-house, that knows no shade ;
Here Amphitrite sails through myrtle bowers ;
There Gladiators fight, or die in flowers ;
Un-watered see the drooping sea-horse mourn,   125
And swallows roost in Nilus' dusty Urn.

My Lord advances with majestic mien,
Smit with the mighty pleasure, to be seen :
But soft,—by regular approach,—not yet,—
First through the length of yon hot Terrace sweat ; 130
And when up ten steep slopes you've dragged your
        thighs,
Just at his Study-door he'll bless your eyes.

His Study ! with what Authors is it stored ?
In Books, not Authors, curious is my Lord ;
To all their dated Backs he turns you round :   135
These Aldus printed, those Du Sueil has bound.
Lo, some are Vellum, and the rest as good
For all his Lordship knows, but they are Wood.
For Locke or Milton 'tis in vain to look,
These shelves admit not any modern book.   140
And now the Chapel's silver bell you hear,
That summons you to all the Pride of Prayer :
Light quirks of Music, broken and uneven,

Gladiators fight.—The two Statues of the *Gladiator pugnans* and
Gladiator moriens.
Terrace sweat.—The *Approaches* and *Communications* of house with
garden, or of one part with another, ill judged, and inconvenient.
His Study ! etc.—The false Taste in Books ; a satire on the vanity
in collecting them, more frequent in men of Fortune than the study to
understand them. Many delight chiefly in the elegance of the print,
or of the binding ; some have carried it so far, as to cause the upper
shelves to be filled with painted books of wood ; others pique themselves so much upon books in a language they do not understand,
as to exclude the most useful in one they do.
Pride of Prayer.—The false Taste in *Music*, improper to the subjects,
as of light airs in churches, often practised by the organists, etc.

Make the soul dance upon a Jig to Heaven.
On painted Ceilings you devoutly stare,   145
Where sprawl the Saints of Verrio or Laguerre,
On gilded clouds in fair expansion lie,
And bring all Paradise before your eye.
To rest, the Cushion and soft Dean invite,
Who never mentions Hell to ears polite.   150
    But hark ! the chiming Clocks to dinner call :
A hundred footsteps scrape the marble Hall :
The rich Buffet well-coloured Serpents grace,
And gaping Tritons spew to wash your face.
Is this a dinner ? this a Genial room ?   155
No, 'tis a Temple, and a Hecatomb.
A solemn Sacrifice, performed in state,
You drink by measure, and to minutes eat.
So quick retires each flying course, you'd swear
Sancho's dread Doctor and his Wand were there. 160
Between each Act the trembling salvers ring,
From soup to sweet-wine, and God bless the King.
In plenty starving, tantalized in state,
And complaisantly helped to all I hate,
Treated, caressed, and tired, I take my leave,   165
Sick of his civil Pride from Morn to Eve ;
I curse such lavish cost, and little skill,

Painted Ceilings.—And in *Painting* (from which even Italy is not free) of naked figures in Churches, etc., which has obliged some Popes to put draperies on some of those of the best masters.

Verrio or Laguerre.—Verrio (Antonio) painted many ceilings, etc., at Windsor, Hampton Court, etc., and Laguerre at Blenheim Castle and other places.

Who never mentions Hell to ears polite.—This is a fact ; a reverend Dean, preaching at Court, threatened the sinner with punishment in " a place which he thought it not decent to name in so polite an assembly."

Serpents grace.—Taxes the incongruity of *Ornaments* (though sometimes practised by the ancients) where an open mouth ejects the water into a fountain, or where the shocking images of serpents, etc., are introduced in Grottos or Buffets.

Is this a dinner, etc.—The proud Festivals of some men are here set forth to ridicule, where pride destroys the ease, and formal regularity all the pleasurable enjoyment of the entertainment.

Sancho's dread Doctor.—See *Don Quixote*, chap. xlvii.

And swear no Day was ever past so ill.

Yet hence the Poor are clothed, the Hungry fed ;
Health to himself, and to his Infants bread ·170
The Lab'rer bears : What his hard Heart denies,
His charitable Vanity supplies.

Another age shall see the golden Ear
Embrown the Slope, and nod on the Parterre,
Deep Harvests bury all his pride has planned, 175
And laughing Ceres re-assume the land.

Who then shall grace, or who improve the Soil ?
Who plants like BATHURST, or who builds like BOYLE.
'Tis Use alone that sanctifies Expense,
And Splendour borrows all her rays from Sense. 180

His Father's Acres who enjoys in peace,
Or makes his Neighbours glad, if he increase :
Whose cheerful Tenants bless their yearly toil,
Yet to their Lord owe more than to the soil ;
Whose ample Lawns are not ashamed to feed 185
The milky heifer and deserving steed ;
Whose rising Forests, not for pride or show,
But future Buildings, future Navies, grow :
Let his plantations stretch from down to down,
First shade a Country, and then raise a Town. 190

You too proceed ! make falling Arts your care,
Erect new wonders, and the old repair ;
Jones and Palladio to themselves restore,
And be whate'er Vitruvius was before :
'Til Kings call forth th' Ideas of your mind, 195
(Proud to accomplish what such hands designed,)
Bid Harbours open, public Ways extend,

Yet hence the Poor, etc.—The *Moral* of the whole, where PROVIDENCE
is justified in giving Wealth to those who squander it in this manner.
A bad Taste employs more hands, and diffuses Expense more than a
good one.

Another age, etc.—Had the Poet lived but three Years longer, he had
seen this prophecy fulfilled.

'Til Kings—Bid Harbours open, etc.—The poet after having touched
upon the proper objects of Magnificence and Expense, in the private
works of great men, comes to those great and public works which
become a prince. This Poem was published in the year 1732, when

Bid Temples, worthier of the God, ascend ;
Bid the broad Arch the dang'rous Flood contain,
The Mole projected break the roaring Main ; 200
Back to his bounds their subject Sea command,
And roll obedient Rivers through the Land :
These Honours Peace to happy Britain brings,
These are Imperial Works, and worthy Kings.

EPISTLE V

To Mr. Addison

Occasioned by his Dialogues on Medals

Epistle V.—This was originally written in the year 1715, when Mr.
Addison intended to publish his book of medals ; it was sometime
before he was Secretary of State ; but not published till Mr. Tickell's
Edition of his works ; at which time the verses on Mr. Craggs, which
conclude the poem, were added, viz. in 1720.

See the wild Waste of all-devouring years !
How Rome her own sad Sepulchre appears,
With nodding arches, broken temples spread !
The very Tombs now vanished like their dead !
Imperial wonders raised on Nations spoiled, 5
Where mixed with Slaves the groaning Martyr toiled :

some of the new-built Churches, by the act of Queen Anne, were ready
to fall, being founded on boggy land (which is satirically alluded to in
our author's imitation of Horace, Lib. ii. Sat. 2,—
      Shall half the new-built Churches round thee fall) ;
others were vilely executed, through fraudulent cabals between under-
takers, officers, etc. Dagenham-breach had done very great mischiefs ;
many of the Highways throughout England were hardly passable ; and
most of those which were repaired by Turnpikes were made jobs for
private lucre, and infamously executed, even to the entrances of London
itself : The proposal of building a Bridge at Westminster had been
petitioned against and rejected ; but in two years after the publication
of this poem, an Act for building a Bridge passed through both houses.
After many debates in the committee, the execution was left to the
carpenter above-mentioned, who would have made it a wooden one :
to which our author alludes in these lines,—
      Who builds a Bridge that never drove a pile ?
      Should Ripley venture, all the world would smile.
See the notes on that place.

Huge Theatres, that now unpeopled Woods,
Now drained a distant country of her Floods :
Fanes, which admiring Gods with pride survey,
Statues of Men, scarce less alive than they !   10
Some felt the silent stroke of mould'ring age,
Some hostile fury, some religious rage.
Barbarian blindness, Christian zeal conspire,
And Papal piety, and Gothic fire.
Perhaps, by its own ruins saved from flame,   15
Some buried marble half preserves a name ;
That name the learned with fierce disputes pursue
And give to Titus old Vespasian's due.
  Ambition sighed : She found it vain to trust
The faithless Column and the crumbling Bust :   20
Huge moles, whose shadow stretched from shore to shore,
Their ruins perished, and their place no more !
Convinced, she now contracts her vast design,
And all her triumphs shrink into a Coin.
A narrow orb each crowded conquest keeps ;   25
Beneath her Palm here sad Judæa weeps ;
Now scantier limits the proud Arch confine,
And scarce are seen the prostrate Nile or Rhine :
A small Euphrates through the piece is rolled,
And little Eagles wave their wings in gold.   30
  The Medal, faithful to its charge of fame,
Through climes and ages bears each form and name :
In one short view subjected to our eye
Gods, Emp'rors, Heroes, Sages, Beauties, lie.
With sharpened sight pale Antiquaries pore,   35
Th' inscription value, but the rust adore.
This the blue varnish, that the green endears,
The sacred rust of twice ten hundred years !
To gain Pescennius one employs his schemes,
One grasps a Cecrops in ecstatic dreams.   40

   The proud Arch.—That is, the triumphal Arch, which was generally
an enormous mass of building.
   This the blue varnish, that the green endears.—That is, this a collector
of silver ; that, of brass coins.

Poor Vadius, long with learned spleen devoured,
Can taste no pleasure since his Shield was scoured ;
And Curio, restless by the Fair-one's side,
Sighs for an Otho, and neglects his bride.

Theirs is the Vanity, the Learning thine :　　45
Touched by thy hand, again Rome's glories shine ;
Her Gods, and god-like Heroes rise to view,
And all her faded garlands bloom anew.
Nor blush, these studies thy regard engage ;
These pleased the Fathers of poetic rage ;　　50
The verse and sculpture bore an equal part,
And Art reflected images to Art.

Oh when shall Britain, conscious of her claim,
Stand emulous of Greek and Roman fame ?
In living medals see her wars enrolled,　　55
And vanquished realms supply recording gold ?
Here, rising bold, the Patriot's honest face ;
There Warriors frowning in historic brass ?
Then future ages with delight shall see
How Plato's, Bacon's, Newton's looks agree ;　　60
Or in fair series laurelled Bards be shewn,
A Virgil there, and here an Addison.
Then shall thy CRAGGS (and let me call him mine)
On the cast ore, another Pollio, shine ;
With aspect open, shall erect his head,　　65
And round the orb in lasting notes be read,
" Statesman, yet friend to Truth ! of soul sincere,

Sighs for an Otho.—Charles Patin was banished from the Court
because he sold Louis XIV. an Otho that was not genuine.

Oh when shall Britain, etc.—A compliment to one of Mr. Addison's
papers in the *Spectator* on this subject.

Statesman, yet friend to truth ! etc.—It should be remembered
that this poem was written to be printed before Mr. Addison's
Discourse on Medals, in which there is the following censure of long
legends upon coins : " The first fault I find with a modern legend is
its diffusiveness. You have sometimes the whole side of a medal
over-run with it. One would fancy the Author had a Design of being
Ciceronian—but it is not only the tediousness of these inscriptions
that I find fault with ; supposing them of a moderate length, why
must they be in verse ? We should be surprised to see the title of a
serious book in rhyme."—Dial. iii.

In action faithful, and in honour clear ;
Who broke no promise, served no private end,
Who gained no title, and who lost no friend ;   70
Ennobled by himself, by all approved,
And praised, unenvied, by the Muse he loved."

And praised, unenvied, by the Muse he loved.—Craggs had died the
year before this poem appeared. He is spoken of as *unenvied*, doubtless
because he had died (of small pox) at a moment when he was in disgrace
because of scandals in connection with the South Sea scheme. The
magnificent compliments here paid Craggs are not the only evidences of
Pope's affection for him. Almost twenty years later he paid Pelham
the compliment of likening him to Craggs. See *Epilogue to the Satires*,
Dialogue II., line 70 and note.

EPISTLE TO DR. ARBUTHNOT

ADVERTISEMENT

To the First Publication of this Epistle

THIS paper is a sort of bill of complaint, begun many years since, and drawn up by snatches, as the several occasions offered. I had no thoughts of publishing it, till it pleased some Persons of Rank and Fortune (the Authors of *Verses to the Imitator of Horace*, and of an *Epistle to a Doctor of Divinity from a Nobleman at Hampton Court*) to attack, in a very extraordinary manner, not only my Writings (of which, being public, the Public is judge) but my *Person*, *Morals*, and *Family*, whereof, to those who know me not, a truer information may be requisite. Being divided between the necessity to say something of *myself*, and my own laziness to undertake so awkward a task, I thought it the shortest way to put the last hand to this Epistle. If it have anything pleasing, it will be that by which I am most desirous to please, the *Truth* and the *Sentiment ;* and if anything offensive, it will be only to those I am least sorry to offend, *the vicious* or *the ungenerous*.

Many will know their own pictures in it, there being not a circumstance but what is true ; but I have, for the most part, spared their *Names*, and they may escape being laughed at, if they please.

I would have some of them know, it was owing to the request of the learned and candid Friend to whom it is inscribed, that I make not as free use of theirs as they

Verses to the Imitator of Horace, etc.—Of these squibs the former was said to be a joint production of Lady Mary Wortley Montagu and Lord Hervey ; the latter was written by Hervey alone. **See Carruthers'** *Life of Pope*, ch. VIII.

have done of mine. However, I shall have this advantage, and honour, on my side, that whereas, by their proceeding, any abuse may be directed at any man, no injury can possibly be done by mine, since a nameless character can never be found out, but by its *truth* and *likeness*.

P. SHUT, shut the door, good John! fatigued, I said,
Tie up the knocker, say I'm sick, I'm dead.
The Dog-star rages! nay 'tis past a doubt,
All Bedlam, or Parnassus, is let out:
Fire in each eye, and papers in each hand,   5
They rave, recite, and madden round the land.
    What walls can guard me, or what shades can hide?
They pierce my thickets, through my Grot they glide;
By land, by water, they renew the charge;
They stop the chariot, and they board the barge.   10
No place is sacred, not the Church is free;
Even Sunday shines no Sabbath-day to me;
Then from the Mint walks forth the Man of rhyme,
Happy to catch me just at Dinner-time.
    Is there a Parson, much bemused in beer,   15
A maudlin Poetess, a rhyming Peer,
A Clerk, foredoomed his father's soul to cross,
Who pens a Stanza, when he should *engross?*
Is there, who, locked from ink and paper, scrawls
With desp'rate charcoal round his darkened walls?   20
All fly to TWIT'NAM, and in humble strain
Apply to me, to keep them mad or vain.

Shut, shut the door, good John!—John Searl, his old and faithful servant: whom he has remembered, under that character, in his Will.
    Mint.—A place to which insolvent debtors retired to enjoy an illegal protection, which they were there suffered to afford one another from the persecution of their creditors.
    Much bemused in beer.—Some lines in this Epistle had been used in a letter to Thomson [the author of the *Seasons*] when he was in Italy, and transferred from him to Arbuthnot, which naturally displeased the former, though they lived always on terms of civility and friendship: and Pope earnestly exerted himself, and used all his interest to promote the success of Thomson's *Agamemnon*.

Arthur, whose giddy son neglects the Laws,
Imputes to me and my damned works the cause:
Poor Cornus sees his frantic wife elope,   25
And curses Wit, and Poetry, and Pope.

Friend to my Life ! (which did not you prolong,
The world had wanted many an idle song)
What *Drop* or *Nostrum* can this plague remove ?
Or which must end me, a Fool's wrath or love ?   30
A dire dilemma ! either way I'm sped,
If foes, they write, if friends, they read me dead.
Seized and tied down to judge, how wretched I !
Who can't be silent, and who will not lie.
To laugh, were want of goodness and of grace,   35
And to be grave, exceeds all Power of face.
I sit with sad civility, I read
With honest anguish, and an aching head ;
And drop at last, but in unwilling ears,   39
This saving counsel, " Keep your piece nine years."

" Nine years ! " cries he, who high in Drury-lane,
Lulled by soft Zephyrs through the broken pane,
Rhymes ere he wakes, and prints before *Term* ends,
Obliged by hunger, and request of friends :
" The piece, you think, is incorrect ? why, take it, 45
I'm all submission, what you'd have it, make it."

Three things another's modest wishes bound,
My Friendship, and a Prologue, and ten pound.

Pitholeon sends to me : " You know his Grace,
I want a Patron ; ask him for a Place."   50
' Pitholeon libelled me,'—" but here's a letter

Arthur.—Arthur Moore, a leading politician of Queen Anne's time, who had raised himself by ability and unscrupulousness to place and power. His son James Moore (afterwards James Moore-Smythe), a small placeman and poetaster, and an acquaintance of the Blount family, became a noted object of Pope's scorn.

Seized and tied down to judge.—Alluding to the scene in [Wycherley's] *Plain-Dealer*, where *Oldfox* gags, and ties down the Widow to hear his *well-penned stanzas.*

Pitholeon.—The name taken from a foolish Poet of Rhodes, who pretended much to *Greek.* Schol. in Horat. l. i. Dr. Bentley pretends that this Pitholeon libelled Cæsar also.

Informs you, Sir, 'twas when he knew no better.
Dare you refuse him ?   Curll invites to dine,
He'll write a *Journal*, or he'll turn Divine."
  Bless me ! a packet.—" 'Tis a stranger sues,   55
A Virgin Tragedy, an Orphan Muse."
If I dislike it, " Furies, death and rage ! "
If I approve, " Commend it to the Stage."
There (thank my stars) my whole Commission ends,
The Players and I are, luckily, no friends.   60
Fired that the house reject him, " 'Sdeath I'll print it,
And shame the fools——Your Int'rest, Sir, with Lintot ! "
' Lintot, dull rogue ! will think your price too much : '
" Not, Sir, if you revise it, and retouch."
All my demurs but double his Attacks ;   65
At last he whispers, " Do ; and we go snacks."
Glad of a quarrel, straight I clap the door,
" Sir, let me see your works and you no more."
  'Tis sung, when Midas' Ears began to spring,
(Midas, a sacred person and a king)   70
His very Minister who spied them first,
(Some say his Queen) was forced to speak, or burst.
And is not mine, my friend, a sorer case,
When every coxcomb perks them in my face ?
A.   Good friend, forbear ! you deal in dang'rous things.
I'd never name Queens, Ministers, or Kings ;   76
Keep close to Ears, and those let asses prick ;
'Tis nothing— P.   Nothing ? if they bite and kick ?
Out with it, DUNCIAD ! let the secret pass,
That secret to each fool, that he's an Ass :   80
The truth once told (and wherefore should we lie ?)
The Queen of Midas slept, and so may I.

  Journal.—Meaning the *London Journal ;* a paper in favour of Sir
R. Walpole's ministry.
  A Virgin Tragedy.—Alludes to a tragedy called the *Virgin Queen*,
by Mr. R. Barford, published 1729, who displeased Pope by daring to
adopt the fine machinery of his Sylphs in an heroi-comical poem called
The Assembly.
  Queen.—The story is told, by some, of his Barber, but by *Chaucer*
of his Queen. See Wife of Bath's Tale in Dryden's *Fables.*

You think this cruel ? take it for a rule,
No creature smarts so little as a fool.
Let peals of laughter, Codrus ! round thee break,　　85
Thou unconcerned canst hear the mighty crack :
Pit, Box, and gall'ry in convulsions hurled,
Thou stand'st unshook amidst a bursting world.
Who shames a Scribbler ? break one cobweb through,
He spins the slight, self-pleasing thread anew :　　90
Destroy his fib or sophistry, in vain,
The creature's at his dirty work again,
Throned in the centre of his thin designs,
Proud of a vast extent of flimsy lines !
Whom have I hurt ? has Poet yet, or Peer,　　95
Lost the arched eye-brow, or Parnassian sneer ?
And has not Colley still his Lord, and whore ?
His Butchers Henley, his free-masons Moore ?
Does not one table Bavius still admit ?
Still to one Bishop Philips seem a wit ?　　100
Still Sappho— A. Hold ! for God's sake—you'll offend,
No Names !—be calm !—learn prudence of a friend !
I too could write, and I am twice as tall ;
But foes like these— P. One Flatt'rer 's worse than all.
Of all mad creatures, if the learned are right,　　105
It is the slaver kills, and not the bite.
A fool quite angry is quite innocent :
Alas ! 'tis ten times worse when they *repent*.
　　One dedicates in high heroic prose,
And ridicules beyond a hundred foes :　　110
One from all Grubstreet will my fame defend,
And, more abusive, calls himself my friend.
This prints my *Letters*, that expects a bribe,
And others roar aloud, " Subscribe, subscribe."
　　There are, who to my person pay their court :　　115
I cough like *Horace*, and, though lean, am short,

Free-masons Moore.—He was of this society, and frequently headed
their processions.
　Bishop Philips.—Boulter, afterwards Primate of all Ireland, was
Ambrose Philips' great friend and patron.

Ammon's great son one shoulder had too high,
Such *Ovid's* nose, and " Sir ! you have an Eye "—
Go on, obliging creatures, make me see
All that disgraced my Betters, met in me.   120
Say for my comfort, languishing in bed,
" Just so immortal *Maro* held his head : "
And when I die, be sure you let me know
Great *Homer* died three thousand years ago.
   Why did I write ? what sin to me unknown   125
Dipt me in ink, my parents', or my own ?
As yet a child, nor yet a fool to fame,
I lisped in numbers, for the numbers came.
I left no calling for this idle trade,
No duty broke, no father disobeyed.   130
The Muse but served to ease some friend, not Wife,
To help me through this long disease, my Life,
To second, ARBUTHNOT ! thy Art and Care,
And teach the Being you preserved, to bear.
   But why then publish ? *Granville* the polite,   135
And knowing *Walsh,* would tell me I could write ;
Well-natured *Garth* inflamed with early praise ;
And *Congreve* loved, and *Swift* endured my lays ;
The courtly *Talbot, Somers, Sheffield* read ;

Sir ! you have an Eye.—It is remarkable that amongst these compliments on his infirmities and deformities, he mentions his *eye*, which
was fine, sharp, and piercing.
No father disobeyed.—When Mr. Pope was yet a Child, his Father,
though no Poet, would set him to make English verses. He was
pretty difficult to please, and would often send the boy back to new
turn them. When they were to his mind, he took great pleasure in
them, and would say, *These are good rhymes.*
Talbot, etc.—All these were Patrons or Admirers of Mr. *Dryden ;*
though a scandalous libel against him entitled, *Dryden's Satyr to his
Muse,* has been printed in the name of the Lord *Somers,* of which
he was wholly ignorant.
   These are the persons to whose account the author charges the
publication of his first pieces : persons with whom he was conversant
(and he adds beloved) at 16 or 17 years of age ; an early period for
such acquaintance. The catalogue might be made yet more illustrious,
had he not confined it to that time when he writ the *Pastorals* and
Windsor Forest, on which he passes a sort of censure in the lines following,—
      While pure description held the place of Sense, etc.

Even mitred *Rochester* would nod the head,   140
And *St. John's* self (great *Dryden's* friends before)
With open arms received one Poet more.
Happy my studies, when by these approved !
Happier their author, when by these beloved !
From these the world will judge of men and books,
Not from the *Burnets*, *Oldmixons*, and *Cookes*.   146
 Soft were my numbers ; who could take offence,
While pure Description held the place of Sense ?
Like gentle *Fanny's* was my flowery theme,
A painted mistress, or a purling stream.   150
Yet then did *Gildon* draw his venal quill ;—
I wished the man a dinner, and sat still.
Yet then did *Dennis* rave in furious fret ;
I never answered,—I was not in debt.
If want provoked, or madness made them print,   155
I waged no war with *Bedlam* or the *Mint*.
 Did some more sober Critic come abroad ;
If wrong, I smiled ; if right, I kissed the rod.
Pains, reading, study, are their just pretence,
And all they want is spirit, taste, and sense.   160
Commas and points they set exactly right,
And 'twere a sin to rob them of their mite.
Yet ne'er one sprig of laurel graced these ribalds,
From slashing *Bentley* down to pidling *Tibalds :*
Each wight, who reads not, and but scans and spells,
Each Word-catcher, that lives on syllables,   166
Even such small Critics some regard may claim,
Preserved in *Milton's* or in *Shakespeare's* name.
Pretty ! in amber to observe the forms
Of hairs, or straws, or dirt, or grubs, or worms !   170

Burnets, etc.—Authors of secret and scandalous History.
 Burnets, Oldmixons, and Cookes.—By no means Authors of the same class, though the violence of party might hurry them into the same mistakes. But if the first offended this way, it was only through an honest warmth of temper, that allowed too little to an excellent understanding. The other two, with very bad heads, had hearts still worse.
 A painted mistress, etc.—Meaning the *Rape of the Lock* and *Windsor Forest*.

The things, we know, are neither rich nor rare,
But wonder how the devil they got there.
  Were others angry : I excused them too ;
Well might they rage, I gave them but their due.
A man's true merit 'tis not hard to find ;   175
But each man's secret standard in his mind,
That Casting-weight pride adds to emptiness,
This, who can gratify ? for who can *guess ?*
The Bard whom pilfered Pastorals renown,
Who turns a Persian tale for half a Crown,   180
Just writes to make his barrenness appear,
And strains, from hard-bound brains, eight lines a
    year ;
He, who still wanting, though he lives on theft,
Steals much, spends little, yet has nothing left :
And He, who now to sense, now nonsense leaning, 185
Means not, but blunders round about a meaning :
And He, whose fustian 's so sublimely bad,
It is not Poetry, but prose run mad :
All these, my modest Satire bade *translate,*
And owned that nine such Poets made a *Tate.*   190
How did they fume, and stamp, and roar, and chafe !
And swear, not ADDISON himself was safe.
  Peace to all such ! but were there One whose fires
True Genius kindles, and fair Fame inspires ;
Blest with each talent and each art to please,   195
And born to write, converse, and live with ease :
Should such a man, too fond to rule alone,
Bear, like the Turk, no brother near the throne.
View him with scornful, yet with jealous eyes,
And hate for arts that caused himself to rise ;   200
Damn with faint praise, assent with civil leer,
And without sneeiing, teach the rest to sneer ;

    Means not, but blunders round about a meaning.—A case common
both to *Poets* and *Critics* of a certain order ; only with this difference,
that the *Poet* writes himself out of his *own meaning ;* and the *Critic*
never gets into *another man's.* Yet both keep going on, and *blundering
round about* their subject, as benighted people are wont to do, who
seek for an entrance which they cannot find.

Willing to wound, and yet afraid to strike,
Just hint a fault, and hesitate dislike ;
Alike reserved to blame, or to commend,   205
A tim'rous foe, and a suspicious friend ;
Dreading even fools, by Flatt'rers besieged,
And so obliging, that he ne'er obliged ;
Like *Cato*, give his little Senate laws,
And sit attentive to his own applause ;   210
While Wits and Templars every sentence raise,
And wonder with a foolish face of praise :—
Who but must laugh, if such a man there be ?
Who would not weep, if ATTICUS were he ?
   What though my Name stood rubric on the walls, 215
Or plaistered posts, with claps, in capitals ?
Or smoking forth, a hundred hawkers' load,
On wings of winds came flying all abroad ?
I sought no homage from the Race that write ;
I kept, like *Asian* Monarchs, from their sight :   220
Poems I heeded (now be-rhymed so long)
No more than thou, great GEORGE ! a birth-day song.
I ne'er with wits or witlings passed my days,
To spread about the itch of verse and praise ;
Nor like a puppy, daggled through the town,   225
To fetch and carry sing-song up and down ;
Nor at Rehearsals sweat, and mouthed, and cried,
With handkerchief and orange at my side ·
But sick of fops, and poetry, and prate,
To *Bufo* left the whole *Castalian* state.   230
   Proud as *Apollo* on his forkèd hill,
Sat full-blown *Bufo*, puffed by every quill ;
Fed with soft Dedication all day long,
Horace and he went hand in hand in song.
His Library (where busts of Poets dead   235
And a true *Pindar* stood without a head,)
Received of wits an undistinguished race,

   A true Pindar stood without a head.—Ridicules the affectation of
Antiquaries, who frequently exhibit the headless *Trunks* and *Torsos*
of Statues, for Plato, Homer, Pindar, etc.

Who first his judgment asked, and then a place :
Much they extolled his pictures, much his seat,
And flattered every day, and some days eat : 240
Till grown more frugal in his riper days,
He paid some bards with port, and some with praise ;
To some a dry rehearsal was assigned,
And others (harder still) he paid in kind.
Dryden alone (what wonder ?) came not nigh, 245
Dryden alone escaped this judging eye :
But still the *Great* have kindness in reserve,
He helped to bury whom he helped to starve.
    May some choice patron bless each grey goose quill !
May every *Bavius* have his *Bufo* still ! 250
So, when a Statesman wants a day's defence,
Or Envy holds a whole week's war with Sense,
Or simple pride for flatt'ry makes demands,
May dunce by dunce be whistled off my hands !
Blest be the *Great !* for those they take away, 255
And those they left me ; for they left me GAY ;
Left me to see neglected Genius bloom,
Neglected die, and tell it on his tomb :
Of all thy blameless life the sole return
My Verse, and QUEENSB'RY weeping o'er thy urn ! 260
    Oh let me live my own, and die so too !
(To live and die is all I have to do :)
Maintain a Poet's dignity and ease,
And see what friends, and read what books I please ;
Above a Patron, though I condescend 265
Sometimes to call a minister my friend.
I was not born for Courts or great affairs ;
I pay my debts, believe, and say my prayers ;
Can sleep without a Poem in my head ;
Nor know, if *Dennis* be alive or dead. 270
    Why am I asked what next shall see the light ?
Heavens ! was I born for nothing but to write ?

Helped to bury.—Mr. *Dryden*, after having lived in exigencies,
had a magnificent Funeral bestowed upon him by the contribution
of several persons of quality.

Has Life no joys for me ? or, (to be grave)
Have I no friend to serve, no soul to save ?
" I found him close with *Swift* "—' Indeed ? no doubt,'
(Cries prating *Balbus*) ' something will come out.'   276
'Tis all in vain, deny it as I will.
' No, such a Genius never can lie still ; '
And then for mine obligingly mistakes
The first Lampoon Sir *Will.* or *Bubo* makes.   280
Poor guiltless I ! and can I choose but smile,
When every Coxcomb knows me by my *Style ?*
　　Curst be the verse, how well soe'er it flow,
That tends to make one worthy man my foe,
Give Virtue scandal, Innocence a fear,   285
Or from the soft-eyed Virgin steal a tear !
But he who hurts a harmless neighbour's peace,
Insults fallen worth, or Beauty in distress,
Who loves a Lie, lame slander helps about,
Who writes a Libel, or who copies out :   290
That Fop, whose pride affects a patron's name,
Yet absent, wounds an author's honest fame :
Who can *your* merit *selfishly* approve
And show the *sense* of it without the *love ;*
Who has the vanity to call you friend,   295
Yet wants the honour, injured, to defend ;
Who tells whate'er you think, whate'er you say,
And, if he lie not, must at least betray :
Who to the *Dean,* and *silver bell* can swear,
And sees at *Canons* what was never there ;   300
Who reads, but with a lust to misapply,
Make Satire a Lampoon, and Fiction, Lie.
A lash like mine no honest man shall dread,
But all such babbling blockheads in his stead.
　　Let *Sporus* tremble— A. What ? that thing of
　　silk,   305

Who to the Dean, and silver bell, etc.—Meaning the man who would
have persuaded the Duke of Chandos that Mr. P. meant him in those
circumstances ridiculed in the Epistle on *Taste.* See Mr. Pope's Letter
to the Earl of Burlington concerning this matter.

Sporus, that mere white curd of Ass's milk ?
Satire or sense, alas ! can *Sporus* feel ?
Who breaks a butterfly upon a wheel ?
P.   Yet let me flap this bug with gilded wings,
This painted child of dirt, that stinks and stings ; 310
Whose buzz the witty and the fair annoys,
Yet wit ne'er tastes, and beauty ne'er enjoys :
So well-bred spaniels civilly delight
In mumbling of the game they dare not bite.
Eternal smiles his emptiness betray,   315
As shallow streams run dimpling all the way.
Whether in florid impotence he speaks,
And, as the prompter breathes, the puppet squeaks ;
Or at the ear of *Eve,* familiar Toad,
Half froth, half venom, spits himself abroad,   320
In puns, or politics, or tales, or lies,
Or spite, or smut, or rhymes, or blasphemies.
His wit all see-saw, between *that* and *this,*
Now high, now low, now master up, now miss,
And he himself one vile Antithesis.   325
Amphibious thing ! that acting either part,
The trifling head or the corrupted heart,
Fop at the toilet, flatt'rer at the board,
Now trips a Lady, and now struts a Lord.
Eve's tempter thus the Rabbins have exprest,   330
A Cherub's face, a reptile all the rest ;
Beauty that shocks you, parts that none will trust ;
Wit that can creep, and pride that licks the dust.
    Not Fortune's worshipper, nor fashion's fool,
Not Lucre's madman, nor Ambition's tool,   335
Not proud, nor servile ;—be one Poet's praise,
That, if he pleased, he pleased by manly ways :
That Flatt'ry, even to Kings, he held a shame,
And thought a Lie in verse or prose the same.

Half froth.—Alluding to those *frothy* excretions, called by the people
Toad-spits, seen in summer-time hanging upon plants, and emitted by
young insects which lie hid in the midst of them, for their preservation, while in their helpless state.

That not in Fancy's maze he wandered long,　340
But stooped to Truth, and moralized his song :
That not for Fame, but Virtue's better end,
He stood the furious foe, the timid friend,
The damning critic, half approving wit,
The coxcomb hit, or fearing to be hit ;　345
Laughed at the loss of friends he never had,
The dull, the proud, the wicked, and the mad ;
The distant threats of vengeance on his head
The blow unfelt, the tear he never shed ;
The tale revived, the lie so oft o'erthrown,　350
Th' imputed trash, and dulness not his own ;
The morals blackened when the writings scape,
The libelled person, and the pictured shape ;
Abuse, on all he loved, or loved him, spread,
A friend in exile, or a father, dead ;　355
The whisper, that to greatness still too near,
Perhaps, yet vibrates on his Sov'reign's ear :—
Welcome for thee, fair *Virtue !* all the past ;
For thee, fair Virtue ! welcome even the *last !*
　　A.　But why insult the poor, affront the great ?
　　P.　A knave 's a knave, to me, in every state :　361
Alike my scorn, if he succeed or fail,
Sporus at court, or *Japhet* in a jail,
A hireling scribbler, or a hireling peer,
Knight of the post corrupt, or of the shire ;　365

But stooped to Truth.—The term is from falconry ; and the allusion to one of those untamed birds of spirit, which sometimes wantons at large in airy circles before it regards, or *stoops to*, its prey.

The lie so oft o'erthrown.—As, that he received subscriptions for Shakespeare, that he set his name to Mr. Broome's verses, etc., which, though publicly disproved, were nevertheless shamelessly repeated in the Libels, and even in that called *the Nobleman's Epistle.*

Th' imputed trash.—Such as profane *Psalms*, *Court-Poems*, and other scandalous things, printed in his Name by Curll and others.

Abuse, on all he loved, or loved him, spread.—Namely on the Duke of Buckingham, the Earl of Burlington, Lord Bathurst, Lord Bolingbroke, Bishop Atterbury, Dr. Swift, Dr. Arbuthnot, Mr. Gay, his Friends, his Parents, and his very Nurse, aspersed in printed papers, by James Moore, G. Ducket, L. Welsted, Tho. Bentley, and other obscure persons.

If on a Pillory, or near a Throne,
He gain his Prince's ear, or lose his own.

   Yet soft by nature, more a dupe than wit,
Sappho can tell you how this man was bit ;
This dreaded Sat'rist *Dennis* will confess   370
Foe to his pride, but friend to his distress :
So humble, he has knocked at *Tibbald's* door,
Has drunk with *Cibber,* nay, has rhymed for *Moore.*
Full ten years slandered, did he once reply ?
Three thousand suns went down on *Welsted's* lie. 375
To please a Mistress one aspersed his life ;
He lashed him not, but let her be his wife.
Let *Budgel* **charge** low *Grubstreet* on his quill,
And write whate'er he pleased, except his Will ;
Let the two *Curlls* of Town and Court, abuse   380
His father, mother, body, soul, and muse.

Ten years.—It was so long after many libels before the Author of the *Dunciad* published that poem, till when, he never writ a word in answer to the many scurrilities and falsehoods concerning him.

Welsted's lie.—This man had the impudence to tell in print that Mr. P. had occasioned a *Lady's death,* and to name a person he never heard of. He also published that he libelled the Duke of Chandos ; with whom (it was added) that he had lived in familiarity, and received from him a present of *five hundred pounds :* the falsehood of both which is known to his Grace. Mr. P. never received any present, farther than the subscription for Homer, from him, or from *Any great Man* whatsoever.

Let Budgel.—*Budgel,* in a weekly pamphlet called the *Bee,* bestowed much abuse on him, in the imagination that he writ some things about the *Last Will* of Dr. *Tindal,* in the *Grub-street Journal ;* a Paper wherein he never had the least hand, direction, or supervisal, nor the least knowledge of its Author.

Except his Will.—Alluding to Tindal's Will : by which, and other indirect practices, Budgel, to the exclusion of the next heir, a nephew, got to himself almost the whole fortune of a man entirely unrelated to him.

His father, mother, etc.—In some of Curll's and other pamphlets, Mr. Pope's father was said to be a Mechanic, a Hatter, a Farmer, nay a Bankrupt. But, what is stranger, a *Nobleman* (if such a Reflection could be thought to come from a Nobleman) had dropped an allusion to that pitiful untruth, in a paper called an *Epistle to a Doctor of Divinity :* and the following line,—

      Hard as thy Heart, and as thy Birth obscure,
had fallen from a like *Courtly* pen, in certain *Verses to the Imitator of Horace.* Mr. Pope's Father was of a Gentleman's Family in Oxford-

Yet why? that Father held it for a rule,
It was a sin to call our neighbour fool :
That harmless Mother thought no wife a whore :
Hear this, and spare his family, *James Moore !*   385
Unspotted names, and memorable long !
If there be force in Virtue, or in Song.

Of gentle blood (part shed in Honour's cause,
While yet in *Britain* Honour had applause)
Each parent sprung— A. What fortune, pray?—   P.
    Their own,   390
And better got, than *Bestia's* from the throne.
Born to no Pride, inheriting no Strife,
Nor marrying Discord in a noble wife,
Stranger to civil and religious rage,
The good man walked innoxious through his age.   395
Nor Courts he saw, no suits would ever try,
Nor dared an Oath, nor hazarded a Lie.
Un-learned, he knew no schoolman's subtle art,
No language, but the language of the heart.
By Nature honest, by Experience wise,   400
Healthy by temp'rance, and by exercise ;

shire, the head of which was the Earl of Downe, whose sole Heiress
married the Earl of Lindsey.   His mother was the daughter of William
Turnor, Esq. of York : she had three brothers, one of whom was
killed, another died in the service of King Charles ; the eldest following
his fortunes, and becoming a general officer in Spain, left her what
estate remained after the sequestrations and forfeitures of her family—
Mr. Pope died in 1717, aged 75 ; she in 1733, aged 93, a very few
weeks after this poem was finished.   The following inscription was
placed by their son on their Monument in the parish of Twickenham,
in Middlesex :—

D. O. M.

ALEXANDRO . POPE . VIRO . INNOCVO . PROBO . PIO .
QVI . VIXIT . ANNOS . LXXV . OB . MDCCXVII .
ET . EDITHAE . CONIVGI . INCVLPABILI .
PIENTISSIMAE . QVAE . VIXIT . ANNOS .
XCIII . OB . MDCCXXXIII .
PARENTIBVS . BENEMERENTIBVS . FILIVS . FECIT .
ET . SIBI .

A noble wife.—Alluding to Addison's marriage with the Countess of
Warwick, and Dryden's with Lady Elizabeth Howard.
    Hazarded a Lie.—He was a nonjuror, and would not take the oath
of allegiance or supremacy, or the oath against the Pope.

His life, though long, to sickness past unknown,
His death was instant, and without a groan.
O grant me, thus to live, and thus to die!
Who sprung from Kings shall know less joy than I.   405
  O Friend! may each domestic bliss be thine!
Be no unpleasing Melancholy mine:
Me, let the tender office long engage,
To rock the cradle of reposing Age,
With lenient arts extend a Mother's breath,   410
Make Languor smile, and smooth the bed of Death,
Explore the thought, explain the asking eye,
And keep a while one parent from the sky!
On cares like these if length of days attend,
May Heaven, to bless those days, preserve my friend
Preserve him social, cheerful, and serene,   416
And just as rich as when he served a QUEEN.
A.   Whether that blessing be denied or given,
Thus far was right, the rest belongs to Heaven.

   And just as rich as when he served a Queen.—An honest compliment
to his Friend's real and unaffected disinterestedness, when he was the
favourite Physician of Queen Anne.

SATIRES AND EPISTLES OF HORACE IMITATED

ADVERTISEMENT

THE occasion of publishing these imitations was the clamour rais'd on some of my Epistles. An answer from Horace was both more full, and of more Dignity than any I could have made in my own person ; and the example of much greater Freedom in so eminent a Divine as Dr. Donne, seem'd a proof with what indignation and contempt a Christian may treat vice or folly in ever so low, or ever so high, a station. Both these Authors were acceptable to the Princes and Ministers under whom they lived. The Satires of Dr. Donne I versified at the desire of the Earl of Oxford while he was Lord Treasurer, and of the Duke of Shrewsbury, who had been Secretary of State ; neither of whom look'd upon a satire on vicious courts as any reflection on those they serv'd in. And indeed there is not in the world a greater error than that which fools are so apt to fall into, and knaves with good reason to encourage— the mistaking a Satirist for a Libeller ; whereas to a *true Satirist* nothing is so odious as a *Libeller*, for the same reason as to a man *truly virtuous* nothing is so hateful as a hypocrite.

Uni æquus virtuti atque eius amicis.—POPE.

The clamour rais'd on some of my Epistles.—Notably (and possibly solely) on the one addressed to the Earl of Burlington.

At the desire of the Earl of Oxford.—This, in spite of the doubts of some of Pope's unfriendly editors, is shown to be the case by a letter from the son of the earl to Pope, March 11, 1726. These reworkings of Donne (not included in this volume) were revised before their publication in the thirties. Pope's mention of Oxford, as well as other details of this Advertisement, shows that the recurrent political animus in the Imitations of Horace is quite conscious.

THE FIRST SATIRE OF THE SECOND
BOOK OF HORACE

To Mr. Fortescue

P. THERE are (I scarce can think it, but am told),
There are, to whom my Satire seems too bold :
Scarce to wise Peter complaisant enough,
And something said of Chartres much too rough.
The lines are weak, another's pleas'd to say,   5
Lord Fanny spins a thousand such a day.
Tim'rous by nature, of the rich in awe,
I come to Council learned in the Law :
You'll give me, like a friend, both sage and free,

Mr. Fortescue.—William Fortescue (1687–1749), an eminent barrister,
later judge and Master of the Rolls, was the firm friend of Pope and of
Gay for many years.

Wise Peter and *Chartres.*—These men had been mentioned in the
third *Moral Epistle* (see pages 175 and 181).

Lord Fanny.—The name was promptly taken as referring to Lord
Hervey, who since 1728 had been embroiled with Pope. This line (or
other grievances) led Hervey to print in August 1733 *An Epistle to a
Doctor of Divinity*, which attacked Pope, who rejoined in his *Letter to a
Noble Lord* (November 1733). Here (quoting Satire x. of Horace's
Book I.) Pope writes : " *Fanny* (my Lord) is the plain English of
Fannius, a real person, who was a foolish critic, and an enemy of
Horace, perhaps a noble one. . . . This Fannius was, it seems, ex-
tremely fond of both his *poetry* and his *person*. . . . He was moreover
of a delicate or effeminate complexion, and constant at the assemblies
and operas of those days, where he took it into his head to slander poor
Horace . . . till it provoked him at last just to name him, give him a
lash, and send him whimpering to the ladies." On Hervey see also the
character of Sporus in the *Epistle to Dr. Arbuthnot* (pages 212–213).

219

Advice ; and (as you use) without a fee.   10
   F.   I'd write no more.
   P.   Not write ? but then I think,
And for my soul I cannot sleep a wink.
I nod in company, I wake at night,
Fools rush into my head, and so I write.
   F.   You could not do a worse thing for your life.   15
Why, if the nights seem tedious, take a wife :
Or rather truly, if your point be rest,
Lettuce and cowslip wine ; *probatum est.*
But talk with Celsus, Celsus will advise
Hartshorn, or something that shall close your eyes.   20
Or if you needs must write, write Cæsar's praise,
You'll gain at least a *Knighthood*, or the *Bays.*
   P.   What ? like Sir Richard, rumbling, rough, and
       fierce,
With ARMS, and GEORGE, and BRUNSWICK crowd the
       verse,
Rend with tremendous sound your ears asunder,   25
With Gun, Drum, Trumpet, Blunderbuss, and Thunder ?
Or nobly wild, with Budgell's fire and force,
Paint angels trembling round his falling horse ?
   F.   Then all your Muse's softer art display,
Let CAROLINA smooth the tuneful lay,   30
Lull with AMELIA's liquid name the Nine,
And sweetly flow thro' all the Royal Line.
   P.   Alas ! few verses touch their nicer ear ;
They scarce can bear their *Laureate* twice a year ;
And justly Cæsar scorns the poet's lays :   35
It is to *history* he trusts for praise.
   F.   Better be Cibber, I'll maintain it still,

   Sir Richard.—Blackmore appears also in the braying contest in the
second book of the *Dunciad.*
   Paint angels.—The angels are Pope's heightening of a moderately
absurd passage on the battle of Oudenarde in Budgell's poem *On His
Majesty's Late Journey to Cambridge and Newmarket.*
   Their Laureate twice a year.—Cibber, who had " the Bays " (the
laureateship) after 1730, wrote bad but official odes for New Year's
and for the Royal Birthdays, which were generally subjects of banter.

Than ridicule all taste, blaspheme quadrille,
Abuse the City's best good men in metre,
And laugh at Peers that put their trust in Peter. 40
Ev'n those you touch not, hate you.
    P.   What should ail them ?
F.   A hundred smart in Timon and in Balaam :
The fewer still you name, you wound the more ;
Bond is but one, but Harpax is a score.
    P.   Each mortal has his pleasure : none deny 45
Scarsdale his bottle, Darty his Ham-pye ;
Ridotta sips and dances, till she see
The doubling lustres dance as fast as she ;
F—— loves the Senate, Hockley-hole his brother,
Like in all else, as one egg to another. 50
I love to pour out all my self, as plain
As downright Shippen, or as old Montaigne :
In them, as certain to be lov'd as seen,
The Soul stood forth, nor kept a thought within ;
In me what spots (for spots I have) appear, 55
Will prove at least the medium must be clear.
In this impartial glass, my Muse intends
Fair to expose myself, my foes, my friends ;
Publish the present age ; but where my text
Is vice too high, reserve it for the next : 60
My foes shall wish my life a longer date,
And ev'ry friend the less lament my fate.
My head and heart thus flowing thro' my quill,
Verse-man or prose-man, term me which you will,
Papist or Protestant, or both between, 65
Like good Erasmus in an honest mean,
In moderation placing all my glory,
While Tories call me Whig, and Whigs a Tory.
    Satire's my weapon, but I'm too discreet
To run a muck, and tilt at all I meet ; 70

    Timon, Balaam, Bond.—See *Moral Essays,* iii., lines 91, 100, 342 ;
and iv., line 99.
    Hockley-hole.—Now Ray Street. In Pope's day it was famous for
its bear-baitings and prize-fights.

I only wear it in a land of Hectors,
Thieves, supercargoes, sharpers, and directors.
Save but our *army* ! and let Jove incrust
Swords, pikes, and guns, with everlasting rust !
Peace is my dear delight—not FLEURY'S more :   75
But touch me, and no minister so sore.
Whoe'er offends, at some unlucky time
Slides into verse, and hitches in a rhyme,
Sacred to ridicule his whole life long,
And the sad burthen of some merry song.   80

    Slander or poison dread from Delia's rage,
Hard words or hanging, if your judge be Page.
From furious Sappho scarce a milder fate,
P—x'd by her love, or libell'd by her hate.
Its proper power to hurt, each creature feels ;   85
Bulls aim their horns, and asses lift their heels ;
'Tis a bear's talent not to kick, but hug ;
And no man wonders he's not stung by Pug.
So drink with Walters, or with Chartres eat,
They'll never poison you, they'll only cheat.   90

    Then, learned sir ! (to cut the matter short)
Whate'er my fate, or well or ill at Court,
Whether old age, with faint but cheerful ray,
Attends to gild the ev'ning of my day,

Fleury.—Premier of France at the time.
Whoe'er offends.—Pope's apparent vindictiveness is borrowed from
Boileau :

    Et malheur a tout nom qui propre à la censure,
    Peut entrer dans un vers sans rompre la mesure.

Page.—Sir Francis Page had presided at the trial of Pope's (and
Johnson's) friend Savage for murder in 1728. Fielding also satirizes
Page in *Tom Jones* (Book VIII., chap. ii.).
Furious Sappho.—This was applied to Lady Mary Wortley Montagu.
She protested to Pope's friend, Lord Peterborough, who conveyed
Pope's galling reply in a letter : " He [Pope] said to me, what I had
taken the liberty to say to you, that he wondered how the town would
apply these lines to any but some noted common woman ; that he
would be yet more surprised if you should take them to yourself."
The grounds of the bitter enmity between Pope and Lady Mary (which
in 1727 or 1728 broke their former close intimacy, and which caused
several covert mentions of the lady in Pope's lines) have never been
determined.

Or death's black wing already be display'd, 95
To wrap me in the universal shade ;
Whether the darken'd room to muse invite,
Or whiten'd wall provoke the skew'r to write :
In durance, exile, Bedlam, or the Mint,
Like Lee or Budgell, I will rhyme and print. 100
    F.   Alas, young man ! your days can ne'er be long,
In flower of age you perish for a song !
Plums and directors, Shylock and his wife,
Will club their testers, now, to take your life ! 104
    P.   What ? arm'd for virtue when I point the pen,
Brand the bold front of shameless guilty men ;
Dash the proud gamester in his gilded car ;
Bare the mean heart that lurks beneath a *Star* ;
Can there be wanting, to defend her cause,
Lights of the Church, or guardians of the laws ? 110
Could pension'd Boileau lash in honest strain
Flatt'rers and bigots ev'n in Louis' reign ?
Could laureate Dryden pimp and fry'r engage,
Yet neither Charles nor James be in a rage ?
And I not strip the gilding off a knave, 115
Unplac'd, unpension'd, no man's heir, or slave ?
I will, or perish in the gen'rous cause :
Hear this, and tremble ! you who 'scape the laws.
Yes, while I live, no rich or noble knave
Shall walk the world, in credit, to his grave. 120
To virtue only and her friends a friend,
The world beside may murmur, or commend.
Know, all the distant din that world can keep,
Rolls o'er my grotto, and but soothes my sleep.
There, my retreat the best companions grace, 125

   Like Lee or Budgell.—Both were insane ; Lee was for a time in Bedlam (Bethlehem Hospital), and Budgell was " in durance " in Fleet prison.
   To Virtue only.—Pope's " device " as satirist. The original in Horace is : *Uni æquus virtuti atque ejus amicis.*
   My grotto.—This was a decorated passageway under the King's Road to Hampton Court. Its practical utility was to give Pope easy access to his gardens.

Chiefs out of war, and statesmen out of place.
There St. John mingles with my friendly bowl
The feast of reason and the flow of soul :
And He, whose lightning pierc'd th' Iberian lines,
Now forms my quincunx, and now ranks my vines,   130
Or tames the genius of the stubborn plain,
Almost as quickly as he conquer'd Spain.
   Envy must own, I live among the great,
No pimp of pleasure, and no spy of state.
With eyes that pry not, tongue that ne'er repeats,   135
Fond to spread friendships, but to cover heats ;
To help who want, to forward who excel ;
This, all who know me, know ; who love me, tell ;
And who unknown defame me, let them be
Scribblers or peers, alike are mob to me.   140
This is my plea, on this I rest my cause—
What saith my council, learned in the laws ?
   F. Your plea is good ; but still I say, beware !
Laws are explain'd by men—so have a care.
It stands on record, that in Richard's times   145
A man was hang'd for very honest rhymes ;
Consult the statute, *quart.* I think it is,
Edwardi sext. or *prim. et quint. Eliz.*
See *Libels, Satires*—here you have it—read.
   P. *Libels* and *satires* ! lawless things indeed !   150
But grave *epistles*, bringing vice to light,
Such as a king might read, a bishop write ;

<hr>

He, whose lightning.—" Charles Mordaunt, Earl of Peterborough, who, in the year 1705, took Barcelona, and in the winter following, with only 280 horse and 900 foot, enterprised and accomplished the conquest of Valentia."—POPE.
  Consult the statute.—Crocker's note illuminates the methods of Pope : " There is no statute ' *quart. Edwardi sext.*,' but there were statutes *tert.* and *quart.* of Edward VI., and *prim.* and *quint. Eliz.*, against writing, printing, or singing seditious words. The reference is more exact than could have been expected in rhyme."
  Grave epistles.—A fortnight after this satire was published Pope wrote Swift (April 2, 1733) : " You call your satires libels ; I would rather call my satires epistles ; they will consist more of morality than wit, and grow graver, which you will call duller."

Such as Sir ROBERT would approve—

    F.   Indeed ?

The case is alter'd—you may then proceed ;

In such a cause the plaintiff will be hiss'd,   155

My lords the judges laugh, and you're dismiss'd.

Sir Robert.—Walpole's expected approval is the " revolution and discovery " which brings the comedy to a close.

THE FIRST EPISTLE OF THE SECOND BOOK OF HORACE: TO AUGUSTUS

ADVERTISEMENT

THE reflections of Horace, and the judgments past in his Epistle to Augustus, seem'd so seasonable to the present times, that I could not help applying them to the use of my own country. The author thought them considerable enough to address them to his Prince; whom he paints with all the great and good qualities of a monarch upon whom the Romans depended for the encrease of an *absolute empire*. But to make the poem entirely English, I was willing to add one or two of those which contribute to the happiness of a *free people*, and are consistent with the welfare of *our neighbours*.

This epistle will show the learned world to have fallen into two mistakes: one, that *Augustus was a patron of poets in general*; whereas he not only prohibited all but the best writers to name him, but recommended that care even to the civil magistrate: *Admonebat prætores ne paterentur nomen suum obsolefieri*, etc. The other, that this piece was only a *general discourse of poetry*; whereas it was an *Apology for the poets*, in order to render Augustus more their patron. Horace here pleads the cause of his contemporaries, first against the taste of the *town*, whose humour it was to magnify the authors of the preceding age; secondly against the *court* and *nobility*, who encouraged only the writers for the theatre; and lastly against the *emperor* himself, who had conceived them of little use to the government.

He shews (by a view of the progress of learning, and the change of taste among the Romans) that the introduction of the polite arts of Greece had given the writers of his time great advantages over their predecessors ; that their morals were much improved, and the licence of those ancient poets restrained ; that satire and comedy were become more just and useful ; that whatever extravagances were left on the stage were owing to the *ill taste* of the *nobility* ; that poets, under due regulations, were in many respects useful to the state, and concludes, that it was upon them the emperor himself must depend for his fame with posterity.

We may farther learn from this Epistle that Horace made his court to this Great Prince by writing with a decent freedom toward him, with a just contempt of his low flatterers, and with a manly regard to his own character.   POPE.

WHILE you, great Patron of Mankind ! sustain
The balanc'd world, and open all the main ;
Your country, chief, in arms abroad defend,
At home, with morals, arts, and laws amend ;
How shall the Muse, from such a monarch steal   5
An hour, and not defraud the public weal ?
   Edward and Henry, now the boast of fame,
And virtuous Alfred, a more sacred name,
After a life of gen'rous toils endur'd,
The Gaul subdu'd, or property secur'd,   10
Ambition humbled, mighty cities storm'd,
Or laws establish'd, and the world reform'd ;
Clos'd their long glories with a sigh, to find
Th' unwilling gratitude of base mankind !
All human virtue, to its latest breath.   15
Finds envy never conquer'd, but by death.
The great Alcides, ev'ry labour past,
Had still this monster to subdue at last.
Sure fate of all, beneath whose rising ray
Each star of meaner merit fades away !   20

Oppress'd we feel the beam directly beat,
Those suns of glory please not till they set.

    To thee the world its present homage pays,
The harvest early, but mature the praise :
Great friend of LIBERTY ! in *Kings* a name   25
Above all Greek, above all Roman fame :
Whose word is truth, as sacred and rever'd,
As Heav'n's own oracles from altars heard.
Wonder of Kings ! like whom, to mortal eyes
None e'er has risen, and none e'er shall rise.   30

    Just in one instance, be it yet confest
Your people, Sir, are partial in the rest :
Foes to all living worth except your own,
And advocates for folly dead and gone.
Authors, like coins, grow dear as they grow old ;   35
It is the rust we value, not the gold.
Chaucer's worst ribaldry is learn'd by rote,
And beastly Skelton heads of houses quote :
One likes no language but the Faery Queen ;
A Scot will fight for Christ's Kirk o' the Green :   40
And each true Briton is to Ben so civil,
He swears the Muses met him at the Devil.

    Tho' justly Greece her eldest sons admires,
Why should not we be wiser than our sires ?
In ev'ry public virtue we excel :   45
We build, we paint, we sing, we dance as well,
And learned Athens to our art must stoop,
Could she behold us tumbling thro' a hoop.

    If time improve our wit as well as wine,
Say at what age a Poet grows divine ?   50
Shall we, or shall we not, account him so,
Who dy'd, perhaps, an hundred years ago ?

And beastly Skelton.—Skelton, poet laureate to Henry VIII., a
volume of whose verses has been lately reprinted, consisting almost
wholly of ribaldry, obscenity, and scurrilous language.—POPE.

   Christ's Kirk o' the Green.—A Ballad made by a King of Scotland.—
POPE.

   At the Devil.— The Devil Tavern, where Ben Jonson held his Poetical
Club.—POPE.

End all dispute ; and fix the year precise
When British bards begin t'immortalize ?
" Who lasts a century can have no flaw,   55
I hold that wit a classic, good in law."
     Suppose he wants a year, will you compound ?
And shall we deem him Ancient, right and sound,
Or damn to all eternity at once,
At ninety-nine, a Modern and a Dunce ?   60
     " We shall not quarrel for a year or two ;
By courtesy of England, he may do."
     Then by the rule that made the horse-tail bare,
I pluck out year by year, as hair by hair,
And melt down Ancients like a heap of snow :   65
While you, to measure merits, look in Stowe,
And estimating authors by the year,
Bestow a garland only on a bier.
     Shakespear (whom you and ev'ry play-house bill
Style the divine, the matchless, what you will)   70
For gain, not glory, wing'd his roving flight,
And grew immortal in his own despight.
Ben, old and poor, as little seem'd to heed
The life to come, in ev'ry poet's creed,
Who now reads Cowley ? if he pleases yet,   75
His moral pleases, not his pointed wit ;
Forgot his epic, nay Pindaric art,
But still I love the language of his heart.
     " Yet surely, surely, these were famous men !
What boy but hears the sayings of old Ben ?   80
In all debates where critics bear a part,
Not one but nods, and talks of Jonson's Art,
Of Shakespear's Nature, and of Cowley's Wit ;
How Beaumont's judgment check'd what Fletcher writ ;
How Shadwell hasty, Wycherley was slow ;   85

By courtesy of England.—Loosely used, the phrase means that out of
politeness the case against the poet will not be pressed.   In law the
phrase covers only the privilege of the husband during his life to enjoy
his dead wife's estate.

Stowe.—John Stowe's *Summary of English Chronicles,* 1565, etc.

But, for the passions, Southern sure and Rowe.
These, only these, support the crowded stage,
From eldest Heywood down to Cibber's age."
    All this may be ; the people's voice is odd,
It is, and it is not, the voice of God.   90
To *Gammer Gurton* if it give the bays,
And yet deny the *Careless Husband* praise,
Or say our fathers never broke a rule ;
Why then, I say, the public is a fool.
But let them own, that greater faults than we   95
They had, and greater virtues, I'll agree.
Spenser himself affects the obsolete,
And Sidney's verse halts ill on Roman feet :
Milton's strong pinion now not Heav'n can bound,
Now serpent-like, in prose he sweeps the ground,   100
In quibbles, angel and archangel join,
And God the Father turns a school-divine.
Not that I'd lop the beauties from his book,
Like slashing Bentley with his desp'rate hook,
Or damn all Shakespear, like th' affected fool   105
At court, who hates whate'er he read at school.
    But for the wits of either Charles's days,
The mob of gentlemen who wrote with ease ;
Sprat, Carew, Sedley, and a hundred more,
(Like twinkling stars the Miscellanies o'er)   110
One simile, that solitary shines
In the dry desert of a thousand lines,
Or lengthen'd thought that gleams through many a page,
Has sanctify'd whole poems for an age.
I lose my patience, and I own it too,   115
When works are censur'd, not as bad but new ;
While if our elders break all reason's laws,

   Gammer Gurton.—Some " dunce " must have commended this play ;
Pope's note calls it " a piece of very low humour, one of the first
printed plays in English, and therefore much valued by some antiquaries."
   The Careless Husband.—Cibber's popular comedy (1704) seems to be
complimented here.
   Slashing Bentley.—Bentley's much emended text of *Paradise Lost*
(1732) occasioned general ridicule.

These fools demand not pardon, but applause.
  On Avon's bank, where flow'rs eternal blow,
If I but ask if any weed can grow ?   120
One tragic sentence if I dare deride,
Which Betterton's grave action dignify'd,
Or well-mouth'd Booth with emphasis proclaims
(Tho' but, perhaps, a muster-roll of names),
How will our fathers rise up in a rage,   125
And swear, all shame is lost in George's age !
You'd think no fools disgrac'd the former reign,
Did not some grave examples yet remain,
Who scorn a lad should teach his father skill,
And, having once been wrong, will be so still.   130
He who to seem more deep than you or I,
Extols old bards, or Merlin's Prophecy,
Mistake him not ; he envies, not admires,
And to debase the sons, exalts the sires.
Had ancient times conspir'd to disallow   135
What then was new, what had been ancient now ?
Or what remain'd, so worthy to be read
By learned critics, of the mighty dead ?
  In days of ease, when now the weary sword
Was sheath'd, and luxury with Charles restor'd ; 140
In ev'ry taste of foreign courts improv'd,
" All, by the King's example, liv'd and lov'd."
Then peers grew proud in horsemanship t'excel,
Newmarket's glory rose, as Britain's fell ;
The soldier breath'd the gallantries of France, 145
And ev'ry flow'ry courtier writ romance.
Then Marble, soften'd into life, grew warm,
And yielding metal flow'd to human form :
Lely on animated canvas stole
The sleepy eye, that spoke the melting soul.   150
No wonder then, when all was love and sport,

Betterton.—The great tragic actor had had a farm near Reading, and had been Pope's friend from Binfield days. With Booth—in a sense Betterton's successor—Pope was perhaps less intimate.
  All, by the King's example.—" A verse of the Lord Lansdowne."—
POPE.

The willing Muses were debauch'd at court :
On each enervate string they taught the note
To pant or tremble thro' an eunuch's throat.
But Britain, changeful as a child at play,　　155
Now calls in princes, and now turns away :
Now Whig, now Tory, what we lov'd we hate ;
Now all for pleasure, now for Church and State ;
Now for Prerogative, and now for Laws ;
Effects unhappy ! from a noble cause.　　160
　Time was, a sober Englishman would knock
His servants up, and rise by five o'clock,
Instruct his family in ev'ry rule,
And send his wife to church, his son to school.
To worship like his fathers was his care ;　　165
To teach their frugal virtues to his heir ;
To prove that luxury could never hold ;
And place, on good security, his gold.
Now times are chang'd, and one poetic itch
Has seiz'd the Court and City, poor and rich :　　170
Sons, sires, and grandsires, all will wear the bays,
Our wives read Milton, and our daughters plays,
To theatres, and to rehearsals throng.
And all our grace at table is a song.
I, who so oft renounce the Muses, lie,　　175
Not ——'s self e'er tells more fibbs than I ;
When sick of Muse, our follies we deplore,
And promise our best friends to rhyme no more ;
We wake next morning in a raging fit,
And call for pen and ink to show our wit.　　180
　He serv'd a 'prenticeship who sets up shop ;
Ward try'd on puppies and the poor, his drop ;
Ev'n Radcliffe's doctors travel first to France,

Ward.—A famous empiric, whose pill and drop had several surprising effects, and were one of the principal subjects of writing and conversation at this time.—Pope.
Radcliffe's doctors.—The Radcliffe Fellows, who studied medicine abroad on the foundation left Oxford by Dr. John Radcliffe ; or, with more general implication, based on the career of Radcliffe himself, fashionable practitioners.

Nor dare to practise till they've learn'd to dance.
Who builds a bridge that never drove a pile ?   185
(Should Ripley venture, all the world would smile)
But those who cannot write, and those who can,
All rhyme, and scrawl, and scribble, to a man.
Yet, Sir, reflect, the mischief is not great ;
These madmen never hurt the Church or State :   190
Sometimes the folly benefits mankind ;
And rarely avarice taints the tuneful mind.
Allow him but his plaything of a pen,
He ne'er rebels, or plots, like other men :
Flight of cashiers, or mobs, he'll never mind ;   195
And knows no losses while the Muse is kind.
To cheat a friend, or Ward, he leaves to Peter ;
The good man heaps up nothing but mere metre,
Enjoys his garden and his book in quiet ;
And then—a perfect hermit in his diet.   200
    Of little use the man you may suppose,
Who says in verse what others say in prose ;
Yet let me show, a poet's of some weight,
And (tho' no soldier) useful to the State.
What will a child learn sooner than a song ?   205
What better teach a foreigner the tongue ?
What's long or short, each accent where to place,
And speak in public with some sort of grace.
I scarce can think him such a worthless thing,
Unless he praise some monster of a king ;   210
Or virtue or religion turn to sport,
To please a lewd, or unbelieving Court.
Unhappy Dryden !—In all Charles's days,
Roscommon only boasts unspotted bays ;
And in our own (excuse some courtly stains)   215
No whiter page than Addison remains.

Ripley.—See the *Moral Essays*, iv., 18.
Courtly stains.—Probably "party writing" is meant. Addison, of
course, prided himself on freedom from this, and did largely escape it :
but it breaks into his work unexpectedly—as, for instance, the praise
of Marlborough in the libretto of *Rosamond.*

He, from the taste obscene reclaims our youth,
And sets the passions on the side of truth,
Forms the soft bosom with the gentlest art,
And pours each human virtue in the heart.   220
Let Ireland tell, how wit upheld her cause,
Her trade supported, and supplied her laws ;
And leave on SWIFT this grateful verse engrav'd,
" The Rights a Court attack'd, a Poet sav'd."
Behold the hand that wrought a nation's cure,   225
Stretch'd to relieve the idiot and the poor,
Proud Vice to brand, or injur'd Worth adorn,
And stretch the ray to ages yet unborn.
Not but there are, who merit other palms ;
Hopkins and Sternhold glad the heart with Psalms : 230
The boys and girls whom charity maintains,
Implore your help in these pathetic strains :
How could devotion touch the country pews,
Unless the Gods bestow'd a proper Muse ?
Verse cheers their leisure, verse assists their work, 235
Verse prays for peace, or sings down Pope and
          Turk.
The silenc'd preacher yields to potent strain,
And feels that grace his pray'r besought in vain ;
The blessing thrills thro' all the lab'ring throng,
And Heav'n is won by violence of song.   240
     Our rural ancestors, with little blest,
Patient of labour when the end was rest,
Indulg'd the day that hous'd their annual grain,
With feasts, and off'rings, and a thankful strain :
The joy their wives, their sons, and servants share, 245
Ease of their toil, and part'ners of their care :
The laugh, the jest, attendants on the bowl,
Smooth'd ev'ry brow, and open'd ev'ry soul :
With growing years the pleasing licence grew,

Pope and Turk.—A hymn in the Queen Anne Prayer Book (1703)
began :
     " Preserve us, Lord, by Thy dear word,
        From Turk and Pope defend us, Lord."

And taunts alternate innocently flew. 250
But times corrupt, and nature, ill-inclin'd,
Produc'd the point that left a sting behind ;
Till friend with friend, and families at strife,
Triumphant malice rag'd thro' private life.
Who felt the wrong, or fear'd it, took th' alarm, 255
Appeal'd to law, and justice lent her arm.
At length, by wholesome dread of statutes bound,
The poets learn'd to please, and not to wound :
Most warp'd to flattery's side ; but some, more nice,
Preserv'd the freedom, and forbore the vice. 260
Hence satire rose, that just the medium hit,
And heals with morals what it hurts with wit.
    We conquer'd France, but felt our captive's charms ;
Her arts victorious triumph'd o'er our arms ;
Britain to soft refinements less a foe, 265
Wit grew polite, and numbers learn'd to flow.
Waller was smooth ; but Dryden taught to join
The varying verse, the full-resounding line,
The long majestic march, and energy divine.
Tho' still some traces of our rustic vein 270
And splay-foot verse remain'd, and will remain.
Late, very late, correctness grew our care,
When the tir'd nation breath'd from civil war.
Exact Racine, and Corneille's noble fire,
Show'd us that France had something to admire. 275
Not but the tragic spirit was our own,
And full in Shakespear, fair in Otway shone :
But Otway fail'd to polish or refine,
And fluent Shakespear scarce effac'd a line.
Ev'n copious Dryden wanted, or forgot, 280
The last and greatest art, the art to blot.
Some doubt, if equal pains, or equal fire

Correctness.—The approximation of perfect propriety or decorum, especially in metrics. Of his early adviser, William Walsh, Pope told Spence : " He used to encourage me much, and used to tell me that there was one way left of excelling ; for though we had several great poets, we never had any one great poet that was correct ; and he desired me to make that my study and aim."

The humbler Muse of comedy require.
But in known images of life, I guess
The labour greater, as th' indulgence less.   285
Observe how seldom ev'n the best succeed :
Tell me if Congreve's fools are fools indeed ?
What pert, low dialogue has Farqu'ar writ !
How Van wants grace, who never wanted wit !
The stage how loosely does Astræa tread,   290
Who fairly puts all characters to bed !
And idle Cibber, how he breaks the laws,
To make poor Pinky eat with vast applause !
But fill their purse, our poet's work is done,
Alike to them, by pathos or by pun.   295
    O you ! whom vanity's light bark conveys
On fame's mad voyage by the wind of praise,
With what a shifting gale your course you ply,
For ever sunk too low, or borne too high !
Who pants for glory finds but short repose,   300
A breath revives him, or a breath o'erthrows.
Farewell the stage ! if just as thrives the play,
The silly bard grows fat, or falls away.
    There still remains, to mortify a wit,
The many-headed monster of the pit :   305
A senseless, worthless, and unhonour'd crowd ;
Who, to disturb their betters mighty proud,
Clatt'ring their sticks before ten lines are spoke,
Call for the farce, the bear, or the black-joke.
What dear delight to Britons farce affords !   310
Ever the taste of mobs, but now of lords ;
(Taste, that eternal wanderer, which flies
From heads to ears, and now from ears to eyes.)
The play stands still ; damn action and discourse,
Back fly the scenes, and enter foot and horse ;   315

Van.—Sir John Vanbrugh.
Astræa.—" A name taken by Mrs. [Aphra] Behn, authoress of several obscene plays."—POPE.
Pinky.—William Penkethman, a famous low comedian who, says the *Tatler*, No. 188, " devours a cold chick with great applause."
The black-joke.—An indecent popular song.

Pageants on pageants, in long order drawn,
Peers, heralds, bishops, ermine, gold, and lawn ;
The Champion too ! and, to complete the jest,
Old Edward's armour beams on Cibber's breast.
With laughter sure Democritus had dy'd,   320
Had he beheld an audience gape so wide.
Let bear or elephant be e'er so white,
The people, sure, the people are the sight !
Ah luckless poet ! stretch thy lungs and roar,
That bear or elephant shall heed thee more ;   325
While all its throats the gallery extends,
And all the thunder of the pit ascends !
Loud as the wolves, on Orcas' stormy steep,
Howl to the roarings of the Northern deep.
Such is the shout, the long-applauding note,   330
At Quin's high plume, or Oldfield's petticoat ;
Or when from Court a birth-day suit bestow'd,
Sinks the lost actor in the tawdry load.
Booth enters—hark ! the universal peal !
" But has he spoken ? " Not a syllable.   335
What shook the stage, and made the people stare ?
Cato's long wig, flow'r'd gown, and lacquer'd chair.

    Yet lest you think I rally more than teach,
Or praise malignly arts I cannot reach,
Let me for once presume t'instruct the times,   340
To know the poet from the man of rhymes :
'Tis he, who gives my breast a thousand pains,
Can make me feel each passion that he feigns ;
Enrage, compose, with more than magic art,
With pity and with terror tear my heart ;   345

Old Edward's armour.—The coronation of Henry VIII. and Anne
Boleyn, in which the playhouses vied with each other to represent all
the pomp of a coronation. In this noble contention the armour of one
of the kings of England was borrowed from the Tower to dress the
champion.—POPE.

Quin.—(1693–1766.) A famous actor of the day. The even more
famous Anne Oldfield had died in 1730.

Cato's long wig.—A contemporary drawing of this curiously garbed
Cato is reproduced in R. W. Lowe's edition of Cibber's *Apology* (1899),
II., 117.

And snatch me o'er the earth or thro' the air,
To Thebes, to Athens, when he will, and where.
    But not this part of the poetic state
Alone, deserves the favour of the great :
Think of those authors, Sir, who would rely   350
More on a reader's sense, than gazer's eye.
Or who shall wander where the Muses sing ?
Who climb their mountain, or who taste their spring ?
How shall we fill a library with wit,
When Merlin's Cave is half unfurnish'd yet ?   355
My Liege ! why writers little claim your thought,
I guess ; and, with their leave, will tell the fault :
We poets are (upon a poet's word)
Of all mankind, the creatures most absurd :
The season, when to come, and when to go,   360
To sing, or cease to sing, we never know ;
And if we will recite nine hours in ten,
You lose your patience, just like other men.
Then too we hurt ourselves when to defend
A single verse, we quarrel with a friend ;   365
Repeat unask'd ; lament, the wit's too fine
For vulgar eyes, and point out ev'ry line.
But most, when straining with too weak a wing,
We needs will write epistles to the King ;
And from the moment we oblige the town,   370
Expect a place, or pension from the Crown ;
Or dubb'd historians by express command,
T'enroll your triumphs o'er the seas and land,
Be call'd to Court to plan some work divine,
As once for Louis, Boileau and Racine.   375
    Yet think, great Sir ! (so many virtues shown)
Ah think, what poet best may make them known ?
Or chuse at least some Minister of Grace,
Fit to bestow the Laureate's weighty place.
    Charles, to late times to be transmitted fair,   380

Merlin's Cave.—" A building in the royal gardens of Richmond, where is a small but choice collection of books," is Pope's ironic comment.

Assign'd his figure to Bernini's care ;
And great Nassau to Kneller's hand decreed
To fix him graceful on the bounding steed ;
So well in paint and stone they judg'd of merit :
But kings in wit may want discerning spirit.   385
The hero William, and the martyr Charles,
One knighted Blackmore, and one pension'd Quarles ;
Which made old Ben, and surly Dennis swear,
" No Lord's anointed, but a Russian bear."
    Not with such majesty, such bold relief,   390
The forms august, of king, or conqu'ring chief,
E'er swell'd on marble ; as in verse have shin'd
(In polish'd verse) the manners and the mind.
Oh ! could I mount on the Mæonian wing,
Your arms, your actions, your repose to sing !   395
What seas you travers'd, and what fields you fought !
Your country's peace, how oft, how dearly bought !
How barb'rous rage subsided at your word,
And nations wonder'd while they dropp'd the sword !
How, when you nodded, o'er the land and deep,   400
Peace stole her wing, and wrapt the world in sleep ;
Till earth's extremes your mediation own,
And Asia's tyrants tremble at your throne—
But verse, alas ! your Majesty disdains ;
And I'm not us'd to panegyric strains :   405
The zeal of fools offends at any time,
But most of all, the zeal of fools in rhyme,
Besides, a fate attends on all I write,
That when I aim at praise, they say I bite.
A vile encomium doubly ridicules :   410
There's nothing blackens like the ink of fools.
If true, a woeful likeness ; and if lies,
" Praise undeserv'd is scandal in disguise : "
Well may he blush, who gives it, or receives ;
And when I flatter, let my dirty leaves   415

Oh ! could I mount.—The extreme of Pope's satire on George II. is
here concentrated in such words as *repose* and *bought*.

(Like journals, odes, and such forgotten things
As Eusden, Philips, Settle, writ of Kings)
Clothe spice, line trunks, or flutt'ring in a row
Befringe the rails of Bedlam and Soho.

Bedlam and Soho.—About Bethlehem Hospital (Bedlam) and in Wardour Street (" Old Soho "), as well as in Duck Lane, gathered dealers in old books.

EPILOGUE TO THE SATIRES
(*In Two Dialogues*)

Written in MDCCXXXVIII

DIALOGUE I

Fr. NOT twice a twelve-month you appear in print,
And when it comes, the Court see nothing in't.
You grow correct, that once with rapture writ,
And are, besides, too *moral* for a wit.
Decay of parts, alas ! we all must feel—   5
Why now, this moment, don't I see you steal ?
'Tis all from Horace ; Horace long before ye
Said, " Tories called him Whig and Whigs a Tory ; "
And taught his Romans, in much better metre,
" To laugh at fools who put their trust in Peter."   10
    But Horace, Sir, was delicate, was nice ;
Bubo observes, he lashed no sort of *vice* :
Horace would say, Sir Billy *served the Crown*,
Blunt could *do bus'ness*, H–ggins *knew the Town* ;
In Sappho touch the *failings of the sex*,   15
In rev'rend bishops note some *small neglects*,
And own, the Spaniard did a *waggish thing*,

Tories called him Whig.—See Satire 1. (to Fortescue), line 68. Line 10
is an echo from line 40 of Satire 1.
    Bubo observes.—Some guilty person, very fond of making such an
observation.—POPE. Bubo, Warton said, was Bubb Doddington.
    Sir Billy . . . H–ggins.—Sir Billy was Sir William Yonge. Huggins,
Pope says, " formerly jaylor of the Fleet prison, enriched himself by
many exactions, for which he was tried and expelled."

Who cropt our ears, and sent them to the King.
His sly, polite, insinuating style
Could please at Court, and make Augustus smile :   20
An artful manager, that crept between
His friend and shame, and was a kind of screen.
But 'faith your very friends will soon be sore ;
Patriots there are, who wish you'd jest no more—
And where's the glory ? 'twill be only thought   25
The Great Man never offered you a groat,
Go see Sir Robert——

    P.   See Sir Robert !—hum—
And never laugh—for all my life to come ?
Seen him I have, but in his happier hour
Of social pleasure, ill-exchanged for power ;   30
Seen him, uncumbered with the venal tribe,
Smile without art, and win without a bribe.
Would he oblige me ? let me only find,
He does not think me what he thinks mankind.
Come, come, at all I laugh he laughs, no doubt ;   35
The only difference is, I dare laugh out.

    F. Why yes : with Scripture still you may be free ;
A horse-laugh, if you please, at honesty ;
A joke on Jekyl, or some odd Old Whig
Who never changed his principle, or wig :   40
A patriot is a fool in ev'ry age,
Whom all Lord Chamberlains allow the stage :
These nothing hurts ; they keep their fashion still,

Who cropt our ears.—Said to be executed by the captain of a Spanish ship on one Jenkins, a captain of an English one. He cut off his ears, and bid him carry them to the King, his master.—POPE. [Jenkins, whose ear was thus amputated in 1731, exhibited it to Parliament in 1738 ; and in October 1739 Walpole, to the delight of the patriot group, was compelled to declare war.]

Patriots there are.—This appellation was generally given to those in opposition to the Court. Tho' some of them (which our author hints at) had views too mean and interested to deserve that name.—POPE.

What he thinks mankind.—That is, venal. One of Walpole's best-known sayings was, " Every man has his price."

All Lord Chamberlains.—This officer controlled the theatres, and just after the Licensing Act of 1737 was busy suppressing " patriot " plays—such as, for example, those of Henry Fielding.

And wear their strange old virtue, as they will.
    If any ask you, " Who's the man, so near   45
His Prince, that writes in verse, and has his ear ? "
Why, answer, Lyttelton, and I'll engage
The worthy youth shall ne'er be in a rage :
But were his verses vile, his whisper base,
You'd quickly find him in Lord Fanny's case.   50
Sejanus, Wolsey, hurt not honest Fleury,
But well may put some statesmen in a fury.
    Laugh then at any, but at fools or foes ;
These you but anger, and you mend not those.
Laugh at your friends, and, if your friends are sore,   55
So much the better, you may laugh the more ;
To vice and folly to confine the jest,
Sets half the world, God knows, against the rest ;
Did not the sneer of more impartial men
At sense and virtue, balance all again.   60
Judicious wits spread wide the ridicule,
And charitably comfort knave and fool.
    P.   Dear Sir, forgive the prejudice of youth :
Adieu distinction, satire, warmth, and truth !
Come, harmless characters that no one hit ;   65
Come, Henley's Oratory, Osborn's wit !
The honey dropping from Favonio's tongue,
The flowers of Bubo, and the flow of Y—ng !
The gracious dew of pulpit eloquence,

Why, answer, Lyttelton.—George Lyttelton, Secretary to the Prince
of Wales, distinguished both for his writings and speeches in the spirit
of Liberty.
    Sejanus, Wolsey.—The one the wicked minister of Tiberius ; the
other of Henry VIII. The writers against the Court usually bestowed
these and other odious names on the Minister, without distinction, and
in the most injurious manner. See Dialogue II., line 137.
    Henley's Oratory.—See *Dunciad*, Book III., line 199 ; and for Osborn,
see *ibid.*, Book II., lines 167, 312, and notes.
    The gracious dew.—Alludes to some court sermons, and florid pane-
gyrical speeches ; particularly one very full of puerilities and flatteries ;
which afterwards got into an address in the same pretty style ; and
was lastly served up in an Epitaph, between Latin and English, published by its author.—POPE. (The occasion was the death of the Queen
in 1737.)

And all the well-whipt cream of courtly sense,   70
That first was H—vy's, F—'s next, and then
The St—te's, and then H—vy's once again.
O come, that easy Ciceronian style,
So Latin, yet so English all the while,
As, tho' the pride of Middleton and Bland,   75
All boys may read, and girls may understand !
Then might I sing without the least offence,
And all I sung should be the *Nation's sense* ;
Or teach the melancholy muse to mourn,
Hang the sad verse on Carolina's urn,   80
And hail her passage to the realms of rest,
All parts performed, and *all* her children blest !
So—Satire is no more—I feel it die—
No gazetteer more innocent than I—
And let, a-God's name, ev'ry fool and knave   85
Be graced thro' life, and flattered in his grave.
  F.   Why so ?   If Satire knows its time and place,
You still may lash the greatest—in disgrace :
For merit will by turns forsake them all ;
Would you know when ?   exactly when they fall.   90
But let all Satire in all changes spare
Immortal S——k, and grave De——re !
Silent and soft, as saints remove to Heaven,
All ties dissolved, and ev'ry sin forgiven,

That first was H—vy's.—Lord Hervey, Henry Fox, and the " Senate "
had apparently all passed on the eulogies pronounced upon the Queen.
Cf. Pope's note to line 69.   He proceeds now to criticize the epitaph
for its Anglo-Ciceronian style, and to ascribe it to Middleton (author of
the *Life of Cicero*), and Bland (formerly master of Eton College).   See
the *Dunciad*, Book i., line 231 and note.

All parts performed.—Gossip said that the Queen had declined on her
deathbed to receive the Sacraments, and to become reconciled to the
Prince of Wales.

No gazetteer.—Steele, who had written the government newspaper,
The London Gazette, said in his *Apology* (page 103) that he did so " without ever erring against the rule observed by all ministries, to keep that
paper very innocent and very insipid."   But here the innocence may
be alleged ironically.

Immortal S——k.—The Earl of Selkirk had been an officer of the
royal household under William and the first two Hanoverian monarchs.
" Grave Delaware " was a court favourite.

These may some gentle ministerial wing 95
Receive, and place forever near a king !
There, where no passion, pride, or shame transport,
Lulled with the sweet Nepenthe of a Court ;
There, where no father's, brother's, friend's disgrace 99
Once break their rest, or stir them from their place :
But past the sense of human miseries,
All tears are wiped for ever from all eyes ;
No cheek is known to blush, no heart to throb,
Save when they lose a question, or a job.
 P. Good Heaven forbid, that I should blast their
   glory, 105
Who know how like Whig ministers to Tory,
And when three sov'reigns died, could scarce be vext,
Consid'ring what a *gracious Prince* was next.
Have I in silent wonder, seen such things
As pride in slaves, and avarice in kings ; 110
And at a peer, or peeress, shall I fret,
Who starves a sister, or forswears a debt ?
Virtue, I grant you, is an empty boast ;
But shall the dignity of *Vice* be lost ?
Ye Gods ! shall Cibber's son, without rebuke, 115
Swear like a Lord, or Rich out-whore a Duke ?
A fav'rite's porter with his master vie,
Be bribed as often, and as often lie ?
Shall Ward draw contracts with a statesman's skill ?
Or Japhet pocket, like his Grace, a will ? 120
Is it for Bond, or Peter, (paltry things)
To pay their debts, or keep their faith, like kings ?
If Blunt dispatched himself, he played the man,
And so may'st thou, illustrious Passeran !

 Ward . . . Or Japhet.—See notes to the *Dunciad*, Book III., line 34,
and *Moral Essays*, III., line 86. On *Bond*, see *Moral Essays*, III., line 100.
 If Blunt.—Author of an impious, foolish book called *The Oracles of
Reason*, who being in love with a near kinswoman of his, and rejected,
gave himself a stab in the arm, as pretending to kill himself, of the
consequence of which he really died. Passeran, Warburton describes
as " Author of another book of the same stamp, called *A Philosophical
Discourse on Death*, being a defence of suicide."

But shall a printer, weary of his life,   125
Learn from their books, to hang himself and wife ?
This, this, my friend, I cannot, must not bear ;
Vice thus abused, demands a nation's care :
This calls the Church to deprecate our sin,
And hurls the thunder of the laws on gin.   130
    Let modest Foster, if he will, excell
Ten Metropolitans in preaching well ;
A simple Quaker, or a Quaker's wife,
Outdo Landaff in doctrine,—yea in life :
Let humble Allen, with an awkward shame,   135
Do good by stealth, and blush to find it fame.
Virtue may choose the high or low degree,
'Tis just alike to virtue, and to me ;
Dwell in a monk, or light upon a king,
She's still the same, beloved, contented thing.   140
Vice is undone, if she forgets her birth,
And stoops from angels to the dregs of earth :
But 'tis the fall degrades her to a whore ;
Let *Greatness* own her, and she's mean no more,
Her birth, her beauty crowds and courts confess,   145
Chaste matrons praise her, and grave bishops bless ;
In golden chains the willing world she draws,
And hers the Gospel is, and hers the Laws,
Mounts the tribunal, lifts her scarlet head,
And sees pale Virtue carted in her stead.   150
Lo ! at the wheels of her triumphal car,
Old England's Genius, rough with many a scar,

Laws on gin.—A spirituous liquor, the exorbitant use of which had
almost destroyed the lowest rank of the people, till it was restrained by
an Act of Parliament in 1736.—POPE.

Let modest Foster.—" A celebrated Anabaptist preacher, who lectured
Sunday evenings in the Old Jewry."

Outdo Landaff.—A poor bishopric in Wales, as poorly supplied.—
POPE.   The Quaker's wife was a Mrs. Drummond.

Let humble Allen.—Ralph Allen of Prior Park, near Bath, was friend
and benefactor of Pope and Henry Fielding, among others.   Fielding
later idealized him as Squire Allworthy in *Tom Jones.*

Pale Virtue carted.—Modern readers may require to be reminded
that in Pope's days carting, or exhibiting from a cart, was a punishment
of prostitutes and procuresses.—CROKER.

Dragged in the dust ! his arms hang idly round,
His flag inverted trails along the ground !
Our youth, all liveried o'er with foreign gold,   155
Before her dance : behind her, crawl the old !
See thronging millions to the pagod run,
And offer country, parent, wife, or son !
Hear her black trumpet thro' the land proclaim,
That NOT TO BE CORRUPTED IS THE SHAME.   160
In soldier, churchman, patriot, man in power,
'Tis avarice all, ambition is no more !
See, all our nobles begging to be slaves !
See, all our fools aspiring to be knaves !
The wit of cheats, the courage of a whore,   165
Are what ten thousand envy and adore :
All, all look up, with reverential awe,
At crimes that 'scape, or triumph o'er the law :
While truth, worth, wisdom, daily they decry—
" Nothing is sacred now but villainy."   170
      Yet may this verse (if such a verse remain)
Show there was one who held it in disdain.

DIALOGUE II

      Fr.   'Tis all a libel—Paxton (Sir) will say.
P.   Not yet, my friend ! to-morrow 'faith it may ;
And for that very cause I print to-day.
How should I fret to mangle ev'ry line,
In rev'rence to the sins of *Thirty-nine* !   5
Vice with such giant strides comes on amain,
Invention strives to be before in vain ;
Feign what I will, and paint it e'er so strong,
Some rising genius sins up to my song.
      F.   Yet none but you by name the guilty lash :   10

To the pagod run.—Vice is imaged as a monstrous Hindoo idol.
Paxton.—Nicholas Paxton, once Solicitor to the Treasury.
I print to-day.—Dialogue II. appeared about two months later than
Dialogue I., in the summer of 1738.

Ev'n Guthry saves half Newgate by a dash.
Spare then the person, and expose the vice.
P. How, Sir ! not damn the sharper, but the dice ?
Come on then, Satire ! general, unconfined,
Spread thy broad wing, and souse on all the kind.　　15
Ye statesmen, priests, of one religion all !
Ye tradesmen, vile, in Army, Court, or Hall ;
Ye rev'rend atheists.　F.　Scandal ! name them, Who ?
　　P.　Why that's the thing you bid me not to do.
Who starved a sister, who forswore a debt,　　20
I never named ; the Town's inquiring yet.
The poisoning dame—　F. You mean—　P. I don't.—
　　F.　You do.
P.　See, now I keep the secret, and not you !
The bribing statesman—　F.　Hold, too high you go. 24
P.　The bribed elector—　F.　There you stoop too low.
P.　I fain would please you, if I knew with what ;
Tell me, which knave is lawful game, which not ?
Must great offenders, once escaped the Crown,
Like royal harts, be never more run down ?
Admit your law to spare the knight requires,　　30
As beasts of nature may we hunt the squires ?
Suppose I censure—you know what I mean—
To save a bishop, may I name a dean ?
　　F.　A dean, Sir ? no : his fortune is not made
You hurt a man that's rising in the trade.　　35
　　P.　If not the tradesman who set up to-day,
Much less the 'prentice who to-morrow may.
Down, down, proud Satire ! tho' a realm be spoiled,
Arraign no mightier thief than wretched Wild ;

Ev'n Guthry.—The ordinary of Newgate, who publishes the memoirs of the malefactors, and is often prevailed upon to be so tender of their reputation as to set down no more than the initials of their name.—POPE.
　　Who starved a sister.—See Dialogue i., line 11 . Sometimes this is thought to refer to Lady Mary Wortley Montagu.
　　Wretched Wild.—Jonathan Wild, a famous thief and thief impeacher, who was at last caught in his own train and hanged.—POPE. Did Pope know that Fielding was soon to arraign a mightier person in Wild's name ?

Or, if a Court or country's made a job,   40
Go drench a pick-pocket, and join the mob.
    But, Sir, I beg you (for the love of vice !)
The matter's weighty, pray consider twice ;
Have you less pity for the needy cheat,
The poor and friendless villain, than the great ?   45
Alas ! the small discredit of a bribe
Scarce hurts the lawyer, but undoes the scribe.
Then better sure it charity becomes
To tax directors, who (thank God) have plums ;
Still better, ministers ; or, if the thing   50
May pinch ev'n there—why, lay it on a king.
    F.   Stop ! stop !
    P.   Must satire, then, nor rise nor fall ?
Speak out, and bid me blame no rogues at all.
    F.   Yes, strike that Wild, I'll justify the blow.   54
    P.   Strike ? why, the man was hanged ten years ago :
Who now that obsolete example fears ?
Ev'n Peter trembles only for his ears.
    F.   What, always Peter ?   Peter thinks you mad,
You make men desperate, if they once are bad :
Else might he take to virtue some years hence——   60
    P.   As S——k, if he lives, will love the Prince.
    F.   Strange spleen to S——k !
    P.   Do I wrong the man ?
God knows, I praise a Courtier where I can.
When I confess, there is who feels for fame,
And melts to goodness, need I Scarb'row name ?   65
Pleased let me own in Esher's peaceful grove

Will love the Prince.—Hypocritical Peter Walter (whom, under the aliases of Peter Pounce and Petrus Gualterus, Fielding later depicted in *Joseph Andrews*, Book III., chap. xii., and in *The Golden Chrysipus*) is as likely to take to virtue as Selkirk is to love the Prince of Wales.

Scarb'row.—Earl of, and Knight of the Garter, whose personal attachments to the king appeared from his steady adherence to the royal interest, after his resignation of his great employment of Master of the Horse : and whose known honour and virtue made him esteemed of all parties.—POPE.

Esher's peaceful grove.—The house and gardens of Esher, in Surrey, belonging to the Honourable Mr. Pelham, brother to the Duke of New-

(Where Kent and Nature vie for Pelham's love)
The scene, the master, opening to my view,
I sit and dream I see my Craggs anew !
   Ev'n in a bishop I can spy desert ;   70
Secker is decent, Rundle has a heart,
Manners with candour are to Benson given,
To Berkley, ev'ry virtue under Heaven.
   But does the Court a worthy man remove ?
That instant, I declare, he has my love :   75
I shun his zenith, court his mild decline ;
Thus Somers once, and Halifax, were mine.
Oft, in the clear, still mirror of retreat,
I studied Shrewsbury, the wise and great :
Carleton's calm sense, and Stanhope's noble flame,   80
Compared, and knew their gen'rous end the same :
How pleasing Atterbury's softer hour !
How shined the soul, unconquered in the Tower !
How can I Pult'ney, Chesterfield forget,
While Roman spirit charms, and Attic wit :   85
Argyll, the State's whole thunder born to wield,
And shake alike the Senate and the field :
Or Wyndham, just to freedom and the throne,
The master of our passions, and his own.
Names, which I long have loved, nor loved in vain,   90
Ranked with their friends, not numbered with their
       train ;

castle. The author could not have given a more amiable idea of his character, than in comparing him to Mr. Craggs.—POPE. Esher was designed by William Kent, who was Pope's friend.

   Secker . . . Rundle, etc.—Thomas Secker was later Archbishop of Canterbury ; Thomas Rundle was Bishop of Derry ; George Benson, Bishop of Gloucester. George Berkeley (1684–1753), Bishop of Cloyne, was the celebrated philosopher, and a friend of Pope.

   Thus Somers once.—Somers, Halifax, Shrewsbury, and James, Earl Stanhope, were all among Pope's early titled friends.

   Atterbury's softer hour.—In Atterbury's trial for treason (1723), Pope testified to the non-political nature of such hours. Atterbury was exiled, and died abroad.

   Pult'ney, Chesterfield.—These men, as well as Wyndham, were among Pope's " patriot " friends. Argyll the patriots hoped to win away from Walpole.

And if yet higher the proud list should end,
Still let me say ! No follower, but a friend.
   Yet think not, friendship only prompts my lays ;
I follow Virtue ; where she shines, I praise :   95
Point she to priest or elder, Whig or Tory,
Or round a Quaker's beaver, cast a glory.
I never (to my sorrow I declare)
Dined with the Man of Ross, or my Lord May'r.   99
Some, in their choice of friends (nay, look not grave)
Have still a secret bias to a knave :
To find an honest man I beat about,
And love him, court him, praise him, in or out.
   F.   Then why so few commended ?
   P.   Not so fierce ;
Find you the virtue, and I'll find the verse.   105
But random praise—the task can ne'er be done ;
Each mother asks it for her booby son,
Each widow asks it for *the best of men*,
For him she weeps, and him she weds again.
Praise cannot stoop, like satire, to the ground ;   110
The number may be hanged, but not be crowned.
Enough for half the greatest of these days,
To 'scape my censure, not expect my praise.
Are they not rich ? what more can they pretend ?
Dare they to hope a poet for their friend ?   115
What Richelieu wanted, Louis scarce could gain,
And what young Ammon wished, but wished in vain.
No pow'r the Muse's friendship can command ;
No pow'r when virtue claims it, can withstand :
To Cato, Virgil paid one honest line ;   120
O let my country's friends illumine mine !
—What are you thinking ?   F.   Faith, the thought's
       no sin,
I think your friends are out, and would be in ;

   My Lord May'r.—Sir John Barnard, Lord Mayor in 1738.
   What young Ammon wished.—That is, when he congratulated
Achilles, with a mixture of regret for his own failure in this respect, on
such a herald of his fame as Homer, at a visit to the tomb of that
hero.—WAKEFIELD.

 P. If merely to come in, Sir, they go out,
The way they take is strangely round about. 125
  F. They too may be corrupted, you'll allow ?
  P. I only call those knaves who are so now.
 Is that too little ? Come then, I'll comply—
Spirit of Arnall ! aid me while I lie.
Cobham's a coward, Polwarth is a slave, 130
And Lyttelton a dark, designing knave,
St. John has ever been a wealthy fool—
But let me add, Sir Robert's mighty dull,
Has never made a friend in private life,
And was, besides, a tyrant to his wife. 135
 But, pray, when others praise him, do I blame ?
Call Verres, Wolsey, any odious name ?
Why rail they then, if but a wreath of mine,
Oh all-accomplished St. John ! deck thy shrine ? 139
 What ! shall each spur-galled hackney of the day,
When Paxton gives him double pots and pay,
Or each new-pensioned sycophant, pretend
To break my windows if I treat a friend ;
Then wisely plead, to me they meant no hurt,
But 'twas my guest at whom they threw the dirt ? 145
Sure, if I spare the minister, no rules
Of honour bind me, not to maul his tools ;
Sure, if they cannot cut, it may be said
His saws are toothless, and his hatchet's lead.
 It angered Turenne, once upon a day, 150
To see a footman kicked that took his pay :
But when he heard th' affront the fellow gave,
Knew one a man of honour, one a knave ;
The prudent Gen'ral turned it to a jest,

 Spirit of Arnall.—See Pope's note on *Dunciad*, Book II., line 315.
 Cobham's a coward.—Compare this with the conclusion of the first *Moral Essay.*
 Polwarth.—The Hon. Hugh Hume, son of Alexander, Earl of March-mont, grandson of Patrick, Earl of Marchmont, and distinguished, like them, in the cause of liberty.—Pope.
 Lyttelton.—See Dialogue I., line 47.
 To break my windows.—Which was done when Lord Bolingbroke and Lord Bathurst were one day dining with him at Twickenham.—Warton.

And begged, he'd take the pains to kick the rest :   155
Which not at present having time to do——
    F.   Hold, Sir ! for God's sake, where's th' affront to
    you ?
Against your worship when had S——k writ ?
Or P—ge poured forth the torrent of his wit ?
Or grant the bard whose distich all commend   160
[*In pow'r a servant, out of pow'r a friend*]
To W—le guilty of some venial sin ;
What's that to you who ne'er was out nor in ?
   The priest whose flattery bedropt the Crown,
How hurt he you ? he only stained the gown.   165
And how did, pray, the florid youth offend,
Whose speech you took, and gave it to a friend ?
P.   Faith, it imports not much from whom it came ;
Whoever borrowed, could not be to blame,
Since the whole House did afterwards the same.   170
Let courtly wits to wits afford supply,
As hog to hog in huts of Westphaly ;
If one, thro' Nature's bounty or his Lord's,
Has what the frugal, dirty soil affords,
From him the next receives it, thick or thin,   175
As pure a mess almost as it came in ;
The blessed benefit, not there confined,
Drops to the third, who nuzzles close behind ;
From tail to mouth, they feed and they carouse :
The last full fairly gives it to the *House*.   180
    F.   This filthy simile, this beastly line
Quite turns my stomach——
    P.   So does flatt'ry mine ;
And all your courtly civet-cats can vent,
Perfume to you, to me is excrement.

Had S——k writ.—On Selkirk and Page see Dialogue I., line 92, and
the *Imitation of Horace*, Book II., Satire I., line 82 ; also *The Dunciad*,
Book IV., line 30.
  The bard.—Bubb Doddington.
  The priest.—Spoken not of any particular priest, but of many
priests.—POPE.
  The florid youth.—*Cf.* Dialogue I., line 70 (Henry Fox).

But hear me further—Japhet, 'tis agreed, 185
Writ not, and Chartres scarce could write or read,
In all the Courts of Pindus guiltless quite ;
But pens can forge, my friend, that cannot write ;
And must no egg in Japhet's face be thrown,
Because the deed he forged was not my own ? 190
Must never patriot then declaim at gin,
Unless, good man ! he has been fairly in ?
No zealous pastor blame a failing spouse,
Without a staring reason on his brows ?
And each blasphemer quite escape the rod, 195
Because the insult's not on man, but God ?
 Ask you what provocation I have had ?
The strong antipathy of good to bad.
When truth or virtue an affront endures, 199
Th' affront is mine, my friend, and should be yours.
Mine, as a foe professed to false pretence,
Who think a coxcomb's honour like his sense ;
Mine, as a friend to ev'ry worthy mind ;
And mine as man, who feel for all mankind. 204
 F. You're strangely proud.
 P.   So proud, I am no slave :
So impudent, I own myself no knave :
So odd, my country's ruin makes me grave.
Yes, I am proud ; I must be proud to see
Men not afraid of God, afraid of me :
Safe from the bar, the pulpit, and the throne, 210
Yet touched and shamed by ridicule alone.
 O sacred weapon ! left for truth's defence,
Sole dread of folly, vice, and insolence !
To all but Heav'n-directed hands denied,
The Muse may give thee, but the Gods must guide : 215
Rev'rent I touch thee ! but with honest zeal ;
To rouse the watchmen of the public weal,
To virtue's work provoke the tardy Hall,
And goad the prelate slumb'ring in his stall.
Ye tinsel insects ! whom a court maintains, 220
That counts your beauties only by your stains,

Spin all your cobwebs o'er the eye of day !
The Muse's wing shall brush them all away :
All his Grace preaches, all his Lordship sings,   224
All that makes Saints of Queens, and Gods of Kings,
All, all but truth, drops dead-born from the press,
Like the last Gazette, or the last Address.

When black ambition stains a public cause,
A monarch's sword when mad vain-glory draws,
Not Waller's wreath can hide the nation's scar,   230
Nor Boileau turn the feather to a star.
Not so, when diadem'd with rays divine,
Touched with the flame that breaks from virtue's shrine,
Her priestess muse forbids the good to die,
And opes the Temple of Eternity.   235
There, other trophies deck the truly brave,
Than such as Anstis casts into the grave ;
Far other stars than   *   and   *   *   wear,
And may descend to Mordington from Stair :
(Such as on Hough's unsullied mitre shine,   240
Or beam, good Digby, from a heart like thine)
Let Envy howl, while Heaven's whole chorus sings,
And bark at honour not conferred by kings ;
Let Flatt'ry sick'ning see the incense rise,
Sweet to the world, and grateful to the skies :   245
Truth guards the poet, sanctifies the line,
And makes immortal, verse as mean as mine.

Yes, the last pen for freedom let me draw,
When truth stands trembling on the edge of law ;

Not Waller's wreath.—His *Panegyric on the Protector*.
Nor Boileau turn.—See his Ode on Namur, where (to use his own words), " il a fait un astre de la plume blanche que le roi porte ordinairement à son chapeau, et qui est en effet une espèce de comète, fatale à nos ennemis."—POPE.
Anstis.—The chief herald at arms. It is the custom, at the funeral of great peers, to cast into the grave the broken staves and ensigns of honour.—POPE.
Far other stars.—The asterisks were put for *George* (the King), and *Frederick* (the Prince of Wales).
To Mordington.—Lord Mordington kept a gaming house.
Such as on Hough's.—Hough was Bishop of Worcester. " Good Digby " was one of Pope's friends, Edward, Lord Digby (died 1737).

Here, last of Britons ! let your names be read ;   250
Are none, none living ? let me praise the dead,
And for that cause which made your fathers shine,
Fall by the votes of their degen'rate line.

    F.   Alas ! aias ! pray end what you began,
And write next winter more *Essays on Man.*   255

THE DUNCIAD
IN FOUR BOOKS

THE DUNCIAD

PREFACE

Prefixed to the five first imperfect Editions of the
DUNCIAD, in three books, printed at DUBLIN and
LONDON, in octavo and duodecimo, 1727.

THE PUBLISHER TO THE READER

IT will be found a true observation, though somewhat
surprising, that when any scandal is vented against a
man of the highest distinction and character, either in
the state or in literature, the public in general afford it a
most quiet reception ; and the larger part accept it as
favourably as if it were some kindness done to themselves : whereas if a known scoundrel or blockhead but
chance to be touched upon, a whole legion is up in arms,

The Publisher.—Who he was is uncertain ; but Edward Ward tells
us, in his preface to *Durgen*, " that most judges are of opinion this
preface is not of English extraction, but Hibernian," etc. He means
it was written by Dr. Swift, who, whether publisher or not, may be
said in a sort to be author of the poem. For when he, together with
Mr. Pope (for reasons specified in the preface to their *Miscellanies*)
determined to own the most trifling pieces in which they had any hand,
and to destroy all that remained in their power ; the first sketch of this
poem was snatched from the fire by Dr. Swift, who persuaded his
friend to proceed in it, and to him it was therefore inscribed. But
the occasion of printing it was as follows :

There was published in those *Miscellanies* a treatise of the *Bathos,
or Art of Sinking in Poetry*, in which was a chapter, where the species
of bad writers were ranged in classes, and initial letters of names
prefixed, for the most part at random. But such was the Number of
Poets eminent in that art, that some one or other took every letter
to himself. All fell into so violent a fury, that for half a year, or more,
the common Newspapers (in most of which they had some property, as
being hired writers) were filled with the most abusive falsehoods and
scurrilities they could possibly devise ; a liberty no ways to be wondered at in those people, and in those papers, that for many years,
during the uncontrolled Licence of the press, had aspersed almost

and it becomes the common cause of all scribblers, book-sellers, and printers whatsoever.

Not to search too deeply into the reason hereof, I will only observe as a fact, that every week for these two months past, the town has been persecuted with pamphlets, advertisements, letters, and weekly essays, not only against the wit and writings, but against the character and person of Mr. Pope. And that of all those men who have received pleasure from his works, which by modest computation may be about a hundred thousand in these kingdoms of England and Ireland ; (not to mention Jersey, Guernsey, the Orcades, those in the new world and foreigners, who have translated him into their languages) of all this number not a man hath stood up to say one word in his defence.

The only exception is the author of the following poem, who doubtless had either a better insight into the grounds of this clamour, or a better opinion of Mr.

all the great characters of the age ; and this with impunity, their own persons and names being utterly secret and obscure. This gave Mr. Pope the thought, that he had now some opportunity of doing good, by detecting and dragging into light these common Enemies of mankind ; since to invalidate this universal slander, it sufficed to shew what contemptible men were the authors of it. He was not without hopes, that by manifesting the dulness of those who had only malice to recommend them ; either the booksellers would not find their account in employing them, or the men themselves, when discovered, want courage to proceed in so unlawful an occupation. This it was that gave birth to the Dunciad ; and he thought it an happiness, that, by the late flood of slander on himself, he had acquired such a peculiar right over their Names as was necessary to his design.

About a hundred thousand.—It is surprising with what stupidity this preface, which is almost a continued irony, was taken by those authors. All such passages as these were understood by Curl, Cook, Cibber, and others, to be serious. Hear the Laureate (Letter to Mr. Pope, p. 9) : " Though I grant the Dunciad a better poem of its kind than ever was writ ; yet, when I read it with those *vain-glorious* encumbrances of Notes and Remarks upon it, etc., it is amazing, that you, who have writ with such masterly spirit upon the ruling Passion, should be so blind a slave to your own, as not to see how far *a low avarice of Praise*," etc. (taking it for granted that the notes of Scriblerus and others were the author's own).

The author of the following poem, etc.—A very plain irony, speaking of Mr. Pope himself.

Pope's integrity, joined with a greater personal love for him, than any other of his numerous friends and admirers.

Farther, that he was in his peculiar intimacy, appears from the knowledge he manifests of the most private authors of all the anonymous pieces against him, and from his having in this poem attacked no man living, who had not before printed, or published, some scandal against this gentleman.

How I came possest of it, is no concern to the reader ; but it would have been a wrong to him had I detained the publication ; since those names which are its chief ornaments die off daily so fast, as must render it too soon unintelligible. If it provoke the author to give us a more perfect edition, I have my end.

Who he is I cannot say, and (which is a great pity) there is certainly nothing in his style and manner of writing, which can distinguish or discover him : For if it bears any resemblance to that of Mr. Pope, 'tis not improbable but it might be done on purpose, with a view to have it pass for his. But by the frequency of his allusions to Virgil, and a laboured (not to say affected) *shortness* in imitation of him, I should think him more an admirer of the Roman poet than of the Grecian, and in that not of the same taste with his friend.

I have been well informed, that this work was the labour of full six years of his life, and that he wholly retired himself from all the avocations and pleasures of the world, to attend diligently to its correction and

---

Attacked no man living.—The publisher in these words went a little too far ; but it is certain, whatever names the reader finds that are unknown to him, are of such ; and the exception is only of two or three, whose dulness, impudent scurrility, or self-conceit, all mankind agreed to have justly entitled them to a place in the Dunciad.

There is certainly nothing in his style, etc.—This irony had small effect in concealing the author. The Dunciad, imperfect as it was, had not been published two days, but the whole Town gave it to Mr. Pope.

The labour of full six years, etc.—This was also honestly and seriously believed by divers gentlemen of the Dunciad.

perfection ; and six years more he intended to bestow upon it, as it should seem by this verse of Statius, which was cited at the head of his manuscript,

Oh mihi bissenos multum vigilata per annos,
Duncia !

Hence also we learn the true title of the poem ; which with the same certainty as we call that of Homer the Iliad, of Virgil the Æneid, of Camoens the Lusiad, we may pronounce, could have been, and can be no other than

The DUNCIAD.

It is styled *Heroic*, as being *doubly* so ; not only with respect to its nature, which, according to the best rules of the ancients, and strictest ideas of the moderns, is critically such ; but also with regard to the heroical disposition and high courage of the writer, who dared to stir up such a formidable, irritable, and implacable race of mortals.

There may arise some obscurity in chronology from the *Names* in the poem, by the inevitable removal of some authors, and insertion of others, in their niches. For whoever will consider the unity of the whole design will be sensible, that the *poem was not made for these authors, but these authors for the poem.* I should judge that they were clapped in as they rose, fresh and fresh, and changed from day to day ; in like manner as when the old boughs wither, we thrust new ones into a chimney.

I would not have the reader too much troubled or anxious, if he cannot decipher them ; since when he shall have found them out, he will probably know no more of the persons than before.

Yet we judged it better to preserve them as they are, than to change them for fictitious names ; by which the satire would only be multiplied, and applied to many instead of one. Had the hero, for instance, been called Codrus, how many would have affirmed him to have been Mr. T., Mr. E., Sir R. B., etc., but now all that unjust scandal is saved by calling him by a name, which by good luck happens to be that of a real person.

ADVERTISEMENT

To the FIRST EDITION with Notes, in Quarto, 1729

IT will be sufficient to say of this edition, that the reader has here a much more correct and complete copy of the DUNCIAD, than has hitherto appeared. I cannot answer but some mistakes may have slipt into it ; but a vast number of others will be prevented by the names being now not only set at length, but justified by the authorities and reasons given. I make no doubt, the author's own motive to use real rather than feigned names, was his care to preserve the innocent from any false application ; whereas in the former editions, which had no more than the initial letters, he was made, by keys printed here, to hurt the inoffensive ; and (what was worse) to abuse his friends, by an impression at Dublin.

The commentary which attends this poem was sent me from several hands, and consequently must be unequally written ; yet will have one advantage over most commentaries, that it is not made upon conjectures, or at a remote distance of time : And the reader cannot but derive one pleasure from the very *Obscurity* of the persons it treats of, that it partakes of the nature of a *Secret*, which most people love to be let into, though the men or the things be ever so inconsiderable or trivial.

Of the *Persons* it was judged proper to give some account : For since it is only in this monument that they must expect to survive (and here survive they will, as long as the English tongue shall remain such as it was in the reigns of Queen ANNE and King GEORGE) it seemed but humanity to bestow a word or two upon each, just to tell what he was, what he writ, when he lived, and when he died.

If a word or two more are added upon the chief offenders, 'tis only as a paper pinned upon the breast, to mark the enormities for which they suffered ; lest the correction only should be remembered, and the crime forgotten.

In some articles it was thought sufficient, barely to transcribe from Jacob, Curl, and other writers of their own rank, who were much better acquainted with them than any of the authors of this comment can pretend to be. Most of them had drawn each other's characters on certain occasions ; but the few here inserted are all that could be saved from the general destruction of such works.

Of the part of Scriblerus I need say nothing ; his manner is well enough known, and approved by all but those who are too much concerned to be judges.

The Imitations of the Ancients are added, to gratify those who either never read, or may have forgotten them ; together with some of the parodies and allusions to the most excellent of the Moderns. If, from the frequency of the former, any man think the poem too much a Cento, our Poet will but appear to have done the same thing in jest which Boileau did in earnest ; and upon which Vida, Fracastorius, and many of the most eminent Latin poets, professedly valued themselves.

A LETTER TO THE PUBLISHER

OCCASIONED BY THE

FIRST CORRECT EDITION OF THE DUNCIAD

IT is with pleasure I hear, that you have procured a correct copy of the DUNCIAD, which the many surreptitious ones have rendered so necessary ; and it is yet with more, that I am informed it will be attended with a COMMENTARY : a Work so requisite, that I cannot think the Author himself would have omitted it, had he approved of the first appearance of this Poem.

Such *Notes* as have occurred to me, I herewith send you : you will oblige me by inserting them amongst those which are, or will be, transmitted to you by others ; since not only the Author's friends, but even strangers, appear engaged by humanity, to take some care of an Orphan of so much genius and spirit, which its parent seems to have abandoned from the very beginning, and suffered to step into the world naked, unguarded, and unattended.

It was upon reading some of the abusive papers lately published, that my great regard to a Person, whose Friendship I esteem as one of the chief honours of my life, and a much greater respect to Truth, than to him or any man living, engaged me in inquiries, of which the enclosed *Notes* are the fruit.

I perceived, that most of these authors had been (doubtless very wisely) the first aggressors. They had tried, 'til they were weary, what was to be got by railing at each other : Nobody was either concerned or surprised, if this or that scribbler was proved a dunce. But every one was curious to read what could be said to prove Mr. Pope one, and was ready to pay something for such a discovery : A stratagem, which would they fairly own, it might not only reconcile them to me, but screen them from the resentment of their lawful Superiors, whom they daily abuse, only (as I charitably hope) to get that *by* them, which they cannot get *from* them.

I found this was not all : Ill success in that had transported them to Personal abuse, either of himself, or (what I think he could less forgive) of his Friends. They had called Men of virtue and honour bad Men, long before he had either leisure or inclination to call them bad Writers : and some had been such old offenders, that he had quite forgotten their persons as well as their slanders, 'til they were pleased to revive them.

Now what had Mr. Pope done before to incense them ?

9*a*

He had published those works which are in the hands of everybody, in which not the least mention is made of any of them. And what has he done since? He has laughed, and written the DUNCIAD. What has that said of them? A very serious truth, which the public had said before, that they were dull: and what it had no sooner said, but they themselves were at great pains to procure or even purchase room in the prints, to testify under their hands to the truth of it.

I should still have been silent, if either I had seen any inclination in my friend to be serious with such accusers, or if they had only meddled with his Writings; since whoever publishes, puts himself on his trial by his Country. But when his Moral character was attacked, and in a manner from which neither truth nor virtue can secure the most innocent,—in a manner, which, though it annihilates the credit of the accusation with the just and impartial, yet aggravates very much the guilt of the accusers; I mean by Authors *without names*: then I thought, since the danger was common to all, the concern ought to be so; and that it was an act of justice to detect the Authors, not only on this account, but as many of them are the same who for several years past have made free with the greatest names in Church and State, exposed to the world the private misfortunes of Families, abused all, even to Women, and whose prostituted papers (for one or other party, in the unhappy divisions of their Country) have insulted the Fallen, the Friendless, the Exiled, and the Dead.

Besides this, which I take to be a public concern, I have already confessed I had a private one. I am one of that number who have long loved and esteemed Mr. POPE; and had often declared it was not his capacity or writings (which we ever thought the least valuable part of his character), but the honest, open, and beneficent man, that we most esteemed, and loved in him. Now, if what these people say were believed, I must appear to all my friends either a fool, or a knave; either imposed on myself, or imposing on them ; so that I am as much interested in the confutation of these calumnies, as he is himself.

I am no Author, and consequently not to be suspected either of jealousy or resentment against any of the Men, of whom scarce one is known to me by sight ; and as for their Writings, I have sought them (on this one occasion) in vain, in the closets and libraries of all my acquaintance. I had still been in the dark, if a Gentleman had not procured me (I suppose from some of themselves, for they are generally much more dangerous friends than enemies) the passages I send you. I solemnly protest I have added nothing to the malice or absurdity of them ; which it behoves me to declare, since the vouchers themselves will be so soon and so irrecoverably lost. You may in some measure prevent it, by preserving at least their Titles, and discovering (as far as you can depend on the truth of your information) the Names of the concealed authors.

The first objection I have heard made to the Poem is, that the persons are too *obscure* for satire. The persons themselves, rather than allow the objection, would forgive the satire ; and if one could be tempted to afford it a serious answer, were not all assassinates, popular insurrections, the insolence of the rabble without doors, and of domestics within, most wrongfully chastised, if the Meanness of offenders indemnified them from punishment ? On the contrary, Obscurity renders them more dangerous, as less thought of ; Law can pronounce judgment only on open facts ; Morality alone can pass censure on intentions of mischief ; so that for secret calumny, or the arrow flying in the dark, there is no public punishment left, but what a good Writer inflicts.

The next objection is, that these sort of authors are *poor*. That might be pleaded as an excuse at the Old Bailey, for lesser crimes than Defamation (for 'tis the

Titles.—Which we have done in a List printed in the Appendix.

case of almost all who are tried there) ; but sure it can be none : for who will pretend that the robbing another of his Reputation supplies the want of it in himself? I question not but such authors are poor, and heartily wish the objection were removed by any honest livelihood.　But Poverty is here the accident, not the subject : He who describes Malice and Villainy to be pale and meagre, expresses not the least anger against Paleness or Leanness, but against Malice and Villainy.　The Apothecary in *Romeo and Juliet* is poor ; but is he therefore justified in vending poison ?　Not but Poverty itself becomes a just subject of satire, when it is the consequence of vice, prodigality, or neglect of one's lawful calling ; for then it increases the public burden, fills the streets and highways with Robbers, and the garrets with Clippers, Coiners, and Weekly Journalists.

But admitting that two or three of these offend less in their morals, than in their writings : must Poverty make nonsense sacred ?　If so, the fame of bad authors would be much better consulted than that of all the good ones in the world ; and not one of an hundred had ever been called by his right name.

They mistake the whole matter : It is not charity to encourage them in the way they follow, but to get them out of it : for men are not bunglers because they are poor, but they are poor because they are bunglers.

Is it not pleasant enough to hear our authors crying out on the one hand, as if their persons and characters were too sacred for Satire ; and the public objection on the other, that they are too mean even for Ridicule ? But whether Bread or Fame be their end, it must be allowed, our Author, by and in this Poem, has mercifully given them a little of both.

There are two or three, who by their rank and fortune have no benefit from the former objections, supposing them good, and these I was sorry to see in such company. But if, without any provocation, two or three Gentlemen will fall upon one, in an affair wherein his interest and reputation are equally embarked ; they cannot certainly, after they have been content to print themselves his enemies, complain of being put into the number of them.

Others, I am told, pretend to have been once his Friends. Surely they are their enemies who say so, since nothing can be more odious than to treat a friend as they have done. But of this I cannot persuade myself, when I consider the constant and eternal aversion of all bad writers to a good one.

Such as claim a merit from being his Admirers I would gladly ask, if it lays him under a personal obligation ? At that rate he would be the most obliged humble servant in the world. I dare swear for these in particular he never desired them to be his admirers, nor promised in return to be theirs. That had truly been a sign he was of their acquaintance ; but would not the malicious world have suspected such an approbation of some motive worse than ignorance, in the author of the *Essay on Criticism ?* Be it as it will, the reasons of their Admiration and of his Contempt are equally subsisting ; for his works and theirs are the very same that they were.

One, therefore, of their assertions, I believe may be true : " That he has a contempt for their writings." And there is another, which would probably be sooner allowed by himself than by any good judge beside : " That his own have found too much success with the public." But as it cannot consist with his modesty to claim this as a justice, it lies not on him, but entirely on the public, to defend its own judgment.

There remains what in my opinion might seem a better plea for these people than any they have made use of. If Obscurity or Poverty were to exempt a man from satire, much more should Folly or Dulness, which are still more involuntary ; nay, as much so as personal Deformity. But even this will not help them ; De-

formity becomes an object of Ridicule when a man sets
up for being handsome ; and so must Dulness when he
sets up for a Wit. They are not ridiculed, because
Ridicule in itself is, or ought to be, a pleasure ; but
because it is just to undeceive and vindicate the honest
and unpretending part of mankind from imposition ;
because particular interest ought to yield to general, and
a great number, who are not naturally Fools, ought
never to be made so, in complaisance to a few who are.
Accordingly we find that in all ages, all vain pretenders, were they ever so poor or ever so dull, have
been constantly the topics of the most candid
satirists, from the Codrus of JUVENAL to the Damon
of BOILEAU.

Having mentioned BOILEAU, the greatest Poet and
most judicious Critic of his age and country, admirable
for his Talents, and yet perhaps more admirable for his
Judgment in the proper application of them ; I cannot
help remarking the resemblance betwixt him and our
Author, in Qualities, Fame, and Fortune ; in the dis-
tinctions shewn them by their Superiors, in the general
esteem of their Equals, and in their extended reputation
amongst Foreigners ; in the latter of which ours has
met with the better fate, as he has had for his Translators persons of the most eminent rank and abilities
in their respective nations. But the resemblance holds
in nothing more, than in their being equally abused by
the ignorant pretenders to Poetry of their times ; of
which not the least memory will remain but in their own
Writings, and in the Notes made upon them. What
BOILEAU has done in almost all his poems, our Author
has only in this : I dare answer for him he will do it in
no more ; and on this principle of attacking few but
who had slandered him, he could not have done it at all,
·had he been confined from censuring obscure and worthless persons, for scarce any other were his enemies. However, as the parity is so remarkable, I hope it will continue to the last ; and if ever he shall give us an edition

of this Poem himself, I may see some of them treated as gently, on their repentance or better merit, as Perrault and Quinault were at last by BOILEAU.

In one point I must be allowed to think the character of our English Poet the more amiable. He has not been a follower of Fortune or Success ; he has lived with the Great without flattery ; been a friend to Men in power without pensions ; from whom, as he asked, so he received no favour, but what was done Him in his Friends. As his Satires were the more just for being delayed, so were his Panegyrics ; bestowed only on such persons as he had familiarly known, only for such virtues as he had long observed in them, and only at such times as others cease to praise, if not begin to calumniate them,— I mean when out of power or out of fashion. A satire, therefore, on writers so notorious for the contrary practice, became no man so well as himself ; as none, it is plain, was so little in their friendships, or so much in that of those whom they had most abused, namely the Greatest and Best of all Parties. Let me add a further reason, that, though engaged in their Friendships, he never espoused their Animosities ; and can almost singly challenge this honour, not to have written a line of any man, which, through Guilt, through Shame, or through Fear, through variety of Fortune, or change of Interest, he was ever unwilling to own.

I shall conclude with remarking what a pleasure it must be to every reader of Humanity, to see all along, that our Author in his very laughter is not indulging his own ill-nature, but only punishing that of others. As to his Poem, those alone are capable of doing it justice, who, to use the words of a great writer, know how hard it is (with regard both to his subject and his manner)

Out of fashion.—As Mr. Wycherley, at the time the Town declaimed against his book of Poems ; Mr. Walsh, after his death ; Sir William Trumbull, when he had resigned the office of Secretary of State ; Lord Bolingbroke, at his leaving England after the Queen's death ; Lord Oxford, in his last decline of life ; Mr. Secretary Craggs, at the end of the South Sea year, and after his death : others only in Epitaphs.

VETUSTIS DARE NOVITATEM, OBSOLETIS NITOREM, OB-
SCURIS LUCEM, FASTIDITIS GRATIAM.—I am

ST. JAMES'S,   Your most humble servant,
Dec. 22, 1728.   WILLIAM CLELAND.

ADVERTISEMENT

To the First Edition of the Fourth Book of the
DUNCIAD, when printed separately in the Year
1742.

WE apprehend it can be deemed no injury to the author
of the three first books of the Dunciad, that we publish
this Fourth. It was found merely by accident, in taking
a survey of the *Library* of a late eminent nobleman ; but
in so blotted a condition, and in so many detached pieces,
as plainly shewed it not only to be *incorrect*, but *unfinished*. That the author of the three first books had
a design to extend and complete his poem in this manner,
appears from the dissertation prefixed to it, where it is
said, that *the design is more extensive, and that we may
expect other episodes to complete it :* and from the declaration in the argument to the third book, that *the accomplishment of the prophecies therein, would be the theme
hereafter of a greater Dunciad.* But whether or no he
be the author of this, we declare ourselves ignorant.
If he be, we are no more to be blamed for the publication
of it, than Tucca and Varius for that of the last six books
of the Æneid, though perhaps inferior to the former.

William Cleland.—This Gentleman was of Scotland, and bred at
the University of Utrecht, with the Earl of Mar. He served in Spain
under Earl Rivers. After the Peace, he was made one of the Com-
missioners of the Customs in Scotland, and then of Taxes in England,
in which having shewn himself for twenty years diligent, punctual,
and incorruptible, though without any other assistance of Fortune,
he was suddenly displaced by the Minister in the sixty-eighth year
of his age ; and died two months after, in 1741. He was a person
of Universal Learning, and an enlarged Conversation ; no man had a
warmer heart for his Friend, or a sincerer attachment to the Constitution of his Country. And yet for all this, the Public will not
allow him to be the author of this Letter.

If any person be possessed of a more perfect copy of
this work, or of any other fragments of it, and will com-
municate them to the publisher, we shall make the next
edition more complete : In which we also promise to
insert any *Criticisms* that shall be published (if at all to
the purpose) with the *Names* of the *Authors ;* or any
letters sent us (though not to the purpose) shall yet be
printed under the title of *Epistolæ Obscurorum Virorum ;*
which, together with some others of the same kind
formerly laid by for that end, may make no unpleasant
addition to the future impressions of this poem.

MARTINUS SCRIBLERUS
Of the POEM

THIS poem, as it celebrateth the most grave and ancient
of things, Chaos, Night, and Dulness : so is it of the most
grave and ancient kind. Homer (saith Aristotle) was
the first who gave the *Form*, and (saith Horace) who
adapted the *Measure*, to heroic poesy. But, even before
this, may be rationally presumed from what the Ancients
have left written, was a piece by Homer composed, of
like nature and matter with this of our poet. For of
Epic sort it appeareth to have been, yet of matter surely
not unpleasant, witness what is reported of it by the
learned archbishop Eustathius, in Odyss. x. And accordingly Aristotle, in his Poetic, chap. iv., doth further
set forth, that as the Iliad and Odyssey gave example
to Tragedy, so did this poem to Comedy its first idea.

From these authors also it should seem, that the Hero,
or chief personage of it, was no less *obscure*, and his understanding and sentiments no less quaint and strange (if
indeed not more so) than any of the actors of our poem.
MARGITES was the name of this personage, whom Antiquity recordeth to have been *Dunce the first ;* and
surely, from what we hear of him, not unworthy to
be the root of so spreading a tree, and so numerous a
posterity. The poem, therefore, celebrating him was

properly and absolutely a *Dunciad ;* which though now unhappily lost, yet is its nature sufficiently known by the infallible tokens aforesaid. And thus it doth appear, that the first Dunciad was the first Epic poem, written by Homer himself, and anterior even to the Iliad or Odyssey.

Now, forasmuch as our poet had translated those two famous works of Homer which are yet left, he did conceive it in some sort his duty to imitate that also which was lost : and was therefore induced to bestow on it the same form which Homer's is reported to have had, namely that of Epic poem : with a title also framed after the ancient Greek manner, to wit, that of *Dunciad.*

Wonderful it is, that so few of the moderns have been stimulated to attempt some Dunciad ! since, in the opinion of the multitude, it might cost less pain and oil than an imitation of the greater Epic. But possible it is also, that, on due reflection, the maker might find it easier to paint a Charlemagne, a Brute, or a Godfrey, with just pomp and dignity heroic, than a Margites, a Codrus, or a Flecknoe.

We shall next declare the occasion and the cause which moved our poet to this particular work. He lived in those days, when (after providence had permitted the invention of Printing as a scourge for the sins of the learned) Paper also became so cheap, and Printers so numerous, that a deluge of Authors covered the land : Whereby, not only the peace of the honest unwriting subject was daily molested, but unmerciful demands were made of his applause, yea of his money, by such as would neither earn the one, nor deserve the other. At the same time, the licence of the Press was such, that it grew dangerous to refuse them either ; for they would forthwith publish slanders unpunished, the authors being anonymous, and skulking under the wings of Publishers, a set of men who never scrupled to vend either Calumny or Blasphemy, as long as the Town would call for it.

Now our author, living in those times, did conceive it

an endeavour well worthy an honest Satirist, to dissuade the dull, and punish the wicked, *the only way that was left.* In that public-spirited view he laid the plan of his Poem, as the greatest service he was capable (without much hurt, or being slain) to render his dear country. First, taking things from their original, he considereth the Causes creative of such Authors, namely *Dulness* and *Poverty ;* the one born with them, the other contracted by neglect of their proper talents, through self-conceit of greater abilities. This truth he wrappeth in an *Allegory* (as the construction of Epic poesy requireth) and feigns that one of these Goddesses had taken up her abode with the other, and that they jointly inspired all such writers and such works. He proceedeth to shew the *qualities* they bestow on these authors, and the *effects* they produce : then the *materials*, or *stock* with which they furnish them ; and (above all) that *self-opinion* which causeth it to seem to themselves vastly greater than it is, and is the prime motive of their setting up in this sad and sorry merchandise. The great power of these Goddesses acting in alliance (whereof as the one is the mother of Industry, so is the other of Plodding), was to be exemplified in some *one, great* and *remarkable Action :* and none could be more so than that which our poet hath chosen, viz. the restoration of the reign of Chaos and Night, by the ministry of Dulness their Daughter, in the removal of her imperial seat from the City to the polite World ; as the Action of the Æneid is the restoration of the empire of Troy, by the removal of the race from thence to Latium. But as Homer singing only the *Wrath* of Achilles, yet includes in his poem the whole history of the Trojan war ; in like manner our author hath drawn into this *single Action* the whole history of Dulness and her children.

A *Person* must next be fixed upon to support this Action. This *Phantom* in the poet's mind must have a *Name :* He finds it to be ――― ; and he becomes of course the Hero of the Poem.

The *Fable* being thus, according to the best Example, one and entire, as contained in the Proposition ; the *Machinery* is a continued chain of Allegories, setting forth the whole Power, Ministry, and Empire of Dulness, extended through her subordinate instruments, in all her various operations.

This is branched into *Episodes*, each of which hath its Moral apart, though all conducive to the main end.   The Crowd assembled in the second book demonstrates the design to be more extensive than to bad poets only, and that we may expect other Episodes of the Patrons, Encouragers, or Paymasters of such authors, as occasion shall bring them forth.   And the third book, if well considered, seemeth to embrace the whole World.   Each of the Games relateth to some or other vile class of writers : The first concerneth the Plagiary, to whom he giveth the name of Moore ;   the second, the libellous Novelist, whom he styleth Eliza ;   the third, the flattering Dedicator ;   the fourth, the bawling Critic, or noisy Poet ;   the fifth, the dark and dirty Party-writer ; and so of the rest ; assigning to each some *proper name* or other, such as he could find.

As for the *Characters*, the public hath already acknowledged how justly they are drawn : the manners are so depicted, and the sentiments so peculiar to those to whom applied, that surely to transfer them to any other or wiser personages would be exceeding difficult : and certain it is that every person concerned, being consulted apart, hath readily owned the resemblance of every portrait, his own excepted.   So Mr. Cibber calls them, " a parcel of *poor wretches*, so many *silly flies :* but adds, our Author's Wit is remarkably more bare and barren, whenever it would fall foul on *Cibber*, than upon any other Person whatever."

The *Descriptions* are singular, the *Comparisons* very quaint, the *Narration* various, yet of one colour : The purity and chastity of *Diction* is so preserved, that in the places most suspicious not the *words* but only the

images have been censured, and yet are those images no
other than have been sanctified by ancient and classical
Authority (though, as was the manner of those good
times, not so curiously wrapped up), yea, and commented
upon by the most grave Doctors, and approved
Critics.

As it beareth the name of *Epic*, it is thereby subjected
to such severe indispensable rules as are laid on all
Neoterics, a strict imitation of the Ancients ; insomuch
that any deviation, accompanied with whatever poetic
beauties, hath always been censured by the sound Critic.
How exact that Imitation hath been in this piece,
appeareth not only by its general structure, but by
particular allusions infinite, many whereof have escaped
both the commentator and poet himself ; yea divers by
his exceeding diligence are so altered and interwoven
with the rest, that several have already been, and more
will be, by the ignorant abused, as altogether and origin·
ally his own.

In a word, the whole poem proveth itself to be the
work of our Author, when his faculties were in full vigour
and perfection ; at that exact time when years have
ripened the Judgment, without diminishing the Imagination : which, by good Critics, is held to be punctually
at *forty*. For, at that season it was that Virgil finished
his Georgics ; and Sir Richard Blackmore, at the like
age composing his Arthurs, declared the same to be the
very *Acme* and pitch of life for Epic poesy : Though
since he hath altered it to *sixty*, the year in which he
published his Alfred. True it is, that the talents for
Criticism, namely, smartness, quick censure, vivacity
of remark, certainty of asseveration, indeed all but
acerbity, seem rather the gifts of Youth than of riper
Age. But it is far otherwise in *Poetry ;* witness the
works of Mr. Rymer and Mr. Dennis, who, beginning
with Criticism, became afterwards such Poets as no age
hath paralleled. With good reason therefore did our
author choose to write his Essay on that subject at

twenty, and reserve for his maturer years this great and
wonderful work of the Dunciad.

BY AUTHORITY

𝔅𝔶 virtue of the Authority in Us vested by the Act for
subjecting Poets to the power of a Licenser, we have revised
this Piece; where finding the style and appellation of
KING to have been given to a certain Pretender, Pseudo-
Poet, or Phantom, of the name of TIBBALD; and apprehending the same may be deemed in some sort a reflection
on Majesty, or at least an insult on that Legal Authority
which has bestowed on another Person the Crown of
Poesy: We have ordered the said Pretender, Pseudo-Poet,
or Phantom, utterly to vanish and evaporate out of this
work: And do declare the said Throne of Poesy from
henceforth to be abdicated and vacant, unless duly and
lawfully supplied by the LAUREATE himself.   And it is
hereby enacted, that no other Person do presume to fill
the same.   ƆC. Ch.

THE DUNCIAD

To Dr. Jonathan Swift

BOOK THE FIRST

ARGUMENT

The Proposition, the Invocation, and the Inscription. Then the Original of the great Empire of *Dulness*, and cause of the continuance thereof. The College of the *Goddess* in the City, with her private Academy for Poets in particular ; the Governors of it, and the four Cardinal Virtues. Then the Poem *hastes into the midst of things*, presenting her, on the evening of a Lord Mayor's day, revolving the long succession of her Sons, and the glories past and to come. She fixes her eye on *Bays* to be the Instrument of that great Event which is the Subject of the Poem. He is described pensive among his Books, giving up the Cause, and apprehending the Period of her Empire : After debating whether to betake himself to the Church, or to Gaming, or to Party-writing, he raises an Altar of proper books, and (making first his solemn prayer and declaration) purposes thereon to sacrifice all his unsuccessful writings. As the pile is kindled, the Goddess, beholding the flame from her seat, flies and puts it out, by casting upon it the poem of *Thule*. She forthwith reveals herself to him, transports him to her Temple, unfolds her Arts, and initiates him into her Mysteries ; then denouncing the death of *Eusden* the Poet Laureate, anoints him, carries him to Court, and proclaims him Successor.

The Mighty Mother, and her Son, who brings
The Smithfield Muses to the ear of Kings,
I sing. Say you, her instruments the Great !
Called to this work by Dulness, Jove, and Fate :
You by whose care, in vain decried and curst,   5

The Smithfield Muses.—*Smithfield* is the place where Bartholomew Fair was kept, whose shows, machines, and dramatical entertainments, formerly agreeable only to the taste of the Rabble, were, by the Hero of this poem and others of equal genius, brought to the Theatres of Covent Garden, Lincolns Inn Fields, and the Haymarket, to be the reigning pleasures of the Court and Town. This happened in the reigns of King George I. and II. See Book III.

By Dulness, Jove, and Fate.—That is, by their *Judgments*, their *Interests*, and their *Inclinations*.

Still Dunce the second reigns like Dunce the first ;
Say, how the Goddess bade Britannia sleep,
And poured her Spirit o'er the land and deep.
    In eldest time, ere mortals writ or read,
Ere Pallas issued from the Thund'rer's head,   10
Dulness o'er all possessed her ancient right,
Daughter of Chaos and eternal Night :
Fate in their dotage this fair Idiot gave,
Gross as her sire, and as her mother grave,
Laborious, heavy, busy, bold, and blind,   15
She ruled, in native Anarchy, the mind.
    Still her old Empire to restore she tries,
For, born a Goddess, Dulness never dies.
    O Thou ! whatever title please thine ear,
Dean, Drapier, Bickerstaff, or Gulliver !   20
Whether thou choose Cervantes' serious air,
Or laugh and shake in Rab'lais' easy chair,
Or praise the Court, or magnify Mankind,
Or thy grieved Country's copper chains unbind ;
From the Bœotia though her Power retires,   25
Mourn not, my SWIFT, at aught our Realm acquires.
Here pleased behold her mighty wings outspread
To hatch a new Saturnian age of Lead.

Drapier, Bickerstaff, or Gulliver.—The several names and characters he assumed in his ludicrous, his splenetic, or his party-writings ; which take in all his works.

Or praise the Court, or magnify Mankind.—*Ironicè*, alluding to *Gulliver's* representations of both.—The next line relates to the papers of the *Drapier* against the currency of *Wood's* copper coin in *Ireland*, which, upon the great discontent of the people, his Majesty was graciously pleased to recall.

Bœotia.—Bœotia of old lay under the raillery of the neighbouring wits, as Ireland does now ; though each of those nations produced one of the greatest wits and greatest generals of their age.

Mourn not, my Swift, at aught our Realm acquires.—*Ironicè iterum.* The Politics of *England* and *Ireland* were at this time by some thought to be opposite, or interfering with each other : Dr. *Swift* of course was in the interest of the latter, our Author of the former.

To hatch a new Saturnian age of Lead.—The ancient Golden Age is by Poets styled *Saturnian*, as being under the reign of Saturn ; but in the Chemical language *Saturn* is Lead. She is said here only to be spreading her wings to hatch this age ; which is not produced completely till the fourth book.

Close to those walls where Folly holds her throne.
And laughs to think Monroe would take her down,   30
Where o'er the gates, by his famed father's hand,
Great Cibber's brazen, brainless brothers stand ;
One Cell there is, concealed from vulgar eye,
The Cave of Poverty and Poetry.
Keen, hollow winds howl through the bleak recess,   35
Emblem of Music caused by Emptiness.
Hence Bards, like Proteus long in vain tied down,
Escape in Monsters, and amaze the town.
Hence Miscellanies spring, the weekly boast
Of Curl's chaste press, and Lintot's rubric post :   40
Hence hymning Tyburn's elegiac lines,
Hence Journals, Medleys, Merc'ries, MAGAZINES ;

Father's hand.—Mr. Caius Gabriel Cibber, father of the Poet
Laureate. The two Statues of the Lunatics over the gates of Bedlam
Hospital were done by him, and (as the son justly says of them) are no
ill monuments of his fame as an artist.

Poverty and Poetry.—I cannot here omit a remark that will greatly
endear our Author to every one, who shall attentively observe that
Humanity and Candour, which everywhere appear in him towards
those unhappy objects of the ridicule of all mankind, the bad Poets.
He here imputes all scandalous rhymes, scurrilous weekly papers,
base flatteries, wretched elegies, songs, and verses (even from those
sung at Court to ballads in the streets), not so much to malice or ser-
vility as to Dulness ; and not so much to Dulness as to Necessity.
And thus, at the very commencement of his Satire, makes an apology
for all that are to be satirized.

Curl's chaste press, and Lintot's rubric post.—Two Booksellers, of
whom see Book II. The former was fined by the Court of King's
Bench for publishing obscene books ; the latter usually adorned his
shop with titles in red letters.

Hence hymning Tyburn's elegiac lines.—It is an ancient English custom
for the Malefactors to sing a Psalm at their execution at Tyburn ; and no
less customary to print Elegies on their deaths, at the same time, or
before.

Magazines.—The common name of those upstart collections in prose
and verse ; in which, at some times,—
    —*new born nonsense first is taught to cry ;*
at others, dead-born Scandal has its monthly funeral, where Dulness
assumes all the various shapes of Folly to draw in and cajole the Rabble.
The eruption of every miserable Scribbler ; the scum of every dirty
Newspaper ; or Fragments of Fragments, picked up from every
Dunghill, under the title of *Papers, Essays, Reflections, Confutations,
Queries, Verses, Songs, Epigrams, Riddles, etc.*, equally the disgrace
of human Wit, Morality, Decency, and Common Sense.

Sepulchral Lies, our holy walls to grace,
And New-year Odes, and all the Grub-street race.
In clouded Majesty here Dulness shone ;   45
Four guardian Virtues, round, support her throne :
Fierce champion Fortitude, that knows no fears
Of hisses, blows, or want, or loss of ears :
Calm Temperance, whose blessings those partake
Who hunger, and who thirst for scribbling sake :   50
Prudence, whose glass presents th' approaching jail :
Poetic Justice, with her lifted scale,
Where, in nice balance, truth with gold she weighs,
And solid pudding against empty praise.
Here she beholds the Chaos dark and deep,   55
Where nameless Somethings in their causes sleep,
'Til genial Jacob, or a warm Third day,
Call forth each mass, a Poem, or a Play :
How hints, like spawn, scarce quick in embryo lie,
How new-born nonsense first is taught to cry,   60
Maggots half-formed in rhyme exactly meet,
And learn to crawl upon poetic feet.
Here one poor word an hundred clenches makes,
And ductile Dulness new mæanders takes ;
There motley images her fancy strike,   65

Sepulchral Lies.—Is a just satire on the Flatteries and Falsehoods
admitted to be inscribed on the walls of Churches, in Epitaphs.
New-year Odes.—Made by the Poet Laureate for the time being,
to be sung at Court on every New-year's day, the words of which are
happily drowned in the voices and instruments. The *New-year Odes*
of the Hero of this work were of a cast distinguished from all that pre-
ceded him, and made a conspicuous part of his character as a writer, which
doubtless induced our Author to mention them here so particularly.
Here one poor word an hundred clenches makes.—It may not be
amiss to give an instance or two of these operations of *Dulness* out of
the works of her Sons, celebrated in the Poem.   A great Critic formerly
held these clenches (puns) in such abhorrence that he declared, " he
that would pun, would pick a pocket."   Yet Mr. Dennis's works
afford us notable examples in this kind : " *Alexander Pope* hath sent
abroad into the world as many *Bulls* as his namesake Pope *Alexander.*
—Let us take the initial and final letters of his name, viz. *A . P*—*E*, and
they give you the idea of an *Ape.*—*Pope* comes from the Latin word
Popa, which signifies a little Watt ; or from *poppysma*, because he was
continually *popping* out squibs of wit, or rather *Popysmata*, or *Popisms.*"
—DENNIS on *Hom.* and *Daily Journal, June 11,* 1728.

Figures ill paired, and Similes unlike.
She sees a Mob of Metaphors advance,
Pleased with the madness of the mazy dance ;
How Tragedy and Comedy embrace ;
How Farce and Epic get a jumbled race ;   70
How Time himself stands still at her command,
Realms shift their place, and Ocean turns to land.
Here gay Description Egypt glads with showers,
Or gives to Zembla fruits, to Barca flowers ;
Glitt'ring with ice here hoary hills are seen,   75
There painted valleys of eternal green ;
In cold December fragrant chaplets blow,
And heavy harvests nod beneath the snow.
  All these and more the cloud-compelling Queen
Beholds through fogs, that magnify the scene.   80
She, tinselled o'er in robes of varying hues,
With self-applause her wild creation views ;
Sees momentary monsters rise and fall,
And with her own fools-colours gilds them all.
  'Twas on the day when * * rich and grave,   85
Like Cimon, triumphed both on land and wave :
(Pomps without guilt, of bloodless swords and maces,
Glad chains, warm furs, broad banners, and broad faces)
Now Night descending, the proud scene was o'er,
But lived in Settle's numbers one day more.   90

How Farce and Epic.—How Time himself, etc.—Allude to the trans-
gressions of the *Unities* in the Plays of such Poets. For the Miracles
wrought upon *Time* and *Place*, and the mixture of Tragedy and Comedy,
Farce and Epic, see Pluto and Proserpine, Penelope, etc., if yet extant.

Thorold, rich and grave.—Sir George Thorold, Lord Mayor of London
in the year 1720. The Procession of a Lord Mayor is made partly
by land, and partly by water.—Cimon, the famous Athenian General,
obtained a victory by sea, and another by land, on the same day, over
the Persians and Barbarians.

But lived in Settle's numbers one day more.—A beautiful manner of
speaking, usual with poets in praise of poetry. Settle was poet to the
City of London. His office was to compose yearly panegyrics upon
the Lord Mayors, and verses to be spoken in the pageants : But that
part of the shows being at length frugally abolished, the employment
of City-poet ceased ; so that upon Settle's demise there was no successor to that place.

Now May'rs and Shrieves all hushed and satiate
　　lay,
Yet ate, in dreams, the custard of the day ;
While pensive Poets painful vigils keep,
Sleepless themselves, to give their readers sleep.
Much to the mindful Queen the feast recalls　　95
What City Swans once sung within the walls ;
Much she revolves their arts, their ancient praise,
And sure succession down from Heywood's days.
She saw, with joy, the line immortal run,
Each sire imprest, and glaring in his son :　　100
So watchful Bruin forms, with plastic care,
Each growing lump, and brings it to a Bear.
She saw old Prynne in restless Daniel shine,
And Eusden eke out Blackmore's endless line ;
She saw slow Philips creep like Tate's poor page,　　105
And all the mighty Mad in Dennis rage.

Heywood's.—John Heywood, whose Interludes were printed in the time of Henry VIII.
　Old Prynne in restless Daniel.—The first edition had it,—
　　　She saw in Norton all his father shine :
a great mistake ! for Daniel De Foe had parts, but Norton De Foe was a wretched writer, and never attempted Poetry. Much more justly is Daniel himself made successor to W. Pryn, both of whom wrote Verses as well as Politics. And both these authors had a semblance in their fates as well as writings, having been alike sentenced to the Pillory.
　And Eusden eke out, etc.—Laurence Eusden, Poet Laureate [before Cibber]. Mr. Jacob gives a catalogue of some few only of his works, which were very numerous. Of Blackmore, see Book II. Of Philips, Book I. 262 and Book III. *prope fin.*
　Nahum Tate was Poet Laureate, a cold writer, of no invention ; but sometimes translated tolerably when befriended by Mr. Dryden. In his second part of Absalom and Achitophel are above two hundred admirable lines together of that great hand, which strongly shine through the insipidity of the rest. Something parallel may be observed of another author here mentioned.
　And all the mighty Mad.—This is by no means to be understood literally, as if Mr. Dennis were really mad, according to the Narrative of Dr. Norris in Swift and Pope's *Miscellanies.* No—it is spoken of that *Excellent* and *Divine Madness,* so often mentioned by Plato : that poetical rage and enthusiasm, with which Mr. D. hath, in his time, been highly possessed ; and of those *extraordinary hints and motions* whereof he himself so feelingly treats in his preface to the *Rem. on Pr. Arth.* Mr. John Dennis was the son of a Saddler in

In each she marks her Image full exprest,
But chief in BAYS's monster-breeding breast :
Bays, formed by nature Stage and Town to bless,
And act, and be, a Coxcomb with success.   110
Dulness, with transport eyes the lively Dunce,
Rememb'ring she herself was Pertness once.
Now (shame to Fortune !) an ill Run at Play
Blanked his bold visage. and a thin Third day :
Swearing and supperless the Hero sate,   115
Blasphemed his Gods, the Dice, and damned his Fate ;
Then gnawed his pen, then dashed it on the ground,
Sinking from thought to thought, a vast profound !
Plunged for his sense, but found no bottom there ;
Yet wrote and floundered on in mere despair.   120
Round him much Embryo, much Abortion lay,
Much future Ode, and abdicated Play ;
Nonsense precipitate, like running Lead,
That slipped through Cracks and Zig-zags of the
     Head ;

London born in 1657. He paid court to Mr. Dryden ; and having
obtained some correspondence with Mr. Wycherley and Mr. Congreve,
he immediately obliged the public with their Letters. He made
himself known to the Government by many admirable schemes and
projects ; which the Ministry, for reasons best known to themselves,
constantly kept private. For his character as a writer, it is given
us as follows : " Mr. Dennis is *excellent* at Pindaric writings, *perfectly
regular* in all his performances, and a person of *sound Learning.* That
he is master of a great deal of *Penetration* and *Judgment,* his criticisms
(particularly on *Prince Arthur*) do sufficiently demonstrate." From
the same account it also appears " that he writ Plays more to get
Reputation than *Money.*"—DENNIS of himself.

Bays, formed by nature, etc.—It is hoped the poet here hath done full
justice to his Hero's character, which it were a great mistake to imagine was wholly sunk in stupidity : he is allowed to have supported it
with a wonderful mixture of Vivacity. This character is heightened
according to his own desire, in a Letter he wrote to our author :
" Pert and dull at least you might have allowed me. What ! am I
only to be dull, and dull still, and again, and for ever." He then
solemnly appealed to his own conscience, " that he could not think
himself so, nor believe that our Poet did ; but that he spoke worse of
him than he could possibly think ; and concluded it must be merely
to show his *Wit,* or for some *Profit* or *Lucre* to himself."

Shame to Fortune.—Because she usually shews favour to persons
of this Character, who have a three-fold pretence to it.

All that on Folly Frenzy could beget,   125
Fruits of dull Heat, and Sooterkins of Wit,
Next, o'er his Books his eyes began to roll,
In pleasing memory of all he stole,
How here he sipped, how there he plundered snug,
And sucked all o'er, like an industrious Bug.   130
Here lay poor Fletcher's half-eat scenes, and here
The Frippery of crucified Moliere ;
There hapless Shakespear, yet of Tibbald sore,
Wished he had blotted for himself before.
The rest on Out-side merit but presume,   135
Or serve (like other Fools) to fill a room ·
Such with their shelves as due proportion hold,
Or their fond parents drest in red and gold ;
Or where the pictures for the page atone,
And Quarles is saved by Beauties not his own.   140

Poor Fletcher's half-eat scenes.—A great number of them taken out
to patch up his Plays.
   The Frippery.—"When I fitted up an old play, it was as a good housewife will mend old linen, when she has not better employment."
   Hapless Shakespear, etc.—It is not to be doubted but Bays was a
subscriber to Tibbald's Shakespear. He was frequently liberal this
way ; and, as he tells us, "subscribed to Mr. Pope's Homer, out of
pure Generosity and Civility : but when Mr. Pope did so to his Nonjuror, he concluded it could be nothing but a joke."
   This Tibbald, or Theobald, published an edition of Shakespear,
of which he was so proud himself as to say, in one of Mist's Journals,
June 8, "That to expose any Errors in it was impracticable." And
in another, April 27, "That whatever care might for the future be taken
by any other Editor, he would still give above five hundred emenda-
tions, that *shall* escape them all."
   Wished he had blotted.—It was a ridiculous praise which the Players
gave to Shakespear, "that he never blotted a line." Ben Jonson
honestly wished he had blotted a thousand ; and Shakespear would
certainly have wished the same, if he had lived to see those alterations
in his works, which, not the Actors only (and especially the daring Hero
of this poem) have made on the *Stage*, but the presumptuous Critics
of our days in their *Editions*.
   The rest on Out-side merit, etc.—This Library is divided into three
parts ; the first consists of those authors from whom he stole, and
whose works he mangled ; the second, of such as fitted the shelves,
or were gilded for show, or adorned with pictures ; the third class
our author calls solid learning, old Bodies of Divinity, old Commentaries, old English Printers, or old English Translations ; all very
voluminous, and fit to erect altars to Dulness.

Here swells the shelf with Ogilby the great ;
There, stamped with arms, Newcastle shines complete :
Here all his suff'ring brotherhood retire,
And 'scape the martyrdom of jakes and fire :
A Gothic Library ! of Greece and Rome   145
Well purged, and worthy Settle, Banks, and Broome.

But, high above, more solid Learning shone,
The Classics of an Age that heard of none ;
There Caxton slept, with Wynkyn at his side,
One clasped in wood, and one in strong cow-hide ;   150

Ogilby the great.—" John Ogilby was one, who, from a late initiation into literature, made such a progress as might well style him the prodigy of his time ! sending into the world so many large *Volumes !* His translations of Homer and Virgil done *to the life*, and *with such excellent sculptures :* And (what added great grace to his works) he printed them all on *special good paper*, and in a *very good letter*."—*Winstanly, Lives of Poets.*

There, stamped with arms, Newcastle shines complete.—" The *Duchess of Newcastle* was one who busied herself in the ravishing delights of Poetry ; leaving to posterity in print three *ample Volumes* of her studious endeavours."—*Winstanly,* ibid. Langbane reckons up *eight* Folios of her Grace's ; which were usually adorned with gilded covers, and had her coat of arms upon them.

Worthy Settle, Banks, and Broome.—The Poet has mentioned these three authors in particular, as they are parallel to our Hero in three capacities : 1. Settle was his brother Laureate : only indeed upon half-pay, for the City instead of the Court ; but equally famous for unintelligible flights in his poems on public occasions, such as Shows, Birth-days, etc. 2. Banks was his Rival in *Tragedy* (though more successful) in one of his Tragedies, the *Earl of Essex*, which is yet alive : *Anna Boleyn*, the *Queen of Scots*, and *Cyrus the Great*, are dead and gone. These he drest in a sort of *Beggar's Velvet*, or a happy Mixture of the thick Fustian and thin Prosaic ; exactly imitated in *Perolla and Isidora*, *Cæsar in Egypt*, and the *Heroic Daughter*. 3. Broome was a serving-man of Ben Jonson, who once picked up a *Comedy* from his Betters, or from some cast scenes of his Master, not entirely contemptible.

More solid Learning.—Some have objected, that books of this sort suit not so well the library of our Bays, which they imagine consisted of Novels, Plays, and obscene books ; but they are to consider, that he furnished his shelves only for ornament, and read these books no more than the *Dry Bodies of Divinity*, which, no doubt, were purchased by his father, when he designed him for the Gown.

Caxton.—A Printer in the time of Edward IV., Richard III., and Henry VII. ; Wynkyn de Word, his successor, in that of Henry VII. and VIII. The former translated into prose Virgil's Æneis, as a history ; of which he speaks, in his Proeme, in a very singular manner, as of a book hardly known.

There saved by spice, like mummies, many a year,
Dry Bodies of Divinity appear ;
De Lyra there a dreadful front extends,
And here the groaning shelves Philemon bends.

    Of these twelve volumes, twelve of amplest size,
Redeemed from tapers and defrauded pies,   156
Inspired he seizes ; these an altar raise ;
An hecatomb of pure unsullied lays
That altar crowns ; A folio Common-place
Founds the whole pile, of all his works the base ; 160
Quartos, octavos, shape the less'ning pyre ;
A twisted Birth-day Ode completes the spire.

    Then he : " Great Tamer of all human art !
First in my care, and ever at my heart ;
Dulness ! whose good old cause I yet defend,   165
With whom my Muse began, with whom shall end.
E'er since Sir Fopling's Periwig was Praise,
To the last honours of the Butt and Bays :
O thou ! of Business the directing soul !
To this our head like bias to the bowl,   170
Which, as more pond'rous, made its aim more true,
Obliquely waddling to the mark in view :
O ! ever gracious to perplexed mankind,
Still spread a healing mist before the mind ;
And, lest we err by Wit's wild dancing light,   175
Secure us kindly in our native night.
Or, if to Wit a coxcomb make pretence,

De Lyra.—Nich. de Lyra, or Harpsfield, a very voluminous commentator, whose works, in five vast folios, were printed in 1472.

Philemon.—Philemon Holland, Doctor in Physic. He translated *so many books*, that a man would think he had done *nothing else ;* insomuch that he might be called *Translator general of his age.* The books alone of his turning into English are sufficient to make a *Country Gentleman* a *complete Library.*

A twisted, etc.—In the former Edition :
       " And last, a little Ajax tips the spire."
A little Ajax, in *duodecimo,* translated from Sophocles by Tibbald.

E'er since Sir Fopling's Periwig.—The first visible cause of the passion of the Town for our Hero was a fair flaxen full-bottomed periwig, which, he tells us, he wore in his first play of the *Fool in fashion.* This remarkable Periwig usually made its entrance upon the stage in a sedan, brought in by two chairmen, with infinite approbation of the audience.

Guard the sure barrier between that and Sense ;
Or quite unravel all the reas'ning thread,
And hang some curious cobweb in its stead ! 180
As, forced from wind-guns, lead itself can fly,
And pond'rous slugs cut swiftly through the sky ;
As clocks to weight their nimble motion owe,
The wheels above urged by the load below :
Me Emptiness, and Dulness could inspire, 185
And were my Elasticity and Fire.
Some Dæmon stole my pen (forgive th' offence)
And once betrayed me into common sense :
Else all my Prose and Verse were much the same;
This prose on stilts, that poetry fallen lame. 190
Did on the stage my Fops appear confined ?
My life gave ampler lessons to mankind.
Did the dead letter unsuccessful prove ?
The brisk Example never failed to move.
Yet sure had Heaven decreed to save the State, 195
Heaven had decreed these works a longer date.
Could Troy be saved by any single hand,
This grey-goose weapon must have made her stand.
What can I now ? my Fletcher cast aside,
Take up the Bible, once my better guide ? 200
Or tread the path by vent'rous Heroes trod,
This Box my Thunder, this right hand my God ?
Or chaired at White's amidst the Doctors sit,

As, forced from wind-guns, etc.—The thought of these four verses is found in a poem of our Author's of a very early date (namely written at fourteen years old, and soon after printed) to the author of a poem called *Successio*.

My Fletcher.—A familiar manner of speaking, used by modern Critics, of a favourite author. Bays might as justly speak thus of Fletcher, as a French Wit did of Tully, seeing his works in his library, "Ah ! mon cher Ciceron ; je le connois bien ; c'est le même que Marc Tulle." But he had a better title to call Fletcher *his own*, having made so free with him.

Take up the Bible, once my better guide.—When, according to his Father's intention, he had been a *Clergyman*, or (as he thinks himself) a *Bishop* of the Church of England.

Amidst the Doctors sit.—Scriblerus comments thus : The Doctors in this place mean no more than *false Dice*, a Cant phrase used amongst Gamesters. So the meaning of these four sonorous lines is only this, " Shall I play fair or foul ? "

Teach Oaths to Gamesters, and to Nobles Wit ?
Or bidst thou rather Party to embrace ?   205
(A friend to Party thou, and all her race ;
'Tis the same rope at diff'rent ends they twist ;
To Dulness Ridpath is as dear as Mist.)
Shall I, like Curtius, desp'rate in my zeal,
O'er head and ears plunge for the Commonweal ?   210
Or rob Rome's ancient geese of all their glories,
And cackling save the Monarchy of Tories ?
Hold—to the Minister I more incline ;
To serve his cause, O Queen ! is serving thine.
And see ! thy very Gazetteers give o'er,   215
Even Ralph repents, and Henley writes no more.
What then remains ? Ourself. Still, still remain
Cibberian forehead, and Cibberian brain.
This brazen Brightness, to the 'Squire so dear ;
This polished Hardness, that reflects the Peer :   220
This arch Absurd, that wit and fool delights ;
This Mess, tossed up of Hockley-hole and White's ;
Where Dukes and Butchers join to wreathe my crown,
At once the Bear and Fiddle of the town.
    " O born in sin, and forth in folly brought !   225
Works damned, or to be damned ! (your father's fault)
Go, purified by flames ascend the sky,
My better and more Christian progeny !
Unstained, untouched, and yet in maiden sheets ;
While all your smutty sisters walk the streets.   230

Ridpath—Mist.—George Ridpath, author of a Whig paper, called the
Flying-post ; Nathaniel Mist, of a famous Tory Journal.
    Gazetteers.—A band of ministerial writers, who, on the very day their
patron quitted his post, laid down their paper, and declared they would
never more meddle in Politics.
    O born in sin, etc.—This is a tender and passionate Apostrophe to
his own works, which he is going to sacrifice agreeable to the nature of
man in great affliction ; and reflecting like a parent on the many
miserable fates to which they would otherwise be subject.
    My better and more Christian progeny.—" It may be observable, that
my muse and my spouse were equally prolific ; that the one was seldom
the mother of a Child, but in the same year the other made me father
of a Play. I think we had a dozen of each sort between us ; of both
which kinds some *died* in their *Infancy*," etc.—*Life of C. C.*

Ye shall not beg, like gratis-given Bland,
Sent with a Pass, and vagrant through the land ;
Not sail with Ward, to Ape-and-monkey climes,
Where vile Mundungus trucks for viler rhymes :
Not sulphur-tipt, emblaze an Ale-house fire ;   235
Not wrap up Oranges, to pelt your sire !
O ! pass more innocent, in infant state,
To the mild Limbo of our Father Tate :
Or peaceably forgot, at once be blest
In Shadwell's bosom with eternal Rest !   240
Soon to that mass of Nonsense to return,
Where things destroyed are swept to things unborn."

   With that, a Tear (portentous sign of Grace !)
Stole from the Master of the sevenfold Face ;
And thrice he lifted high the Birth-day brand,   245
And thrice he dropt it from his quiv'ring hand ;
Then lights the structure, with averted eyes :
The rolling smoke involves the sacrifice.
The opening clouds disclose each work by turns :
Now flames the Cid, and now Perolla burns ;   250
Great Cæsar roars, and hisses in the fires ;

  Gratis-given Bland, Sent with a Pass.—It was a practice so to give
the Daily Gazetteer and ministerial pamphlets (in which this B. was a
writer), and to send them *Post-free* to all the Towns in the kingdom.
Bland was the Provost of Eton.
  With Ward, to Ape-and-monkey climes.—" Edward Ward, a very
voluminous Poet in Hudibrastic verse, but best known by *The London
Spy*, in prose. He has of late years kept a public house in the City
(but in a genteel way), and with his wit, humour, and good liquor
(ale) afforded his guests a pleasurable entertainment, especially those
of the high-church party."—JACOB, *Lives of Poets*, vol. II. p. 225. Great
number of his works were yearly sold into the Plantations.—Ward, in a
book called *Apollo's Maggot*, declared this account to be a great falsity,
protesting that his public house was not in the *City*, but in *Moorfields*.
  Tate—Shadwell.—Two of his predecessors in the Laurel.
  Now flames the Cid, etc.—In the first notes on the Dunciad it was
said, that this Author was particularly excellent at Tragedy. " This
(says he) is as unjust as to say I could not dance on a Rope." But
certain it is that he had attempted to dance on this Rope, and fell
most shamefully, having produced no less than four Tragedies (the
names of which the Poet preserves in these few lines) : the three first
of them were fairly printed, acted, and damned ; the fourth suppressed, in fear of the like treatment.

King John in silence modestly expires;
No merit now the dear Nonjuror claims,
Moliere's old stubble in a moment flames.
Tears gushed again, as from pale Priam's eyes   255
When the last blaze sent Ilion to the skies.
   Roused by the light, old Dulness heaved the head,
Then snatched a sheet of Thule from her bed;
Sudden she flies, and whelms it o'er the pyre;
Down sink the flames, and with a hiss expire.   260
   Her ample presence fills up all the place;
A veil of fogs dilates her awful face:
Great in her charms! as when on Shrieves and May'rs
She looks, and breathes herself into their airs.
She bids him wait her to her sacred Dome: 265
Well pleased he entered, and confessed his home.
So Spirits ending their terrestrial race
Ascend, and recognize their Native Place.
This the Great Mother dearer held than all
The clubs of Quidnuncs, or her own Guildhall: 270
Here stood her Opium, here she nursed her Owls,
And here she planned th' Imperial seat of Fools.
   Here to her Chosen all her works she shews;
Prose swelled to verse, verse loit'ring into prose:

The dear Nonjuror—Moliere's old stubble.—A Comedy threshed out of Moliere's *Tartuffe*, and so much the Translator's favourite, that he assures us all our author's dislike to it could only arise from *disaffection to the Government.*

When the last blaze sent Ilion to the skies.—See Virgil, Æneid II., where *I.* would advise the reader to peruse the story of Troy's destruction, rather than in Wynkyn.—Scribl.

Thule.—An unfinished poem of that name, of which one sheet was printed many years ago, by Amb. Philips, a northern author. It is an usual method of putting out a fire, to cast wet sheets upon it. Some critics have been of opinion that this sheet was of the nature of the Asbestos, which cannot be consumed by fire: but I rather think it an allegorical allusion to the coldness and heaviness of the writing.

Sacred Dome.—Where he no sooner enters, but he reconnoitres the place of his original: as Plato says the spirits shall, at their entrance into the celestial regions.

Great Mother.—*Magna mater,* here applied to *Dulness.* The *Quidnuncs,* a name given to the ancient members of certain political clubs, who were constantly inquiring *quid nunc?* what news?

How random thoughts now meaning chance to find, 275
Now leave all memory of sense behind ;
How Prologues into Prefaces decay,
And these to Notes are frittered quite away :
How Index-learning turns no student pale,
Yet holds the eel of science by the tail :   280
How, with less reading than makes felons 'scape,
Less human genius than God gives an ape,
Small thanks to France, and none to Rome or Greece,
A vast, vamped, future, old, revived, new piece,
'Twixt Plautus, Fletcher, Shakespear, and Corneille, 285
Can make a Cibber, Tibbald, or Ozell.

 The Goddess then, o'er his anointed head,
With mystic words, the sacred Opium shed.
And lo ! her bird (a monster of a fowl,
Something betwixt a Heideggre and Owl)   290
Perched on his crown. " All hail ! and hail again,
My son : the promised land expects thy reign.
Know, Eusden thirsts no more for sack or praise ;
He sleeps among the dull of ancient days ;
Safe, where no Critics damn, no duns molest,   295
Where wretched Withers, Ward, and Gildon rest,

Tibbald.—Lewis Tibbald (as pronounced) or Theobald (as written)
was bred an Attorney, and son to an Attorney (says Mr. Jacob) of
Sittenburn in Kent. He was author of some forgotten Plays, Translations, and other pieces. He was concerned in a paper called the
Censor, and a Translation of Ovid.
 Ozell.—" Mr. John Ozell (if we credit Mr. Jacob) did go to school in
Leicestershire, where *somebody* left him *something* to live on, when he
shall retire from business. He was designed to be sent to Cambridge,
in order for priesthood ; but he chose rather to be placed in an *office
of accounts,* in the City, being qualified for the same by his skill in
arithmetic, and writing the necessary *hands.* He has obliged the world
with many translations of French Plays."—JACOB, *Lives of Dram.
Poets,* p. 198.
 A Heideggre.—A strange bird from Switzerland, and not (as some
have supposed) the name of an eminent person who was a man of
parts, and, as was said of Petronius, *Arbiter Elegantiarum.*
 Withers.—" George Withers was a great pretender to poetical zeal
against the vices of the times, and abused the greatest personages in
power, which brought upon him *frequent correction.* The Marshalsea
and Newgate were no strangers to him."—*Winstanley.*
 Gildon.—Charles Gildon, a writer of criticisms and libels of the last

And high-born Howard, more majestic sire,
With Fool of Quality completes the quire.
Thou, Cibber ! thou, his Laurel shalt support,
Folly, my son, has still a Friend at Court.   300
Lift up your Gates, ye Princes, see him come !
Sound, sound, ye Viols ; be the Cat-call dumb !
Bring, bring the madding Bay, the drunken Vine ;
The creeping, dirty, courtly Ivy join.
And thou ! his Aid-de-camp, lead on my sons,   305
Light-armed with Points, Antitheses, and Puns.
Let Bawdry, Billingsgate, my daughters dear,
Support his front, and Oaths bring up the rear :
And under his, and under Archer's wing,
Gaming and Grub-street skulk behind the King.   310
  " O ! when shall rise a Monarch all our own,
And I, a Nursing-mother, rock the throne ;
'Twixt Prince and People close the Curtain draw,
Shade him from Light, and cover him from Law ;
Fatten the Courtier, starve the learnèd band,   315
And suckle Armies, and dry-nurse the land :

age, bred at St. Omer's with the Jesuits ; but renouncing popery, he
published Blount's books against the divinity of Christ, the *Oracles
of Reason*, etc. He signalized himself as a critic, having written some
very bad plays ; abused Mr. P. very scandalously in an anonymous
pamphlet of the *Life of Mr. Wycherley*, printed by Curl ; in another
called the *New Rehearsal*, printed in 1714 ; in a third, entitled, the
Complete Art of English Poetry, in two volumes ; and others.
  Howard.—Hon. Edward Howard, author of the *British Princes*,
and a great number of wonderful pieces, celebrated by the late Earls
of Dorset and Rochester, Duke of Buckingham, Mr. Waller, etc.
  Under Archer's wing—Gaming, etc.—When the Statute against
Gaming was drawn up, it was represented, that the King, by ancient
custom, plays at Hazard one night in the year ; and therefore a clause
was inserted, with an exception as to that particular. Under this
pretence, the Groom-porter had a room appropriated to Gaming all
the summer the Court was at Kensington, which his Majesty acci-
dentally being acquainted of with a just indignation prohibited. It is
reported the same practice is yet continued wherever the Court resides,
and the Hazard Table there open to all the professed Gamesters in
town.
     " Greatest *and* justest Sov'reign ! *know you this ?
     Alas ! no more than* Thames' *calm* head *can know
     Whose meads his* arms *drown or whose* corn *o'erflow*."
                              Donne to Queen Eliz.

Till Senates nod to Lullabies divine,
And all be sleep, as at an Ode of thine."
  She ceased. Then swells the Chapel-royal throat:
" God save King Cibber ! " mounts in every note. 320
Familiar White's, " God save King Colley ! " cries ;
" God save King Colley ! " Drury-lane replies :
To Needham's quick the voice triumphal rode,
But pious Needham dropt the name of God ;
Back to the Devil the last echoes roll, 325
And " Coll ! " each Butcher roars at Hockley-hole.
  So when Jove's block descended from on high
(As sings thy great forefather Ogilby)
Loud thunder to its bottom shook the bog,
And the hoarse nation croaked, " God save King Log ! "

  Chapel-royal.—The voices and instruments used in the service of
the Chapel-royal being also employed in the performance of the Birth-
day and New-year Odes.
  But pious Needham.—A Matron of great fame, and very religious in
her way ; whose constant prayer it was, that she might " get enough
by her profession to leave it off in time, and make her peace with
God." But her fate was not so happy ; for being convicted and set
in the pillory, she was (to the lasting shame of all her great Friends
and Votaries) so ill used by the populace, that it put an end to her days.
  Back to the Devil.—The Devil Tavern in Fleet-street, where these
Odes are usually rehearsed before they are performed at Court.
  Ogilby—God save King Log.—See Ogilby's *Æsop's Fables*, where,
in the story of the Frogs and their King, this excellent hemistic is to
be found.

BOOK THE SECOND

ARGUMENT

The King being proclaimed, the solemnity is graced with public *Games*, and sports of various kinds ; not instituted by the Hero, as by Æneas in Virgil, but for greater honour by the *Goddess* in person (in like manner as the games Pythia, Isthmia, etc., were anciently said to be ordained by the Gods, and as Thetis herself appearing, according to Homer, Odyss. xxiv., proposed the prizes in honour of her son Achilles). Hither flock the Poets and Critics, attended, as is but just, with their Patrons and Booksellers. The Goddess is first pleased, for her disport, to propose games to the *Booksellers*, and setteth up the Phantom of a *Poet*, which they contend to overtake. The Races described, with their divers accidents. Next, the game for a *Poetess*. Then follow the Exercises for the *Poets*, of *tickling, vociferating, diving* : The first holds forth the arts and practices of *Dedicators*, the second of *Disputants* and *fustian Poets*, the third of *profound, dark*, and *dirty Party-writers*. Lastly, for the *Critics*, the Goddess proposes (with great propriety) an Exercise, not of their parts, but their patience, in hearing the works of two voluminous Authors, one in *verse*, and the other in *prose*, deliberately read without sleeping : The various effects of which, with the several degrees and manners of their operation, are here set forth ; till the whole number, not of Critics only, but of spectators, actors, and all present, fall asleep ; which naturally and necessarily ends the games.

HIGH on a gorgeous seat, that far out-shone
Henley's gilt tub, or Fleckno's Irish throne,

Henley's gilt tub.—The pulpit of a Dissenter is usually called a Tub ; but that of Mr. Orator Henley was covered with velvet, and adorned with gold. He had also a fair altar, and over it this extraordinary inscription, *The Primitive Eucharist.* See the history of this person, Book III.

Or Fleckno's Irish throne.—Richard Fleckno was an Irish priest, but had laid aside (as himself expressed it) the mechanic part of priesthood. He printed some plays, poems, letters, and travels. I doubt not our Author took occasion to mention him in respect to the poem of Mr. Dryden, to which this bears some resemblance, though of a character more different from it than that of the Æneid from the Iliad, or the Lutrin of Boileau from the Défait de Bouts rimées of Sarazin.

It may be just worth mentioning, that the Eminence, from whence the ancient Sophists entertained their auditors, was called by the pompous name of a throne ;—ἐπὶ θρόνον τινὸς ὑψηλοῦ μάλα σοφιστικῶς καὶ σοβαρῶς. Themistius, Orat. 1

Or that where on her Curls the Public pours,
All-bounteous, fragrant Grains and Golden showers,
Great Cibber sate : The proud Parnassian sneer,　　5
The conscious simper, and the jealous leer,
Mix on his look : All eyes direct their rays
On him, and crowds turn Coxcombs as they gaze :
His Peers shine round him with reflected grace,
New edge their dulness, and new bronze their face.　　10
So from the Sun's broad beam in shallow urns
Heaven's twinkling Sparks draw light, and point their
　　horns.

Not with more glee, by hands pontific crowned,
With scarlet hats wide-waving circled round,
Rome in her Capitol saw Querno sit,　　15
Throned on seven hills, the Antichrist of wit.

And now the Queen, to glad her sons, proclaims,
By herald Hawkers, high heroic Games.
They summon all her Race : an endless band
Pours forth, and leaves unpeopled half the land.　　20

Or that where on her Curls the Public pours.—Edmund Curl stood in the pillory at Charing-cross, in March 1727–8. "This (saith Edmund Curl) is a false assertion——I had indeed the corporal punishment of what the Gentlemen of the long robe are pleased jocosely to call *mounting the Rostrum* for one hour ; but that scene of action was not in the month of *March*, but in *February*." And of *the History of his being tost in a Blanket*, he saith, "Here, *Scriblerus !* thou leeseth in what thou assertest concerning the blanket ; it was not a *blanket*, but a *rug*." Much in the same manner Mr. *Cibber* remonstrated, that his Brothers, at Bedlam, mentioned Book 1., were not *Brazen*, but *Blocks ;* yet our Author let it pass unaltered, as a trifle that no way altered the relationship.—*Scriblerus.*

Rome in her Capitol saw Querno sit.—Camillo Querno was of Apulia, who, hearing the great Encouragement which Leo X. gave to poets, travelled to Rome with a harp in his hand, and sung to it twenty thousand verses of a poem called *Alexias.* He was introduced *as a Buffoon* to Leo, and promoted to the honour of the *Laurel ;* a jest which the Court of Rome and the Pope himself entered into so far, as to cause him to ride on an elephant to the Capitol, and to hold a solemn festival on his coronation ; at which it is recorded the Poet himself was so transported as to *weep for joy.* He was ever after a constant frequenter of the Pope's table, drank abundantly, and poured forth verses without number.—Paulus Jovius. Some idea of his poetry is given by Fam. Strada, in his Prolusions.

A motley mixture ! in long wigs, in bags,
In silks, in crapes, in Garters, and in Rags,
From drawing-rooms, from colleges, from garrets,
On horse, on foot, in hacks, and gilded chariots :
All who true Dunces in her cause appeared,   25
And all who knew those Dunces to reward.
  Amid that area wide they took their stand,
Where the tall may-pole once o'er-looked the Strand.
But now (so ANNE and Piety ordain)
A Church collects the saints of Drury-lane.   30
  With Authors, Stationers obeyed the call,
(The field of glory is a field for all).
Glory, and gain, th' industrious tribe provoke;
And gentle Dulness ever loves a joke.
A Poet's form she placed before their eyes,   35
And bade the nimblest racer seize the prize;
No meagre, muse-rid mope, adust and thin,
In a dun night-gown of his own loose skin;
But such a bulk as no twelve bards could raise,
Twelve starveling bards of these degen'rate days.   40
All as a partridge plump, full-fed, and fair,
She formed this image of well-bodied air;
With pert flat eyes she windowed well its head:
A brain of feathers, and a heart of lead;
And empty words she gave, and sounding strain,   45
But senseless, lifeless ! idol void and vain!
Never was dashed out, at one lucky hit,
A fool, so just a copy of a wit;
So like, that critics said, and courtiers swore,
A Wit it was, and called the phantom Moore.   50
  All gaze with ardour : some a poet's name,
Others a sword-knot and laced suit inflame.
But lofty Lintot in the circle rose :

But lofty Lintot.—We enter here upon the episode of the Booksellers : Persons, whose names being more known and famous in the
learned world than those of the Authors in this poem, do therefore
need less explanation.   The action of Mr. Bernard Lintot here imitates
that of Dares in Virgil, rising just in this manner to lay hold on a *Bull*.
This eminent Bookseller printed the *Rival Modes* before-mentioned.

" This prize is mine ; who tempt it are my foes;
With me began this genius, and shall end." 55
He spoke : and who with Lintot shall contend ?
   Fear held them mute. Alone, untaught to fear,
Stood dauntless Curl ; " Behold that rival here !
The race by vigour, not by vaunts is won ;
So take the hindmost, Hell," he said, and run. 60
Swift as a bard the bailiff leaves behind,
He left huge Lintot, and out-stripped the wind.
As when a dab-chick waddles through the copse
On feet and wings, and flies, and wades, and hops :
So lab'ring on, with shoulders, hands, and head, 65
Wide as a wind-mill all his figure spread,
With arms expanded Bernard rows his state,
And left-legged Jacob seems to emulate.
Full in the middle way there stood a lake,
Which Curl's Corinna chanced that morn to make : 70
(Such was her wont, at early dawn to drop
Her evening cates before his neighbour's shop,)
Here fortuned Curl to slide ; loud shout the band,
And " Bernard ! Bernard ! " rings through all the
      Strand.

Stood dauntless Curl.—We come now to a character of much respect, that of Mr. Edmund Curl. As a plain repetition of great actions is the best praise of them, we shall only say of this eminent man, that he carried the Trade many lengths beyond what it ever before had arrived at ; and that he was the envy and admiration of all his profession. He possessed himself of a command over all authors whatever ; he caused them to write what he pleased ; they could not call their very *Names* their own. He was not only famous among these ; he was taken notice of by the *State*, the *Church*, and the *Law*, and received particular marks of distinction from each.

Curl's Corinna.—This name, it seems, was taken by one Mrs. T——, who procured some private letters of Mr. Pope, while almost a boy, to Mr. Cromwell, and sold them without the consent of either of those Gentlemen to Curl, who printed them in 12mo, 1727. We only take this opportunity of mentioning the manner in which those letters got abroad, which the author was ashamed of as very trivial things, full not only of levities, but of wrong judgments of men and books, and only excusable from the youth and inexperience of the writer.—POPE. Mrs. Elizabeth Thomas was first styled Corinna by Dryden, to whom she sent a copy of verses. She died, in want, in 1730.—CARRUTHERS.

Obscene with filth the miscreant lies bewrayed,   75
Fallen in the plash his wickedness had laid :
Then first (if Poets aught of truth declare)
The caitiff Vaticide conceived a prayer.

" Hear, Jove ! whose name my bards and I adore,
As much at least as any God's, or more ;   80
And him and his if more devotion warms,
Down with the Bible, up with the Pope's Arms."

A place there is, betwixt earth, air, and seas,
Where, from Ambrosia, Jove retires for ease,
There in his seat two spacious vents appear,   85
On this he sits, to that he leans his ear,
And hears the various vows of fond mankind;
Some beg an eastern, some a western wind :
All vain petitions, mounting to the sky,
With reams abundant this abode supply ;   90
Amused he reads, and then returns the bills
Signed with that Ichor which from Gods distils.

In office here fair Cloacina stands,
And ministers to Jove with purest hands.
Forth from the heap she picked her Vot'ry's prayer,
And placed it next him, a distinction rare !   96
Oft had the Goddess heard her servants call,
From her black grottos near the Temple-wall,
List'ning delighted to the jest unclean
Of link-boys vile, and watermen obscene ;   100
Where as he fished her nether realms for Wit,
She oft had favoured him, and favours yet.
Renewed by ordure's sympathetic force,
As oiled with magic juices for the course,
Vig'rous he rises ; from th' effluvia strong   105
Imbibes new life, and scours and stinks along ;
Re-passes Lintot, vindicates the race,
Nor heeds the brown dishonours of his face.

Down with the Bible, up with the Pope's Arms.—The Bible, Curl's
sign ; the Cross-keys, Lintot's.
As oiled with magic juices.—Alluding to the opinion that there are
ointments used by witches to enable them to fly in the air. etc.

And now the victor stretched his eager hand,
Where the tall Nothing stood, or seemed to stand ;
A shapeless shade, it melted from his sight,　　III
Like forms in clouds, or visions of the night.
To seize his papers, Curl, was next thy care ;
His papers light fly diverse, tost in air ;
Songs, sonnets, epigrams the winds uplift,　　115
And whisk 'em back to Evans, Young, and Swift.
Th' embroidered suit at least he deemed his prey ;
That suit an unpaid tailor snatched away.
No rag, no scrap, of all the beau, or wit,
That once so fluttered, and that once so writ.　　120
　　Heaven rings with laughter. Of the laughter vain,
Dulness, good Queen, repeats the jest again.
Three wicked imps of her own Grubstreet choir,
She decked like Congreve, Addison, and Prior ;
Mears, Warner, Wilkins run : delusive thought !　　125
Breval, Bond, Besaleel, the varlets caught.
Curl stretches after Gay, but Gay is gone :
He grasps an empty Joseph for a John ;

An unpaid tailor.—This line has been loudly complained of in Mist,
June 8, Dedic. to Sawney, and others, as a most inhuman satire on the
poverty of *Poets :* But it is thought our Author would be acquitted
by a jury of *Tailors.* To me this instance seems unluckily chosen ;
if it be a satire on anybody, it must be on a bad *paymaster,* since the
person to whom they have here applied it was a man of fortune. Not
but poets may well be jealous of so great a prerogative as *non-payment ;*
which Mr. Dennis so far asserts, as boldly to pronounce, that "if
Homer himself was not in debt, it was because nobody would trust
him."

Like Congreve, Addison, and Prior.—These authors being such whose
names will reach posterity, we shall not give any account of them,
but proceed to those of whom it is necessary.—Besaleel Morris was
author of some satires on the translators of Homer, with many other
things printed in newspapers.—" Bond writ a satire against Mr. P.—
Capt. Breval was author of the Confederates, an ingenious dramatic
performance, to expose Mr. P., Mr. Gay, Dr. Arb., and some ladies of
quality," says Curl.

Mears, Warner, Wilkins.—Booksellers, and Printers of much anonymous stuff.

Joseph.—Joseph Gay, a fictitious name put by Curl before several
pamphlets, which made them pass with many for Mr. Gay's. The
antiquity of the word *Joseph,* which likewise signifies a loose upper-
coat, gives much pleasantry to the idea.

So Proteus, hunted in a nobler shape,
Became, when seized, a puppy, or an ape,   130
    To him the Goddess : " Son ! thy grief lay down,
And turn this whole illusion on the town :
As the sage dame, experienced in her trade,
By names of Toasts retails each battered jade ;
(Whence hapless Monsieur much complains at Paris
Of wrongs from Duchesses and Lady Maries ;)   136
Be thine, my stationer ! this magic gift ;
Cook shall be Prior, and Concanen, Swift :
So shall each hostile name become our own,
And we too boast our Garth and Addison."   140
    With that she gave him (piteous of his case,
Yet smiling at his rueful length of face)
A shaggy Tap'stry, worthy to be spread
On Codrus' old, or Dunton's modern bed :

And turn this whole illusion on the town.—It was a common practice of this bookseller to publish vile pieces of obscure hands under the names of eminent authors.

Cook shall be Prior.—The man here specified writ a thing called *The Battle of Poets,* in which Philips and Welsted were the Heroes, and Swift and Pope utterly routed. He also published some malevolent things in the British, London, and Daily Journals ; and at the same time wrote letters to Mr. Pope, protesting his innocence. His chief work was a translation of Hesiod, to which Theobald writ notes and half notes, which he carefully owned.

And we too boast our Garth and Addison.—Nothing is more remarkable than our author's love of praising good writers. He has in this very poem celebrated Mr. Locke, Sir Isaac Newton, Dr. Barrow, Dr. Atterbury, Mr. Dryden, Mr. Congreve, Dr. Garth, Mr. Addison ; in a word, almost every man of his time that deserved it ; even Cibber himself (presuming him to be author of the *Careless Husband*). It was very difficult to have that pleasure in a poem on this subject, yet he has found means to insert their panegyric, and has made even Dulness out of her own mouth pronounce it. It must have been particularly agreeable to him to celebrate Dr. Garth ; both as his constant friend, and as he was his predecessor in this kind of satire.

A shaggy Tap'stry.—A sorry kind of Tapestry frequent in old inns, made of worsted or some coarser stuff, like that which is spoken of by Donne—*Faces as frightful as theirs who whip Christ in old hangings.* The imagery woven in it alludes to the mantle of Cloanthus, in *Æneid* v. [v. 250, ff.]

On Codrus' old, or Dunton's modern bed.—Of Codrus the poet's bed, see Juvenal, describing his *poverty* very copiously, *Sat.* iii. 103, etc. But Mr. Concanen, in his dedication of the letters, advertisements

Instructive work ! whose wry-mouthed portraiture 145
Displayed the fates her confessors endure.
Earless on high, stood unabashed De Foe,
And Tutchin flagrant from the scourge below.
There Ridpath, Roper, cudgelled might ye view ;
The very worsted still look black and blue. 150
Himself among the storied chiefs he spies,
As, from the blanket, high in air he flies ;
And " Oh ! " (he cried) " what street, what lane but
    knows
Our purgings, pumpings, blankettings, and blows ?
In every loom our labours shall be seen, 155
And the fresh vomit run for ever green ! "
    See in the circle next, Eliza placed,
Two babes of love close clinging to her waist ;
Fair as before her works she stands confessed,
In flowers and pearls by bounteous Kirkall dressed. 160
The Goddess then : " Who best can send on high
The salient spout, far-streaming to the sky ;
His be yon Juno of majestic size,

etc., to the author of the Dunciad, assures us, " that Juvenal never satirized the Poverty of Codrus."

John Dunton was a broken bookseller, and abusive scribbler ; he writ *Neck or Nothing*, a violent satire on some ministers of state ; a libel on the Duke of Devonshire and the Bishop of Peterborough, etc.

And Tutchin flagrant from the scourge.—John Tutchin, author of some vile verses, and of a weekly paper called the *Observator :* He was sentenced to be whipped through several towns in the west of England, upon which he petitioned King James II. to be hanged. When that prince died in exile, he wrote an invective against his memory, occasioned by some humane elegies on his death. He lived to the time of Queen Anne.

There Ridpath, Roper.—Authors of the *Flying-post* and *Post-boy*, two scandalous papers on different sides, for which they equally and alternately deserved to be cudgelled, and were so.

Himself among the storied chiefs he spies.—The history of Curl's being tossed in a blanket, and whipped by the scholars of Westminster, is well known.

Eliza.—Eliza Haywood. This woman was authoress of those most scandalous books called the *Court of Carimania*, and the new *Utopia*.

Kirkall.—The name of an Engraver. Some of this Lady's works were printed in four volumes in 12mo, with her picture thus dressed up before them.

With cow-like udders, and with ox-like eyes.
This China Jordan let the chief o'ercome   165
Replenish, not ingloriously, at home."
   Osborne and Curl accept the glorious strife,
(Though this his Son dissuades, and that his Wife).
One on his manly confidence relies ;
One on his vigour and superior size.   170
First Osborne leaned against his lettered post ;
It rose, and laboured to a curve at most.
So Jove's bright bow displays its wat'ry round,
(Sure sign that no spectator shall be drowned).
A second effort brought but new disgrace :   175
The wild Mæander washed the Artist's face ;
Thus the small jet, which hasty hands unlock,
Spirts in the gard'ner's eyes who turns the cock.
Not so from shameless Curl ; impetuous spread
The stream, and smoking flourished o'er his head. 180
So (famed like thee for turbulence and horns)
Eridanus his humble fountain scorns ;
Through half the heavens he pours th' exalted urn ;
His rapid waters in their passage burn.
   Swift as it mounts, all follow with their eyes : 185
Still happy Impudence obtains the prize.
Thou triumph'st, Victor of the high-wrought day,
And the pleased dame, soft smiling, lead'st away.
Osborne, through perfect modesty o'ercome,
Crowned with the Jordan, walks contented home.   190
   But now for Authors nobler palms remain ;
" Room for my Lord ! " three jockeys in his train ;
Six huntsmen with a shout precede his chair :

Osborne.—Thomas Osborne, a bookseller in Gray's-inn, very well
qualified by his impudence to act this part ; and therefore placed here
instead of a less deserving Predecessor. This man published advertisements for a year together, pretending to sell Mr. Pope's subscription
books of Homer's Iliad at half the price : Of which books he had none,
but cut to the size of them (which was Quarto) the common books in
folio, without Copper-plates, on a worse paper, and never above half
the value.—*Pope.* Of Osborne, Johnson used to say, that he had no
sense of any shame, but that of being poor.—*Bannister.*

He grins, and looks broad nonsense with a stare.
His Honour's meaning Dulness thus exprest,   195
" He wins this Patron, who can tickle best."
He chinks his purse, and takes his seat of state ;
With ready quills the Dedicators wait ;
Now at his head the dext'rous task commence,
And, instant, fancy feels th' imputed sense ;   200
Now gentle touches wanton o'er his face,
He struts Adonis, and affects grimace :
Rolli the feather to his ear conveys,
Then his nice taste directs our Operas :
Bentley his mouth with classic flatt'ry opes,   205
And the puffed orator bursts out in tropes.
But Welsted most the Poet's healing balm
Strives to extract from his soft, giving palm ;
Unlucky Welsted ! thy unfeeling master,
The more thou ticklest, gripes his fist the faster.   210
    While thus each hand promotes the pleasing pain,
And quick sensations skip from vein to vein ;
A youth unknown to Phœbus in despair,

Rolli.—Paolo Antonio Rolli, an Italian Poet, and writer of many Operas in that language, which, partly by the help of his genius, prevailed in England near twenty years. He taught Italian to some fine Gentlemen, who affected to direct the Operas.

Bentley his mouth, etc.—Not spoken of the famous Dr. Richard Bentley, but of one Tho. Bentley, a small critic, who aped his uncle in a *little Horace*. The great one who was intended to be dedicated to the Lord Halifax, but (on a change of the Ministry) was given to the Earl of Oxford ; for which reason the little one was dedicated to his son the Lord Harley.

Welsted.—Leonard Welsted, author of the *Triumvirate*, or a *Letter in Verse from Palæmon to Cælia at Bath*, which was meant for a satire on Mr. P. and some of his friends about the year 1718. He writ other things which we cannot remember. You have him again in Book III.

A youth unknown to Phœbus, etc.—The satire of this Episode, being levelled at the base flatteries of authors to worthless wealth or greatness, concludes here with an excellent lesson to such men : That although their pens and praises were as exquisite as they conceit of themselves, yet (even in their own mercenary views) a creature unlettered, who serveth the passions, or pimpeth to the pleasures of such vain, braggart, puft Nobility, shall with those patrons be much more inward, and of them much higher rewarded.—SCRIBL.

Puts his last refuge all in heaven and prayer.
What force have pious vows ! The Queen of Love 215
His sister sends, her vot'ress, from above.
As, taught by Venus, Paris learnt the art
To touch Achilles' only tender part ;
Secure, through her, the noble prize to carry,
He marches off his Grace's Secretary. 220
" Now turn to diff'rent sports," (the Goddess cries)
" And learn, my sons, the wond'rous power of Noise.
To move, to raise, to ravish every heart,
With Shakespear's nature, or with Jonson's art,
Let others aim : 'tis yours to shake the soul 225
With Thunder rumbling from the mustard-bowl,
With horns and trumpets now to madness swell,
Now sink in sorrows with a tolling bell ;
Such happy arts attention can command,
When fancy flags, and sense is at a stand. 230
Improve we these. Three Cat-calls be the bribe
Of him, whose chatt'ring shames the monkey-tribe ;
And his this Drum, whose hoarse heroic bass
Drowns the loud clarion of the braying Ass."
    Now thousand tongues are heard in one loud din ; 235
The monkey-mimics rush discordant in ;
'Twas chatt'ring, grinning, mouthing, jabb'ring all,
And Noise and Norton, Brangling and Breval,
Dennis and Dissonance, and captious Art,
And Snip-snap short, and Interruption smart, 240
And Demonstration thin, and Theses thick,

With Thunder rumbling from the mustard-bowl.—The old way of
making Thunder and Mustard were the same ; but since, it is more
advantageously performed by troughs of wood with stops in them.
Whether Mr. Dennis was the inventor of that improvement, I know
not ; but it is certain, that being once at a Tragedy of a new author,
he fell into a great passion at hearing some, and cried, " 'Sdeath !
that is *my* ' Thunder.' "
    With a tolling bell.—A mechanical help to the Pathetic, not unuse-
ful to the modern writers of Tragedy.
    Three Cat-calls.—Certain musical instruments used by one sort of
Critics to confound the Poets of the Theatre.
    Norton.—See page 276.—*J. Durant Breval,* author of a very extra-
ordinary Book of Travels, and some Poems.

And Major, Minor, and Conclusion quick.
" Hold!" (cried the Queen), " a Cat-call each shall **win:**
Equal your merits! equal is your din!
But that this well-disputed game may end,   245
Sound forth, my Brayers, and the welkin rend."
    As, when the long-eared milky mothers wait
At some sick miser's triple bolted gate,
For their defrauded, absent foals they make
A moan so loud, that all the guild awake;   250
Sore sighs sir Gilbert, starting at the bray,
From dreams of millions, and three groats to **pay.**
So swells each wind-pipe; Ass intones to Ass;
Harmonic twang! of leather, horn, and brass;
Such as from lab'ring lungs th' Enthusiast blows,   255
High Sound, attempered to the vocal nose;
Or such as bellow from the deep Divine;
There, Webster! pealed thy voice, and Whitfield! **thine.**
But far o'er all, sonorous Blackmore's strain;
Walls, steeples, skies, bray back to him again.   260
In Tot'nham fields, the brethren, with amaze,
Prick all their ears up, and forget to graze;
Long Chanc'ry-lane retentive rolls the sound,
And courts to courts return it round and round;
Thames wastes it thence to Rufus' roaring hall,   265
And Hungerford re-echoes bawl for bawl.
All hail him victor in both gifts of song,
Who sings so loudly, and who sings so long.

    Webster—and Whitfield.—The one the writer of a Newspaper **called**
the *Weekly Miscellany*, the other a Field-preacher.—*Warburton.*
    Long Chanc'ry-lane.—The place where the offices of Chancery are
kept. The long detention of Clients in that Court, and the difficulty
of getting out, is humorously allegorized in these lines.
    Who sings so loudly, and who sings so long.—A just character of Sir
Richard Blackmore knight, who (as Mr. Dryden expresseth it)
            Writ to the rumbling of the coach's wheels,
and whose indefatigable Muse produced no less than six Epic poems;
Prince and King Arthur, twenty books; *Eliza,* ten; *Alfred,* twelve;
the *Redeemer,* six; besides *Job,* in folio; the whole book of *Psalms;*
the *Creation,* seven books; *Nature of Man,* three books; and many
more. 'Tis in this sense he is styled afterwards the *everlasting Black-*
more.

This labour past, by Bridewell all descend,
(As morning prayer and flagellation end)   270
To where Fleet-ditch with disemboguing streams
Rolls the large tribute of dead dogs to Thames,
The king of dykes ! than whom no sluice of mud
With deeper sable blots the silver flood.
" Here strip, my children ! here at once leap in, 275
Here prove who best can dash through thick and **thin.**
And who the most in love of dirt excel,
Or dark dexterity of groping well.
Who flings most filth, and wide pollutes around
The stream, be his the Weekly Journals bound ; 280
A pig of lead to him who dives the best ;
A peck of coals a-piece shall glad the rest."
In naked majesty Oldmixon stands,

As morning prayer and flagellation end.—It is between eleven and
twelve in the morning, after church service, that the criminals are
whipt in Bridewell.—This is to mark punctually the *time* of the day :
Homer does it by the circumstance of the Judges rising from court,
or of the Labourer's dinner ; our author by one very proper both to
the *Persons* and the *Scene* of his poem, which we may remember
commenced in the evening of the Lord-mayor's day : The first book
passed in that *night ;* the next *morning* the games begin in the Strand,
thence along Fleet-street (places inhabited by Booksellers) ; then they
proceed by Bridewell toward Fleet-ditch, and lastly through Ludgate
to the City and the Temple of the Goddess.

Dash through thick and thin—love of dirt—dark dexterity.—The
three chief qualifications of Party-writers : to stick at nothing, to
delight in flinging dirt, and to slander in the dark by guess.

The Weekly Journals.—Papers of news and scandal intermixed, on
different sides and parties, and frequently shifting from one side to
the other, called the *London Journal, British Journal, Daily Journal,*
etc., the concealed writers of which for some time were Oldmixon,
Roome, Arnall, Concanen, and others ; persons never seen by our
Author.

In naked majesty Oldmixon stands.—Mr. JOHN OLDMIXON, next to
Mr. Dennis, the most ancient Critic of our nation ; and unjust censurer
of Mr. Addison. In his *Essay on Criticism,* and the *Arts of Logic
and Rhetoric,* he frequently reflects on our Author. But the top of his
character was a Perverter of History, in that scandalous one of the
Stuarts, in folio, and his *Critical History of England,* two volumes,
octavo. Being employed by Bishop Kennet, in publishing the
Historians in his Collection, he falsified Daniel's *Chronicle* in numberless places. He was all his life a virulent Party-writer for hire, and
received his reward in a small place, which he enjoyed to his death.
He is here likened to Milo, in allusion to Ovid [*Metam.* Bk. xv. v. 229].

And Milo-like surveys his arms and hands ;
Then, sighing, thus, " And am I now three-score ? 285
Ah why, ye Gods, should two and two make four ? "
He said, and climbed a stranded lighter's height,
Shot to the black abyss, and plunged downright.
The Senior's judgment all the crowd admire,
Who but to sink the deeper, rose the higher.   290
    Next Smedley dived ; slow circles dimpled o'er
The quaking mud, that closed, and oped no more,
All look, all sigh, and call on Smedley lost ;
" Smedley " in vain resounds through all the coast.
    Then * essayed ; scarce vanished out of sight, 295
He buoys up instant, and returns to light :
He bears no token of the sabler streams,
And mounts far off among the Swans of Thames.
    True to the bottom see Concanen creep,
A cold, long-winded native of the deep ;   300
If perseverance gain the Diver's prize,
Not everlasting Blackmore this denies ;

Next Smedley dived.—The person here mentioned, an Irishman,
was author and publisher of many scurrilous pieces, a weekly White-
hall Journal, in the year 1722, in the name of Sir James Baker ; and
particularly whole volumes of Billingsgate against Dr. Swift and Mr.
Pope, called *Gulliveriana* and *Alexandriana*, printed in octavo, 1728.
    Jonathan Smedley, a staunch Whig, and Dean of Clogher.—*Car-
ruthers.*
    *Then * essayed.*—A gentleman of genius and spirit, who was secretly
dipt in some papers of this kind, on whom our Poet bestows a
panegyric instead of a satire, as deserving to be better employed than
in party quarrels, and personal invectives.—*Pope.* Supposed to be
Aaron Hill ; but Pope denied it.—*Warton.*
    Concanen.—MATTHEW CONCANEN, an Irishman, bred to the law.
He was author of several dull and dead scurrilities in the *British* and
London Journals, and in a paper called the *Speculatist.* In a pamphlet,
called a *Supplement to the Profound*, he dealt very unfairly with our
Poet, not only frequently imputing to him Mr. Broome's verses (for
which he might indeed seem in some degree accountable, having
corrected what that gentleman did) but those of the Duke of Buckingham and others : To this rare piece somebody humorously caused him
to take for his motto, *De profundis clamavi.* He was since a hired
scribbler in the *Daily Courant*, where he poured forth much Billingsgate against the Lord Bolingbroke, and others ; after which this man
was surprisingly promoted to administer Justice and Law in Jamaica.
This is the scribbler to whom Warburton wrote his famous Letter,
published by Dr. Akenside.

No noise, no stir, no motion canst thou make,
Th' unconscious stream sleeps o'er thee like a lake.
    Next plunged a feeble, but a desp'rate pack,   305
With each a sickly brother at his back :
Sons of a Day ! just buoyant on the flood,
Then numbered with the puppies in the mud.
Ask ye their names ? I could as soon disclose
The names of these blind puppies as of those.   310
Fast by, like Niobe (her children gone)
Sits Mother Osborne, stupefied to stone !
And Monumental brass this record bears,
" These are,—ah no ! these were, the Gazetteers ! "
    Not so bold Arnall ; with a weight of skull,   315
Furious he dives, precipitately dull.
Whirlpools and storms his circling arm invest,
With all the might of gravitation blest.
No crab more active in the dirty dance,
Downward to climb, and backward to advance.   320
He brings up half the bottom on his head,
And loudly claims the Journals and the Lead.

With each a sickly brother at his back : Sons of a Day ! etc.—These were daily papers, a number of which, to lessen the expense, were printed one on the back of another.

Like Niobe.—See the story in Ovid, *Met.* vii., where the miserable petrifaction of this old Lady is pathetically described.

Osborne.—A name assumed by the eldest and gravest of these writers, who at last, being ashamed of his Pupils, gave his paper over, and in his age remained silent.

Arnall.—WILLIAM ARNALL, bred an Attorney, was a perfect Genius in this sort of work. He began under twenty with furious Party-papers ; then succeeded Concanen in the *British Journal.* At the first publication of the Dunciad, he prevailed on the Author not to give him his due place in it, by a letter professing his detestation of such practices as his predecessor's. But since, by the most unexampled insolence, and personal abuse of several great men, the Poet's particular friends, he most amply deserved a nitch in the Temple of Infamy : He writ for hire, and valued himself upon it ; not indeed without cause, it appearing by the REPORT on Walpole, that he received " for *Free Britons,* and other writings, in space of *four years,* no less than *ten thousand nine hundred and ninety-seven pounds, six shillings, and eight pence,* out of the Treasury." But frequently, through his fury or folly, he exceeded all the bounds of his commission, and obliged his honourable Patron to disavow his scurrilities.

The plunging Prelate, and his pond'rous Grace,
With holy envy gave one Layman place.
When lo ! a burst of thunder shook the flood ;   325
Slow rose a form, in majesty of Mud ;
Shaking the horrors of his sable brows,
And each ferocious feature grim with ooze.
Greater he looks, and more than mortal stares ;
Then thus the wonders of the deep declares.   330
    First he relates, how sinking to the chin,
Smit with his mien the Mud-nymphs sucked him
          in :
How young Lutetia, softer than the down,
Nigrina black, and Merdamante brown,
Vied for his love in jetty bowers below,   335
As Hylas fair was ravished long ago.
Then sung, how shewn him by the Nut-brown
          maids
A branch of Styx here rises from the Shades,
That tinctured as it runs with Lethe's streams,
And wafting Vapours from the Land of dreams,   340
(As under seas Alpheus' secret sluice
Bears Pisa's off'rings to his Arethuse)
Pours into Thames : and hence the mingled wave
Intoxicates the pert, and lulls the grave :
Here brisker vapours o'er the TEMPLE creep,   345
There, all from Paul's to Aldgate drink and sleep.
Thence to the banks where rev'rend Bards repose,
They led him soft ; each rev'rend Bard arose ;

Plunging Prelate.—Sir Robert Walpole, who was Bishop Sherlock's
contemporary at Eton College, used to relate, that when some of the
scholars, going to bathe in the Thames, stood shivering on the bank,
S. plunged in immediately over head and ears.—*Warton.*

As Hylas fair.—Who was ravished by the water-nymphs and drawn
into the river.

A branch of Styx, etc.—Cf. Homer. *Il.* II. [vv. 751–5]. Of the land
of Dreams in the same region he makes mention, *Odyss.* XXIV. See
also Lucian's True History. *Lethe* and the *Land of Dreams* allegorically
represent the *Stupefaction* and *visionary Madness* of Poets, equally
dull and extravagant. Of Alpheus's waters gliding secretly under the
sea of Pisa, to mix with those of Arethuse in Sicily, see Moschus, *Idyl.*
VIII. Virg. *Ecl.* X. vv. 3, 4. And again, *Æn.* III. vv. 693–5.

And Milbourn chief, deputed by the rest,
Gave him the cassock, surcingle, and vest.   350
" Receive " (he said) " these robes which once were mine,
Dulness is sacred in a sound divine."
    He ceased, and spread the robe ; the crowd confess
The rev'rend Flamen in his lengthened dress.
Around him wide a sable Army stand,   355
A low-born, cell-bred, selfish, servile band,
Prompt or to guard or stab, to saint or damn,
Heaven's Swiss, who fight for any God, or Man.
        Through Lud's famed gates, along the well-known
            Fleet,
Rolls the black troop, and overshades the street ;   360
'Til showers of Sermons, Characters, Essays,
In circling fleeces whiten all the ways :
So clouds, replenished from some bog below,
Mount in dark volumes, and descend in snow.
Here stopt the Goddess ; and in pomp proclaims   365
A gentler exercise to close the games.
    " Ye Critics ! in whose heads, as equal scales,
I weigh what author's heaviness prevails ;
Which most conduce to sooth the soul in slumbers,
My H—ley's periods, or my Blackmore's numbers ;   370
Attend the trial we propose to make :
If there be man, who o'er such works can wake,
Sleep's all-subduing charms who dares defy,
And boasts Ulysses' ear with Argus' eye ;
To him we grant our amplest powers to sit   375
Judge of all present, past, and future wit ;
To cavil, censure, dictate, right or wrong ;
Full and eternal privilege of tongue."

    And Milbourn.—Luke Milbourn, a Clergyman, the fairest of Critics ;
who, when he wrote against Mr. Dryden's Virgil, did him justice in
printing at the same time his own translations of him, which were
intolerable. His manner of writing has a great resemblance with
that of the Gentlemen of the Dunciad against our Author.
    Heaven's Swiss, who fight for any God, or Man.—The expression is
taken from Dryden's *Hind and Panther :* " Those Swisses fight for any
side for pay."—*Warton.*

Three College Sophs, and three pert Templars came,
The same their talents, and their tastes the same ; 380
Each prompt to query, answer, and debate,
And smit with love of Poesy and Prate,
The pond'rous books two gentle readers bring ;
The heroes sit, the vulgar form a ring.
The clam'rous crowd is hushed with mugs of **Mum**, 385
'Til all, tuned equal, send a gen'ral hum.
Then mount the Cierks, and in one lazy tone
Through the long, heavy, painful page drawl on ;
Soft creeping, words on words, the sense compose ;
At every line they stretch, they yawn, they doze. 390
As to soft gales top-heavy pines bow low
Their heads, and lift them as they cease to blow :
Thus oft they rear, and oft the head decline,
As breathe, or pause, by fits, the airs divine ;
And now to this side, now to that they nod, 395
As verse, or prose, infuse the drowsy God.
Thrice Budgel aimed to speak, but thrice supprest
By potent Arthur, knocked his chin and breast.
Toland and Tindal, prompt at priests to jeer,
Yet silent bowed to *Christ's No kingdom here.* 400
Who sate the nearest, by the words o'ercome,
Slept first ; the distant nodded to the hum.

Thrice Budgel aimed to speak.—Famous for his speeches on many
occasions about the South Sea scheme, etc. " He is a very ingenious
gentleman, and hath written some excellent Epilogues to Plays, and
one small piece on Love, which is very pretty."—Jacob, *Lives of Poets.*
But this Gentleman since made himself much more eminent, and
personally well known to the greatest Statesmen of all parties, as well
as to all the Courts of Law in this nation. Budgel was a relation of
Addison whom he accompanied as clerk to Ireland. He afterwards
rose to be Under Secretary of State. After Addison's death he was
involved in losses by the South Sea Bubble ; a stain fell on his character in consequence of Tindal's bequest in his favour being set aside,
and he committed suicide in 1737.
Toland and Tindal.—Two persons, not so happy as to be obscure,
who writ against the Religion of their Country. *Toland*, the author
of the Atheist's Liturgy, called *Pantheisticon*, was a spy, in pay to Lord
Oxford. *Tindal* was author of the *Rights of the Christian Church,*
and *Christianity as old as the Creation.*
Christ's No kingdom, etc.—This is said by Curl. Key to Dunc., to
allude to a sermon of a reverend Bishop.

Then down are rolled the books ; stretched o'er 'em lies
Each gentle clerk, and mutt'ring seals his eyes,
As what a Dutchman plumps into the lakes,　　　　405
One circle first, and then a second makes ;
What Dulness dropt among her sons imprest
Like motion, from one circle to the rest ;
So from the mid-most the nutation spreads
Round and more round, o'er all the *sea of heads*.　　410
At last Centlivre felt her voice to fail ;
Motteux himself unfinished left his tale ;
Boyer the State, and Law the Stage gave o'er ;
Morgan and Mandevil could prate no more ;
Norton, from Daniel and Ostrœa sprung,　　　　415
Blessed with his father's front, and mother's tongue,
Hung silent down his never-blushing head ;
And all was hushed, as Folly's self lay dead.

Thus the soft gifts of Sleep conclude the day,
And stretched on bulks, as usual, Poets lay.　　　420
Why should I sing, what bards the nightly Muse

Centlivre.—Mrs. Susanna Centlivre, wife to Mr. Centlivre, Yeoman of the Mouth to his Majesty. She writ many Plays, and a Song (says Mr. Jacob) before she was seven years old. She also writ a Ballad against Mr. Pope's Homer before he began it.

Motteux.—Peter Anthony Motteux, the excellent translator of *Don Quixote,* and author of a number of forgotten dramatic pieces. Dryden addressed a complimentary Epistle to him. He died in 1718.

Boyer the State, and Law the Stage gave o'er.—A. Boyer, a voluminous compiler of Annals, Political Collections, etc.—William Law, A. M., wrote with great zeal against the Stage ; Mr. Dennis answered with as great : Their books were printed in 1726. The same Mr. Law is author of a book, entitled, *An Appeal to all that doubt of or disbelieve the truth of the gospel ;* in which he has detailed a system of the rankest Spinozism, for the most exalted Theology ; and amongst other things as rare, has informed us of this, that Sir Isaac Newton stole the principles of his philosophy from one *Jacob Bœhmen,* a German cobbler.

Morgan.—A man of some learning, and uncommon acuteness, with a strong disposition to Satire, which very often degenerated into scurrility. His most celebrated work is the *Moral Philosopher,* first published in the year 1737.

Norton.—Norton De Foe, offspring of the famous Daniel. *Fortes creantur fortibus.* One of the authors of the *Flying Post,* in which well-bred work Mr. P. has sometime the honour to be abused with his betters ; and of many hired scurrilities and daily papers, to which he never set his name.

Did slumb'ring visit, and convey to stews :
Who prouder marched, with magistrates in state,
To some famed round-house, ever open gate !
How Henley lay inspired beside a sink,   423
And to mere mortals seemed a Priest in drink :
While others, timely, to the neighb'ring Fleet
(Haunt of the Muses) made their safe retreat.

BOOK THE THIRD

ARGUMENT

After the other persons are disposed in their proper places of rest, the Goddess transports the King to her Temple, and there lays him to slumber with his head on her lap ; a position of marvellous virtue, which causes all the visions of wild enthusiasts, projectors, politicians, inamoratos, castle-builders, chemists, and poets. He is immediately carried on the wings of Fancy, and led by a mad Poetical Sibyl to the *Elysian shade* ; where, on the banks of *Lethe*, the souls of the dull are dipped by *Bavius*, before their entrance into this world. There he is met by the ghost of *Settle*, and by him made acquainted with the wonders of the place, and with those which he himself is destined to perform. He takes him to a *Mount of Vision*, from whence he shews him the past triumphs of the Empire of Dulness, then the present, and lastly the future : how small a part of the world was ever conquered by Science, how soon those conquests were stopped, and those very nations again reduced to her dominion. Then distinguishing the Island of *Great-Britain*, shews by what aids, by what persons, and by what degrees it shall be brought to her Empire. Some of the persons he causes to pass in review before his eyes, describing each by his proper figure, character, and qualifications. On a sudden the Scene shifts, and a vast number of miracles and prodigies appear, utterly surprising and unknown to the King himself, till they are explained to be the wonders of his own reign now commencing. On this subject *Settle* breaks into a congratulation, yet not unmixed with concern, that his own times were but types of these. He prophesies how first the nation shall be overrun with *Farces*, *Operas*, and *Shows ;* how the throne of Dulness shall be advanced over the *Theatres*, and set up even at *Court ;* then how her Sons shall preside in the seats of *Arts* and *Sciences :* giving a glimpse or Pisgah-sight of the future Fulness of her Glory, the accomplishment whereof is the subject of the fourth and last book.

BUT in her Temple's last recess enclosed,
On Dulness' lap th' Anointed head reposed.

Fleet.—A prison for insolvent Debtors on the bank of the Ditch.

Him close she curtains round with Vapours blue,
And soft besprinkles with Cimmerian dew.
Then raptures high the seat of Sense o'erflow,   5
Which only heads refined from Reason know.
Hence, from the straw where Bedlam's Prophet nods,
He hears loud Oracles, and talks with Gods :
Hence the Fool's Paradise, the Statesman's Scheme,
The air-built Castle, and the golden Dream,   10
The Maid's romantic wish, the Chemist's flame,
And Poet's vision of eternal Fame.

And now, on Fancy's easy wing conveyed,
The King descending views th' Elysian Shade.
A slip-shod Sibyl led his steps along,   15
In lofty madness meditating song ;
Her tresses staring from Poetic dreams,
And never washed, but in Castalia's streams.
Taylor, their better Charon, lends an oar,
(Once swan of Thames, though now he sings no more.)
Benlowes, propitious still to blockheads, bows ;   21
And Shadwell nods the Poppy on his brows.
Here, in a dusky vale where Lethe rolls,
Old Bavius sits, to dip poetic souls,

Taylor.—John Taylor the Water-poet, an honest man, who owns he learned not so much as the Accidence : A rare example of modesty in a Poet !

> *I must confess I do want eloquence,*
> *And never scarce did learn my Accidence ;*
> *For having got from* possum *to* posset,
> *I there was gravelled, could no farther get.*

He wrote fourscore books in the reign of James I. and Charles I., and afterwards (like Edward Ward) kept an Ale-house in Long-Acre. He died in 1654.

Benlowes.—A country gentleman, famous for his own bad poetry, and for patronizing bad poets, as may be seen from many Dedications of Quarles and others to him. Some of these anagramed his name, *Benlowes* into *Benevolus :* to verify which he spent his whole estate upon them.

And Shadwell nods the Poppy, etc.—Shadwell took Opium for many years, and died of too large a dose, in the year 1692.

Old Bavius sits.—Bavius was an ancient Poet, celebrated by Virgil for the like cause as Bays by our Author, though not in so Christian-like a manner : For heathenishly it is declared by Virgil of Bavius, that he ought to be hated and *detested* for his evil works ; *Qui Bavium*

And blunt the sense, and fit it for a skull 25
Of solid proof, impenetrably dull:
Instant, when dipt, away they wing their flight,
Where Brown and Mears unbar the gates of Light,
Demand new bodies, and in Calf's array
Rush to the world, impatient for the day. 30
Millions and millions on these banks he views,
Thick as the stars of night, or morning dews,
As thick as bees o'er vernal blossoms fly,
As thick as eggs at Ward in pillory. 34
  Wond'ring he gazed: When lo! a Sage appears,
By his broad shoulders known, and length of ears,
Known by the band and suit which Settle wore
(His only suit) for twice three years before:
All as the vest, appeared the wearer's frame,
Old in new state; another, yet the same. 40
Bland and familiar as in life, begun
Thus the great Father to the greater Son.
  "Oh born to see what none can see awake!
Behold the wonders of th' oblivious Lake.
Thou, yet unborn, hast touched this sacred shore; 45
The hand of Bavius drenched thee o'er and o'er.
But blind to former, as to future fate,

non odit; Whereas we have often had occasion to observe our Poet's
great *Good Nature* and *Mercifulness* through the whole course of this
Poem.—SCRIBLERUS.

  Mr. Dennis warmly contends, that Bavius was no inconsiderable
author: nay, that "He and Mævius had (even in Augustus's days) a very
formidable party at Rome, who thought them much superior to Virgil
and Horace: For (saith he) I cannot believe they would have fixed
that eternal brand upon them, if they had not been coxcombs in
more than ordinary credit."—*Rem. on Pr. Arthur*, part II. c. I. An
argument which, if this poem should last, will conduce to the honour
of the gentlemen of the Dunciad.

  Brown and Mears.—Booksellers, Printers for anybody.

  Ward in pillory.—John Ward of Hackney, Esq., Member of Parliament, being convicted of forgery, was first expelled the House, and then
sentenced to the Pillory on February 17, 1727.

  Settle.—Elkanah Settle was once a Writer in vogue as well as Cibber,
both for Dramatic Poetry and Politics. He was author or publisher
of many noted pamphlets in the time of King Charles II. He answered
all Dryden's political poems; and, being carried up on *one side*, succeeded not a little in his Tragedy of the *Empress of Morocco*.

What mortal knows his pre-existent state?
Who knows how long thy transmigrating soul
Might from Bœotian to Bœotian roll?   50
How many Dutchmen she vouchsafed to thrid?
How many stages through old Monks she rid?
And all who since, in mild benighted days,
Mixed the Owl's ivy with the Poet's bays?
As man's Mæanders to the vital spring   55
Roll all their tides; then back their circles bring;
Or whirligigs twirled round by skilful swain,
Suck the thread in, then yield it out again:
All nonsense thus, of old or modern date,
Shall in thee centre, from thee circulate.   60
For this our Queen unfolds to vision true
Thy mental eye, for thou hast much to view:
Old scenes of glory, times long cast behind
Shall, first recalled, rush forward to thy mind:
Then stretch thy sight o'er all her rising reign, 65
And let the past and future fire thy brain.

" Ascend this hill, whose cloudy point commands
Her boundless empire over seas and lands.
See, round the Poles where keener spangles shine,
Where spices smoke beneath the burning Line,   70
(Earth's wide extremes) her sable flag displayed,
And all the nations covered in her shade.

" Far eastward cast thine eye, from whence the Sun
And orient Science their bright course begun:
One god-like Monarch all that pride confounds,   75
He, whose long wall the wand'ring Tartar bounds;
Heavens! what a pile! whole ages perish there,
And one bright blaze turns Learning into air.

" Thence to the south extend thy gladdened eyes
There rival flames with equal glory rise,   80

See, round the Poles, etc.—Almost the whole Southern and Northern
Continent wrapt in ignorance.
Monarch.—Chi Ho-am-ti, Emperor of China, the same who built
the great wall between China and Tartary, destroyed all the books and
learned men of that empire.

From shelves to shelves see greedy Vulcan **roll,**
And lick up all the Physic of the Soul.
How little, mark! that portion of the ball,
Where, faint at best, the beams of Science fall:
Soon as they dawn, from Hyperborean skies   85
Embodied dark, what clouds of Vandals rise!
Lo! where Mæotis sleeps, and hardly flows
The freezing Tanais through a waste of snows,
The North by myriads pours her mighty sons,
Great nurse of Goths, of Alans, and of Huns!   90
See Alaric's stern port! the martial frame
Of Genseric! and Attila's dread name!
See the bold Ostrogoths on Latium fall;
See the fierce Visigoths on Spain and Gaul!
See, where the morning gilds the palmy shore   95
(The soil that arts and infant letters bore)
His conq'ring tribes th' Arabian prophet draws,
And saving Ignorance enthrones by Laws.
See Christians, Jews, one heavy sabbath keep,
And all the western world believe and sleep.   100
" Lo! Rome herself, proud mistress now no **more**
Of arts, but thund'ring against heathen lore;
Her grey-haired Synods damning books unread,
And Bacon trembling for his brazen head.
Padua, with sighs, beholds her Livy burn,   105
And even th' Antipodes Virgilius mourn.
See the Cirque falls, th' unpillared Temple nods,
Streets paved with Heroes, Tiber choked with Gods:
'Til Peter's keys some christened Jove adorn,

Vulcan roll.—The Caliph, Omar I., having conquered Ægypt,
caused his General to burn the Ptolemæan library, on the gates of which
was this inscription, ΨΤΧΗΣΙΑΤΡΕΙΟΝ, the Physic of the Soul.
  The soil that arts and infant letters bore.—Phœnicia, Syria, etc.,
where Letters are said to have been invented. In these countries
Mahomet began his conquests.
  'Til Peter's keys some christened Jove adorn.—After the government
of Rome devolved to the Popes, their zeal was for some time exerted
in demolishing the Heathen Temples and Statues, so that the Goths
scarce destroyed more monuments of Antiquity out of rage, than
these out of devotion. At length they spared some of the temples,

And Pan to Moses lends his pagan horn;   110
See, graceless Venus to a Virgin turned,
Or Phidias broken and Apelles burned.

   " Behold yon' Isle, by Palmers, Pilgrims trod,
Men bearded, bald, cowled, uncowled, shod, unshod,
Peeled, patched, and piebald, linsey-wolsey brothers,
Grave Mummers! sleeveless some, and shirtless others.
That once was Britain—Happy! had she seen   117
No fiercer sons, had Easter never been.
In peace, great Goddess, ever be adored;
How keen the war, if Dulness draw the sword!   120
Thus visit not thy own! on this blest age
Oh spread thy Influence, but restrain thy Rage!

   " And see, my son! the hour is on its way,
That lifts our Goddess to imperial sway:
This fav'rite Isle, long severed from her reign,   125
Dove-like, she gathers to her wings again.
Now look through Fate! behold the scene she draws!
What aids, what armies to assert her cause!
See all her progeny, illustrious sight!
Behold, and count them, as they rise to light.   130
As Berecynthia, while her offspring vie
In homage to the mother of the sky,
Surveys around her, in the blest abode,
An hundred sons, and every son a God:
Not with less glory mighty Dulness crowned   135
Shall take through Grubstreet her triumphant round;
And her Parnassus glancing o'er at once,
Behold an hundred sons, and each a Dunce.

   " Mark first that youth who takes the foremost place,
And thrust his person full into your face.   140

---

by converting them to Churches; and some of the Statues, by modify-
ing them into images of Saints. In much later times, it was thought
necessary to change the statues of Apollo and Pallas, on the tomb
of Sannazarius, into David and Judith; the Lyre easily became a
Harp, and the Gorgon's head turned to that of Holofernes.

   Happy!—had Easter never been.—Wars in England anciently, about
the right time of celebrating Easter.

   Dove-like, she gathers.—This is fulfilled in the fourth book.

With all thy Father's virtues blest, be born!
And a new Cibber shall the stage adorn.
 " A second see, by meeker manners known,
And modest as the maid that sips alone ;
From the strong fate of drams if thou get free,   145
Another Durfey, Ward ! shall sing in thee.
Thee shall each ale-house, thee each gill-house mourn,
And answ'ring gin-shops sourer sights return.
 " Jacob, the scourge of Grammar, mark with awe,
Nor less revere him, blunderbuss of Law.   150
Lo P—p—le's brow, tremendous to the town,
Horneck's fierce eye, and Roome's funereal frown.
Lo sneering Goode, half malice and half whim,
A friend in glee, ridiculously grim.
Each Cygnet sweet, of Bath and Tunbridge race,   155

Jacob, the scourge of Grammar, mark with awe.—" This *Gentleman*
is son of a *considerable Maltster* of Romsey in Southamptonshire, and
bred to the Law under a *very eminent Attorney :* Who, between his
more laborious studies, has *diverted* himself with Poetry. He is a great
admirer of poets and their works, which has occasioned him to try
his genius that way.—He has written in prose the *Lives* of the *Poets,
Essays,* and a great many Law-books, *The Accomplished Conveyancer,
Modern Justice, etc.*—GILES JACOB of himself, *Lives of Poets,* vol. I.
He very grossly, and unprovoked, abused in that book the Author's
Friend, Mr. *Gay.*

Horneck and Roome.—These two were virulent party-writers,worthily
coupled together, and one would think prophetically, since, after the
publishing of this piece, the former dying, the latter succeeded him in
Honour and *Employment.* The first was Philip Horneck, author of a
Billingsgate paper called *The High German Doctor.* Edward Roome
was son of an Undertaker for Funerals in Fleet-street, and writ some
of the papers called *Pasquin,* where by malicious innuendos he endeavoured to represent our Author guilty of malevolent practices with a
great man then under prosecution of Parliament. Of this man was
made the following Epigram :—

 " You ask why Roome diverts you with his jokes,
   Yet if he writes, is dull as other folks ?
   You wonder at it—This, sir, is the case,
   The jest is lost unless he prints his face."

Popple was the author of some vile Plays and Pamphlets. He published abuses on our Author in a paper called the *Prompter.*
 Goode.—An ill-natured Critic, who writ a satire on our Author,
called *The Mock Æsop,* and many anonymous Libels in Newspapers for
hire.

II

Whose tuneful whistling makes the waters pass;
Each Songster, Riddler, every nameless name,
All crowd, who foremost shall be damned to Fame.
Some strain in rhyme ; the Muses, on their racks,
Scream like the winding of ten thousand jacks ;   160
Some free from rhyme or reason, rule or check,
Break Priscian's head, and Pegasus's neck ;
Down, down they larum, with impetuous whirl,
The Pindars, and the Miltons of a Curl.

" Silence, ye Wolves ! while Ralph to Cynthia howls,
And makes night hideous—Answer him, ye Owls !   166
" Sense, speech, and measure, living tongues and dead,
Let all give way, and Morris may be read.
Flow, Welsted, flow ! like thine inspirer, Beer,
Though stale, not ripe ; though thin, yet never clear ;
So sweetly mawkish, and so smoothly dull ;   171
Heady, not strong ; o'erflowing, though not full.
" Ah Dennis ! Gildon ah ! what ill-starred rage

Whose tuneful whistling makes the waters pass.—There were several successions of these sort of minor poets, at Tunbridge, Bath, etc., singing the praise of the Annuals flourishing for that season ; whose names indeed would be nameless, and therefore the Poet slurs them over with others in general.

Ralph.—James Ralph, a name inserted after the first editions, not known to our Author till he writ a swearing-piece called *Sawney*, very abusive of Dr. Swift, Mr. Gay, and himself. These lines allude to a thing of his, entitled, *Night*, a Poem : This low writer attended his own works with Panegyrics in the Journals, and once in particular praised himself highly above Mr. Addison. He was wholly illiterate, and knew no language, not even *French*. Being advised to read the rules of dramatic poetry before he began a play, he smiled and replied, " *Shakespear* writ without rules." He ended at last in the common sink of all such writers, a political Newspaper, to which he was recommended by his friend Arnal, and received a small pittance for pay.

Ah Dennis ! etc.—The reader, who has seen through the course of these notes, what a constant attendance Mr. Dennis paid to our Author and all his works, may perhaps wonder he should be mentioned but twice, and so slightly touched, in this poem. But in truth he looked upon him with some esteem, for having (more generously than all the rest) *set his Name* to such writings. He was also a very old man at this time. By his own account of himself in Mr. *Jacob's Lives*, he must have been above threescore, and happily lived many years after. So that he was senior to Mr. *Durfey*, who hitherto of all our poets enjoyed the longest bodily life.

Divides a friendship long confirmed by age?
Blockheads with reason wicked wits abhor;   175
But fool with fool is barb'rous civil war.
Embrace, embrace, my sons! be foes no more!
Nor glad vile Poets with true Critics' gore.
　" Behold yon Pair, in strict embraces joined;
How like in manners, and how like in mind!   180
Equal in wit, and equally polite,
Shall this a *Pasquin,* that a *Grumbler* write;
Like are their merits, like rewards they share,
That shines a Consul, this Commissioner.
　" But who is he, in closet close y-pent,   185
Of sober face, with learnèd dust besprent?
Right well mine eyes arede the myster wight,
On parchment scraps y-fed, and Wormius hight.
To future ages may thy dulness last,
As thou preserv'st the dulness of the past!   190
　" There, dim in clouds, the poring Scholiasts mark,
Wits, who, like owls, see only in the dark,

Behold yon Pair, etc.—One of these was author of a weekly paper
called the *Grumbler,* as the other was concerned in another called
Pasquin, in which Mr. *Pope* was abused with the Duke of *Buckingham,*
and Bishop of *Rochester.* They also joined in a piece against his first
undertaking, to translate the *Iliad,* intituled *Homerides,* by Sir *Iliad
Doggrel,* printed 1715.
That shines a Consul, this Commissioner.—Such places were given
at this time to such sort of writers.
Arede.—*Read,* or *peruse;* though sometimes used for *counsel.*
Myster wight.—Pope defined the phrase as " uncouth mortal,"
mistaking the meaning of the word myster, used by Spenser, and
meaning manner, craft, or trade.
Wormius.—Let not this name, purely fictitious, be conceited to mean
the learned *Olaus Wormius;* much less (as it was unwarrantably foisted
into the surreptitious editions) our own Antiquary Mr. *Thomas Hearne,*
who had no way aggrieved our Poet, but on the contrary published
many curious tracts which he hath to his great contentment perused.
Hight.—" In Cumberland they say to *hight,* for to *promise,* or *vow;*
but HIGHT usually signifies *was called;* and so it does in the North even
to this day, notwithstanding what is done in Cumberland."—*Hearne.*
Wits, who, like owls, etc.—These few lines exactly describe the right
verbal critic: The darker his author is, the better he is pleased;
like the famous Quack Doctor, who put up in his bills, *he delighted in
matters of difficulty.* Somebody said well of these men, that their
heads were *Libraries out of order.*

A Lumber-house of books in every head,
For ever reading, never to be read!
  " But, where each Science lifts its modern type,
Hist'ry her Pot, Divinity her Pipe,   196
While proud Philosophy repines to show,
Dishonest sight! his breeches rent below;
Embrowned with native bronze, lo! Henley stands,
Turning his voice, and balancing his hands.   200
How fluent nonsense trickles from his tongue!
How sweet the periods, neither said, nor sung!
Still break the benches, Henley! with thy strain,
While Sherlock, Hare, and Gibson preach in vain.
Oh great Restorer of the good old Stage,   205
Preacher at once, and Zany of thy age!
Oh worthy thou of Ægypt's wise abodes,
A decent priest, where monkeys were the gods!
But fate with butchers placed thy priestly stall,
Meek modern faith to murder, hack, and maul;   210
And bade thee live, to crown Britannia's praise,
In Toland's, Tindal's, and in Woolston's days,
  " Yet oh, my sons, a father's words attend:
(So may the fates preserve the ears you lend)
'Tis yours a Bacon or a Locke to blame,   215
A Newton's genius, or a Milton's flame:
But oh! with One, immortal One dispense;
The source of Newton's Light, of Bacon's Sense.
Content, each Emanation of his fires

Lo! Henley stands, etc.—J. Henley the Orator; he preached on the Sundays upon Theological matters, and on the Wednesdays upon all other sciences. Each auditor paid one shilling. He declaimed some years against the greatest persons, and occasionally did our Author that honour. After having stood some Prosecutions, he turned his rhetoric to buffoonery upon all public and private occurrences. This man had an hundred pounds a year given him for the secret service of a weekly paper of unintelligible nonsense, called the *Hyp-Doctor.*
  Sherlock, Hare, Gibson.—Bishops of Salisbury, Chichester, and London; whose Sermons and Pastoral Letters did honour to their country as well as stations.
  Of Toland and *Tindal*, see Book II. *Tho. Woolston* was an impious madman, who wrote in a most insolent style against the Miracles of the Gospel, in the years 1726, etc.

That beams on earth, each Virtue he inspires, 220
Each Art he prompts, each Charm he can create,
Whate'er he gives, are given for you to hate.
Persist, by all divine in Man unawed,
But, ' Learn, ye DUNCES ! not to scorn your God.' "

Thus he, for then a ray of Reason stole 225
Half through the solid darkness of his soul ;
But soon the cloud returned—and thus the Sire :
" See now, what Dulness and her sons admire !
See what the charms, that smite the simple heart
Not touched by Nature, and not reached by Art."

His never-blushing head he turned aside, 231
(Not half so pleased when Goodman prophesied)
And looked, and saw a sable Sorc'rer rise,
Swift to whose hand a wingèd volume flies :
All sudden, Gorgons hiss, and Dragons glare, 235
And ten-horned fiends and Giants rush to war.
Hell rises, Heaven descends, and dance on Earth :
Gods, imps, and monsters, music, rage, and mirth,
A fire, a jig, a battle, and a ball,
'Til one wide conflagration swallows all. 240

But, ' Learn, ye Dunces ! not to scorn your God.'—Virg. *Æn.* VI.
[v. 619]. The hardest lesson a *Dunce* can learn. For being bred to
scorn what he does not understand, that which he understands least
he will be apt to *scorn* most. Of which, to the disgrace of all Government, and (in the Poet's opinion) even of that of DULNESS herself,
we have had a late example in a book entitled, *Philosophical Essays
concerning human Understanding.*—WARBURTON.
" *Not to scorn your God.*"—See this subject pursued in Book IV.
Not half so pleased when Goodman prophesied.—Mr. Cibber tells
us, in his *Life*, p. 149, that Goodman being at the rehearsal of a play,
in which he had a part, clapped him on the shoulder and cried, " If
he does not make a good actor, I'll be d—d."—And (says Mr. Cibber)
I make it a question, whether Alexander himself, or Charles the Twelfth
of Sweden, when at the head of their first victorious armies, could feel
a greater transport in their bosoms than I did in mine.
A sable Sorc'rer.—Dr. Faustus, the subject of a set of Farces, which
lasted in vogue two or three seasons, in which both Play-houses strove
to outdo each other for some years. All the extravagances in the
sixteen lines following were introduced on the Stage, and frequented
by persons of the first quality in England, to the twentieth and thirtieth time.
Hell rises, Heaven descends, and dance on Earth.—This monstrous
absurdity was actually represented in Tibbald's *Rape of Proserpine.*

Thence a new world to Nature's laws unknown,
Breaks out refulgent, with a heaven its own:
Another Cynthia her new journey runs,
And other planets circle other suns.
The forests dance, the rivers upward rise,　　　　　245
Whales sport in woods, and dolphins in the skies;
And last, to give the whole creation grace,
Lo! one vast Egg produces human race.
　　Joy fills his soul, joy innocent of thought;
'What power,' he cries, 'what power these wonders
　　　　wrought?'　　　　　250
"Son, what thou seek'st is in thee! Look, and
　　find
Each monster meets his likeness in thy mind.
Yet wouldst thou more? in yonder cloud behold,
Whose sars'net skirts are edged with flamy gold,
A matchless youth! his nod these worlds controls,　255
Wings the red lightning, and the thunder rolls.
Angel of Dulness, sent to scatter round
Her magic charms o'er all unclassic ground:
Yon stars, yon suns, he rears at pleasure higher,
Illumes their light, and sets their flames on fire.　260
Immortal Rich! how calm he sits at ease
'Mid snows of paper, and fierce hail of pease;
And proud his Mistress' orders to perform,
Rides in the whirlwind, and directs the storm.
　　"But lo! to dark encounter in mid air　　　265
New wizards rise; I see my Cibber there!
Booth in his cloudy tabernacle shrined,
On grinning dragons thou shalt mount the wind.

　　Lo! one vast Egg.—In another of these Farces, Harlequin is hatched
upon the stage out of a large Egg.
　　Immortal Rich.—Mr. John Rich, Master of the Theatre Royal in
Covent-garden, was the first that excelled this way.
　　Booth.—Booth and Cibber were joint managers of the Theatre in
Drury-lane.
　　On grinning dragons thou shalt mount the wind.—In his Letter to
Ir. P. Mr. C. solemnly declares this not to be literally true. We
ope therefore the reader will understand it *allegorically* only.

Dire is the conflict, dismal is the din,
Here shouts all Drury, there all Lincoln's-inn ;　270
Contending Theatres our empire raise,
Alike their labours, and alike their praise.
　" And are these wonders, Son, to thee unknown ?
Unknown to thee ?　these wonders are thy own.
These Fate reserved to grace thy reign divine,　275
Foreseen by me, but ah ! withheld from mine.
In Lud's old walls though long I ruled, renowned
Far as loud Bow's stupendous bells resound ;
Though my own Aldermen conferred the bays,
To me committing their eternal praise,　　280
Their full-fed Heroes, their pacific May'rs,
Their annual trophies, and their monthly wars ;
Though long my Party built on me their hopes,
For writing Pamphlets, and for roasting Popes ;
Yet lo ! in me what authors have to brag on !　285
Reduced at last to hiss in my own dragon.
Avert it, Heaven ! that thou, my Cibber, e'er
Shouldst wag a serpent-tail in Smithfield fair !
Like the vile straw that's blown about the streets,
The needy Poet sticks to all he meets,　　290
Coached, carted, trod upon, now loose, now fast,
And carried off in some Dog's tail at last.
Happier thy fortunes ! like a rolling stone,
Thy giddy dulness still shall lumber on,
Safe in its heaviness, shall never stray,　　295
But lick up every blockhead in the way.

Annual trophies, on the Lord-mayor's day ; and *monthly wars* in the Artillery-ground.
　Though long my Party.—Settle, like most Party-writers, was very uncertain in his political principles. He was employed to hold the pen in the *Character* of a *popish successor*, but afterwards printed his *Narrative* on the other side. He had managed the ceremony of a famous Pope-burning on November 17, 1680 ; then became a trooper in King James's army, at Hounslow-heath. After the Revolution he kept a booth at Bartholomew-fair, where, in the droll called *St. George for England*, he acted in his old age in a Dragon of green leather of his own invention ; he was at last taken into the Charter-house, and there died, aged sixty years.

Thee shall the Patriot, thee the Courtier taste,
And every year be duller than the last.
Till raised from booths, to Theatre, to Court,
Her seat imperial Dulness shall transport.   300
Already Opera prepares the way,
The sure fore-runner of her gentle sway :
Let her thy heart, next Drabs and Dice, engage,
The third mad passion of thy doting age.
Teach thou the warbling Polypheme to roar,   305
And scream thyself as none e'er screamed before !
To aid our cause, if Heaven thou canst not bend,
Hell thou shalt move ; for Faustus is our friend :
Pluto with Cato thou for this shalt join,
And link the Mourning Bride to Proserpine.   310
Grubstreet ! thy fall should men and Gods conspire,
Thy stage shall stand, ensure it but from Fire.
Another Æschylus appears ! prepare
For new abortions, all ye pregnant fair !
In flames, like Semele's, be brought to bed,   315
While opening Hell spouts wild-fire at your head.
    " Now, Bavius, take the poppy from thy brow,
And place it here ! here all ye Heroes bow !
This, this is he, foretold by ancient rhymes :
Th' Augustus born to bring Saturnian times.   320

Thee shall the Patriot, thee the Courtier taste.—It stood in the first
edition with blanks * * *and* * *. Concanen was sure " they must
needs mean no body but *King GEORGE* and *Queen CAROLINE ;*
and said he would insist it was so, till the Poet cleared himself by filling
up the blanks otherwise, agreeably to the context, and consistent with
his *allegiance.*"

Polypheme.—He translated the Italian Opera of *Polifemo ;* but
unfortunately lost the whole jest of the story.

Faustus, Pluto, etc.—Names of miserable Farces, which it was the
custom to act at the end of the best Tragedies, to spoil the digestion
of the audience.

Ensure it but from Fire.—In Tibbald's farce of *Proserpine*, a corn-
field was set on fire : whereupon the other play-house had a barn
burnt down for the recreation of the spectators. They also rivalled
each other in showing the burnings of hell-fire, in *Dr. Faustus.*

Another Æschylus appears.—It is reported of Æschylus, that when
his Tragedy of the *Furies* was acted, the audience were so terrified that
the children fell into fits.

Signs following signs lead on the mighty year!
See! the dull stars roll round and re-appear.
See, see, our own true Phœbus wears the bays!
Our Midas sits Lord Chancellor of Plays!
On Poets' Tombs see Benson's titles writ!   325
Lo! Ambrose Philips is preferred for Wit!
See under Ripley rise a new White-hall,
While Jones' and Boyle's united Labours fall;
While Wren with sorrow to the grave descends;
Gay dies unpensioned with a hundred friends;   330

On Poets' Tombs see Benson's titles writ.—W—m Benson (Surveyor of the Buildings to his Majesty King George I.) gave in a report to the Lords, that their House and the Painted-chamber adjoining were in immediate danger of falling. Whereupon the Lords met in a committee to appoint some other place to sit in, while the House should be taken down. But it being proposed to cause some other builders first to inspect it, they found it in very good condition. In favour of this man, the famous Sir Christopher Wren, who had been Architect to the Crown for above fifty years, who built most of the churches in London, laid the first stone of St. Paul's, and lived to finish it, had been displaced from his employment at the age of near ninety years.

Ambrose Philips.—"He was (saith Mr. JACOB) one of the wits at Button's and a justice of the peace;" But he hath since met with higher preferment in Ireland. He endeavoured to create some misunderstanding between our Author and Mr. Addison, whom also soon after he abused as much. His constant cry was, that Mr. P. was an *Enemy to the government;* and in particular he was the avowed author of a report very industriously spread, that he had a hand in a Party-paper called the *Examiner:* A falsehood well known to those yet living, who had the direction and publication of it.

While Jones' and Boyle's united Labours fall.—At the time when this poem was written, the banqueting-house at White-hall, the church and piazza of Covent-garden, and the palace and chapel of Somerset-house, the works of the famous Inigo Jones, had been for many years so neglected, as to be in danger of ruin. The portico of Covent-garden church had been just then restored and beautified at the expense of the Earl of Burlington [*i.e.* Richard Boyle]; who, at the same time by his publication of the designs of that great Master and Palladio, as well as by many noble buildings of his own, revived the true taste of Architecture in this kingdom.

Gay dies unpensioned, etc.—See Mr. Gay's fable of the *Hare and many Friends.* This gentleman was early in the friendship of our Author, which continued to his death. He wrote several works of humour with great success, the *Shepherd's Week, Trivia,* the *What-d'ye-call-it, Fables;* and, lastly, the celebrated *Beggar's Opera;*

Hibernian Politics, O Swift ! thy fate ;
And Pope's, ten years to comment and translate.
  " Proceed, great days ! till Learning fly the shore,
Till Birch shall blush with noble blood no more,

a piece of satire which hits all tastes and degrees of men, from those of the highest quality to the very rabble.   That verse of Horace,

Primores populi arripuit, populumque tributim,

could never be so justly applied as to this.   The vast success of it was unprecedented, and almost incredible : What is related of the wonderful effects of the ancient music or tragedy hardly came up to it ; Sophocles and Euripides were less followed and famous.   It was acted in London sixty-three days, uninterrupted ; and renewed the next season with equal applauses.   It spread into all the great towns of England, was played in many places to the thirtieth and fortieth time, at Bath and Bristol fifty, etc.   It made its progress into Wales, Scotland, and Ireland, where it was performed twenty-four days together : It was last acted in Minorca.   The fame of it was not confined to the Author only ; the ladies carried about with them the favourite songs of it in fans ; and houses were furnished with it in screens.   The person who acted Polly, till then obscure, became all at once the favourite of the town ; her pictures were engraved, and sold in great numbers ; her life written, books of letters and verses to her published ; and pamphlets made even of her sayings and jests.

  Furthermore, it drove out of England, for that season, the Italian Opera, which had carried all before it for ten years.   That idol of the Nobility and people, which the great Critic Mr. Dennis by the labours and outcries of a whole life could not overthrow, was demolished by a single stroke of this gentleman's pen.   This happened in the year 1728.   Yet so great was his modesty, that he constantly prefixed to all the editions of it this motto, *Nos hæc novimus esse nihil.*

  O Swift ! thy fate.—Ver. 331, in the former Editions thus :
              "——O Swift ! thy doom,
    And Pope's, translating ten whole years with Broome."
On which was the following Note, " He concludes his irony with a stroke upon himself ; for whoever imagines this a sarcasm on the other ingenious person is surely mistaken.   The opinion our Author had of him was sufficiently shewn by his joining him in the undertaking of the *Odyssey ;* in which Mr. Broome, having engaged without any previous agreement, discharged his part so much to Mr. Pope's satisfaction, that he gratified him with the full sum of *Five hundred pounds,* and a present of all those books for which his own interest could procure him subscribers, to the value of *One hundred more.*   The Author only seems to lament, that he was employed in Translation at all."

  And Pope's, ten years to comment and translate.—The Author here plainly laments that he was so long enployed in translating and commenting.   He began the *Iliad* in 1713, and finished it in 1719.   The edition of Shakespear (which he undertook merely because nobody else would) took up near two years more in the drudgery of comparing impressions, rectifying the Scenery, etc., and the translation of half the *Odyssey* employed him from that time to 1725.

Till Thames see Eton's sons for ever play,   335
Till Westminster's whole year be holiday,
Till Isis' Elders reel, their pupils' sport,
And Alma Mater lie dissolved in Port ! "
   ' Enough ! enough ! ' the raptured Monarch cries ;
And through the Iv'ry Gate the Vision flies.   340

BOOK THE FOURTH

Book the Fourth.—This book may properly be distinguished from the former, by the Name of the GREATER DUNCIAD, not so indeed in Size, but in Subject ; and so far contrary to the distinction anciently made of the *Greater* and *Lesser Iliad.* But much are they mistaken who imagine this Work in any wise inferior to the former, or of any other hand than of our Poet ; of which I am much more certain than that the *Iliad* itself was the work of *Solomon,* or the *Batrachomuomachia* of *Homer,* as *Barnes* hath affirmed.—" BENTLEY."

ARGUMENT

The Poet being, in this Book, to declare the *Completion* of the *Prophecies* mentioned at the end of the former, makes a new *Invocation ;* as the greater Poets are wont, when some high and worthy matter is to be sung. He shews the Goddess coming in her Majesty, to destroy *Order* and *Science,* and to substitute the *Kingdom of the Dull* upon earth. How she leads captive the *Sciences,* and silenceth the *Muses,* and *what* they be who succeed in their stead. All her Children, by a wonderful attraction, are drawn about her ; and bear along with them divers others, who promote her Empire by connivance, weak resistance, or discouragement of Arts ; such as Half-wits, tasteless Admirers, vain Pretenders, the Flatterers of Dunces, or the Patrons of them. All these crowd round her ; one of them offering to approach her is driven back by a Rival ; but she commends and encourages both. The first who speak in form are the Geniuses of the *Schools,* who assure her of their care to advance her Cause, by confining Youth to *Words,* and keeping them out of the way of real Knowledge. Their Address, and her gracious Answer ; with her Charge to them and the Universities. The *Universities* appear by their proper Deputies, and assure her that the same method is observed in the progress of *Education.* The speech of *Aristarchus* on this subject. They are drawn off by a band of young Gentlemen returned from *Travel* with their *Tutors ;* one of whom delivers to the Goddess, in a polite oration, an account of the whole Conduct and Fruits of their *Travels :* presenting to her at the same time a young Nobleman perfectly accomplished. She receives him graciously, and endues him with the happy quality of *Want of Shame.*

She sees loitering about her a number of *Indolent Persons* abandoning all business and duty, and dying with laziness : To these approaches the Antiquary *Annius,* entreating her to make them *Virtuoso's,* and assign them over to him : But *Mummius,* another Antiquary, complaining of his fraudulent proceeding, she finds a method to reconcile their difference. Then enter a troop of people fantastically adorned, offering her strange and exotic presents : Amongst them one stands forth and demands justice on another, who had deprived him of one of the greatest Curiosities in nature ; but he justifies himself so well, that the Goddess gives them both her approbation. She recommends to them to find proper employment for the *Indolents* before-mentioned, in the study of *Butterflies, Shells, Birds-nests, Moss, etc.,* but with particular caution, not to proceed beyond *Trifles,* to any useful or extensive views of Nature, or of the Author of Nature. Against the last of these apprehensions, she is secured by a hearty address from the *Minute Philosophers* and *Freethinkers,* one of whom speaks in the name of the rest. The Youth, thus instructed and principled, are delivered to her in a body, by the hands of *Silenus,* and then admitted to taste the cup of the *Magus,* her High Priest, which causes a total blivion of all Obligations, divine, civil, moral, or rational. To these her Adepts she sends *Priests, Attendants,* and *Comforters,* of various kinds ; confers on them *Orders* and *Degrees ;* and then dismissing them with a speech, confirming to each his *Privileges,* and telling what she expects from each, concludes with a *Yawn* of extraordinary virtue : The Progress and Effects whereof on all Orders of men, and the Consummation of all, in the restoration of *Night* and *Chaos,* conclude the Poem.

YET, yet a moment, one dim Ray of Light
Indulge, dread Chaos, and eternal Night !
Of darkness visible so much be lent,
As half to shew, half veil, the deep Intent.
Ye Powers ! whose Mysteries restored I sing,   5
To whom Time bears me on his rapid wing,
Suspend a while your Force inertly strong,
Then take at once the Poet and the Song.
   Now flamed the Dog-star's unpropitious ray,
Smote every Brain, and withered every Bay ;   10
Sick was the Sun, the Owl forsook his bower,
The moon-struck Prophet felt the madding hour :
Then rose the Seed of Chaos, and of Night,
To blot out Order, and extinguish Light,

Force inertly strong.—Alluding to the *Vis inertiæ of Matter,* which, though it really be no Power, is yet the Foundation of all the Qualities and Attributes of that sluggish Substance.

Of dull and venal a new World to mould, 15
And bring Saturnian days of Lead and Gold.
   She mounts the Throne : her head a Cloud concealed,
In broad Effulgence all below revealed ;
('Tis thus aspiring Dulness ever shines)
Soft on her lap her Laureate son reclines. 20
   Beneath her footstool, *Science* groans in Chains,
And *Wit* dreads Exile, Penalties, and Pains.
There foamed rebellious *Logic*, gagged and bound,
There, stript, fair *Rhet'ric* languished on the ground ;
His blunted Arms by *Sophistry* are borne, 25
And shameless *Billingsgate* her Robes adorn.
Morality, by her false Guardians drawn,
Chicane in Furs, and *Casuistry* in Lawn,
Gasps, as they straiten at each end the cord,
And dies, when Dulness gives her Page the word. 30
Mad *Máthesis* alone was unconfined,
Too mad for mere material chains to bind,
Now to pure Space lifts her ecstatic stare,
Now running round the Circle finds it square.
But held in ten-fold bonds the *Muses* lie, 35
Watched both by Envy's and by Flatt'ry's eye :

A new World.—In allusion to the Epicurean opinion, that from the Dissolution of the natural World into Night and Chaos a new one should arise ; this the Poet alluding to, in the Production of a new moral World, makes it partake of its original Principles.

Beneath her footstool, etc.—We are next presented with the pictures of those whom the Goddess leads in captivity. *Science* is only depressed and confined so as to be rendered useless ; but *Wit* or *Genius*, as a more dangerous and active enemy, punished, or driven away : *Dulness* being often reconciled in some degree with learning, but never upon any terms with Wit. And accordingly it will be seen that she admits something *like* each Science, as Casuistry, Sophistry, etc., but nothing like *Wit*, *Opera* alone supplying its place.

Gives her Page the word.—There was a Judge of this name, always ready to hang any Man that came before him, of which he was suffered to give a hundred miserable examples during a long life, even to his dotage.

Mad Máthesis.—Alluding to the strange Conclusions some Mathematicians have deduced from their principles, concerning the *real Quantity of Matter*, the *Reality of Space*, etc.

Running round the Circle *finds it square.*—Regards the wild and fruitless attempts of *squaring the Circle.*

Watched both by Envy's and by Flatt'ry's eye.—One of the mis-

There to her heart sad Tragedy addrest
The dagger wont to pierce the Tyrant's breast;
But sober History restrained her rage,
And promised Vengeance on a barb'rous age.   40
There sunk Thalia, nerveless, cold, and dead,
Had not her Sister Satire held her head:
Nor couldst thou, CHESTERFIELD! a tear refuse,
Thou weptst, and with thee wept each gentle Muse.
When lo! a Harlot form soft sliding by,   45
With mincing step, small voice, and languid eye:
Foreign her air, her robe's discordant pride
In patch-work flutt'ring and her head aside:
By singing Peers up-held on either hand,
She tripped and laughed, too pretty much to stand;
Cast on the prostrate Nine a scornful look,   51
Then thus in quaint Recitativo spoke.
  " O *Cara! Cara!* silence all that train:
Joy to great Chaos! let Division reign:
Chromatic tortures soon shall drive them hence,   55

fortunes falling on Authors from the *Act* for subjecting *Plays* to the
power of a *Licenser*, being the false representations to which they
were exposed, from such as either gratified their Envy to Merit, or
made their Court to Greatness, by perverting general Reflections
against Vice into Libels on particular Persons.
  When lo! a Harlot form.—The Attitude given to this Phantom represents the nature and genius of the *Italian* Opera; its affected airs,
its effeminate sounds, and the practice of patching up these Operas
with favourite Songs, incoherently put together. These things were
supported by the subscriptions of the Nobility. This circumstance
that OPERA should prepare for the opening of the grand Sessions was
prophesied of in Book III.
  Let Division reign.—Alluding to the false taste of playing tricks in
Music with numberless divisions, to the neglect of that harmony which
conforms to the Sense, and applies to the Passions. Mr. *Handel* had
introduced a great number of Hands, and more variety of Instruments
into the Orchestra, and employed even Drums and Cannon to make
a fuller Chorus; which proved so much too manly for the fine Gentlemen of his age, that he was obliged to remove his music into *Ireland*.
After which they were reduced, for want of Composers, to practice the
patch-work above-mentioned.
  Chromatic tortures.—That species of the ancient music called the *Chromatic* was a variation and embellishment, in odd irregularities, of the
Diatonic kind. They say it was invented about the time of *Alexander*,
and that the *Spartans* forbade the use of it, as languid and effeminate.

Break all their nerves, and fritter all their sense:
One Trill shall harmonize joy, grief, and rage,
Wake the dull Church, and lull the ranting Stage;
To the same notes thy sons shall hum, or snore,
And all thy yawning daughters cry, *encore.*   60
Another Phœbus, thy own Phœbus, reigns,
Joys in my jigs, and dances in my chains.
But soon, ah soon, Rebellion will commence,
If Music meanly borrows aid from Sense.
Strong in new Arms, lo ! Giant HANDEL stands,   65
Like bold Briareus, with a hundred hands ;
To stir, to rouse, to shake the soul he comes,
And Jove's own Thunders follow Mars's Drums.
Arrest him, Empress ; or you sleep no more—"
She heard, and drove him to th' Hibernian shore.   70
  And now had Fame's posterior Trumpet blown,
And all the Nations summoned to the Throne.
The young, the old, who feel her inward sway,
One instinct seizes, and transports away.
None need a guide, by sure attraction led,   75
And strong impulsive gravity of Head ;
None want a place, for all their Centre found,
Hung to the Goddess, and cohered around.
Not closer, orb in orb, conglobed are seen
The buzzing Bees about their dusky Queen.   80
  The gath'ring number, as it moves along,
Involves a vast involuntary throng,
Who gently drawn, and struggling less and less,
Roll in her Vortex, and her power confess.

Giant Handel.—It is remarkable, that in the earlier part of his life,
Pope was so very insensible to the charms of music, that he once asked
his friend, Dr. Arbuthnot, who had a fine ear, "whether, at Lord
Burlington's concerts, the rapture which the company expressed upon
hearing the compositions and performance of Handel did not proceed
wholly from affectation."

Fame's posterior Trumpet.—According to Hudibras :—

    " She blows not both with the same Wind,
    But one before and one behind ;
    And therefore modern Authors name
    One good, and t' other evil Fame."

Not those alone who passive own her laws,   85
But who, weak rebels, more advance her cause.
Whate'er of dunce in College or in Town
Sneers at another, in toupee or gown ;
Whate'er of mongrel no one class admits,
A wit with dunces, and a dunce with wits.   90
    Nor absent they, no members of her state,
Who pay her homage in her sons, the Great ;
Who, false to Phœbus, bow the knee to Baal ;
Or, impious, preach his word without a call.
Patrons, who sneak from living worth to dead,   95
Withhold the pension, and set up the head ;
Or vest dull Flatt'ry in the sacred Gown ;
Or give from fool to fool the Laurel crown.
And (last and worst) with all the cant of wit,
Without the soul, the Muse's Hypocrite.   100
    There marched the bard and blockhead, side by side,
Who rhymed for hire, and patronized for pride.
Narcissus, praised with all a Parson's power,
Looked a white lily sunk beneath a shower.
There moved Montalto with superior air ;   105
His stretched-out arm displayed a volume fair ;
Courtiers and Patriots in two ranks divide,
Through both he passed, and bowed from side to side :
But as in graceful act, with awful eye
Composed he stood, bold Benson thrust him by :   110
On two unequal crutches propt he came,
Milton's on this, on that one Johnston's name.
The decent Knight retired with sober rage,

    Looked a white lily sunk beneath a shower.—Means Dr. Middleton's
laboured encomium on Lord Hervey, in his dedication of the *Life of
Cicero.*
    Bowed from side to side.—As being of no *one* party.
    Bold Benson.—This man endeavoured to raise himself to Fame by
erecting monuments, striking coins, setting up heads, and procuring
translations, of *Milton ;* and afterwards by as great passion for *Arthur
Johnston,* a *Scotch* physician's version of the Psalms, of which he
printed many fine editions. See more of him, Book III.
    The decent Knight.—An eminent person, Sir Thomas Hanmer, who
was about to publish a very pompous edition of a great Author, *at his
own expense.*

Withdrew his hand, and closed the pompous page.
But (happy for him as the times went then)   115
Appeared Apollo's Mayor and Aldermen,
On whom three hundred gold-capt youths await,
To lug the pond'rous volume off in state.
   When Dulness, smiling—" Thus revive the Wits!
But murder first, and mince them all to bits ;   120
As erst Medea (cruel, so to save !)
A new Edition of old Æson gave ;
Let standard-authors, thus, like trophies born,
Appear more glorious as more hacked and torn.
And you, my Critics ! in the chequered shade,   125
Admire new light through holes yourselves have made.
" Leave not a foot of verse, a foot of stone,
A Page, a Grave, that they can call their own ;
But spread, my sons, your glory thin or thick,
On passive paper, or on solid brick.   130
So by each Bard an Alderman shall sit,
A heavy Lord shall hang at every Wit,
And while on Fame's triumphal Car they ride,
Some Slave of mine be pinioned to their side."
   Now crowds on crowds around the Goddess press, 135
Each eager to present their first Address.
Dunce scorning Dunce beholds the next advance,
But Fop shews Fop superior complaisance,
When lo ! a Spectre rose, whose index-hand
Held forth the virtue of the dreadful wand ;   140

Thus revive, etc.—The Goddess applauds the practice of tacking the
obscure names of Persons not eminent in any branch of learning, to
those of the most distinguished Writers ; either by printing *Editions*
of their works with impertinent alterations of their Text, as in the
former instances ; or by setting up *Monuments* disgraced with their
own vile names and inscriptions, as in the latter.

Old Æson.—Of whom Ovid (very applicable to these restored authors),
" Æson *miratur*,
Dissimilemque animum *subiit*."

A Page.—*Pagina*, not *Pedissequus*. A Page of a Book ; not a
Servant, Follower, or Attendant ; no Poet having had a *Page* since
the death of Mr. Thomas Durfey.—*Scriblerus*.

An Alderman shall sit.—Alluding to the monument erected for
Butler by Alderman Barber.

His beavered brow a birchen garland wears,
Dropping with Infant's blood, and Mother's tears.
O'er every vein a shudd'ring horror runs ;
Eton and Winton shake through all their Sons.
All Flesh is humbled, Westminster's bold race   145
Shrink, and confess the genius of the place :
The pale Boy-Senator yet tingling stands,
And holds his breeches close with both his hands.
    Then thus. "Since Man from beast by Words is
        known,
Words are Man's province, Words we teach alone.   150
When Reason doubtful, like the Samian letter,
Points him two ways, the narrower is the better.
Placed at the door of Learning, youth to guide,
We never suffer it to stand too wide.
To ask, to guess, to know, as they commence,   155
As Fancy opens the quick springs of Sense,
We ply the Memory, we load the brain,
Bind rebel Wit, and double chain on chain ;
Confine the thought, to exercise the breath ;
And keep them in the pale of Words till death.   160
Whate'er the talents, or howe'er designed,
We hang one jingling padlock on the mind :
A Poet the first day he dips his quill ;
And what the last ? A very Poet still.
Pity ! the charm works only in our wall,   165
Lost, lost too soon in yonder House or Hall.
There truant WYNDHAM every Muse gave o'er,

Like the Samian letter.—The letter Y, used by Pythagoras as an emblem of the different roads of Virtue and Vice.
              " Et tibi quæ Samios diduxit litera ramos."
Pers. [*Sat.* III. v. 56].
    Placed at the door, etc.—This circumstance of the *Genius Loci* (with that of the Index-hand before) seems to be an allusion to the *Table of Cebes*, where the Genius of human Nature points out the road to be pursued by those entering into life.
    To stand too wide.—A pleasant allusion to the description of the door of Wisdom in the *Table of Cebes*.
    In yonder House or Hall.—Westminster-hall and the House of Commons.

There TALBOT sunk, and was a Wit no more!
How sweet an Ovid, MURRAY was our boast!
How many Martials were in PULT'NEY lost! 170
Else sure some Bard, to our eternal praise,
In twice ten thousand rhyming nights and days,
Had reached the Work, the All that mortal can;
And South beheld that Master-piece of Man.
   " Oh " (cried the Goddess) " for some   pedant
     Reign! 175
Some gentle JAMES, to bless the land again;
To stick the Doctor's Chair into the Throne,
Give law to Words, or war with Words alone,
Senates and Courts with Greek and Latin rule,
And turn the Council to a Grammar School! 180
For sure, if Dulness sees a grateful Day,
'Tis in the shade of Arbitrary Sway.
O! if my sons may learn one earthly thing,
Teach but that one, sufficient for a King;
That which my Priests, and mine alone, maintain, 185
Which as it dies, or lives, we fall, or reign:
May you, may Cam and Isis, preach it long!
' The RIGHT DIVINE of Kings to govern wrong.' "
   Prompt at the call, around the Goddess roll
Broad hats, and hoods, and caps, a sable shoal: 190
Thick and more thick the black blockade extends,

That Master-piece of Man.—Namely, an *Epigram.* The famous Dr. South declared a perfect Epigram to be as difficult a performance as an Epic Poem. And the Critics say, " an Epic Poem is the greatest work human nature is capable of."

Some gentle James, etc.—Wilson tells us that this King, *James* the First, took upon himself to teach the Latin tongue to Car, Earl of Somerset; and that Gondomar, the Spanish ambassador, would speak false Latin to him, on purpose to give him the pleasure of correcting it, whereby he wrought himself into his good graces.

This great Prince was the first who assumed the title of *Sacred Majesty.*

Prompt at the call—Aristotle's friends.—The Author, with great propriety, hath made these, who were so *prompt at the call* of Dulness, to become preachers of the Divine Right of Kings, to be the *friends* of *Aristotle;* for this philosopher, in his *politics,* hath laid it down as a principle, that some men were, by nature, made to serve, and others to command.

A hundred head of Aristotle's friends.
Nor wert thou, Isis ! wanting to the day,
[Though Christ-church long kept prudishly away.]
Each staunch Polemic, stubborn as a rock,   195
Each fierce Logician, still expelling Locke,
Came whip and spur, and dashed through thin and thick
On German Crowzaz, and Dutch Burgersdyck.
As many quit the streams that murm'ring fall
To lull the sons of Marg'ret and Clare-hall,   200
Where Bentley late tempestuous wont to sport
In troubled waters, but now sleeps in Port.
Before them marched that awful Aristarch ;
Ploughed was his front with many a deep Remark :
His Hat, which never vailed to human pride,   205
Walker with rev'rence took, and laid aside.
Low bowed the rest : He, kingly, did but nod ;
So upright Quakers please both Man and God.
Mistress ! dismiss that rabble from your throne :

A hundred head of Aristotle's friends.—The Philosophy of *Aristotle* hath suffered a long disgrace in this learned University : being first expelled by the *Cartesian*, which, in its turn, gave place to the *Newtonian*. But it had all this while some faithful followers in secret, who never bowed the knee to *Baal*, nor acknowledged any strange God in Philosophy. These, on this new appearance of the Goddess, come out like Confessors, and made an open profession of the ancient faith, in the *ipse dixit* of their Master.—SCRIBLERUS.

Though Christ-church, etc.—This line is doubtless spurious, and foisted in by the impertinence of the Editor ; and accordingly we have put it between Hooks. For I affirm this College came as early as any other, by its *proper Deputies ;* nor did any College pay homage to Dulness in its *whole body.*—"BENTLEY."

Still expelling Locke.—In the year 1703 there was a meeting of the heads of the University of Oxford to censure Mr. Locke's *Essay on Human Understanding,* and to forbid the reading it. See his Letters in the last Edition.

The streams.—The river Cam, running by the walls of these Colleges, which are particularly famous for their skill in Disputation.

Sleeps in Port.—Namely, "now retired into harbour, after the tempests that had long agitated his society."—So SCRIBLERUS. But the learned *Scipio Maffei* understands it of a certain wine called *Port,* from *Oporto,* a city of Portugal, of which this Professor invited him to drink abundantly.—SCIP. MAFF. *De Compotationibus Academicis.*

Walker.—John Walker, Vice-Master of Trinity College, Cambridge, while Bentley was Master

Avaunt——is Aristarchus yet unknown?   210
Thy mighty Scholiast, whose unwearied pains
Made Horace dull, and humbled Milton's strains.
Turn what they will to Verse, their toil is vain,
Critics like me shall make it Prose again.   214
Roman and Greek Grammarians! know your Better:
Author of something yet more great than Letter;
While tow'ring o'er your Alphabet, like Saul,
Stands our Digamma, and o'er-tops them all.
'Tis true, on Words is still our whole debate,
Disputes of *Me* or *Te*, of *aut* or *at*,   220
To sound or sink in *cano*, O or A,
Or give up Cicero to C or K.
Let Freind affect to speak as Terence spoke,
And Alsop never but like Horace joke:
For me, what Virgil, Pliny may deny,   225
Manilius or Solinus shall supply:
For Attic Phrase in Plato let them seek,

Aristarchus.—A famous Commentator, and Corrector of Homer, whose name has been frequently used to signify a complete Critic. The compliment paid by our Author to this eminent Professor, in applying to him so great a Name, was the reason that he hath omitted to comment on this part which contains his own praises. We shall therefore supply that loss to our best ability.—SCRIBL.

Critics like me.—Alluding to two famous Editions of Horace and Milton: whose richest veins of Poetry he hath prodigally reduced to the poorest and most beggarly prose.—SCRIBL.

Author of something yet more great than Letter.—Alluding to those Grammarians, such as Palamedes and Simonides, who invented *single letters*. But Aristarchus, who had found out a *double* one, was therefore worthy of double honour.—SCRIBL.

While tow'ring o'er your Alphabet, like Saul, Stands our Digamma.—Alludes to the boasted restoration of the Æolic Digamma, in his long projected Edition of Homer.

Of Me or Te.—It was a serious dispute, about which the learned were much divided, and some treatises written: Had it been about *Meum* or *Tuum*, it could not be more contested, than whether at the end of the first Ode of Horace, to read, Me *doctarum hederæ præmia frontium*, or, Te *doctarum hederæ, etc.*—SCRIBL.

Or give up Cicero to C or K.—Grammatical disputes about the manner of pronouncing Cicero's name in Greek.

Freind—Alsop.—Dr. Robert Freind, master of Westminster-school, and canon of Christ-church—Dr. Anthony Alsop, a happy imitator of the Horatian style.

I poach in Suidas for unlicensed Greek.
In ancient Sense if any needs will deal,
Be sure I give them Fragments, not a Meal;   230
What Gellius or Stobæus hashed before,
Or chewed by blind old Scholiasts o'er and o'er.
The critic Eye, that microscope of Wit,
Sees hairs and pores, examines bit by bit:
How parts relate to parts, or they to whole,   235
The body's harmony, the beaming soul,
Are things, which Kuster, Burman, Wasse shall see,
When Man's whole frame is obvious to a *Flea.*
    " Ah, think not, Mistress ! more true Dulness lies
In Folly's Cap, than Wisdom's grave disguise.   240
Like buoys that never sink into the flood,
On Learning's surface we but lie and nod.
Thine is the genuine head of many a house,
And much Divinity without a Νοῦς,
Nor could a BARROW work on every block,   245
Nor has one ATTERBURY spoiled the flock.
See ! still thy own, the heavy Canon roll,
And Metaphysic smokes involve the Pole.
For thee we dim the eyes, and stuff the head
With all such reading as was never read: 250
For thee explain a thing till all men doubt it,
And write about it, Goddess, and about it:

    Suidas, Gellius, Stobæus.—The first a Dictionary-writer, a collector
of impertinent facts and barbarous words ; the second a minute Critic ;
the third an author, who gave his Common-place book to the public,
where we happen to find much Mince-meat of old books.
    Kuster, Burman, and *Wasse.*—Three men of real and useful erudition.
    Barrow, Atterbury.—Isaac Barrow, Master of Trinity, Francis Atter-
bury, Dean of Christ-church, both great Geniuses and eloquent
Preachers ; one more conversant in the sublime Geometry ; the other
in classical Learning ; but who equally made it their care to advance
the polite Arts in their several Societies.
    Canon.—Canon here, if spoken of Artillery, is in the plural number ;
if of the *Canons of the House,* in the singular, and meant only of *one ;*
in which case I suspect the *Pole* to be a false reading, and that it should
be the *Poll,* or *Head* of that Canon. It may be objected, that this
is a mere *Paronomasia* or *Pun.* But what of that ? Is any figure
of speech more apposite to our gentle Goddess, or more frequently
used by her and her Children, especially of the University ?—*Scriblerus.*

So spins the silk-worm small its slender store,
And labours till it clouds itself all o'er.

   " What though we let some better sort of fool   255
Thrid every science, run through every school ?
Never by tumbler through the hoops was shewn
Such skill in passing all, and touching none ;
He may indeed (if sober all this time)
Plague with Dispute, or persecute with Rhyme.   260
We only furnish what he cannot use,
Or wed to what he must divorce, a Muse :
Full in the midst of Euclid dip at once,
And petrify a Genius to a Dunce :
Or set on Metaphysic ground to prance,   265
Show all his paces, not a step advance.
With the same CEMENT, ever sure to bind,
We bring to one dead level every mind.
Then take him to develop, if you can,
And hew the Block off, and get out the Man.   270
But wherefore waste I words ? I see advance
Whore, Pupil, and laced Governor from France.
Walker ! our hat "——nor more he deigned to say,
But, stern as Ajax' spectre, strode away.

   In flowed at once a gay embroidered race,   275
And titt'ring pushed the Pedants off the place :
Some would have spoken, but the voice was drowned
By the French horn, or by the op'ning hound.
The first came forwards, with as easy mien,
As if he saw St. James's and the Queen.   280

   And touching none.—These two verses are verbatim from an epigram
of Dr. Evans, of St. John's College, Oxford ; composed twenty years
before the Dunciad was written.
   And hew the Block off.—A notion of Aristotle, that there was originally
in every block of marble a Statue, which would appear on the removal
of the superfluous parts.
   Stern as Ajax' spectre, strode away.—See Homer, *Odyss.* xi., where
the Ghost of Ajax turns sullenly from Ulysses the *Traveller*, who had
succeeded against him in the dispute for the arms of Achilles. There
had been the same contention between the *Travelling* and the *University*
tutor, for the spoils of our young heroes, and fashion adjudged it to
the former ; so that this might well occasion the sullen dignity in
departure, which Longinus so much admired.—SCRIBL.

When thus th' attendant Orator begun,
" Receive, great Empress ! thy accomplished Son :
Thine from the birth, and sacred from the rod,
A dauntless infant ! never scared with God.
The Sire saw, one by one, his Virtues wake :   285
The Mother begged the blessing of a Rake.
Thou gav'st that Ripeness, which so soon began,
And ceased so soon, he ne'er was Boy nor Man.
Through School and College, thy kind cloud o'ercast,
Safe and unseen the young Æneas past :   290
Thence bursting glorious, all at once let down,
Stunned with his giddy Larum half the town.
Intrepid then, o'er seas and lands he flew :
Europe he saw, and Europe saw him too.
There all thy gifts and graces we display,   295
Thou, only thou, directing all our way !
To where the Seine, obsequious as she runs,
Pours at great Bourbon's feet her silken sons :
Or Tiber, now no longer Roman, rolls,
Vain of I'alian Arts, Italian Souls :   300
To happy Convents, bosomed deep in vines,
Where slumber Abbots, purple as their wines :
To Isles of fragrance, lily-silvered vales,
Diffusing languor in the panting gales :
To lands of singing, or of dancing slaves,   305
Love-whisp'ring woods, and lute-resounding waves.
But chief her shrine where naked Venus keeps,
And Cupids ride the Lion of the Deeps ;
Where, eased of Fleets, the Adriatic main
Wafts the smooth Eunuch and enamoured swain. 310

Unseen the young Æneas past : Thence bursting glorious.—See
Virg. *Æn.* I. [vv. 411–17], where he enumerates the causes why his
mother took this care of him ; to wit (1) that nobody might touch or
correct him ; (2) might stop or detain him ; (3) examine him about the
progress he had made, or so much as guess why he came there.
   Lily-silvered vales.—Tuberoses.
   And Cupids ride the Lion of the Deeps.—The winged Lion, the Arms
of Venice. This Republic heretofore the most considerable in Europe,
for her Naval Force and the extent of her Commerce : now illustrious
for her *Carnivals*.

Led by my hand, he sauntered Europe round,
And gathered every Vice on Christian ground;
Saw every Court, heard every King declare
His royal Sense of Op'ras or the Fair;
The Stews and Palace equally explored,   315
Intrigued with glory, and with spirit whored;
Tried all *hors-d'œuvres*, all *liqueurs* defined,
Judicious drank, and greatly-daring dined;
Dropt the dull lumber of the Latin store,
Spoiled his own language, and acquired no more; 320
All Classic learning lost on Classic ground;
And last turned *Air*, the Echo of a Sound!
See now, half-cured, and perfectly well-bred,
With nothing but a Solo in his head;
As much Estate, and Principle, and Wit,   325
As Jansen, Fleetwood, Cibber shall think fit;
Stolen from a Duel, followed by a Nun,
And, if a Borough choose him not, undone;
See, to my country happy I restore
This glorious Youth, and add one Venus more.   330
Her too receive (for her my soul adores)
So may the sons of sons of sons of whores,
Prop thine, O Empress! like each neighbour Throne,
And make a long Posterity thy own."
Pleased, she accepts the Hero, and the Dame   335
Wraps in her Veil, and frees from sense of Shame.

And last turned Air, the Echo of a Sound.—Yet less a Body than Echo
itself; for Echo reflects *Sense* or *Words* at least, this Gentleman only
Airs and *Tunes*:

     " Sonus *est, qui vivit in* illo."

Ovid, *Met.* [III. v. 401].—SCRIBLERUS.

    With nothing but a Solo in his head.—With nothing but a *Solo?*
Why, if it be a *Solo,* how should there be anything else? Palpable
Tautology! Read boldly an *Opera,* which is enough of conscience for
such a head as has lost all its Latin.—" BENT."

    Jansen, Fleetwood, Cibber.—Three very eminent persons, all Mana-
gers of *Plays;* who, though not Governors by profession, had, each
in his way, concerned themselves in the Education of Youth: and
regulated their Wits, their Morals, or their Finances, at that period of
their age which is the most important, their entrance into the polite
world. Of the last of these, and his Talents for this end, see Book I.

Then looked, and saw a lazy, lolling sort,
Unseen at Church, at Senate, or at Court,
Of ever-listless Loit'rers, that attend
No Cause, no Trust, no Duty, and no Friend.   340
Thee too, my Paridel! she marked thee there,
Stretched on the rack of a too easy chair,
And heard thy everlasting yawn confess
The Pains and Penalties of Idleness.
She pitied! but her Pity only shed   345
Benigner influence on thy nodding head.

But Annius, crafty Seer, with ebon wand,
And well-dissembled em'rald on his hand,
False as his Gems, and cankered as his Coins,
Came, crammed with capon, from where Pollio dines.
Soft, as the wily Fox is seen to creep,   351
Where bask on sunny banks the simple sheep,
Walk round and round, now prying here, now there,
So he ; but pious, whispered first his prayer.

" Grant, gracious Goddess! grant me still to cheat,
O may thy cloud still cover the deceit!   356
Thy choicer mists on this assembly shed,
But pour them thickest on the noble head.
So shall each youth, assisted by our eyes,
See other Cæsars, other Homers rise ;   360
Through twilight ages hunt th' Athenian fowl,
Which Chalcis Gods, and mortals call an Owl.

Thee too, my Paridel.—The Poet seems to speak of this young gentleman with great affection. The name is taken from Spenser, who
gives it to a *wandering Courtly Squire*, that travelled about for the
same reason, for which many young Squires are now fond of travelling,
and especially to *Paris*.

Annius.—The name taken from Annius the Monk of Viterbo, famous
for many Impositions and Forgeries of ancient manuscripts and
inscriptions, which he was prompted to by mere vanity, but our
Annius had a more substantial motive.

Where Pollio dines.—This seems more obscure than almost any other
passage in the whole. Perhaps he meant the Prince of Wales's dinners.

Hunt th' Athenian fowl.—The Owl stamped on the reverse on the
ancient money of Athens.

    " Which *Chalcis* Gods, and mortals call an Owl,"
is the verse by which Hobbes renders that of Homer [*Il.* XIV. 291].

Now see an Atty's, now a Cecrops clear,
Nay, Mahomet ! the Pigeon at thine ear ;
Be rich in ancient brass, though not in gold, 365
And keep his Lares, though his house be sold ;
To headless Phœbe his fair bride postpone,
Honour a Syrian Prince above his own ;
Lord of an Otho, if I vouch it true ;
Blest in one Niger, till he knows of two." 370
    Mummius o'erheard him ; Mummius, Fool-renowned,
Who like his Cheops stinks above the ground,
Fierce as a startled Adder, swelled, and said,
Rattling an ancient Sistrum at his head :
    " Speak'st thou of Syrian Princes ? Traitor base !
Mine, Goddess ! mine is all the hornèd race. 376
True, he had wit, to make their value rise ;
From foolish Greeks to steal them, was as wise ;

Attys, Cecrops.—The first Kings of Athens, of whom it is hard to suppose any Coins are extant ; but not so improbable as what follows, that there should be any of Mahomet, who forbade all Images ; and the story of whose Pigeon was a monkish fable. Nevertheless one of these Anniuses made a counterfeit medal of that Impostor, now in the collection of a learned Nobleman.

Mummius.—This name is not merely an allusion to the Mummies he was so fond of, but probably referred to the Roman General of that name, who burned Corinth, and committed the curious Statues to the Captain of a ship, assuring him, " that if any were lost or broken, he should procure others to be made in their stead : " by which it should seem (whatever may be pretended) that Mummius was no Virtuoso.

Fool-renowned.—A compound epithet in the Greek manner, *renowned by Fools*, or *renowned for making Fools*.

Cheops.—A King of Egypt, whose body was certainly to be known, as being buried alone in his Pyramid, and is therefore more genuine than any of the Cleopatras. This Royal Mummy, being stolen by a wild Arab, was purchased by the Consul of Alexandria, and transmitted to the Museum of Mummius ; for proof of which he brings a passage in Sandys's *Travels*, where that accurate and learned Voyager assures us that he saw the Sepulchre empty ; which agrees exactly (saith he) with the time of the theft above-mentioned. But he omits to observe that Herodotus tells the same thing of it in his time.

Speak'st thou of Syrian Princes, etc.—The strange story following, which may be taken for a fiction of the Poet, is justified by a true relation in Spon's Voyages [of Vaillant, the French historian of the Syrian kings, swallowing twenty gold medals when the ship in which he was returning to France was attacked by Sallee pirates].

More glorious yet, from barb'rous hands to keep,
When Sallee Rovers chased him on the deep.   380
Then taught by Hermes, and divinely bold,
Down his own throat he risked the Grecian gold,
Received each Demi-God, with pious care,
Deep in his Entrails—I revered them there,
I bought them, shrouded in that living shrine,   385
And, at their second birth, they issue mine."
    " Witness, great Ammon ! by whose horns I swore,"
(Replied soft Annius) " this our paunch before
Still bears them, faithful ; and that thus I eat,
Is to refund the Medals with the meat.   390
To prove me, Goddess ! clear of all design,
Bid me with Pollio sup, as well as dine :
There all the Learned shall at the labour stand,
And Douglas lend his soft obstetric hand."
    The Goddess smiling seemed to give consent ;   395
So back to Pollio, hand in hand, they went.
    Then thick as Locusts black'ning all the ground,
A tribe, with weeds and shells fantastic crowned,
Each with some wondrous gift approached the Power,
A Nest, a Toad, a Fungus, or a Flower.   400
But far the foremost, two, with earnest zeal,
And aspect ardent to the Throne appeal.
    The first thus opened : " Hear thy suppliant's call,
Great Queen, and common Mother of us all !
Fair from its humble bed I reared this Flower,   405
Suckled, and cheered, with air, and sun, and shower,
Soft on the paper ruff its leaves I spread,
Bright with the gilded button tipt its head ;

Each Demi-God.—They are called Θεοὶ on their Coins.
    Witness, great Ammon.—Jupiter Ammon is called to witness, as the father of Alexander, to whom those Kings succeeded in the division of the Macedonian Empire, and whose *Horns* they wore on their Medals.
    Douglas.—A Physician of great Learning and no less Taste ; above all curious in what related to *Horace*, of whom he collected every Edition, Translation, and comment, to the number of several hundred volumes.

Then throned in glass, and named it CAROLINE:
Each maid cried, Charming! and each youth, Divine!
Did Nature's pencil ever blend such rays, 411
Such varied light in one promiscuous blaze?
Now prostrate! dead! behold that Caroline:
No maid cries, Charming! and no youth, Divine:
And lo the wretch! whose vile, whose insect lust 415
Laid this gay daughter of the Spring in dust.
Oh punish him, or to th' Elysian shades
Dismiss my soul, where no Carnation fades!"
He ceased, and wep.. With innocence of mien,
Th' Accused stood forth, and thus addressed the Queen.

" Of all th' enamelled race, whose silv'ry wing 421
Waves to the tepid Zephyrs of the spring,
Or swims along the fluid atmosphere,
Once brightest shined this child of Heat and Air.
I saw and started from its vernal bower, 425
The rising game, and chased from flower to flower
It fled, I followed; now in hope, now pain;
It stopt, I stopt; it moved, I moved again.
At last it fixed, 'twas on what plant it pleased,
And where it fixed, the beauteous bird I seized: 430
Rose or Carnation was below my care;
I meddle, Goddess! only in my sphere.
I tell the naked fact without disguise,
And, to excuse it, need but shew the prize;
Whose spoils this paper offers to your eye, 435
Fair even in death! this peerless *Butterfly*."

"My sons!" (she answered) 'both have done your parts:
Live happy both, and long promote our arts!
But hear a Mother, when she recommends
To your fraternal care our sleeping friends. 440

And named it Caroline.—It is a compliment which the Florists usually pay to Princes and great persons, to give their names to the most curious Flowers of their raising: Some have been very jealous of vindicating this honour, but none more than that ambitious Gardener at Hammersmith, who caused his Favourite to be painted on his sign, with this inscription, *This is My Queen Caroline.*

Our sleeping friends.—Of whom see above.

The common Soul, of Heaven's more frugal make,
Serves but to keep fools pert, and knaves awake:
A drowsy Watchman, that just gives a knock,
And breaks our rest, to tell us what's a-clock.
Yet by some object every brain is stirred;   445
The dull may waken to a humming-bird;
The most recluse, discreetly opened, find
Congenial matter in the Cockle-kind;
The mind, in Metaphysics at a loss,
May wander in a wilderness of Moss;   450
The head that turns at super-lunar things,
Poised with a tail, may steer on Wilkins' wings.

   " O! would the Sons of Men once think their Eyes
And Reason given them but to study *Flies!*
See Nature in some partial narrow shape,   455
And let the Author of the Whole escape:
Learn but to trifle; or, who most observe,
To wonder at their Maker, not to serve!"

   " Be that my task " (replies a gloomy Clerk,
Sworn foe to Myst'ry, yet divinely dark;   460
Whose pious hope aspires to see the day
When Moral Evidence shall quite decay,
And damns implicit faith, and holy lies,
Prompt to impose and fond to dogmatize :)
   " Let others creep by timid steps, and slow,   465

   A wilderness of Moss.—Of which the Naturalists count I can't tell
how many hundred species.
   Wilkins' wings.—One of the first Projectors of the Royal Society,
who, among many enlarged and useful notions, entertained the extravagant hope of a possibility to fly to the Moon; which has put some
volatile Geniuses upon making wings for that purpose.
   When Moral Evidence shall quite decay.—Alluding to a ridiculous
and absurd way of some Mathematicians, in calculating the gradual
decay of Moral Evidence by mathematical proportions: according
to which calculation, in about fifty years it will be no longer probable
that Julius Cæsar was in Gaul, or died in the Senate-house. See Craig's
Theologiæ Christianæ Principia Mathematica. But as it seems evident,
that facts of a thousand years old, for instance, are now as probable
as they were five hundred years ago; it is plain that if in fifty more
they quite disappear, it must be owing, not to their Arguments, but
to the extraordinary Power of our Goddess; for whose help therefore
they have reason to pray.

On plain Experience lay foundations low,
By common sense to common knowledge bred,
And last, to Nature's Cause through Nature led.
All-seeing in thy mists, we want no guide,
Mother of Arrogance, and Source of Pride!   470
We nobly take the high Priori Road,
And reason downward, till we doubt of God;
Make Nature still encroach upon his plan;
And shove him off as far as e'er we can:
Thrust some Mechanic Cause into his place;   475
Or bind in Matter, or diffuse in Space.
Or, at one bound o'er-leaping all his laws,
Make God Man's Image, Man the final Cause,
Find Virtue local, all relation scorn,
See all in *Self*, and but for self be born: 480
Of naught so certain as our *Reason* still,
Of naught so doubtful as of *Soul* and *Will*.
Oh hide the God still more! and make us see
Such as Lucretius drew, a God like Thee:
Wrapt up in Self, a God without a Thought,   485
Regardless of our merit or default.

The high Priori Road.—Those who, from the effects in this Visible
world, deduce the Eternal Power and Godhead of the First Cause,
though they cannot attain to an adequate idea of the Deity, yet discover so much of him, as enables them to see the End of their Creation,
and the Means of their Happiness: whereas they who take this high
Priori Road (such as Hobbes, Spinoza, Des Cartes, and some better
Reasoners) for one that goes right, ten lose themselves in Mists, or
ramble after Visions, which deprive them of all sight of their End,
and mislead them in the choice of wrong means.

Make Nature still.—This relates to such as, being ashamed to assert
a mere Mechanic Cause, and yet unwilling to forsake it entirely, have
had recourse to a certain *Plastic Nature, Elastic Fluid, Subtile Matter,*
etc.

*Thrust some Mechanic Cause into his place; or bind in Matter, or
diffuse in Space.*—The first of these Follies is that of Des Cartes; the
second of Hobbes; the third of some succeeding Philosophers. I am
afraid that Pope suffered himself so far to be misled by the malignity
of Warburton, as to aim a secret stab at Newton and Clarke, by
associating their figurative, and not altogether unexceptionable,
language concerning space (which they called the sensorium of the
Deity) with the opinion of Spinoza.—*Dugald Stewart*, cited by
Roscoe.

Or that bright Image to our fancy draw,
Which Theocles in raptured vision saw,
While through Poetic scenes the GENIUS roves,
Or wanders wild in Academic Groves;   490
That NATURE our Society adores,
Where Tindal dictates, and Silenus snores."
  Roused at his name, up rose the bousy Sire,
And shook from out his Pipe the seeds of fire;
Then snapt his box, and stroked his belly down: 495
Rosy and rev'rend, though without a Gown.
Bland and familiar to the throne he came,
Led up the Youth, and called the Goddess *Dame:*
Then thus : " From Priest-craft happily set free,
Lo ! every finished Son returns to thee: 500
First slave to Words, then vassal to a Name,
Then dupe to Party ; child and man the same;
Bounded by Nature narrowed still by Art,
A trifling head, and a contracted heart.
Thus bred, thus taught, how many have I seen,   505
Smiling on all, and smiled on by a Queen?
Marked out for Honours, honoured for their Birth,
To thee the most rebellious things on earth :
Now to thy gentle shadow all are shrunk,
All melted down, in Pension, or in Punk!   510
So K* so B** sneaked into the grave,
A Monarch's half, and half a Harlot's slave.
Poor W** nipt in Folly's broadest bloom,
Who praises now ? his Chaplain on his Tomb.

  Or that bright Image.—Bright Image was the title given by the later
Platonists to that Vision of *Nature,* which they had formed out of
their own fancy, so bright, that they called it Αὔτοπτον Ἄγαλμα,
or the *Self-seen Image*—that is, seen by its own light.—SCRIBL.
  That Nature our Society adores.—See the *Pantheisticon,* with its
liturgy and rubrics, composed by *Toland.*
  Silenus.—Silenus was an Epicurean Philosopher, as appears from
Virgil, *Eclog.* vi., where he sings the principles of that Philosophy in his
drink.
  Seeds of fire.—The Epicurean language, *Semina rerum,* or Atoms,
Virgil, *Eclog.* vi.
               " Semina ignis—semina flammæ."
  Smiled on by a Queen.—That is, This Queen or Goddess of Dulness.

Then take them all, oh take them to thy breast ! 515
Thy *Magus*, Goddess ! shall perform the rest."
  With that, a WIZARD OLD his *Cup* extends ;
Which whoso tastes, forgets his former friends,
Sire, Ancestors, Himself.   One casts his eyes
Up to a *Star*, and like Endymion dies : 520
A *Feather*, shooting from another's head,
Extracts his brain ; and Principle is fled ;
Lost is his God, his Country, every thing :
And nothing left but Homage to a King !
The vulgar herd turn off to roll with Hogs, 525
To run with Horses, or to hunt with Dogs ;
But, sad example ! never to escape
Their Infamy, still keep the human shape.
But she, good Goddess, sent to every child
Firm Impudence, or Stupefaction mild ; 530
And straight succeeded, leaving shame no room,
Cibberian forehead, or Cimmerian gloom.
  Kind Self-conceit to some her glass applies,
Which no one looks in with another's eyes :
But as the Flatt'rer or Dependant paint, 535
Beholds himself a Patriot, Chief, or Saint.
  On others' Int'rest her gay liv'ry flings,
Int'rest that waves on Party-coloured wings :
Turned to the Sun, she casts a thousand dyes,
And, as she turns, the colours fall or rise. 540
  Others the Syren Sisters warble round,
And empty heads console with empty sound.
No more, alas ! the voice of Fame they hear,
The balm of Dulness trickling in their ear.

Lost in his God, his Country—And nothing left but Homage to a King.—
So strange as this must seem to a mere English reader, the famous
Mons. de la Bruyère declares it to be the character of every good
Subject in a Monarchy : "Where (says he) *there is no such thing as Love
of our Country*, the Interest, tne Glory, and Service of the *Prince* supply
its place."—*De la République*, chap. x.
  The balm of Dulness.—The true *Balm of Dulness*, called by the Greek
Physicians Κολακεία, is a *Sovereign* remedy against Inanity, and
has its poetic name from the Goddess herself.   Its ancient Dispensators
were *her Poets :* and for that reason our Author, in his Book II., calls

Great C**, H**, P**, R**, K*,   545
Why all your Toils ? your Sons have learned to sing.
How quick Ambition hastes to ridicule !
The Sire is made a Peer, the Son a Fool.
   On some, a Priest succinct in amice white
Attends ; all flesh is nothing in his sight !   550
Beeves, at his touch, at once to jelly turn,
And the huge Boar is shrunk into an Urn :
The board with specious miracles he loads,
Turns Hares to Larks, and Pigeons into Toads.
Another (for in all what one can shine ?)   555
Explains the *Sève* and *Verdeur* of the Vine.
What cannot copious Sacrifice atone ?
Thy Truffles, Perigord ! thy Hams, Bayonne !
With French Libation, and Italian Strain,
Wash Bladen white, and expiate Hays's stain.   560
KNIGHT lifts the head, for what are crowds undone,
To three essential Partridges in one ?
Gone every blush, and silent all reproach,
Contending Princes mount them in their Coach.
   Next, bidding all draw near on bended knees,   565
The Queen confers her *Titles* and *Degrees*.

it *the Poet's healing balm :* but now it is got into as many hands as
Goddard's Drops or Daffy's Elizir. It is prepared by the *Clergy*, as
appears from several places of this poem : And by previous references
it seems as if the *Nobility* had it made up in their own houses. This,
which *Opera* is here said to administer, is but a spurious sort. See
my Dissertation on the *Silphium* of the *Antients.*—"BENTL."
   Miracles he loads.—This good Scholiast (Scriblerus), not being
acquainted with modern Luxury, was ignorant that these were only
the miracles of *French Cookery*, and that particularly *Pigeons en
crapeau* were a common dish.
   Sève and Verdeur.—French Terms relating to Wines, which signify
their flavour and poignancy.
   Bladen—Hays.—Names of Gamesters. Bladen is a black man,
ROBERT KNIGHT, Cashier of the South-Sea Company, who fled from
England in 1720 (afterwards pardoned in 1742). These lived with the
utmost magnificence at Paris, and kept open Tables frequented by persons of the first Quality of England, and even by Princes of the Blood
of France. Colonel Martin Bladen was a man of some literature and
translated Cæsar's *Commentaries.* I never could learn that he had
offended Pope. He was uncle to Wm. Collins, the poet, whom he left
an estate.

Her children first of more distinguished sort,
Who study Shakespear at the Inns of Court,
Impale a Glow-worm, or Vertú profess,
Shine in the dignity of F.R.S.　　　　　　　　570
Some, deep Free-Masons, join the silent race
Worthy to fill Pythagoras's place:
Some Botanists, or Florists at the least,
Or issue Members of an Annual feast.
Nor past the meanest unregarded, one　　　　575
Rose a Gregorian, one a Gormogon.
The last, not least in honour or applause,
Isis and Cam made DOCTORS of her LAWS.
　　Then, blessing all, " Go children of my care!
To Practice now from Theory repair.　　　　580
All my commands are easy, short, and full:
My Sons! be proud, be selfish, and be dull.
Guard my Prerogative, assert my Throne:
This Nod confirms each Privilege your own.

Her children first of more distinguished sort, Who study Shakespear at the Inns of Court.—Mr. THOMAS EDWARDS, a *Gentleman,* as he is pleased to call himself, of *Lincoln's Inn ;* but, in reality, a Gentleman only of the Dunciad ; or, to speak him better, in the plain language of our honest Ancestors to such Mushrooms, *A Gentleman of the last Edition :* who, nobly eluding the solicitude of his careful Father, very early retained himself in the cause of *Dulness* against *Shakespear,* and with the wit and learning of his Ancestor *Tom Thimble* in the *Rehearsal,* and with the air of good nature and politeness of *Caliban* in the *Tempest,* hath now happily finished the *Dunce's progress* in personal abuse.—SCRIBL.

A Gregorian, one a Gormogon.—A sort of Lay-brothers, *Slips* from the root of the Free-Masons.

Doctors of her Laws.—Pope refused this degree when offered to him on a visit undertaken to Oxford with Warburton, because the University would not confer the degree of D.D. upon Warburton, to whom some of its members had proposed it.

Each Privilege your own, etc.—This speech of Dulness to her Sons at parting may possibly fall short of the Reader's expectation ; who may imagine the Goddess might give them a charge of more consequence, and, from such a Theory as is before delivered, incite them to the practice of something more extraordinary, than to personate Running-Footmen, Jockeys, Stage Coachmen, etc.

But if it be well considered, that whatever inclination they might have to do mischief, her sons are generally rendered harmless by their Inability ; and that it is the common effect of Dulness (even in her

The Cap and Switch be sacred to his Grace;   585
With Staff and Pumps the Marquis lead the Race :
From Stage to Stage the licensed Earl may run,
Paired with his Fellow-Charioteer the Sun ;
The learnèd Baron Butterflies design,
Or draw to silk Arachne's subtile line ;   590
The Judge to dance his brother Sergeant call ;
The Senator at Cricket urge the Ball ;
The Bishop stow (Pontific Luxury !)
An hundred Souls of Turkeys in a pie ;
The sturdy Squire to Gallic masters stoop,   595
And drown his Lands and Manors in a Soupe.
Others import yet nobler arts from France,
Teach Kings to fiddle, and make Senates dance.
Perhaps more high some daring son may soar,
Proud to my list to add one Monarch more !   600
And nobly conscious, Princes are but things
Born for First Ministers, as Slaves for Kings,
Tyrant supreme ! shall three Estates command,
And MAKE ONE MIGHTY DUNCIAD OF THE LAND ! "

    More she had spoke, but yawned—All Nature nods :
What Mortal can resist the Yawn of Gods ?   606
Churches and Chapels instantly it reached ;
(St. James's first, for leaden G—— preached)

greatest efforts) to defeat her own design ; the Poet, I am persuaded,
will be justified, and it will be allowed that these worthy persons, in
their several ranks, do as much as can be expected from them.

    Arachne's subtile line.—This is one of the most ingenious employ-
ments assigned, and therefore recommended only to Peers of Learning.
Of weaving Stockings of the Webs of Spiders, see the *Philosophical
Transactions.*

    The Judge to dance his brother Sergeant call.—Alluding perhaps to
that ancient and solemn *Dance*, intituled, *A Call of Sergeants.*

    Teach Kings to fiddle.—An ancient amusement of Sovereign Princes,
namely, Achilles, Alexander, Nero ; though despised by Themistocles,
who was a Republican.—*Make Senates dance,* either after their Prince,
or to Pontoise, or Siberia.

    What Mortal can resist the Yawn of Gods ?—This verse is truly Homeri-
cal ; as is the conclusion of the Action, where the great Mother composes
all, in the same manner as Minerva at the period of the Odyssey.

    G——.—Dr. Gilbert, Archbishop of York, who had attacked Dr.
King of Oxford whom Pope much respected.

Then catched the Schools ; the Hall scarce kept awake ;
The Convocation gaped, but could not speak : 610
Lost was the Nation's Sense, nor could be found,
While the long solemn Unison went round :
Wide, and more wide, it spread o'er all the realm ;
Even Palinurus nodded at the Helm :
The Vapour mild o'er each Committee crept ; 615
Unfinished Treaties in each Office slept ;
And Chiefless Armies dozed out the Campaign ;
And Navies yawned for Orders on the Main.

  O Muse ! relate (for you can tell alone,
Wits have short Memories, and Dunces none), 620
Relate, who first, who last resigned to rest ;
Whose Heads she partly, whose completely, blest ;
What Charms could Faction, what Ambition lull,
The Venal quiet, and entrance the Dull ;
'Til drowned was Sense, and Shame, and Right, and
      Wrong— 625
O sing, and hush the Nations with thy Song !

  *   *   *   *   *   *

  In vain, in vain—the all-composing Hour
Resistless falls : the Muse obeys the Power.
She comes ! she comes ! the sable Throne behold
Of *Night* primæval and of *Chaos* old ! 630
Before her, *Fancy's* gilded clouds decay,
And all its varying Rain-bows die away.
Wit shoots in vain its momentary fires,

Wits have short Memories.—This seems to be the reason why the
Poets, whenever they give us a Catalogue, constantly call for help on
the Muses, who, as the Daughters of *Memory*, are obliged not to forget
anything. So Homer, *Iliad* II. vv. 788 ff. And Virgil, *Æn.* VII.
[vv. 645–6].—SCRIBL.

  She comes ! she comes ! etc.—Here the Muse, like Jove's Eagle,
after a sudden stoop at ignoble game, soareth again to the skies. As
Prophecy hath ever been one of the chief provinces of Poesy, our Poet
here foretells from what we feel, what we are to fear ; and, in the
style of other prophets, hath used the future tense for the preterite :
since what he says shall be, is already to be seen, in the writings of some
even of our most adored authors, in Divinity, Philosophy, Physics,
Metaphysics, etc., who are too good indeed to be named in such company.

The meteor drops, and in a flash expires.
As one by one, at dread Medea's strain,   635
The sick'ning stars fade off th' ethereal plain;
As Argus' eyes by Hermes' wand opprest,
Closed one by one to everlasting rest;
Thus at her felt approach, and secret might,
Art after *Art* goes out, and all is Night.   640
See skulking *Truth* to her old cavern fled,
Mountains of Casuistry heaped o'er her head!
Philosophy, that leaned on Heaven before,
Shrinks to her second cause, and is no more.
Physic of *Metaphysic* begs defence,   645
And *Metaphysic* calls for aid on *Sense*!
See *Mystery* to *Mathematics* fly!
In vain! they gaze, turn giddy, rave, and die.
Religion blushing veils her sacred fires,
And unawares *Morality* expires.   650
For *public* Flame, nor *private*, dares to shine;
Nor *human* Spark is left, nor Glimpse *divine*!
Lo! thy dread Empire, CHAOS! is restored;
Light dies before thy uncreating word;
Thy hand, great Anarch! lets the curtain fall,   655
And universal Darkness buries All.

Truth to her old cavern fled.—Alluding to the saying of Democritus,
That Truth lay at the bottom of a deep well, from whence he had drawn
her: though Butler says, *He first put her in, before he drew her out.*

A SPECIMEN FROM "THE ILIAD"

BOOK IX

THE ARGUMENT

THE EMBASSY TO ACHILLES

Agamemnon, after the last day's defeat, proposes to the Greeks to quit the siege, and return to their country. Diomed opposes this, and Nestor seconds him, praising his wisdom and resolution. He orders the guard to be strengthened, and a council summoned to deliberate what measures were to be followed in this emergency. Agamemnon pursues this advice, and Nestor farther prevails upon him to send ambassadors to Achilles, in order to move him to a reconciliation. Ulysses and Ajax are made choice of, who are accompanied by old Phœnix. They make, each of them, very moving and pressing speeches, but are rejected with roughness by Achilles, who notwithstanding retains Phœnix in his tent. The ambassadors return unsuccessfully to the camp, and the troops betake themselves to sleep.

This book, and the next following, take up the space of one night, which is the twenty-seventh from the beginning of the poem. The scene lies on the sea-shore, the station of the Grecian ships.

THUS joyful Troy maintained the watch of night;
While Fear, pale comrade of inglorious flight,
And heaven-bred horror, on the Grecian part,
Sat on each face, and saddened every heart.
As from its cloudy dungeon issuing forth,   5
A double tempest of the west and north
Swells o'er the sea, from Thracia's frozen shore,
Heaps waves on waves, and bids the Ægean roar;
This way and that the boiling deeps are tossed;
Such various passions urged the troubled host.   10
Great Agamemnon grieved above the rest,
Superior sorrows swelled his royal breast;
Himself his orders to the heralds bears,
To bid to council all the Grecian peers,

But bid in whispers : these surround their chief,   15
In solemn sadness and majestic grief.
The king amidst the mournful circle rose ;
Down his wan cheek a briny torrent flows :
So silent fountains, from a rock's tall head,
In sable streams soft-trickling waters shed.   20
With more than vulgar grief he stood oppressed ;
Words, mixed with sighs, thus bursting from his breast :
    " Ye sons of Greece ! partake your leader's care,
Fellows in arms, and princes of the war !
Of partial Jove too justly we complain,   25
And heavenly oracles believed in vain.
A safe return was promised to our toils,
With conquest honoured, and enriched with spoils :
Now shameful flight alone can save the host,
Our wealth, our people, and our glory lost.   30
So Jove decrees, almighty lord of all !
Jove, at whose nod whole empires rise or fall,
Who shakes the feeble props of human trust,
And towers and armies humbles to the dust.
Haste then, for ever quit these fatal fields,   35
Haste to the joys our native country yields ;
Spread all your canvas, all your oars employ,
Nor hope the fall of heaven-defended Troy."
    He said ; deep silence held the Grecian band ;
Silent, unmoved, in dire dismay they stand,   40
A pensive scene ! till Tydeus' warlike son
Rolled on the king his eyes, and thus begun :
    " When kings advise us to renounce our fame,
First let him speak, who first has suffered shame.
If I oppose thee, prince ! thy wrath withhold ;   45
The laws of council bid my tongue be bold.
Thou first, and thou alone, in fields of fight,
Durst brand my courage, and defame my might ;
Nor from a friend the unkind reproach appeared,
The Greeks stood witness, all our army heard.   50
The gods, O chief ! from whom our honours spring,
The gods have made thee but by halves a king :

They gave thee sceptres and a wide command,
They gave dominion o'er the seas and land ;
The noblest power that might the world control   55
They gave thee not—a brave and virtuous soul.
Is this a general's voice, that would suggest
Fears like his own in every Grecian breast ?
Confiding in our want of worth he stands,
And if we fly, 'tis what our king commands.   60
Go thou, inglorious ! from the embattled plain,
Ships thou hast store, and nearest to the main ;
A nobler care the Grecians shall employ,
To combat, conquer, and extirpate Troy.
Here Greece shall stay ; or, if all Greece retire,   65
Myself will stay, till Troy or I expire ;
Myself, and Sthenelus, will fight for fame ;
God bade us fight. and 'twas with God we came."
   He ceased ; the Greeks loud acclamations raise,
And voice to voice resounds Tydides' praise.   70
Wise Nestor then his reverend figure reared ;
He spoke : the host in still attention heard :
   " O truly great ! in whom the gods have joined
Such strength of body with such force of mind ;
In conduct, as in courage, you excel,   75
Still first to act what you advise so well.
Those wholesome counsels which thy wisdom moves,
Applauding Greece, with common voice, approves.
Kings thou canst blame ; a bold, but prudent youth ;
And blame e'en kings with praise, because with truth.
And yet those fears that since thy birth have run,   81
Would hardly style thee Nestor's youngest son.
Then let me add what yet remains behind,
A thought unfinished in that generous mind ;
Age bids me speak ; nor shall the advice I bring   85
Distaste the people, or offend the king :
   " Cursed is the man, and void of law and right,
Unworthy property, unworthy light,
Unfit for public rule, or private care,
That wretch, that monster, that delights in war :   90

Whose lust is murder, and whose horrid joy
To tear his country, and his kind destroy!
This night refresh and fortify thy train;
Between the trench and wall let guards remain:
Be that the duty of the young and bold;   95
But thou, O king, to council call the old:
Great is thy sway, and weighty are thy cares;
Thy high commands must spirit all our wars:
With Thracian wines recruit thy honoured guests,
For happy counsels flow from sober feasts.   100
Wise, weighty counsels aid a state distressed
And such a monarch as can choose the best.
See! what a blaze from hostile tents aspires,
How near our fleet approach the Trojan fires!
Who can, unmoved, behold the dreadful light?   105
What eye beholds them, and can close to-night?
This dreadful interval determines all;
To-morrow, Troy must flame, or Greece must fall."
    Thus spoke the hoary sage: the rest obey;
Swift through the gates the guards direct their way.
His son was first to pass the lofty mound,   111
The gen'rous Thrasymed, in arms renowned:
Next him Ascalaphus, Iälmen, stood,
The double offspring of the warrior-god.
Deïpyrus, Aphareus, Merion join,   115
And Lycomed, of Creon's noble line.
Seven were the leaders of the nightly bands,
And each bold chief a hundred spears commands.
The fires they light, to short repasts they fall,
Some line the trench, and others man the wall.   120
    The king of men, on public counsels bent,
Convened the princes in his ample tent;
Each seized a portion of the kingly feast,
But stayed his hand when thirst and hunger ceased.
Then Nestor spoke, for wisdom long approved,   125
And, slowly rising, thus the council moved:
    " Monarch of nations! whose superior sway
Assembled states and lords of earth obey,

The laws and sceptres to thy hand are given,
And millions own the care of thee and heaven.   130
O king ! the counsels of my age attend ;
With thee my cares begin, with thee must end :
Thee, prince ! it fits alike to speak and hear,
Pronounce with judgment, with regard give ear,
To see no wholesome motion be withstood,   135
And ratify the best for public good.
Nor, though a meaner give advice, repine,
But follow it, and make the wisdom thine.
Hear then a thought, not now conceived in haste,
At once my present judgment, and my past :   140
When from Pelides' tent you forced the maid,
I first opposed, and, faithful, durst dissuade ;
But, bold of soul, when headlong fury fired,
You wronged the man, by men and gods admired :
Now seek some means his fatal wrath to end,   145
With prayers to move him, or with gifts to bend."
   To whom the king : " With justice hast thou shewn
A prince's faults, and I with reason own.
That happy man whom Jove still honours most,
Is more than armies, and himself a host.   150
Blessed in his love, this wondrous hero stands,
Heaven fights his war, and humbles all our bands.
Fain would my heart, which erred through frantic rage,
The wrathful chief and angry gods assuage.
If gifts immense his mighty soul can bow,   155
Hear, all ye Greeks, and witness what I vow :
Ten weighty talents of the purest gold,
And twice ten vases of refulgent mould ;
Seven sacred tripods, whose unsullied frame
Yet knows no office, nor has felt the flame :   160
Twelve steeds unmatched in fleetness and in force,
And still victorious in the dusty course :
Rich were the man whose ample stores exceed
The prizes purchased by their wingèd speed :
Seven lovely captives of the Lesbian line,   165
Skilled in each art, unmatched in form divine,

The same I chose for more than vulgar charms,
When Lesbos sunk beneath the hero's arms:
All these, to buy his friendship, shall be paid,
And joined with these the long-contested maid;   170
With all her charms, Briseïs I resign,
And solemn swear those charms were never mine;
Untouched she stayed, uninjured she removes,
Pure from my arms, and guiltless of my loves.
These instant shall be his; and if the powers   175
Give to our arms proud Ilion's hostile towers,
Then shall he store (when Greece the spoil divides)
With gold and brass his loaded navy's sides.
Besides, full twenty nymphs of Trojan race
With copious love shall crown his warm embrace:
Such as himself will choose; who yield to none,   181
Or yield to Helen's heavenly charms alone.
Yet hear me farther: when our wars are o'er,
If safe we land on Argos' fruitful shore,
There shall he live my son, our honours share,   185
And with Orestes' self divide my care.
Yet more—three daughters in my court are bred,
And each well worthy of a royal bed,
Laodicé and Iphigenia fair,
And bright Chrysothemis with golden hair;   190
Her let him choose whom most his eyes approve,
I ask no presents, no reward for love;
Myself will give the dower; so vast a store
As never father gave a child before.
Seven ample cities shall confess his sway,   195
Him Enopé, and Pheræ him obey,
Cardamylé with ample turrets crowned,
And sacred Pedasus for vines renowned;
Æpea fair, the pastures Hira yields,
And rich Antheia with her flowery fields: 200
The whole extent to Pylos' sandy plain,
Along the verdant margin of the main.
There heifers graze, and labouring oxen toil;
Bold are the men, and gen'rous is the soil;

There shall he reign with power and justice crowned,
And rule the tributary realms around.　　206
All this I give, his vengeance to control,
And sure all this may move his mighty soul,
Pluto, the grizly god, who never spares,
Who feels no mercy, and who hears no prayers,　　210
Lives dark and dreadful in deep hell's abodes,
And mortals hate him as the worst of gods.
Great though he be, it fits him to obey:
Since more than his my years, and more my sway."
　　The monarch thus : the reverend Nestor then :　　215
" Great Agamemnon, glorious king of men !
Such are thy offers as a prince may take,
And such as fits a gen'rous king to make.
Let chosen delegates this hour be sent—
Myself will name them—to Pelides' tent :　　220
Let Phœnix lead, revered for hoary age,
Great Ajax next, and Ithacus the sage.
Yet more to sanctify the word you send,
Let Hodius and Eurybates attend.
Now pray to Jove to grant what Greece demands ;　　225
Pray, in deep silence, and with purest hands."
　　He said, and all approved.　The heralds bring
The cleansing water from the living spring.
The youth with wine the sacred goblets crowned,
And large libations drenched the sands around.　　230
The rite performed, the chiefs their thirst allay,
Then from the royal tent they take their way ;
Wise Nestor turns on each his careful eye,
Forbids to offend, instructs them to apply :
Much he advised them all, Ulysses most,　　235
To deprecate the chief, and save the host.
Through the still night they march, and hear the roar
Of murmuring billows on the sounding shore.
To Neptune, ruler of the seas profound,
Whose liquid arms the mighty globe surround,　　240
They pour forth vows, their embassy to bless,
And calm the rage of stern Æacides.

And now arrived, where, on the sandy bay,
The Myrmidonian tents and vessels lay,
Amused at ease, the godlike man they found,   24
Pleased with the solemn harp's harmonious sound;
The well-wrought harp from conquered Thebæ came,
Of polished silver was its costly frame.
With this he soothes his angry soul, and sings
The immortal deeds of heroes and of kings.   250
Patroclus only of the royal train,
Placed in his tent, attends the lofty strain:
Full opposite he sat, and listened long,
In silence waiting till he ceased the song.

Unseen the Grecian embassy proceeds   255
To his high tent; the great Ulysses leads.
Achilles starting, as the chiefs he spied,
Leaped from his seat, and laid the harp aside.
With like surprise arose Menœtius' son:
Pelides grasped their hands, and thus begun: 260
"Princes, all hail! whatever brought you here,
Or strong necessity, or urgent fear;
Welcome, though Greeks! for not as foes ye came;
To me more dear than all that bear the name."

With that, the chiefs beneath his roof he led,   265
And placed in seats with purple carpets spread.
Then thus: "Patroclus, crown a larger bowl,
Mix purer wine, and open every soul.
Of all the warriors yonder host can send,
Thy friend most honours these, and these thy friend."

He said: Patroclus, o'er the blazing fire   271
Heaps in a brazen vase three chines entire:
The brazen vase Automedon sustains,
Which flesh of porket, sheep, and goat contains:
Achilles at the genial feast presides,   275
The parts transfixes, and with skill divides.
Meanwhile Patroclus sweats the fire to raise;
The tent is brightened with the rising blaze:
Then, when the languid flames at length subside,
He strews a bed of glowing embers wide,   280

Above the coals the smoking fragments turns,
And sprinkles sacred salt from lifted urns;
With bread the glittering canisters they load,
Which round the board Menœtius' son bestowed:
Himself, opposed to Ulysses full in sight,   285
Each portion parts, and orders every rite.
The first fat offerings, to the immortals due,
Amidst the greedy flames Patroclus threw;
Then each, indulging in the social feast,
His thirst and hunger soberly repressed.   290
That done, to Phœnix Ajax gave the sign;
Not unperceived; Ulysses crowned with wine
The foaming bowl, and instant thus began,
His speech addressing to the godlike man:
" Health to Achilles! happy are thy guests!   295
Not those more honoured whom Atrides feasts:
Though generous plenty crown thy loaded boards,
That, Agamemnon's regal tent affords;
But greater cares sit heavy on our souls,
Not eased by banquets or by flowing bowls.   300
What scenes of slaughter in yon fields appear!
The dead we mourn, and for the living fear;
Greece on the brink of fate all doubtful stands,
And owns no help but from thy saving hands:
Troy and her aids for ready vengeance call;   305
Their threat'ning tents already shade our wall:
Hear how with shouts their conquest they proclaim,
And point at every ship their vengeful flame!
For them the father of the gods declares,
Theirs are his omens, and his thunder theirs.   310
See, full of Jove, avenging Hector rise!
See! heaven and earth the raging chief defies;
What fury in his breast, what lightning in his eyes!
He waits but for the morn, to sink in flame
The ships, the Greeks, and all the Grecian name.   315
Heavens! how my country's woes distract my mind,
Lest fate accomplish all his rage designed.
And must we, gods! our heads inglorious lay

In Trojan dust, and this the fatal day?
Return, Achilles, oh return, though late,   320
To save thy Greeks, and stop the course of fate;
If in that heart or grief or courage lies,
Rise to redeem ; ah yet, to conquer, rise !
The day may come, when, all our warriors slain,
That heart shall melt, that courage rise in vain.   325
Regard in time, O prince divinely brave,
Those wholesome counsels which thy father gave.
When Peleus in his aged arms embraced
His parting son, these accents were his last :
' My child, with strength, with glory, and success,
Thy arms may Juno and Minerva bless !   331
Trust that to heaven : but thou thy cares engage
To calm thy passions, and subdue thy rage :
From gentler manners let thy glory grow,
And shun contention, the sure source of woe ;   335
That young and old may in thy praise combine,
The virtues of humanity be thine.'
This, now despised, advice thy father gave ;
Ah ! check thy anger, and be truly brave.
If thou wilt yield to great Atrides' prayers,   340
Gifts worthy thee his royal hand prepares ;
If not——but hear me, while I number o'er
The proffered presents, an exhaustless store.
Ten weighty talents of the purest gold,
And twice ten vases of refulgent mould ;   345
Seven sacred tripods, whose unsullied frame
Yet knows no office, nor has felt the flame :
Twelve steeds unmatched in fleetness and in force,
And still victorious in the dusty course :
(Rich were the man whose ample stores exceed   350
The prizes purchased by their wingèd speed :)
Seven lovely captives of the Lesbian line,
Skilled in each art, unmatched in form divine,
The same he chose for more than vulgar charms,
When Lesbos sunk beneath thy conquering arms ;
All these, to buy thy friendship, shall be paid,   356

And joined with these the long-contested maid ;
With all her charms, Briseïs he'll resign,
And solemn swear those charms were only thine ;
Untouched she stayed, uninjured she removes, 360
Pure from his arms, and guiltless of his loves.
These instant shall be thine : and if the powers
Give to our arms proud Ilion's hostile towers,
Then shalt thou store, when Greece the spoil divides,
With gold and brass thy loaded navy's sides. 365
Besides, full twenty nymphs of Trojan race
With copious love shall crown thy warm embrace ;
Such as thyself shalt choose ; who yield to none,
Or yield to Helen's heavenly charms alone.
Yet hear me farther : when our wars are o'er, 370
If safe we land on Argos' fruitful shore,
There shalt thou live his son, his honours share,
And with Orestes' self divide his care.
Yet more—three daughters in his court are bred,
And each well worthy of a royal bed ; 375
Laodicé and Iphigenia fair,
And bright Chrysothemis with golden hair ;
Her shalt thou wed whom most thy eyes approve ;
He asks no presents, no reward for love :
Himself will give the dower : so vast a store 380
As never father gave a child before.
Seven ample cities shall confess thy sway,
Thee Enopé, and Pheræ thee obey,
Cardamylé with ample turrets crowned,
And sacred Pedasus, for vines renowned : 385
Æpea fair, the pastures Hira yields,
And rich Antheia with her flowery fields :
The whole extent to Pylos' sandy plain
Along the verdant margin of the main.
There heifers graze, and labouring oxen toil ; 390
Bold are the men, and gen'rous is the soil.
There shalt thou reign with power and justice crowned,
And rule the tributary realms around.
Such are the proffers which this day we bring,

Such the repentance of a suppliant king.   395
But if all this, relentless, thou disdain,
If honour, and if interest, plead in vain ;
Yet some redress to suppliant Greece afford,
And be, amongst her guardian gods, adored.
If no regard thy suffering country claim,   400
Hear thy own glory, and the voice of fame :
For now that chief, whose unresisted ire
Made nations tremble, and whole hosts retire,
Proud Hector, now, the unequal fight demands,
And only triumphs to deserve thy hands."   405
     Then thus the goddess-born : " Ulysses, hear
A faithful speech, that knows nor art nor fear ;
What in my secret soul is understood,
My tongue shall utter, and my deeds make good.
Let Greece then know, my purpose I retain,   410
Nor with new treaties vex my peace in vain.
Who dares think one thing, and another tell,
My heart detests him as the gates of hell.
     " Then thus in short my fixed resolves attend,
Which nor Atrides, nor his Greeks, can bend :   415
Long toils, long perils, in their cause I bore ;
But now the unfruitful glories charm no more.
Fight or not fight, a like reward we claim,
The wretch and hero finds their prize the same ;
Alike regretted in the dust he lies,   420
Who yields ignobly, or who bravely dies.
Of all my dangers, all my glorious pains,
A life of labours, lo ! what fruit remains ?
As the bold bird her helpless young attends,
From danger guards them, and from want defends ;
In search of prey she wings the spacious air,   426
And with the untasted food supplies her care :
For thankless Greece such hardships have I braved,
Her wives, her infants, by my labours saved ;
Long sleepless nights in heavy arms I stood,   430
And sweat laborious days in dust and blood ;
I sacked twelve ample cities on the main,

And twelve lay smoking on the Trojan plain;
Then at Atrides' haughty feet were laid
The wealth I gathered, and the spoils I made.　435
Your mighty monarch these in peace possessed;
Some few my soldiers had, himself the rest.
Some present too to every prince was paid;
And every prince enjoys the gift he made;
I only must refund of all his train;　　　440
See what pre-eminence our merits gain!
My spoil alone his greedy soul delights;
My spouse alone must bless his lustful nights:
The woman, let him, as he may, enjoy;
But what's the quarrel then of Greece to Troy?　445
What to these shores th' assembled nations draws,
What calls for vengeance but a woman's cause?
Are fair endowments and a beauteous face
Beloved by none but those of Atreus' race?
The wife whom choice and passion both approve, 450
Sure every wise and worthy man will love.
Nor did my fair one less distinction claim;
Slave as she was, my soul adored the dame.
Wronged in my love, all proffers I disdain;
Deceived for once, I trust not kings again.　455
Ye have my answer.　What remains to do,
Your king, Ulysses, may consult with you.
What needs he the defence this arm can make?
Has he not walls no human force can shake?
Has he not fenced his guarded navy round　460
With piles, with ramparts, and a trench profound?
And will not these, the wonders he has done,
Repel the rage of Priam's single son?
There was a time—'twas when for Greece I fought—
When Hector's prowess no such wonders wrought;
He kept the verge of Troy, nor dared to wait　466
Achilles' fury at the Scæan gate;
He tried it once, and scarce was saved by Fate.
But now those ancient enmities are o'er;
To-morrow we the fav'ring gods implore:　　470

Then shall you see our parting vessels crowned,
And hear with oars the Hellespont resound.
The third day hence, shall Pthia greet our sails,
If mighty Neptune send propitious gales ;
Pthia to her Achilles shall restore   475
The wealth he left for this detested shore :
Thither the spoils of this long war shall pass,
The ruddy gold, the steel, and shining brass ;
My beauteous captives thither I'll convey,
And all that rests of my unravished prey.   480
One only valued gift your tyrant gave,
And that resumed, the fair Lyrnessian slave.
Then tell him, loud, that all the Greeks may hear,
And learn to scorn the wretch they basely fear ;
For, armed in impudence, mankind he braves,   485
And meditates new cheats on all his slaves ;
Though, shameless as he is, to face these eyes
Is what he dares not ; if he dares, he dies ;
Tell him, all terms, all commerce, I decline,
Nor share his council, nor his battle join ;   490
For once deceived, was his ; but twice, were mine.
No—let the stupid prince, whom Jove deprives
Of sense and justice, run where frenzy drives ;
His gifts are hateful : kings of such a kind
Stand but as slaves before a noble mind.   495
Not though he proffered all himself possessed,
And all his rapine could from others wrest ;
Not all the golden tides of wealth that crown
The many-peopled Orchomenian town ;
Not all proud Thebes' unrivalled walls contain,   500
The world's great empress on the Egyptian plain,
That spreads her conquests o'er a thousand states,
And pours her heroes through a hundred gates—
Two hundred horsemen and two hundred cars
From each wide portal issuing to the wars—   505
Though bribes were heaped on bribes, in number more
Than dust in fields, or sands along the shore ;
Should all these offers for my friendship call ;

'Tis he that offers, and I scorn them all.
Atrides' daughter never shall be led, 510
An ill-matched consort, to Achilles' bed ;
Like golden Venus though she charmed the heart,
And vied with Pallas in the works of art.
Some greater Greek let those high nuptials grace,
I hate alliance with a tyrant's race. 515
If heaven restore me to my realms with life,
The rev'rend Peleus shall elect my wife ;
Thessalian nymphs there are, of form divine,
And kings that sue to mix their blood with mine,
Blessed in kind love, my years shall glide away, 520
Content with just hereditary sway ;
There, deaf for ever to the martial strife,
Enjoy the dear prerogative of life.
Life is not to be bought with heaps of gold ;
Not all Apollo's Pythian treasures hold, 525
Or Troy once held, in peace and pride of sway,
Can bribe the poor possession of a day !
Lost herds and treasures we by arms regain,
And steeds unrivalled on the dusty plain :
But from our lips the vital spirit fled, 530
Returns no more to wake the silent dead.
My fates long since by Thetis were disclosed,
And each alternate, life or fame, proposed :
Here if I stay, before the Trojan town,
Short is my date, but deathless my renown ; 535
If I return, I quit immortal praise
For years on years, and long-extended days.
Convinced, though late, I find my fond mistake,
And warn the Greeks the wiser choice to make ;
To quit these shores, their native seats enjoy, 540
Nor hope the fall of heaven-defended Troy.
Jove's arm displayed asserts her from the skies ;
Her hearts are strengthened, and her glories rise.
Go then, to Greece report our fixed design :
Bid all your councils, all your armies join, 545
Let all your forces, all your arts conspire,

To save the ships, the troops, the chiefs, from fire.
One stratagem has failed, and others will :
Ye find Achilles is unconquered still.
Go then : digest my message as ye may : 550
But here this night let rev'rend Phœnix stay :
His tedious toils and hoary hairs demand
A peaceful death in Pthia's friendly land.
But whether he remain, or sail with me,
His age be sacred, and his will be free." 555
The son of Peleus ceased : the chiefs around
In silence wrapped, in consternation drowned,
Attend the stern reply.   Then Phœnix rose :
Down his white beard a stream of sorrow flows :
And while the fate of suffering Greece he mourned,
With accent weak these tender words returned : 561
" Divine Achilles ! wilt thou then retire,
And leave our hosts in blood, our fleets on fire ?
If wrath so dreadful fill thy ruthless mind,
How shall thy friend, thy Phœnix, stay behind ? 565
The royal Peleus, when from Pthia's coast
He sent thee early to the Achaian host ;
Thy youth as then in sage debates unskilled,
And new to perils of the direful field ;
He bade me teach thee all the ways of war : 570
To shine in councils and in camps to dare.
Never, ah never, let me leave thy side !
No time shall part us, and no fate divide.
Not though the god, that breathed my life, restore
The bloom I boasted, and the port I bore, 575
When Greece of old beheld my youthful flames,
Delightful Greece, the land of lovely dames.
My father, faithless to my mother's arms,
Old as he was, adored a stranger's charms :
I tried what youth could do, at her desire, 580
To win the damsel, and prevent my sire.
My sire with curses loads my hated head,
And cries, ' Ye furies ! barren be his bed.'
Infernal Jove, the vengeful fiends below,

And ruthless Proserpine, confirmed his vow. 585
Despair and grief attract my lab'ring mind ;
Gods ! what a crime my impious heart designed !
I thought—but some kind God that thought suppressed—
To plunge the poniard in my father's breast :
Then meditate my flight ; my friends in vain 590
With prayers entreat me, and with force detain.
On fat of rams, black bulls, and brawny swine,
They daily feast, with draughts of fragrant wine :
Strong guards they placed, and watched nine nights
    entire :
The roofs and porches flamed with constant fire. 595
The tenth, I forced the gates, unseen of all ;
And, favoured by the night, o'erleaped the wall.
My travels thence through spacious Greece extend :
In Pthia's court at last my labours end.
Your sire received me, as his son caressed, 600
With gifts enriched, and with possessions blessed.
The strong Dolopians thenceforth owned my reign,
And all the coast that runs along the main.
By love to thee his bounties I repaid,
And early wisdom to thy soul conveyed : 605
Great as thou art, my lessons made thee brave,
A child I took thee, but a hero gave.
Thy infant breast a like affection shewed :
Still in my arms, an ever-pleasing load,
Or at my knee, by Phœnix wouldst thou stand ; 610
No food was grateful but from Phœnix' hand.
I pass my watchings o'er thy helpless years,
The tender labours, the compliant cares ;
The gods, I thought, reversed their hard decree,
And Phœnix felt a father's joys in thee : 615
Thy growing virtues justified my cares,
And promised comfort to my silver hairs.
Now be thy rage, thy fatal rage, resigned ;
A cruel heart ill suits a manly mind :
The gods, the only great, and only wise,
Are moved by off'rings, vows, and sacrifice ; 620

Offending man their high compassion wins,
And daily prayers atone for daily sins.
Prayers are Jove's daughters, of celestial race,
Lame are their feet, and wrinkled is their face ;   625
With humble mien, and with dejected eyes,
Constant they follow where Injustice flies :
Injustice, swift, erect, and unconfined,
Sweeps the wide earth, and tramples o'er mankind,
While Prayers, to heal her wrongs, move slow behind.
Who hears these daughters of almighty Jove,   631
For him they mediate to the throne above :
When man rejects the humble suit they make,
The sire revenges for the daughters' sake ;
From Jove commissioned, fierce Injustice then   635
Descends, to punish unrelenting men.
Oh let not headlong passion bear the sway ;
These reconciling goddesses obey :
Due honours to the seed of Jove belong ;
Due honours calm the fierce and bend the strong.   640
Were these not paid thee by the terms we bring,
Were rage still harboured in the haughty king,
Nor Greece, nor all her fortunes, should engage
Thy friend to plead against so just a rage.
But since what honour asks, the gen'ral sends,   645
And sends by those whom most thy heart commends,
The best and noblest of the Grecian train ;
Permit not these to sue, and sue in vain !
Let me, my son, an ancient fact unfold,
A great example drawn from times of old ;   650
Hear what our fathers were, and what their praise,
Who conquered their revenge in former days.

  " Where Calydon on rocky mountains stands,
Once fought the Ætolian and Curetian bands ;
To guard it those, to conquer these, advance ;   655
And mutual deaths were dealt with mutual chance.
The silver Cynthia bade Contention rise,
In vengeance of neglected sacrifice ;
On Œneus' fields she sent a monstrous boar,

That levelled harvests, and whole forests tore : 660
This beast, when many a chief his tusks had slain,
Great Meleager stretched along the plain.
Then, for his spoils, a new debate arose,
The neighbour nations thence commencing foes.
Strong as they were, the bold Curetes failed, 665
While Meleager's thundering arm prevailed :
Till rage at length inflamed his lofty breast,
For rage invades the wisest and the best.
Cursed by Althæa, to his wrath he yields,
And, in his wife's embrace, forgets the fields. 670
" She from Marpessa sprung, divinely fair,
And matchless Idas, more than man in war ;
The god of day adored the mother's charms :
Against the god the father bent his arms :
Th' afflicted pair, their sorrows to proclaim, 675
From Cleopatra changed this daughter's name,
And called Alcyone ; a name to shew
The father's grief, the mourning mother's woe.
To her the chief retired from stern debate,
But found no peace from fierce Althæa's hate : 680
Althæa's hate the unhappy warrior drew,
Whose luckless hand his royal uncle slew ;
She beat the ground, and called the powers beneath
On her own son to wreak her brother's death :
Hell heard her curses from the realms profound, 685
And the red fiends that walked the nightly round.
In vain Ætolia her deliverer waits,
War shakes her walls, and thunders at her gates.
She sent ambassadors, a chosen band,
Priests of the gods, and elders of the land, 690
Besought the chief to save the sinking state :
Their prayers were urgent, and their proffers great—
Full fifty acres of the richest ground,
Half pasture green, and half with vineyards crowned—
His suppliant father, aged Œneus, came ; 695
His sisters followed : e'en the vengeful dame
Althæa sues : his friends before him fall :

He stands relentless, and rejects them all.
Meanwhile the victors' shouts ascend the skies ;
The walls are scaled ; the rolling flames arise ;   700
At length his wife, a form divine, appears,
With piercing cries, and supplicating tears ;
She paints the horrors of a conquered town ;
The heroes slain, the palaces o'erthrown,
The matrons ravished, the whole race enslaved :   705
The warrior heard, he vanquished, and he saved.
The Ætolians, long disdained, now took their turn,
And left the chief their broken faith to mourn.
Learn hence, betimes to curb pernicious ire,
Nor stay, till yonder fleets ascend in fire :   710
Accept the presents ; draw thy conq'ring sword :
And be amongst our guardian gods adored.''
  Thus he : the stern Achilles thus replied :
" My second father, and my rev'rend guide !
Thy friend, believe me, no such gifts demands,   715
And asks no honours from a mortal's hands :
Jove honours me, and favours my designs :
His pleasure guides me, and his will confines :
And here I stay, if such his high behest,
While life's warm spirit beats within my breast.   720
Yet hear one word, and lodge it in thy heart :
No more molest me on Atrides' part :
Is it for him these tears are taught to flow,
For him these sorrows ? for my mortal foe ?
A gen'rous friendship no cold medium knows,   725
Burns with one love, with one resentment glows ;
One should our int'rests, and our passions, be ;
My friend must hate the man that injures me.
Do this, my Phœnix, 'tis a gen'rous part,
And share my realms, my honours, and my heart ;
Let these return : our voyage, or our stay,   731
Rest undetermined till the dawning day.''
  He ceased : then ordered for the sage's bed
A warmer couch with num'rous carpets spread.
With that, stern Ajax his long silence broke,   735

And thus, impatient, to Ulysses spoke :
  " Hence let us go—why waste we time in vain ?
See what effect our low submissions gain !
Liked or not liked, his words we must relate,
The Greeks expect them, and our heroes wait.   740
Proud as he is, that iron heart retains
Its stubborn purpose, and his friends disdains.
Stern, and unpitying ! if a brother bleed,
On just atonement, we remit the deed ;
A sire the slaughter of his son forgives ;   745
The price of blood discharged, the murderer lives :
The haughtiest hearts at length their rage resign,
And gifts can conquer every soul but thine :
The gods that unrelenting breast have steeled,
And cursed thee with a mind that cannot yield.   750
One woman slave was ravished from thy arms :
Lo, seven are offered, and of equal charms.
Then hear, Achilles ! be of better mind ;
Revere thy roof, and to thy guests be kind ;
And know the men, of all the Grecian host,   755
Who honour worth, and prize thy valour most."
  " Oh soul of battles, and thy people's guide ! "
To Ajax thus the first of Greeks replied :
" Well hast thou spoke ; but at the tyrant's name
My rage rekindles and my soul's on flame ;   760
'Tis just resentment, and becomes the brave ;
Disgraced, dishonoured, like the vilest slave !
Return then, heroes ! and our answer bear,
The glorious combat is no more my care ;
Not till amidst yon sinking navy slain,   765
The blood of Greeks shall dye the sable main ;
Not till the flames, by Hector's fury thrown,
Consume your vessels, and approach my own ,
Just there, the impetuous homicide shall stand,
There cease his battle, and there feel our hand." 770
  This said, each prince a double goblet crowned,
And cast a large libation on the ground :
Then to their vessels, through the gloomy shades,

The chiefs return ; divine Ulysses leads.
Meantime Achilles' slaves prepared a bed,   775
With fleeces, carpets, and soft linen spread :
There, till the sacred morn restored the day,
In slumbers sweet the rev'rend Phœnix lay ;
But in his inner tent, an ampler space,
Achilles slept : and in his warm embrace   780
Fair Diomedé of the Lesbian race.
Last, for Patroclus was the couch prepared,
Whose nightly joys the beauteous Iphis shared :
Achilles to his friend consigned her charms,
When Scyros fell before his conquering arms.   785
    And now th' elected chiefs, whom Greece had sent,
Passed through the hosts, and reached the royal tent.
Then rising all, with goblets in their hands,
The peers, and leaders of the Achaian bands,
Hailed their return : Atrides first begun :   790
    " Say, what success ? divine Laertes' son !
Achilles' high resolves declare to all :
Returns the chief, or must our navy fall ? "
    " Great king of nations ! " Ithacus replied,
" Fixed is his wrath, unconquered is his pride ;   795
He slights thy friendship, thy proposals scorns,
And, thus implored, with fiercer fury burns.
To save our army, and our fleets to free,
Is not his care ; but left to Greece and thee.
Your eyes shall view, when morning paints the sky, 800
Beneath his oars the whitening billows fly.
Us too he bids our oars and sails employ,
Nor hope the fall of heaven-protected Troy ;
For Jove o'ershades her with his arm divine,
Inspires her war, and bids her glory shine.   805
Such was his word : what farther he declared,
These sacred heralds and great Ajax heard.
But Phœnix in his tent the chief retains,
Safe to transport him to his native plains,
When morning dawns ; if other he decree,   810
His age is sacred, and his choice is free."

Ulysses ceased : the great Achaian host,
With sorrow seized, in consternation lost,
Attend the stern reply.   Tydides broke
The gen'ral silence, and undaunted spoke :   815
" Why should we gifts to proud Achilles send ?
Or strive with prayers his haughty soul to bend ?
His country's woes he glories to deride,
And prayers will burst that swelling heart with pride.
Be the fierce impulse of his rage obeyed ;   820
Our battles let him or desert or aid ;
Then let him arm when Jove or he think fit ;
That, to his madness, or to heaven, commit :
What for ourselves we can, is always ours :
This night, let due repast refresh our powers ;   825
For strength consists in spirits and in blood,
And those are owed to gen'rous wine and food ;
But when the rosy messenger of day
Strikes the blue mountains with her golden ray,
Ranged at the ships let all our squadrons shine,   830
In flaming arms, a long-extended line :
In the dread front let great Atrides stand,
The first in danger, as in high command."
Shouts of acclaim the list'ning heroes raise,
Then each to heaven the due libations pays ;   835
Till sleep, descending o'er the tents, bestows
The grateful blessings of desired repose.

AIDS TO READERS

THIS volume is built on the theory that it is easy to bury Pope in highly specific footnotes—and unnecessary. His poetry does require notes, but it is well to remember that the reader should get delight from the poems rather than gather information about them. The Elwin-Courthope edition of Pope contains a wealth of critical apparatus, and to it (for want of a better) the student must constantly go. But one can enjoy the poet's brilliance without understanding all the personal allusions, and since some of them have never been understood, it seems possible to spare the reader knowledge of some that are understood. The present volume has devoted a moderate space to footnotes explaining factual details of the poems. In the belief that it is more important for most readers to grasp the general import of a poem than it is to understand the minutiae of individual lines these General Notes are here added. Most of Pope's poems are loosely organized: the truth is that, especially in his later work, he writes *sermones* or "conversations" in the manner of Horace, and conversations, properly enough, have no structure. Throughout his career Pope composed first fragments and then later cemented them together into poems; hence discussion of his poems tends to become discussion of fragments rather than of wholes. Because of these facts it is thought that general introductory statements may prove more useful than would added footnotes.

It may be remarked here that the footnotes in general have been drawn from those of Pope himself or from his early editors. Only a few are original.

PASTORALS

According to Pope these poems were written when he was only sixteen years of age. They were of course later revised after having been submitted to many of the leading wits of the day. They passed into the hands of the publisher Tonson in 1706, and in the spring of 1709 they were printed in the "sixth part" of the *Poetical Miscellanies* commonly called Dryden's or Tonson's *Miscellanies*. The volume opened with a group of pastorals by Ambrose Philips, a friend of Addison's; it concluded with Pope's group of four eclogues. Although Pope's poems were doubtless praised privately, in print Philips was much more commonly extolled. Philips' *Pastorals* were reprinted in 1710 with a preface that concluded: "Theocritus, Virgil, and Spenser, are the only Writers, that seem to have hit upon the true Nature of Pastoral Poems. So that it will be Honour sufficient for me, if I have not altogether fail'd in my attempt." Philips seems to have been a pompous ass, and though Pope at first liked his pastorals very much, utterances such as these, together with the later praise of Philips by Welsted, Dennis, Gildon, and especially that by Steele in *Guardians* 22, 23, 30, and 32, wearied Pope into writing a paper (*Guardian,* No. 40) demonstrating, ironically, the inferiority of his own pastorals to those of Philips, whose anger thereat drove Pope away from Button's coffee house, and widened the breach between Pope and the Whig friends of Addison who frequented Button's. Congreve and Rowe, among the Whigs, seem to have continued to prefer Pope's work to that of Philips.

The pastoral was among the most imitative and artificial of the neo-classic *genres*. Pope follows the elegant tradition of Virgil; and his theory of the pastoral (aping that of Rapin and Fontenelle) makes the poem aim not at realistic description of nature but at a portrayal of the manners of the Golden Age. The result is a confusion of the Golden Age and Windsor Forest that is bewildering but not unpleasant. The chief merit of the poems is their smooth versification—seen perhaps at its best in *Autumn,* the last of the

four to be written. Lines 73-76 of *Summer* are, thanks
to a compliment to Handel in the *Dunciad* (IV, 65),
immortalized in that composer's *Semele*. They will
probably remain in consequence the best known lines
of these poems.

The last paragraph of Pope's "Discourse on Pastoral Poetry" (page 8) leads one to suggest the following comparisons with other pastorals: The song
contest in *Spring* may be compared with the eighth
idyll of Theocritus and the third and seventh of Virgil's eclogues—and possibly with Spenser's *August*.
Pope's *Summer* as a love complaint is related to the
eleventh idyll of Theocritus, the second eclogue of
Virgil, and the first eclogue of Spenser. *Autumn,* because of its refrains, may be compared with Theocritus
II, and Virgil VIII. *Winter* belongs to the same
family of pastoral elegies as Moschus' Lament for
Bion; Bion's Lament for Adonis, Theocritus' idylls I
and XV, Virgil's fifth eclogue and Spenser's *November*.

The elaborate scheme of making each pastoral represent not merely a season but a typical hour of the day
is quite like Pope, who frequently gives us poetic structures built on plans more pretentious than vital. The
scheme that makes shepherds sing in the springtime
and die in the winter is obvious, but certainly artificial.

MESSIAH

This poem had the good fortune to be printed for
the first time in the *Spectator* on May 14, 1712; it
consequently enjoyed a wide circulation amongst the
most reputable readers. Of its composition little is
known, though it is a plausible assumption that the
moral influence of Steele and the *Spectator* encouraged
the poet to attempt what the age commended as
"sacred poetry." The "Advertisement" indicates the

main derivation of the poem, but one ought also to note the tone and at times the phrasing of Milton. The school of Milton, led by John Dennis, had elaborate theories as to the aesthetic worthiness of Biblical paraphrase and as to the use of religious materials in poetry. Dennis in his *Advancement and Reformation of Poetry* (1701) asserts that the actual preeminence of the ancient poets is derived "from joining their religion with their poetry," and he goes on to urge "that the moderns, by incorporating poetry with the religion revealed to us in Sacred Writ, may come to equal the ancients." The use of true Christian, as opposed to heathen, inspiration for poetry was a favorite precept of "reform" in the days of Dennis and Blackmore.

Because of this preparation in criticism and because of Pope's literary enthusiasm for the prophecies of Isaiah, the poem was bound to be a success. It was almost immediately useful to Pope as a hostage for a righteous reputation. There can be no doubt that he loved his tavern companions, such as Tidcombe (who valued Pope for his "atheistical jests"), as much as he did the soberer Addison; under the influence of such companions he wrote an indecent burlesque of the first Psalm—not intended for publication but published, nevertheless, by Curll in 1716. Pope repeatedly disowned the Psalm, and found it useful to point with pride to *Messiah* as showing his true religious fervor. A composite of the two poems would well represent not merely Pope but also the literary society of his day. *Messiah* formed contacts between the poet and a new class of readers, for whom many of his early works lacked specific appeal. Throughout the century the poem was much praised, and it certainly does present in its short compass the poet's most sustained achievement in "full organ" tones. It begins robustly and increases to a noble *fortissimo* in

the final apostrophe to "imperial Salem." Warton
thought the poem the "most animated and sublime" of
Pope's works, and even Bowles is highly commenda-
tory. Later critics, however, have taken less pleasure
in the paraphrase, which at times seems flat, at times
too ornate, and seldom or never seems an improvement on the Hebrew prophet. Every one may choose
his pet aversions amongst the florid phrases; line 78,
as a debased version of "And a little child shall lead
them" has been often pointed out.

WINDSOR FOREST

According to Pope's statement the first part of this
poem, "which relates to the country," was written at
the same time with his *Pastorals;* the latter part,
which celebrates Lord Lansdowne and the Treaty of
Utrecht, was apparently completed shortly before the
poem was published, March 7, 1713. The two parts
of the poem were inspired by two of Pope's friends.
Sir William Trumbull had suggested the theme of
Windsor—apparently to be treated in the fashion of
Denham's *Cooper's Hill* and Waller's poem *On St.
James's Park*. Lord Lansdowne had later given the
poem timeliness by suggesting the intrusion into it of
lines celebrating the peace of Utrecht. This "peace,"
the major accomplishment perhaps of the Tory government of 1710-14, had been in process of negotia-
tion for some months, and though not yet signed, had
been celebrated by Tickell and other poets before
Pope's composition appeared. Granville as a Tory
bard, one of the newly created peers, and one of Pope's
close friends, was a natural person to whom to dedicate the poem. The glowing compliment to Trumbull
(235-58) as well as the praise of Walsh in the *Essay
on Criticism* is prophetic of the vast amount of eulogy

Pope was to spend on his personal friends. Addison's reputed chagrin at the poem would probably be due to the alignment of Pope with the Tories, which the poem implied. Addison was more or less charged with keeping writers of promise well affected towards Whig principles, and while Pope as a Catholic was admittedly a doubtful person from the start, both Steele and Addison had paid him unusual court. He advised Addison on *Cato* and wrote the Prologue, and Addison might well feel annoyed that Swift and Arbuthnot should now have as a Tory asset the fame which the *Spectator* had helped confer. Addison early in 1713 must have been encouraging Pope to translate Homer, but by the end of the year when Swift and others were getting subscribers to the project, Addison did nothing to aid it. *Windsor Forest* and the formation of the Scriblerus Club must have caused a decline in his friendliness for Pope, even if there had been no other reasons.

The poem, quite typically, falls into fragments and does not make a unit. Curiously enough the break between the Trumbull and the Granville sections of the poem is not clearly marked. Pope states that the first part ended with verse 289 (291 in later editions), but verse 258 seems the logical conclusion to the section, as it represents a poetic climax dealing with Trumbull, and is immediately followed by a passage on the swans of Windsor, in which praise of Granville marks a climax.

The poem has a duality quite apart from its dual inspiration. In the 1717 edition of Pope's *Works* the ornamental head-piece for the poem contains a view of Windsor Castle, and the poem certainly stresses the "castle" associations of Windsor fully as much as the sporting pleasures of the forest. The gloomy waste of Norman forestation (43-92) is turned as a com-

pliment to the "peace and plenty" (42) of Queen
Anne's "golden years" (92). The retired statesman
Trumbull is not the happiest man near Windsor; that
post is his "whom this bright Court approves" (235).
And a whole section (299-328) deals with royal heroes
notably connected with Windsor.

But the "forest" aspects of the poem have usually
excited more comment than the "castle" aspects.
Wordsworth found the poem had more original natural images than most of the work of its century, but
Warton and many critics have been more severe and
have thought the poem showed Pope's lack of love for
nature. It very likely does show this, but the poem
must be interpreted in the light of its own day when
human values were, for a poet, of greater import than
were visual images. At various points in the poem
(lines 21-27, 65-73, and 111-118) Pope shows, possibly, that the study and the practice of painting had
trained his eye, but even the much-praised death of
the pheasant stresses humane rather than pictorial qualities. Even in this, the most descriptive of Pope's
poems, pure description never for long holds the place
of "sense."

Melody and the "sense" of fragmentary passages
combined to make the poem very popular. It is interesting to note the more or less casual agreements
with important loci of the century in passages dealing briefly with such topics as the harmony of the universe (11-16), the gloom of ruins (65-72), the praise
of industry and commerce (41-42; 385-412), the inhumanity of the hunter (55-64; 121-24), or the beauty
of rural retirement (237-58). In expressing for readers of Pope's day such melodious commonplaces as
these the poem achieved its best ends. Not description, but rather "reflections upon life and political in-

stitutions" such as he had admired in *Cooper's Hill*
constituted Pope's real aim.

ODE ON ST. CECILIA'S DAY

Grove's *Dictionary of Music* (3rd. ed., 1927; I, 590)
tells us that in 1683 The Musical Society held at London its first annual celebration of St. Cecilia's Day
(November 22). On the continent such celebrations
had long been common; now for a few years they
were to be regular in London, but after 1703 they were
occasional only. The celebration consisted usually of
an anthem at St. Bride's Church, after which, commonly in Stationers Hall, an ode was sung "by the
best voices." Such odes in honor of St. Cecilia were
written by Dryden, Shadwell, Congreve, D'Urfey,
Hughes, and others. Similar celebrations were held
at Oxford, and for one of these Addison wrote his ode.

The immediate genesis of Pope's poem is obscure.
His statement that it was written in 1708 is possibly
wrong; he frequently mistakes the dates of composition of his poems. If, as he told Spence (*Anecdotes,*
page 158), it was written at Steele's request, it was
pretty certainly written later than 1708. In July, 1711,
Steele asked Pope for words that Clayton might set
to music "against winter." If Pope submitted anything, it was probably this poem. In any case, the
poem was published in the summer of 1713, and was
not set to music until much later. An altered form
was set by Maurice Greene and performed at Cambridge in 1730, and even later the first form was set
by other composers. It has never been definitely connected with The Musical Society and its celebrations
of St. Cecilia's Day.

It is perhaps easy to see why any musician to whom
it may have been submitted early would be loth to

attempt a musical setting. Not merely do the first three strophes stagger about, rather than prepare for the Orpheus story which follows; the moods of the strophes shift violently with a rapidity that no music could coherently follow. As a libretto the poem may almost be described as inept.

As a poem the ode won Pope vague compliments for versatility: he could "boldly follow Pindar's pathless way." It was reprinted frequently and consequently must have been in demand. The poet's more hostile critics saw in the ode only an impudent and unsuccessful attempt to rival Dryden, and concerning both the indebtedness and the inferiority of the poem to Dryden's odes there can be no doubt. Dr. Johnson in the *Rambler* for July 30, 1751, pointed out a possible borrowing from Boethius. On the whole the poem is interesting mainly as an attempt in a metrical form unusual for Pope and unsuited to his art. It was translated into Latin by Christopher Smart.

ODE ON SOLITUDE

This poem is Pope at his best and not at the age of twelve. It may have been written originally at that age; but we first find it in a letter sent to Cromwell, July 17, 1709. Its first printed form (1717), as Professor Case's reprinting shows differs notably from the perfect finish which Pope's mature genius gave to the poem. One would like to imagine that the "paternal acres" mean Binfield, and that the poem represents the boy's reaction to the home in the forest, to which he was taken at about the age of twelve. There is, however, very little probability of much autobiographic detail in the poem: it is simply Pope's variation on a theme popular since the days of Virgil and of Horace, to whose second epode it is clearly indebted. It is one of the very best Horatian imitations in English, and shows Pope's unsurpassed skill in the musical manipulation of metrical pauses.

THE DYING CHRISTIAN TO HIS SOUL

A version of this poem was sent to Caryll in a letter from Pope under date of June 12, 1713. In substantially the same form it was first printed in Lewis' Miscellany in 1730. Between that year and 1736, when the present text of the poem was first printed in Pope's *Works,* the stanzas underwent the sort of polishing revision that gave so many of his pieces neatness, elegance, and perfection of finish. The original stimulus to found a poem on the verses of Hadrian came from a conversation summarized in a letter by Pope printed in the *Spectator* for November 10, 1712. Pope was amiably inclined to defend the dignity and effectiveness of Hadrian's verses, and it was doubtless in the desire to illustrate languishing effects combined with dignity that he made his version. Warton in the *Adventurer,* No. 63, pointed out Pope's indebtedness in lines 3, 4, 7, and 8 to Thomas Flatman's "Thought of Death." None ever knew better than Pope how to salvage a golden phrase from the mud of "minor" poetry. Successful "thefts" of this sort were warranted by neo-classic theories of imitation and were not especially furtive, as some have thought. In their finished form the verses do not lack grace or emotional appeal. Evangelically minded authors such as Mrs. Elizabeth Rowe and Henry Brooke were early and enthusiastic admirers of the poem.

The letter to Steele, printed by Pope in 1737, and purporting to send the poem to Steele in December, 1712, is probably not genuine. If the poem had reached Steele at that time, it would very likely have been printed in the *Guardian,* on which Pope was helping Steele in 1713. Pope seems not to have thought the poem ready for publication at that time.

AN ESSAY ON CRITICISM

It is certain that this poem was first published in May, 1711, before Pope was quite twenty-three. The period of its composition, however, is obscured by the conflicting statements of the poet himself. His most commonly printed statement was "Written in 1709," but he told Spence that he showed it to Walsh, and Walsh died in March, 1708. Dennis in 1711 attacked the poem as very immature, and some critics have thought Pope intentionally pushed back the period of composition, so that his youthfulness might excuse this immaturity. On the other hand, as we have seen, Pope was always getting his dates wrong without intention. Since the conclusion is so glowing a tribute to Walsh, one suspects it may have been written not long after his death, and it certainly would not be strange if some passages were written early enough to be submitted to his criticism. Pope's letters to Walsh show that they frequently discussed matters relating to literary criticism. In any case, revision of the poem probably continued until it was sent to press. Even then it was not finished; for after Dennis' attack Pope improved the phrasing to avoid censure where it could easily be avoided. The changes in the printed texts are most interesting. In part they may be explained by rapidity of original execution. Pope told Spence: "The things that I have written fastest, have always pleased the most. I wrote the *Essay on Criticism* fast; for I had digested all the matter in prose, before I began upon it in verse." (*Anecdotes,* page 142.)

The essential nature of the poem—in spite of some

critics—really offers little difficulty. In Pope's day the word *essay* meant "an imperfect attempt at a subject," and it consequently carries modest implications befitting youth. The word also warns us to expect a lack of structure such as will surprise no one who has read other of Pope's poems; it by no means warrants one in expecting an ordered treatment. The thought, however, is unusually well organized for Pope, and no one ought to go further than Addison, who found the observations following "one another like those in Horace's Art of Poetry without that methodical regularity which would have been requisite in a prose author." (*Spectator,* No. 253.) The difficulties of the poem are verbal rather than structural.

It has, to be sure, been urged that Pope got the creative artist and the critic confused, and wrote now for one, now for the other. In view of his assertion (lines 15, 16) that only artists should be critics, such confusion might not be criminal; but the supposed confusion is due to the fact that Pope's readers have not always tried to think in his terms. His position is (lines 11-14) that just as genius is indispensable to the poet, so taste is essential to the critic; but both genius and taste must proceed in accord with Nature, and hence it is quite proper to bid the critic, "First follow Nature," and to advise him as to the training of taste much as one might advise the poet as to the training of his genius. "Nature," of course, meant various things, and so did "wit"; and it is by the vague and elusive uses of such words that the reader is perplexed.

These two terms, as ultimates, parallel each other in some meanings; in general, Nature is cosmic or generic, while Wit is specific. Nature as the universe, "the scale of being," is the material source of all art (see lines 89, 243, 297); while Wit, though very com-

monly (see lines 28, 238, 406, 447, 456, 652) meaning material proper for use in literature, tends to mean
material that has passed through the mind of the artist.
Nature is the *vin cru;* Wit is the *vin travaillé.* But
Nature is also the normal, the "natural," and in art
as in morals conformity to this norm (70-73) is the
test of excellence. Nature is the objective ideal which
the individual strives to approach. Wit is usually either
a faculty within the individual, or is the product of the
individual mind. As a faculty of the mind Wit may
have the meaning, common in earlier English, of *pure
intellect* (53, 61); it also very commonly means *artistic intelligence,* or even at times *genius* (17, 209, 238,
259, 396, 421, 494, 500, 539, 717); and it less frequently approaches something like *invention* or *fancy*
(80, 657). As witticism or conceit (292, 429) it may
be excessive or inept. In general, behind the word may
be glimpsed the popular definition of the term by John
Locke and others as *the quick perception of resem-
blances* (compare Congreve's Witwoud), or the definition of the French equivalent, *esprit,* by the Père Bou-
hours: *c'est un corps solide qui brille* (292, 302, 421,
468). Wit is literary imagination, as process or as
product; brilliance is its peculiar quality.

The *Essay* combines with some tact ideas not always regarded as congruous. On the one hand it
stresses the subjective criterion of excellence, taste;
and again it insists that literature must follow the
"rules of nature"—which are not subjective. But if
we conceive taste, or "the seeds of judgment" (20),
as in part innate and yet as in need of nurture and
training, the apparent contradiction becomes an obvious piece of sense. The "rules" which methodize
the experience of the ancients (88-91) are simply the
result of the experience of the best writers, and are
consequently the best guides for taste. They are the

rules of nature or reason, not of Horace. It is only in servile France that

> Boileau still *in right of Horace* sways.

Pope, it should be noted also, is not here completely rationalistic: he recognizes with customary deference the appeal to nameless "graces beyond the reach of art" (141-55), to the irrational *je ne sais quoi* as a basis of delight.

The poem is a storehouse of popular quotation, and in spite of critics like De Quincey who have stressed the essentially commonplace nature of its ideas, no piece of English criticism except Hamlet's advice to the players has become so thoroughly a part of our thought and utterance about letters. Perhaps the most popular lines are the "sound to sense" passage (364-83). The apostrophe to the ancients (189-200) is in Pope's best vein of enthusiasm. Dr. Johnson thought the simile on the Alps (225-32) the best in the language. The poem is unusually rich in the aphoristic quality which is one of Pope's distinguishing traits.

THE RAPE OF THE LOCK

In the summer of 1711, at a time when he was exasperated by Dennis' *Reflections Critical and Satyrical on a late Rhapsody call'd an Essay upon Criticism,* Pope came to the assistance of his friend Caryll (see page 75) in an attempt to reconcile Lady Arabella Fermor to Caryll's relative, Lord Petre. The *Rape of the Lock* was quickly composed, and is quoted in a letter to Henry Cromwell as early as July 15. Manuscript copies were doubtless circulating by August, and the poem was published (May, 1712) in Lintot's Miscellany. In this first form the poem was cast in two

cantos, which contain together 334 verses. It was received with immediate enthusiasm. Addison in *Spectator,* No. 523, commended it, and privately called it
merum sal. Sir William Trumbull wrote in his letters that it was something which "all men of good
taste, notwithstanding the jarring of parties, must and
do universally applaud." Even the Reverend George
Berkeley, future bishop and philosopher, (who had
commended, to Percival, Pope's wit *and learning*),
wrote the poet: "I am charmed with the magic of your
invention, with all those images, illusions, and inexplicable beauties, which you raise so surprisingly, and
at the same time so naturally out of a trifle." Without doubt the poem scored an enormous success.

Few poets would have trifled with this success, and
perhaps Pope would not have done so had the poem
been altogether pleasing to the persons involved in it.
Sir George Brown ("Sir Plume") was naturally offended, and it may be that Miss Fermor anticipated
the ill-nature of Gildon and Dennis by perceiving the
facts that Belinda's beauty was largely artificial, that
her Othello-like roarings at the loss of the lock lacked
due restraint, and that on occasion she was made to
"talk bawdy." For some reason Pope decided to make
the poem less personal and certainly more fabulous,
fantastic, and exquisitely mock-heroic, by the addition
of burlesque "machines," or supernatural agents. So
in the later months of 1713 he recast his fragile mas-
terpiece into five cantos, introducing the sylphs and
gnomes, and adding many notable episodes such as
the toilet in Canto I, the game of ombre, and the Cave
of Spleen. The speech of Clarissa in Canto V was
added in 1717, ostensibly to give the poem moral significance! The revision succeeded astonishingly; for
upon publication early in 1714, it sold, so Pope wrote,
"in four days' time . . . to the number of three thou-

sand." There were three editions within the year. For the first form of the poem Lintot had paid seven pounds; for the revised form he gave fifteen, and in 1715 he paid over thirty-two for Pope's delightful *Key to the Lock*—a prose pamphlet which gravely demonstrated a dangerous political significance in the poem, the lock being the Barrier Treaty; Belinda, Great Britain; the baron, the Earl of Oxford; Thalestris, the Duchess of Marlborough, and Sir Plume, Prince Eugene. It was an extraordinary burlesque of the political stupidities of the day.

The *Rape of the Lock* remains perhaps Pope's most delightful work, though perhaps not his most significant. Its success, so far as matter goes, lies in the perfection with which it embodies a phase of the social life of the day. *Tom Jones* and *The School for Scandal* later do the same thing more fully, but not more exquisitely. The tone of the poem was certainly learned from those sober discourses on the foibles of women that adorned the *Tatler* and *Spectator*. Steele was at the moment the apostle to the fair sex, and Pope by sending to Caryll (whose son was about to marry) the injunction, "Let him fear the Lord, love his lady, and read the *Tatler*," shows his appreciation of Steele's work. Pope was himself by nature very susceptible to feminine charm, and his treatment of feminine foibles is the more pleasing because like that of Steele it lacks any malice. He preserves throughout a delicious lightness of touch almost unparalleled in English literature. It is even difficult to believe that Clarissa's moralizing is added in "sober sadness"; she sounds too perfectly the duenna.

Historically the poem has interest as lying in the tradition of the mock epic. This tradition, as Pope knew it, was founded on the pseudo-Homeric *Battle of the Frogs and Mice, The Game of Chess* by Vida,

Boileau's *Lutrin,* Addison's Latin poem on the wars of
the pygmies and the cranes, and Garth's *Dispensary.*
Much of the wit in Pope's poem, however, is due to
his clever parodies of well-known passages in Homer,
Virgil. and Milton. In general English mock-heroic
is strongly colored by the grotesque and by caricature:
it is the tradition of Cervantes, of Butler, of Hogarth.
Pope, however, except in the Cave of Spleen, depends
hardly at all on the grotesque; he scores through a
disparate exaltation of mere *petitesse* and of elegance.
The romantics of a hundred years ago thought this
depiction of artificiality a limitation in appeal; rightly
understood it becomes the source of the most delightful details in Pope's satire. His genius enabled him,
with mock-heroic as a vehicle, to make sophisticated
society seem as ludicrous as any romantic could think
it and at the same time as likable as any fop could
wish it. This achievement is due to Pope's sure lightness of touch and to his happy conception of the mock-
heroic as deriving from human pettiness rather than
from human grotesqueness.

Writing in an imitative tradition and using frequently the device of parody Pope naturally brings
upon himself here as elsewhere the charge that he
lacked creative imagination. The game of ombre is
suggested by Vida; Belinda's bodkin was once the
sceptre of Agamemnon; the whole, in fact, has a journalistic foundation in a family quarrel at Hampton Court.
We are even reminded that Pope got his sylphs and
gnomes from a Rosicrucian novel by the Abbé de
Villars. But obviously such charges do not really un-
dermine the individuality and excellence of the work.
Pope frankly uses hints from fairly obvious sources,
and yet gives the hints always a new turn or force.
The sylphs of the Abbé de Villars are, according to
Rosicrucian doctrine, emanations from the four ele-

ments, earth, air, fire, and water; how exquisitely has Pope embodied in these beings rather the "ruling passions" of ladies dead and gone (Canto I, lines 51-56)—and how tactfully has he effaced the highly sexed traits that would have been too gross for the airy gossamer of *his* sylphs. After all, whether the poem is "original" or not matters little; it is delightful, and it stands apart from other poems of its type so as almost to seem unique. It placed Pope at the head of the poets of his day—and of his century.

ELEGY TO THE MEMORY OF AN UNFORTUNATE LADY

Beginning with 1714 Pope was for something more than a decade much occupied with the work of translating the *Iliad* (6 vols., 1715-20) and the *Odyssey* (5 vols., 1725-26), and with editing the plays of Shakespeare (6 vols., 1725). During this same period there were published from his pen some things like the *Temple of Fame* (1715), which had been written earlier, some things of more or less scurrilous nature—almost certainly published against Pope's will by Edmund Curll and others—and in 1717 appeared a collected volume of his poems, which in a sense marks the end of the early period of his work. The later poetic period—after that of translation and editing—is that of the satires and epistles (1727·43). In this volume were first printed two important poems, the *Elegy* and the *Eloisa to Abelard,* which were probably composed after 1715, and which are of interest as written in a more tender and pathetic vein than any of Pope's other works.

The long task of translation was in itself depressing, but there were added causes that gave these two important poems of 1717 a mood of sadness resulting from a sense of frustration. Pope's enemies—persons for the most part to whom he had given slight cause of offense except by being a (tolerant) Roman Catholic and a dangerously gifted Tory—were ever at his heels. If he advertised in the newspapers that a poem from his pen was imminent, Dennis, Gildon, Tom Burnet, Ducket, or some other frequenter of Button's coffee-house prepared to yelp. Their comments were usually absurd and ill natured; but they were always disheartening. Pope withdrew from London to concentrate on Homer; but considering his age, it is natural that thoughts of love should creep in; and considering his ill-health and deformity, it was natural that frustration should mark the end of these thoughts. His correspondence with various ladies at this period (chiefly, however, with Lady Mary Wordey Montagu) shows him to have been in love with love. It was after 1717, apparently, that he definitely centered his affection on Martha Blount. (Cf. *Of the Characters of Women.*)

The eighteenth-century reader, with his love for the *roman à clef* and for scandal generally, naturally busied himself to discover the identity of the unfortunate whom Pope celebrated in this *Elegy.* He never succeeded. It has later appeared probable that Pope's friendly but hardly intimate interest in the woes of a certain Mrs. Weston, who having married unhappily was early separated from her husband, treated unsympathetically by an uncle, was half-moved to enter a convent (but did not), and who died a natural death in 1724, may have given stimulus to the composition of the *Elegy*—though it gave few details. Much of the external inspiration probably came from the tragedies of the time;—the monologue form, the ghost, the dagger, and the simple, direct style, can be thus accounted for.

The poem represents the poet as a lover meeting the ghost of the unfortunate lady, who had stabbed herself. She had loved above her rank, though she herself was of noble blood (70); her family, especially her guardian-uncle, had treated her harshly, and on them the poet heaps somewhat childish imprecations (35-46). The pathos is heightened by the fact that at death she is surrounded only by "foreigners" (i.e., strangers?). There is an obvious, though not close, similarity to the story of Miss Clarissa Harlowe. The last eight lines end with the poet speaking undramatically in his own person. Pope frequently uses this manner of conclusion.

Wakefield says that the poem shows no textual revisions. This is true of but few poems by Pope, and it is somewhat astonishing that he should hit so satisfactorily at first attempt upon a style and mood quite new to him. There are few phrases that seem artificially elegant; the style is direct and emotional without being so obviously rhetorical as the style usual in tragedy of 1717. The tone, the sympathy for the beauteous victim of family tyranny, and the defense of suicide are typically "romantic", and have been called prophetic of Shelley himself. Meanwhile Dr. Johnson's amusing common-sense verdict was that "Poetry has not often been worse employed than in dignifying the amorous fury of a raving girl."

ELOISA TO ABELARD

This is the second "important" poem first published in the 1717 *Works*. About Easter time, 1716, Pope wrote Miss Martha Blount: "I am here studying ten hours a day, but thinking of you in spite of all the learned. The Epistle of Eloisa grows warm, and begins to have some breathings of the heart in it, which

may make posterity think I was in love. I can scarce
find in my heart to leave out the conclusion I once
intended for it." This was apparently about the time
the Popes were quitting Binfield reluctantly for Chiswick, and *Eloisa* is very likely the last of the poet's
works to be written in the Forest. It contains, as
matter of fact, fully as striking images from nature as
did *Windsor Forest*. Upon publication Pope sent his
Works to Lady Mary Wortley Montagu, then in Constantinople, with the message: "There are few things
in them but what you have seen, except the Epistle
of Eloisa to Abelard, in which you will find one passage [probably the conclusion!] that I cannot tell
whether to wish you should understand, or not."

There is little doubt but that Pope was more gen-
uinely in love with "Patty" Blount than with Lady
Mary; but Lady Mary was the more dazzling and
alluring, and his passion for her probably inspired
Pope to motivate the Epistle of Eloisa by the themes
of devotion persisting in absence (Lady Mary was in
Constantinople) and by the need of struggling against
forbidden love (Lady Mary was married!). Eloisa's
tirade against matrimony (73-98) is not purely romantic; it is in effect a tirade against Lady Mary's married state, and is the sort of utterance Pope longed
to hear from her. The mysterious quarrel between
Pope and Lady Mary, which left them after 1727
such ardent enemies, may account for Pope's later de-
preciation of this poem. It may be interesting to note
that in spite of this enmity Pope till his death kept
portraits of Lady Mary hanging in the most important
rooms of his Twickenham villa.

The poem is based upon an English version of the
Latin letters of Abelard and Heloise, published in
1713 by John Hughes. Most of the foundation details of Pope's poem came from this volume; but his

genius alone is responsible for the emotional glow cast over the chosen details. Hughes makes his Heloise say: "Even into holy places before the altar I carry with me the memory of our guilty loves. They are my whole business . . . " Compare Pope's elaboration in lines 264-76. Again where the prose Heloise says: "We have bound ourselves to severe austerities, and must follow them, let them cost us ever so dear," Pope parallels the passage with such pathetic lines as 240-43. It is by no means true, as some of Hughes's friends tried to say, that Pope owed the affecting quality of his verse to the prose original.

Not merely has he heightened the pathos of the situation. He has in lines 59-176 presented a series of pictures that seem the chaotic workings of Eloisa's mind, and yet present the crucial episodes in her story. This narrative element is perfectly blended in tone and matter with the incoherent wanderings of Eloisa's mind. Finally, it is in the depiction of opposite motives—the earthly and the spiritual—working simultaneously in the mind of the nun that Pope has surpassed himself in psychological insight. Warton, who of course undervalued satire, thought Pope's reputation would ultimately depend on *Windsor Forest, The Rape of the Lock,* and *Eloisa.* This is almost the only poem by Pope to satisfy the Wartonian criteria of the sublime and the pathetic, obviously all critics who value poetry on the intensity of the emotion expressed, must place this poem very high among Pope's works.

AN ESSAY ON MAN

Between January 15, 1733, and January 24, 1734, Pope published a larger number of important new pieces than in any other year of his life. It may be worth while to list these pieces, from Professor Griffith's data, and indicate which ones had the author's name on the titlepage.

1733

Jan. 15. Of the Use of Riches, an Epistle to . . . Lord Bathurst. By Mr. Pope.

Feb. 15. The First Satire of the Second Book of Horace Imitated in a Dialogue between Alexander Pope . . . and his Learned Council [Fortescue].

Feb. 20. An Essay on Man. Part I.

March 29. An Essay on Man. Epistle II.

April 17. An Essay on Man. Epistle III.

Nov. 5. The Impertinent, Or a Visit to the Court. A Satyr By an Eminent Hand. [Satire of Dr. Donne Versified.]

1734

Jan. 16. An Epistle to the . . . Lord Visct. Cobham. By Mr. Pope.

Jan. 24. An Essay on Man. Epistle IV.

Between the *Dunciad* and this constellation Pope had published only one important new poem, and that one had been most harshly received. With characteristic shrewdness he set about to make certain that no such fate should befall the *Essay on Man*. Between the years 1728-33 he had composed the eight poems just listed; he now began to publish them in such a way as to make the public think the *Essay on Man* probably not his. It was published anonymously by one bookseller—whose name is also on the titlepage of the *Impertinent*. The other three had Pope's name attached and were published by his regular booksellers. Three poems in a year was "large-scale production" for him, and he expected the rest might be ascribed to other poets—and praised. The scheme worked, and on March 2, 1733, he wrote Jonathan Richardson, "I see that a glut of praise succeeds to a glut of reproach. I am as much overpaid this way now, as I was injured that way before." And to Fortescue on March

8: "In many places it [the *Essay*] is set up as a piece far excelling anything of mine, and commended, I think, more in opposition to me, than in their real judgment it deserves." This innocent revenge was doubtless sweet—and certainly the poem deserved fair play.

The story of the composition of the *Essay* is interestingly complex. It begins, perhaps remotely, in the days after Bolingbroke returned from banishment (1723-24). He came, as every one knows, with that dual pose of farmer and philosopher which was to be so popular later in the century—and he wished Pope to do something philosophical. By 1730 an elaborate plan—here discussed in connection with the Moral Essays—had been drawn up, and work on it had begun. Of this plan the *Essay on Man* was the first of four parts, and the only part to be written as planned. On November 23, 1731, Atterbury inquired in a letter: "Do you pursue the moral plan you marked out, and seemed sixteen months ago so intent upon?" This question puts back the philosophical project—perhaps the first labor on the *Essay on Man* itself—to the summer of 1729, and since Bolingbroke was then in France perhaps it must go back even earlier. Bolingbroke doubtless refers to the *Essay* in November, 1729, when writing to Swift, who in March, 1730, inquires concerning its progress. In October Bolingbroke informs Bathurst, "We are at present deep in metaphysics," and by the end of 1730 Pope could say: "I have many fragments which I am beginning to put together, but nothing perfect or finished." Another letter, to Fortescue, and certain MSS of the poem serve to indicate the confusion of the work in this state. An important letter from Bolingbroke to Swift, August 2, 1731—by which date the poem seems to be approaching a final but yet unpolished form—deserves extensive quotation as showing Bolingbroke's conception of the work:

> Does Pope talk to you of the noble work, which, at my instigation he has begun in such a manner, that he must be convinced by this time, I judged better of his talents than he did? The first epistle, which considers man, and the habitation of man, relatively to the whole system of universal being: the second, which considers him in his own habitation, in himself, and relatively to his particular system: and the third, which shows how
>
> a universal cause
> Works to one end, but works by various laws;
>
> how man, and beast, and vegetable, are linked in a mutual dependency, parts necessary to each other, and necessary to the whole: how human societies were formed; from what spring true religion and true policy are derived; how God has made our greatest interest and our plainest duty indivisibly the same—these three epistles, I say, are finished. The fourth he is now intent upon. It is a noble subject. He pleads the cause of God (I use Seneca's expression) against that famous charge which atheists in all ages have brought—the supposed unequal dispensations of Providence—a charge which I cannot heartily forgive your divines for admitting. You admit it indeed for an extreme good purpose, and you build on this admission the necessity of a future state of rewards and punishments. But what if you should find, that this future state will not account, in opposition to the atheist, for God's justice in the present state, which you give up?

This account of the poem shows that Bolingbroke knew intimately what Pope was doing, so intimately that he could summarize the third epistle accurately, and indicate the basic ideas that were to go into the fourth. Was Bolingbroke, then, in a sense, holding the pen? He gives us no hint of such a thing, and in spite of considerable evidence it seems improbable. Long after both Pope and Bolingbroke were dead Lord Bathurst in 1763 said that the *Essay* was put into verse by Pope from a prose version in Bolingbroke's handwriting. It is generally agreed that Bathurst probably overstated the case. Of Bolingbroke's great influence on the poem there can be no doubt; it is likewise true that Pope at times worked on a rough draft in prose before attempting verse; it may very well be that Bolingbroke wrote, as Spence tells us, some scraps of prose that Pope followed: but since the two were so frequently together there would seem to be little need for Bolingbroke to write extensively—especially since conversation was his best "medium"—and there is little probability, aside from Bathurst's statement, that he would so write.

In fact it is clear that the two friends, finding their philosophic ideas congenial, agreed that each should express these ideas, the one writing in verse and the other in prose and each addressing his work to the other. The beginning of Bolingbroke's essay "A Letter to Mr. Pope" (1753) not only makes these facts clear but also shows that Pope wrote first and that Bolingbroke, being somewhat lazy about the task, began shortly after Pope. Letters from Bolingbroke and Pope to Swift during the years 1732-34 show these years as the period of Bolingbroke's metaphysical work. And the *Essay on Man* was in form before 1732. Some have thought that the "Fragments" by Bolingbroke—printed, like all his philosophic works, after his death—were the materials which Pope "versified," but a careful study of these will convince anyone that they contain so many extensive references to works or editions of works or to events postdating August, 1731, that they could not have been in Pope's hands before then. It was in 1732, according to Bolingbroke, that Pope was urging him to write. The few striking parallels between the *Essay* and the "Fragments" are reminiscences rather than prophecies of the poem. Pope was not unread in philosophy. He revered the names of Erasmus, Montaigne, Charron, and Pascal, and had read, perhaps more widely than intelligently, in such writers as Archbishop King and Shaftesbury, and even in Cudworth, Chubb, and Clarke. In other words, he knew the topics of philosophic or theological argument of his day. His father's library — inherited from a clerical grandfather — had consisted of "polemic divinity," and though one doubts if the poet troubled these volumes much, there is no reason to imagine his mind a philosophic blank upon which Bolingbroke could write at will. His difficulties lay partly, no doubt, in the fact that an early and apparently careful Roman Catholic training was bad preparation for an attempt, under the influence of a clever free-thinker, to make an inoffensive statement of the fashionable heterodoxy of the time. A greater difficulty lay in the fact that these ideas, being the popular, floating ideas of the day, were none too precisely or coherently stated by even the more practised thinkers who held them.

The first three epistles of the *Essay* deal with the place of man in the universe, with his psychology, and with his social relations; and the fourth, on the basis of the three preceding, deduces the nature of happiness. It is an essay on *man,* and in spite of urging from Caryll and others, Pope felt it improper here to mention Jesus Christ or to discuss the "moral attributes" of the Deity, concerning which there were arguments then in process which interested Bolingbroke very much. Pope somewhat disingenuously insisted to Caryll, before Epistle IV was published, that the poem taught Christian love and charity, and depended thus on the doctrine of the Gospel. There can be little doubt, however, that Pope believed in God, in immortality, and vaguely at least, in the more important doctrines of his Church; but he is here silent concerning them. Apparently moved by arguments over

Pope's heterodoxy, Henry Brooke (author of *The Fool of Quality*) wrote to ask just what his friend the poet did believe. The reply (December 1, 1739) is worth quoting both as a statement of the popular pre-dispositions of the day and as a statement of what Pope personally liked to announce as his "creed." The plural "revelations" in the second phrase is interesting as including both the "natural" and "scriptural" channels of revelation:

> I sincerely worship God, believe in his revelations, resign to his dispensations, love all his creatures, am in charity with all denominations of Christians, however violently they treat each other, and detest none so much as that profligate race who would loosen the bands of morality, either under the pretence of religion or freethinking. I hate no man as a man, but I hate vice in any man; I hate no sect, but I hate un-charitableness in any sect; this much I say, merely in com-pliance with your desire that I should say something of myself.

In this "creed," as in the *Essay on Man*, Pope slights theology and metaphysics and stresses ethics. In the poem he seeks for ethics a rationalistic basis which was not, he thought, necessarily hostile to Christianity —in fact, it might supplement orthodox bases of morals.

The ideas in the first epistle of the *Essay* are funda-mental. Pope at once ranges himself with that school of thinkers who stressed the limitations of human reason.

What can we reason but from what we know?

he asks—but he straightway proceeds, after the fashion of Archbishop King's *Origin of Evil*, to give us an account of the universe that is hardly empirical. "Wis-dom infinite," he postulates, must create the best of all possible worlds, a system of creatures forming a vast chain of being, which to be the best possible must be full (and so diverse) and coherent. All possible essences must exist in this chain; for each creature has need of all creatures, however opposite. So the nice bee

From pois'nous herbs extracts the healing dew (220).

But this infinite diversity of creation is ordered, is a "system," admirable for its perfect subordination of part to part and part to whole. In this complete and ordered scale of being obviously

There must be, somewhere, such a rank as man (48).

The principle of plenitude, as Professor Lovejoy aptly names this alleged lust of the Creator for the utmost abundance and diversity, would furthermore demand all kinds of men, poisonous herbs as well as honey bees, the unhappy and vicious as well as the magnanimous —each in his place. With his limited powers man may not always see the necessity of evil (except on *a priori* grounds) ; but only pride and presumption will question the infinite Wisdom that has formed a scale too vast and full to be comprehended by so small a part of it as man. Partial evil (the poisonous herb) is universal good; and hence Pope arrives, through admiration of "Creation's ample range" with its "strong connections, nice dependencies," and "gradations just," to the one clear truth that "Whatever is, is right." This is no denial of the existence of evil; it is an enthusiastic expression of cosmic faith in spite of evil; and the enthusiasm is admiration for the plenitude and order of the universe—certainly not for individual creatures as such. In this universe the great error of man is that pride which, violating the ideal of fullness within the proper sphere, where the individual is "free," urges man to think himself wrongly placed in the scale and worthy of something higher. The duty of man (for whom as such the poet shows little enthusiasm) is summed up in the one word (line 285), at first sight harsh: "Submit!"

After thus expounding the universe as an ordered *continuum,* the poet in Epistle II turns to an analysis of men. He gives us some reflections on pride of learning, which imply the difficulties of analyzing man's mind, and then passes on to the psychological dualism—

> This light and darkness in our chaos join'd—

which so perplexes him. The contrast here is between self-love and reason. Self-love stimulates to action; reason is judicious, corrective, and restraining. Both are indispensable, but the poet is at times contradictory as to the relative strength of each—now one is said to rule, now the other. The truth probably meant is that ideally reason ought to dominate, but that actually self-love and the passions usually do. The passions are called (93) "modes of self-love," a relationship possibly based on Joseph Butler's recent (1726) distinction "between the passions and appetites *themselves* and the *endeavouring* after the means of their gratification." Self-love dictates the method of endeavor through particular passions, and is thus above them. At times the passions are seen at war with reason, though good passions

> List under Reason, and deserve her care.

The poet here first states the doctrine of the "ruling passion," elaborated at about the same time in the Epistle to Cobham. This passion, by definition, dominates the mind completely, and reason itself can only take a conciliatory attitude towards it (162-64). It is practically innate (137), and is quite ineluctable; it may be "the mind's disease," but usually is ("Th' Eter-

nal Art educing good from ill") a source of single-
ness of purpose and constancy (175-80). Self-love,
the passions, especially the "ruling passion," on the
one hand, and reason, on the other, are elements in
man's "system." Their relationships seem chaotic, and
yet only once in the epistle (204) does Pope turn
towards anything like Moral Sense or Conscience or
transcendent Reason as dictator over these elements.
Even the "ruling passion" holds sway in a sort of constitutional monarchy where a system of "checks and
balances" blends and tempers the elements of the mind.
In this process of tempering one thing by its opposite,
he finds (doubtless in the "necessary" order of things)
a principle of compensation that alleviates man's lot.
Throughout the epistle Pope takes a "realistic" view
of man's nature as a

> Chaos of Thought and Passion, all confus'd.

Some elements of man's system are left for treatment in Epistle III, which deals with Man and Society.
We find here a contrast of reason and instinct, and,
more important, a treatment of man's social affections,
or benevolence, which found no place in Epistle II,
possibly because benevolence is regarded as actually
identical with self-love. In basing society, *contra*
Hobbes, on a natural gregariousness or social appetite
in man, Pope of course only follows the dominant
views of his time as stated by Locke, Shaftesbury, and
others. The necessary interdependence of all creatures, "all serv'd, all serving," leads the poet to call
the chain of being (I, 237) a chain of love (III, 7).
While man is again deterred from "pride" by the re-
minder that he exists for the goose just as much as
the goose for him, and that his proper bliss is to be
found within the bounds of his own nature (110).
this epistle presents man in a better light than hereto-

fore in the poem. Man is not benevolent, however, because of any natural goodness within himself but because of the rational and universal law of coherence. The chain must be full and above all coherent (I, 45); hence is "creature link'd to creature, man to man."

Pope founds human society, according to the usual views of his day [See A. O. Lovejoy, in the *Journal of Philosophy*, XIX (1922), 381.] on the longer care necessary to rear "Man's helpless kind" as compared with brutes (123-46). His account of the evolution of society from this animal state to a political organism follows a general tradition reaching at least from Epicurus to Shaftesbury. To Pope this animal state (123-46) is psychologically elemental but not savage or warlike as in Hobbes; development here is guided by "natural love" and by the preservation of the kind. Under the name "State of Nature" Pope next blends, somewhat grotesquely, details from the Book of Genesis, from the classical myth of the Golden Age, and from patriarchal society. This era Pope, like Shaftesbury and similar thinkers, idealizes. After it, political states were formed either peacefully (199-210) or by conquest (241-48). The poem hardly warrants this precise analysis, for Pope is less interested in marking stages of development than he is in indicating the rational basis on which state and church are founded. Religion developed in patriarchal times when the benevolence of the father of the tribe led to a traditionary belief in "one great first father," the creator of the universe. There is here no hint of supernatural revelation. The state, when dominated by the patriarch, or "second Providence", was not based on "right divine" (236) nor on

> Th' enormous faith of many made for one—

which violated the cosmic principle of "all served, all

serving." Such corruption of the state was caused by tyranny and superstition, which are feelingly denounced in a fashion that doubtless pleased Bolingbroke. Tyranny and superstition, in turn, are due to self-love; but self-love also produces the corrective in the "studious head" of the poet or patriot, who shows man the ancient light of true faith and liberty, and leads to the achievement in late days of a "well-mix'd State."

> Such is the World's great harmony, that springs
> From Order, Union, full Consent of things!

At the end of Epistle III Pope announces the identity of "self-love and social" and this may serve as the thesis of the last epistle. Man's greatest interest, or self-love, is served only by the good of all (IV, 37-38); hence the basis of happiness is social. In the scale of being, where "Order [subordination] is Heaven's first law," the one place where equality naturally appears is in happiness:

> Bliss is the same in subject or in king.

After this announcement the poet is naturally quick to assert that happiness does not lie in externals (IV, 57-76), though, curiously enough, it has intimate relations with "health, peace, and competence" (80), and we are again coldly comforted with the idea that "partial Ill is universal Good" (114), and (at some length) that virtue asks no external reward.

> What nothing earthly gives, or can destroy,
> The soul's calm sunshine, and the heart-felt joy,
> Is Virtue's prize.

And this prize, as the poet shows in an elevated passage depends on and is "one close system of benevolence" (358).

So much for the chief ideas of the poem. It is

obvious even in a summary that there are amongst
them antagonistic and self-contradictory notions. The
universe as conceived is so mechanistic as almost to
preclude free-will; and yet choice must be the basis
of morals. We are told that "all subsists by elemental
strife" (I, 169), and yet the "all" is called a *chain of
love;* we are told that "Whatever is, is right," by a
man who is chiefly (though not here) a satirist. Brute
instinct seems exalted above human reason. "Nature"
and other terms are used in shifting and doubtful
senses.

These confusions have led some critics to think that
Pope, following Bolingbroke blindly, hardly knew
what he was saying, and was even unaware that his
poem was deistic in tendency. Such a charge it is
impossible to sustain. It met Pope, from Caryll, Richardson, and others, before the poem was printed. Pope
may not have realized how far towards deism he had
gone; for the word *deist* was in those days much more
reprehensible than the ideas behind the word. Even
clergymen found the ideas not in themselves objec-
tionable; but not even Pope liked to be called a deist.
He knew, however, that he had consciously excluded
from the poem any reference to scriptural revelation,
to the Fall of Man or to his redemption. He knew
that the last epistle placed happiness here and now and
not in a future life: he thus followed the aversion
of Bolingbroke to a moral system of rewards and punishments. But he had tactfully refrained from antag-
onizing and overt denials of these doctrines, and so
while some readers found the poem defective, and some
offensive, more were delighted by the poetry and the
truth of individual passages. The attacks of Crousaz
and Warburton's replies were, as a matter of fact,
largely anticipated in fragmentary utterances made before this heavy artillery came into play. Pope accepted

Warburton's defense because defense was always useful—and probably not because he altogether agreed
with his defender. On the whole the poem succeeded
by being all things to all men. Dr. Johnson found its
ideas commonplace but delightfully phrased. "Never,"
he says, "was penury of knowledge, and vulgarity of
sentiment, so happily disguised." A contemporary of
his was fully as extreme in the other direction when he
quoted Dr. Trapp as asserting that "Pope's discoveries
in the moral world entitle him to as much applause, as
Newton's in the physical one." Brilliance of execution
reconciled Johnson, and it together with the fact that
the substance deals, in fragmentary fashion, with prob-
lems always fascinating to mankind, explains the per-
manent appeal of the poem. A mechanistic universe
may not be a good basis for ethics, but it here makes
a splendid source for poetic imagery.

THE UNIVERSAL PRAYER

The early months of 1738 saw Pope again prolific
in publication. On January 23 appeared an Imitation
of Horace addressed to Murray; in March came the
Pope-Swift Imitation of the Sixth Satire of the Second
Book, and Pope's version of the First Epistle of the
First Book (addressed to Bolingbroke); in May came
the first dialogue of the poem afterwards called the
Epilogue to the Satires, and a new title (*A Sermon
against Adultery*) was in the same month affixed to
the disowned imitation called in 1735 *Sober Advice
from Horace;* in July appeared the second dialogue
of the *Epilogue*—somewhat after the *Universal Prayer,*
which was published on June 22.

Of all these poems the imitation addressed to Bolingbroke alone has a possible relation to the *Universal
Prayer.* In this imitation, as we have seen in the

Introduction to this volume, Pope seems to show consciousness of increasing hostility to some phases of
the *Essay on Man*. It is Warburton, to be sure, and
not Pope, who placed the *Universal Prayer* just after
the *Essay on Man* in the collected works of Pope;
but when all is said, it is a natural position, and it
may be that this poem as well as the Imitation of
Horace addressed to Bolingbroke came into existence
in 1738 because of the critical attitude of the orthodox
towards the *Essay*. There is no clear evidence that
as early as June the *Examen* in which Crousaz had
attacked Pope's fatalism, was known in England, but
in February Pope's friend the Rev. Walter Harte had
preached a notable sermon on the *Union and Harmony
of Reason, Morality and Revealed Religion,* which had
gone through several editions. Harte kept quite away
from the *Essay on Man,* but in one passage of the
sermon after speaking of the skeptical tendencies
among ancient wits he expressed the opinion "That
when persons educated in the Christian faith, make
extraordinary panegyricks upon the *Law of Nature,*
and at the same time speak very coldly, and negligently
about the *Law of the Gospel,* 'Tis much to be feared
. . . that they only honour the *former* in pretence, and
have always a secret ill-will to the *latter*." It was such
utterances as this that, in the absence of Bolingbroke,
suggested to Pope further definition of his position.

In a letter to Ralph Allen (8 September 1736) Pope
included a transcript of the poem, which is there called
"A Prayer to God." Pope says he first wrote the stanzas
in 1715, and that they are now revised as "a Comment
on some verses in my Essay on Man, which has been
mis-construed." This letter, the original of which is in
the University of Chicago Library, indicates an attempt
by Pope to bolster up his views, especially on free will.

The charge of fatalism rather than that of deism is to be combated. The poem was frequently called "The Deist's Prayer," and in his attempt to be *universal* the poet is obviously driven here to house with the type of deist who insisted on universality and was silent about divine revelation. By intention, probably, the poem was neither Christian nor anti-Christian. It is, for example, silent as well with regard to man's depravity as to supernatural revelation. Lines 25-29 hint Pope's settled dislike of the quarrelsome and intolerant relations of various sects. On the other hand, he asserts the goodness, and perhaps the mercy, of the Diety (8), attributes concerning which Bolingbroke took an agnostic position; and the whole poem stresses the (Christian) doctrine of charity. There is even a tactful mention of "grace." His position that following conscience (13) is more important than pursuing Heaven would hardly be very offensive, though obviously heterodox in implication. He followed Butler and other divines of the day when he exalted conscience. Harte's sermon, for example, distinguished an absolute Law of Nature and a relative Law of Nature in a fashion somewhat like Pope's pronouncement in favor of free will (and conscience) and a Nature bound fast in fate.

Pope interestingly continues his avowed habit of housing now with one master and now with another. The poem is perhaps a superlative example of the tendency of his age to incongruous eclecticism and also to an admirable tolerance. Surely, to attempt to express an abstracted essence of all religions, to formulate a petition that all the world could raise to various gods but in one voice, is an imaginative endeavor that is commendable unless the execution is very faulty. The idea of the poem is nobler than the poetry itself, but the high competence of the workmanship can be seen by comparing his poem with a prose attempt at a "Philosopher's Prayer" by Dr. Matthew Tindal found in Budgell's *Bee* for June, 1735. The task is of course supremely difficult and is perhaps as impossible artistically as it has seemed to be intellectually.

MORAL ESSAYS

The four poems grouped under this caption form a fragment of Pope's largest project. In 1729 Fenton reports Pope as intending "to write nothing but epistles in Horace's manner," and it is certain that the *Essay on Man* was then under consideration. But the *Essay on Man* was only one unit in an extensive project, always vague and changing in Pope's mind, but present there from about 1730 almost to the end of his life. His account of the plan, given to Spence after it had been discarded, is as follows:

I had once thoughts of completing my ethic work in four books.—The first, you know, is on the Nature of Man.—The second would have been on Knowledge and its limits:—here would have come in an Essay on Education; part of which I have inserted in the *Dunciad*.—The third was to have treated of Government; both ecclesiastical and civil—and this was what chiefly stopped my going on. I could not have said what I would have said, without provoking every church on the face of the earth: and I did not care for living always in boiling water.—This part would come into my Brutus, which is all planned already; and even some of the most material speeches written in prose.—The fourth would have been on Morality; in eight or nine of the most concerning branches of it: four of which would have been the two extremes to each of the Cardinal Virtues. [*Anecdotes,* page 315.]

The first fourth of this "ethic work" is the *Essay on Man* (1733-34). The second fourth was never attempted. It is possible that the *Essay upon Reason*

(1735) by Pope's protégé the Reverend Walter Harte
—a poem which gave Pope a curious amount of satisfaction—may have forestalled the project at this point.
In the quarto edition of his *Works,* Volume II (1735),
Pope called the *Essay on Man* "Ethic Epistles, Book I,"
and as "Book II" he printed the four Moral Essays,
together with the epistles to Addison, Oxford, and
Arbuthnot.   The octavo editions of the *Works* used
instead of "Book II" the more fitting caption of "Epistles to Several Persons." Obviously the plan was loosely
conceived, and these epistles have for the moment been
substituted for the work on human reason as the second part of the project.   Possibly they were intended
as a part of Book IV originally.   The epic of *Brutus*
(part three of the project) survives only in the prose
plan as printed by Ruffhead and some other editors,
and a few lines composed in blank verse.   The whole
project illustrates Pope's love for large structural effects—and his inability to elaborate the details of
structure.

The four Moral Essays were apparently composed
in exactly the opposite order from that in which they
now stand.   Possibly the Epistle to Bathurst was the
first written.   That to Miss Blount, while written before that to Lord Cobham, was the last to appear in
print.   There is no real point of unity in the four except possibly the treatment in each of the idea of the
"ruling passion."

I.   OF THE KNOWLEDGE AND CHARACTERS OF MEN

The Lord Viscount Cobham (1669?-1749), to whom
this poem is dedicated, had for years been one of Pope's
intimate friends.   A staunch Whig, Cobham had served
under Marlborough in Flanders as lieutenant general,

and was, at the time when this epistle was begun, colonel of the king's own horsemen, and one of the most distinguished officers in the army. His claim on Pope's affections, however, came from his rebuilding of Stowe, an estate whose princely gardens became in Cobham's time "a work to wonder at" (See Moral Essay IV, line 70). It was natural that Pope should address a poem to Cobham; the moment at which he chose to produce the poem is the more significant fact; for it was the time in all Cobham's career when he was most discussed. In March, 1733, he had voted against Walpole's excise, and so broken his long and valuable support of the government. In June he had argued in favor of Lord Bathurst's motion to investigate the disposition of the produce of the forfeited estates (1720) of the South Sea Directors. Immediately he was dismissed as "colonel of his Majesty's own regiment of horse." For months this dismissal caused an uproar, and during this time Pope was working at his epistle. He wrote Swift, April 2, 1733, about a fortnight after Cobham's vote against the excise bill, saying that a poem (probably this) was "finished last week." Quite typically he was still revising it in November — according to Cobham's suggestions. It was published as "by Mr. Pope" in January, 1734, about a week before the anonymously printed fourth epistle of the *Essay on Man* appeared, and at a time when the opposition in Parliament were on the point of introducing a bill to prevent the king from dismissing officers in the army not above the rank of colonels without court martial.

Much later the poem underwent revision by Warburton just before Pope's death. This revision, followed in all later editions of Pope's *Works,* divides the poem into three parts and rearranges the order of various passages to improve structural effect and clarity. In neither version is the poem one of Pope's most scintillating efforts. Except towards the end it is not relieved sufficiently by the brilliant illustrative passages or "characters" that adorn others of his epistles. The first two of the three sections into which Warburton divided the poem really fall together and state somewhat platitudinous reasons why it is difficult to discover a man's true nature. The third section states definitely Pope's central idea that the "ruling passion" is the best key to character-reading, and gives as corollary the idea that men display this passion most clearly on their death-beds. At this rate—if the subject can be analyzed only at death—the use of the "ruling passion" in character analysis cannot have immediate practical results. Pope's century, however, with its interest in universals, wished not to understand men merely, but human nature; and "ruling passion" like our more modern "psychological determinism" is a phrase that can be used abstractly with more effect than in specific application. Cobham thought the satire would have been keener if the ruling passions ridiculed, instead of being those to which all men are a prey—such as gluttony and lechery— had been founded upon some more whimsical or less natural traits. Possibly the epistle *On the Characters of Women* is more interesting because the Augustan conception of feminine foibles answered just this requirement of Cobham's. It is curious to meet, almost on the threshold of Pope's "ethic work" an idea that if forced to its extreme leads to a determinism that precludes all ethics. The treatment of these ideas in the *Essay on Man* (especially Epistle II) is superior in incisiveness and finish to that given here. Considering the circumstances under which the poem was composed—or at least revised—it contains a small amount of political satire, though the conclusion derives all its force from politics.

II. Of the Characters of Women

We are told in a letter to Swift that this poem was composed as early as February, 1733; Pope with characteristic delay kept it by him unpublished for two years. Upon publication he wrote Caryll (February 8, 1735) : "The lady to whom it is addressed had the great modesty to insist on my suppressing her name." Everyone of course knew she was Martha Blount, whom Pope had known almost from childhood, and who, during the last twenty years of his life, was his most intimate friend from the fair sex. As early as 1725 gossip reported them married, and at the publication of this epistle Caryll bluntly asked if the concluding line meant matrimony. Their friendship was the subject of gossip at various times, and in 1743 when after both had been visiting the Allens at Prior Park, Pope left Miss Blount there behind him, Mrs. Allen behaved so discourteously to her guest that Pope later expressed his naturally warm resentment to Allen and left traces of it even in his will—which bequeathed most of his property to Miss Blount. After Pope's death Warburton (who married Allen's niece) had the impudence in his 1751 edition of Pope's *Works* to say, quite falsely, of the conclusion to this epistle: "It is an encomium on an *imaginary* lady to whom the epistle is addressed."

The poem is arranged so as to compliment Miss Blount in contrast with the *varium et mutabile* of her sex. This central concept is stated in the letter to Swift (February 16, 1733) already mentioned: "Your lady friend is *semper eadem,* and I have written an epistle to her on that qualification in a female character." In the poem Pope is saying, "This may be the sex, but you are different." And certainly the last forty-four lines constitute one of the most enthusiastic compliments to a woman that Pope's century produced.

The text of the poem underwent notable changes in an edition, a few copies of which were distributed early in 1744, and which was suppressed at the poet's death. Only one copy, now in the British Museum, is known to survive. In some early editions of the poem Pope had by a footnote indicated that after line 156 (102 in early editions) and in other parts of the poem there was "a want of connection . . . occasioned by the omission of certain examples and illustrations laid down, which may put the reader in mind of what the author has said in his Imitation of Horace,

> Publish the present age, but where the text
> Is vice too high, reserve it for the next."

It was by such a device that Pope the consummate salesman caused his public to await future editions. At first he had advertised that no character portraits in it were drawn from life, and that was depressing news to a public that loved gossip far better than it did poetry.

On his death bed Pope gave certain friends a volume of his works in which this poem appears as it now stands; in which, that is, lines 69-86, 115-150, and 157-198 appeared for the first time. Philomedé was supposed to represent Henrietta, Duchess of Marlborough (in succession to her father, the first Duke; she died in 1733), Atossa to portray Sarah, Duchess of Marlborough (widow of the first Duke), and Chloe was the Countess of Suffolk (Mrs. Howard), formerly mistress of George II and now Pope's neighbor at Twickenham (d. 1767). "Chloe" had been printed in the *Works* of 1738, but not as a part of this poem.

Warburton, probably at the request of Pope's execu-
tors, suppressed the edition containing this version of
the poem, but the character of Atossa was separately
printed in 1746, and in his first "complete" edition of
Pope's *Works* (1751) Warburton used the text of the
suppressed edition—which has since been standard.

Argument over the suppressed edition has centered
only on the Atossa portrait, and has been both violent
and confused. It was apparently common belief after
Pope's death that Sarah, Duchess of Marlborough, had
given Pope a thousand pounds to suppress the character, that he accepted the money and failed to keep his
part of the bargain. This accusation is bluntly made
in the 1746 publication of the Atossa fragment. Sure
proof of any such bargain is naturally wanting (the
evidence of the *Marchmont Papers,* like most of the
story, rests originally on gossip), yet Pope's letters
to the Duchess indicate that in 1743 he did lie under
unique obligations to her. On the other hand, he was
evidently not afraid to publish the portrait during the
lifetime of the Duchess,—a fact which argues against
any bargain such as is alleged. It may well be that
"Atossa" was originally the Duchess of Marlborough,
but that Pope revised the portrait inserting traits that
could not possibly refer to her, but which did hit at
the Duchess of Buckinghamshire—whose recent death
(1743) might seem occasion for "releasing" the character. Under such circumstances he might well feel
free to print the promised characters. A further question is, why, if Pope was desirous of printing the characters, should his friends suppress them? Some of
these friends were not notably tender of Pope's memory, and if they were tender of the Duchess, it was
probably only because she could on occasion contribute
lavishly to campaign expenses. (She died in October,
1744, leaving generous legacies to some of Pope's

friends.) Pope might run risks, but they did not care to do so. The whole incident is very perplexing, and has certainly hurt Pope's reputation—perhaps unduly. A central fact that emerges is the occurrence in the portrait of many details that are quite inapplicable to the Duchess of Marlborough. One would like to know who first thought "Atossa" was she.

III. OF THE USE OF RICHES

Allen, Lord Bathurst (1684-1775) to whom Pope addressed this epistle (to Pope it was an epistle, but he foolishly let Warburton make it a dialogue), was bound to the poet by various ties. He was one of the foremost Tories of the day, and he and Pope were both fascinated by the avocation of gardening. Pope spent the summer of 1718 at Bathurst's estate in Cirencester [*Cicester*] translating Homer, and the two frequently exchanged visits and gave mutual assistance in beautifying their grounds. Long after Pope's death Bathurst lived to retail anecdotes of the poet.

Pope's correspondence gives us fuller details about the composition of this poem than about any other by him. After it was published (January, 1733), he wrote Caryll (March 8) that the epistle was "the work of two years by intervals," and to Swift about the same time he wrote: "I never took more care in my life of anything." A note to line 100 by Pope tells us that the poem was written in 1730. In his letters we find him, in November, 1731, seeking through Tonson to check up on the facts concerning the Man of Ross (lines 249-90), and in January, 1732, he writes to Lord Oxford as if the poem had for some time been ready for printing: "The noise which malice has raised about that epistle [to Burlington] has caused me to suppress a much better concerning the Use of Riches."

Minor revision continued until publication, and the text was again edited for the suppressed 1744 edition. For some reason the copy was in the printer's hands about two months before first publication.

Pope states his conception of the poem in a letter to Caryll (September 27, 1732), where he says the poem deals with

. . . . riches, which seems at present to be the favourite, nay, the only, mistress of mankind, to which all their endeavours are directed, through all the paths of corruption and luxury. My satire will therefore be impartial on both extremes, avarice and profusion. I shall make living examples, which enforce best, and consequently put you once more upon the defence of your friend, against the roar and calumny which I expect, and am ready to suffer in so good a cause.

He deals, then, with wealth as an excessive preoccupation or ruling passion, satirizes both the miser and the spendthrift, and finds the ideal in the wisely benevolent Man of Ross. On the other hand, the complete lack of ability to command wealth is seen in Sir Balaam. The spendthrift and the miser are, it is hinted, not merely opposite but equal in effect. In lines 161-62 (repeated in the *Essay on Man,* II, 205-6) Pope tells us that out of such extremes comes the golden mean, a statement which is his parallel to the Mandevillian paradox that "private vices are public benefits." This conception recurs intermittently in his work and a note to line 150 of *On the Characters of Women* in the last edition revised by Pope speaks of the line as "Alluding and referring to the great principle of his Philosophy, which he never loses sight of, and which teaches, that Providence is incessantly turning the evils arising from the follies and vices of men to general good." Since the poem is a satire no one should be depressed because the more delightful aspects of wealth or of the wealthy are not depicted.

It is natural that writing to a Tory peer, and as a Tory, Pope should indulge in a caustic and partizan indictment of the Whig moneyed interests and of the get-rich-quick citizens, whose trading instincts, to be sure, were rapidly bringing England to the commercial leadership of the world. In general the citizen-trader was a Whig; and so Pope believed that only national disgrace and individual unhappiness could come from the successes of Sir Balaam—and of Sir Robert.

Having suffered from the identification of Timon as Chandos, Pope here determined to use real names and so offend only those who were offensive.

> Bond is but one, but Harpax is a score,

was the lesson he affected to learn. But "Bond" was flatly obvious, while "Harpax" tantalized readers and evoked interest. Furthermore the actual example was not so picturesque or apt as examples with fictitious coloring; hence Pope here, as always, used some pseudonyms. The poem lacks structural coherence and clarity, but it is in detail as brilliantly wrought as any of Pope's works.

IV. OF THE USE OF RICHES

The occasion of this epistle, according to its first titlepage, was the publication by Richard Boyle, Earl of Burlington, of "Palladio's designs of the baths, arches, theatres, etc., of ancient Rome." Lord Burlington (1694-1753) had lived during his young manhood in Italy, where he had acquired a precocious enthusiasm for Palladio. In England he speedily became a leading patron of the arts, and Pope early formed a lasting friendship with him. It was apparently Lord Burlington who drew Pope to a Chiswick residence in 1716, and it was he who helped the poet get his villa at Twickenham. Burlington had the distinction of aiding many geniuses—among whom were Gay, William Kent, and Handel. He was satirized by Lord Hervey, by Hogarth, and doubtless by others of less distinction.

Pope had early manifested a taste in gardening somewhat similar to Burlington's. He had rebelled against the stiff formality of the Dutch school in the *Guardian* for September 29, 1713, and his own grounds at Twickenham were designed to illustrate the best principles of the art of gardening, to which after poetry and politics he owed his greatest devotion. The avocation of all his years after 1718 was in his five acres of Twickenham landscape. A letter of 1725 says: "I am as busy in three inches of gardening as any man can be in threescore acres. I fancy myself like the fellow that spent his life in cutting the twelve apostles in one cherry stone. I have a Theatre, an Arcade, a Bowling-green, a Grove, and what not? in a bit of ground that would have been but a plate of sallet to Nebuchadnezzar, the first day he was turned out to graze."

Concerning the composition of this poem Pope has left us practically no information. In 1730 Burlington printed *Fabriche antiche disegnate da Andrea Palladio Vicentino,* and he there promises a second volume, to which Pope's titlepage seems to refer. Burlington's tone in addressing the prospective reader of the *Fabriche antiche* is quite that of Pope's epistle. In the last sentence of his address he speaks of his age as one (I translate his Italian) "than which perhaps no other has shown a greater inclination to expensive structures, or produced more ignorant pretenders who mislead others from the true pathways of so many fine arts." Such statements gave stimulus, and in fact gave almost a thesis for Pope's poem. The poem was announced as early as March, 1731, in *The Present State of the*

Republic of Letters (VII, 239), as "ready for the press," but it was not published until December.

Of the "red-hot" reception given to the poem, which was Pope's first important effort after the *Dunciad,* mention has been made in the Introduction. There can be no doubt that the identification of Timon with the Duke of Chandos pained the poet. He may have had Chandos' seat, Canons, in mind when he wrote the poem, but he had not thought the fact would be perceived, and he protested against the identification. Bolingbroke in an essay called "A Letter to Mr. Pope" (published in 1753) assumes that the malice was due to Walpole's agents:

You began to laugh at the ridiculous taste, or the no taste in gardening and building, of some men who are at great expence in both. What a clamor was raised instantly? The name of *Timon* was applied to a noble person with double malice, to make him ridiculous, and you, who lived in friendship with him, odious. By the authority that employed itself to encourage this clamor, and by the industry used to spread and support it, one would have thought that you had directed your satire in that epistle to political subjects, and had inveighed against those who impoverish, dishonor, and sell their country, instead of making yourself inoffensively merry at the expence of men who ruin none but themselves, and render none but themselves ridiculous. What will the clamor be, and how will the same authority foment it, when you proceed to lash, in other instances, our want of elegance, even in luxury, and our wild profusion, the source of insatiable rapacity, and almost universal venality?

Pope sought to abate this turmoil by shifts and changes in the poem. The title, at first simply *An Epistle to the Rt. Hon. Richard Earl of Burlington,* etc., became *Of Taste, an Epistle* . . . and then, at the suggestion of Aaron Hill, *Of False Taste.* All this came in the first six weeks; after the Epistle to Bathurst was published, this became its companion and was called, *Of the Use of Riches.* The text, also,

underwent many changes. Most notable was the placing of the passage on Timon. In the first editions this
had come just before the concluding apostrophe to
Burlington, which then included lines 23-38 and 191-
204. In 1735 Pope split this apostrophe into the present two shorter passages, and placed *Timon* in a less
emphatic position immediately following Villario and
Sabinus. Originally lines 169-176, which now serve
to show the good uses of Timon's expenditure, and
so to soften the severity of the picture, came just before the Timon passage where they were less obviously
useful. In all these revisions, as well as in an apolo-
getic letter prefixed to the third edition (1732), Pope
strove to repel charges that he had ungratefully attacked a benefactor.

The poem is remarkable for the excellent satire on
the excessively pompous and elaborate style of some
of Pope's contemporary builders, and for certain central ideas that may be commonplaces, but are commonplaces for architects of the *nouveaux riches* to keep
constantly in mind. Among these are (1) the insist-
ence on taste—which may be trained, but which is
founded only on innate *sense,* "the gift of heaven"
(40-42), (2) the necessity of measure and appropriate-
ness in ornamentation, and (3) the belief in "pleasing
intricacies" as opposed to a flat and obvious regularity.

Pope had expected the *Dunciad* to get rough treatment, but probably the savage welcome given to Timon
really shocked him. He laid aside the Epistle to Bathurst, and presently came out with the first of his
Imitations of Horace, that addressed to Fortescue.
His fighting spirit was roused, and it may very likely
be that his remaining work was given an edge and
force that would have been ill replaced by the abstract
and less incisive technique seen in such poems as his
Epistle to Cobham. General moral precepts were, he

saw, not enough. Shortly after the Epistle to Burlington appeared he wrote Caryll: "My design . . . is rather to ridicule ill men than preach to them. I fear our age is past all other correction."

V. To Mr. Addison

The truthfulness of Pope's statement that this poem (which is not related to the four preceding it), was written in 1715 has been doubted by more than one editor on very slight evidence. It could hardly have been written between 1715 and 1719 (the year of Addison's death), for the two were not on good terms during those years. In fact 1715 is late for such a token of esteem to come into being. The best argument for an early date of composition is lines 35-44, which embody satire on collectors reminiscent of the period of the Scriblerus Club (*ca.* 1713). Lines 41-42, have a direct reference to Dr. Woodward's shield and to Chapter III of the *Memoirs of Martinus Scriblerus,* which would seem possibly more natural before 1715 than after 1719. But there is small basis for argument on either side, and in such a case the poet's statement may as well stand. The lines concerning Craggs, Addison's friend and successor as Secretary of State (1718), could only be added after his death in February, 1721. The poem was published in Tickell's edition of Addison's *Works* in 1721. Certainly the poem, or some other overture, served to reconcile Pope and Tickell. There is some evidence that they remained friendly after this time.

Warburton, whose notes here are unusually inept, says that the poem, as related to the Epistle to Burlington, is a more specialized treatment of *vanity of expense* "as it appears in the common collectors of old coins." Clearly only lines 35-44 deal with this vanity, and the idea is introduced only to be contrasted with Addison's learning (line 45) in such matters. The central idea of the poem is rather the power of "cast metal," or medals, to withstand the conquering force of "all-devouring years" and to memorialize human achievement. At the beginning of this poem, as in *Windsor Forest* and *Eloisa* Pope in a sense anticipates the themes of the "poetry of ruins" popular later in the century. The concluding and natural wish is that not merely warriors but poets may be thus commemorated, and the poem might well terminate with the fine compliment (line 62) that couples Addison with his master Virgil. But the recent death of Craggs, for whom Pope and Addison both had great affection, made it easy to conclude with the glowing Roman lines, which all the critics have had the perspicacity to see are too extensive to be inscribed on a medal. It may be, as some have thought, that Pope is careful to praise Craggs for traits peculiarly lacking in Addison, but that seems to the present commentator a malignant idea. The "Atticus" lines were printed about a year after this epistle, and those who believe that Pope rather than an enemy sent the "Atticus" portrait to the *St. James's Journal* are almost forced to believe that the praise of Craggs in these lines was covertly designed to reflect on Addison. That they did so, no one before Warburton (1751) seems to have thought.

EPISTLE TO DR. ARBUTHNOT

This epistle is justly one of the most famous of Pope's poems. It continues the defense of his satire begun in the Imitation of Horace, Book II, Satire 1 (1733), and is more frankly an apology for his career and personality than anything else he ever wrote. It is important to realize that from 1715 on Pope had been repeatedly the object of attack, and that the *Dunciad* and the Epistle to Burlington had simply intensified the situation, not originated it. In this poem he is defending himself from remote attacks made in the years when he was translating Homer and from enemies of the present, notably Lord Hervey and Lady Mary Wortley Montagu. The reply to early attacks had, as Pope says in the "Advertisement," been drawn up by snatches several years ago; it includes specifically something like lines 147-214 and lines 406-19. Much of the rest of the poem was composed with unusual speed in 1734. The immediate stimulus to writing came from the facts that Arbuthnot, hopelessly ill, had in July written Pope a "last request" that the poet should "continue that noble disdain and abhorrence of vice" in satire, but that he should "study more to reform than chastise, though the one often cannot be effected without the other." Late in August Pope wrote back: "I took very kindly your advice concerning avoiding ill will from writing satire, and it has worked so much upon me, considering the time and state you gave it in, that I determine to address to you one of my epistles, written by piecemeal many years, and which I have now made haste to put together; wherein the question is stated, what were, and are my motives of writing, the objections to them, and my answers. It pleases me much to take this occasion of testifying, to the public at least, if not to posterity, my obligation and friendship for, and from you, for so many years; that is all that is in it; for compliments are fulsome and go for nothing." The poem was in press in December, and was published in January less than two months before Arbuthnot's death.

Dr. John Arbuthnot (1667-1735) was one of the most notable physicians and wits of the day. He was

Queen Anne's favorite doctor and later was said to
hold a similar relation to the Princess of Wales, who
in 1727 became Queen Caroline. He was perhaps the
central figure in the Scriblerus Club, and after Swift's
retirement to Ireland (1714) was Pope's closest literary friend and adviser. Arbuthnot, himself a man of
astonishingly fertile invention, wrote many keen pamphlets, and his "John Bull," in *The History of John
Bull* (1712), has become a national symbol. Arbuthnot
collaborated with Pope more than once, and probably
wrote many of the notes for the *Dunciad Variorum*
(1729).

Discussion of the passages in the poem that were
written early has always centered on the "Atticus"
lines (193-214), which as a portrait of Joseph Addison are among the most famous Pope ever wrote.
Parts of the story of the celebrated "coldness" between
Addison and Pope (there never was an open quarrel)
have been told in connection with other poems; it is
too long a story to be told here in detail. Our best
"original" source for the matter is Spence's *Anecdotes*
(pages 149, 237, 326, 339); in modern times Professor
Nichol Smith and Monsieur Dottin are almost alone in
having written intelligently on the matter. The bases
for the difficulty were at least two. First, an antagonistic difference in the two personalities kept Addison
from anything like intimacy with Pope; in fact Addison made few intimate friends. In company Addison
was formal and taciturn, while Pope seems to have been
impulsive and facetious. Secondly, the politics of the
time thrust the two apart. From about 1714 on, Pope
was frequently attacked by the lesser Whig acquaintance of Addison, whom in line 209 Pope calls the
"little Senate" of Button's coffeehouse. With some
justice and some injustice Pope held Addison responsible. Certainly Addison revised and "toned down"

the attacks of Burnet and Duckett, but whether out of
desire to increase their effectiveness or to soften their
blows, is not clear. There is some truth in the charge
that Addison did "without sneering, teach the rest to
sneer." These sneers mainly concerned Pope's inability to translate Homer; and Pope's chief ground
of complaint against Addison would seem to lie in the
fact that Addison aided—perhaps instigated—Thomas
Tickell to translate the first book of the *Iliad* and publish it simultaneously (some "jockeying" was necessary to bring this about) with the first volume of
Pope's translation (June, 1715). The evident, though
in the event harmless, malice of this incident angered
Pope; and when (in 1718?) he heard, from what
seemed a reliable source, that Addison had paid Gildon
for attacking him (Pope) in Gildon's *Life of Wycherley* (of which a half-dozen copies are now known to
exist) Pope in increased anger wrote the first draft of
this portrait, and, if we may believe him, sent it to
Addison with good effect. Not all the details in Pope's
story of this affair check with now known facts, but
all the essential details do. The equivalent of lines
151-56 and 193-214 was first printed in *St. James's
Journal,* December 15, 1722, probably by some person
unfriendly to Pope but more unfriendly to Dennis.
The Elwin-Courthope edition of Pope does not take
this first-printed version into account, and theorizes
falsely on the supposition that Pope invented after
Addison's death the story of Gildon's venality. In
this earliest version of the portrait Gildon's quill is
"venal"—and there is plenty of evidence that the satire
was written before Addison's death. The portrait in
its final form commences with high compliment and
ends with implied compliment equally high. The lines
in general are an unsympathetic and prejudiced but
in the main sadly truthful portrait. And it is not

merely Addison but also any ungenerous and jealous artist of assured fame who is here castigated to such eternity as the English language may enjoy.

Pope's reply to the attacks of Lady Mary and Lord Hervey is both offensive and defensive. The real grounds of his intense hostility to these two court writers are quite unknown. Several explanations have been given; and others, equally unsatisfactory, can be found; but Pope's animosity is so extreme and his loathing so obviously sincere that we must assume personal as well as political causes. His hatred of Lady Mary, which followed a close intimacy, was first hinted in print in 1727, and in the *Dunciad* (May, 1728) Lord Hervey and Lady Mary both found small niches. In *A Pop upon Pope* (June 1, 1728) two persons whom Pope took to be Lady Mary and Lord Hervey told how they had had Pope beaten as he was out walking. After that there was continual interchange of lampooning courtesies that reflect little credit on any of the three. Such aggressive details are incidental rather than essential to the *Epistle to Arbuthnot*. Lady Mary escapes with a threat (101) and Lord Hervey comes in for something worse than a beating in the character of Sporus (305-33). The editors of Lord Hervey's *Memoirs* have thought the portrait unjust, and it very likely is so; but it should be noted that no detail in the portrait is originated by Pope: he is simply repeating with superior skill what more than one person had said before him.

The most important phase of the poem is Pope's defense of his satire. Pope has usually been painted as an aggressor, who smelt the battle from afar and prepared to shed ink; but the facts are that in 1715 when the first volume of his *Iliad* appeared, in 1717 when *Three Hours after Marriage* was acted, and in 1726 when the Shakespeare edition and his *Odyssey* were the talk of the town, Pope had been excessively attacked and had made relatively small reply. It must be confessed that his alleged passion for peace (lines 261-70) is partly a pose: he did not hate to reply to attacks, but he at times realized the unsatisfactory results from so doing—and in general before 1727 he had restrained himself. He here paints an effective picture of the petty solicitation (1-68) by which he had been victimized, and of the more distressing flattery (104-24). His satire, he urges, touches only fools, who don't feel it (83-104), or only vicious gossips (283-304) who are enemies of mankind. It is devoted, independently, to the cause of virtue (334-59); it does not regard place or person (360-67); and it has not been aggressive (368-87). As an example of his forbearance he mentions the lies told about his dead father—though he goes too far when, to make a good case, he suggests that his family were related to the Popes who had been Earls of Downe. The conclusion, with its tactful praise of the unusually pleasant family life of the Arbuthnots and its mention of the poet's mother, creates perfectly the illusion of kindliness and benevolence with which so skilfully made a poem might well end.

THE FIRST SATIRE OF THE SECOND BOOK OF HORACE IMITATED

To Mr. Fortescue

"When I had a fever one winter in town [Spence makes Pope say], that confined me to my room for five or six days, Lord Bolingbroke, who came to see me, happened to take up a Horace that lay on the table; and in turning it over, dipped on the first satire of the second book, which begins *Sunt quibus in satira,* etc. He observed how well that would hit my case, if I were to imitate it in English. After he was gone, I read it over; translated it in a morning or two and sent it to the press in a week or fortnight after. And this was the occasion of my imitating some other of the satires and epistles afterwards."

The *Epistle to Bathurst* had been published in January, 1733, and the *First Satire* appeared a month later. Both were promptly sent to Swift, to whom Pope said (February 16, 1733): "I never took more care in my life of anything than the former of these, nor less of the latter." It seems, however, highly finished. Possibly there was less care in choosing a moment for publication, a matter to which Pope was usually very attentive. He may have thought that the implication of the poem (that he had best write no more concerning public affairs) would add to the belief that he *was* keeping quiet and was consequently not the author of the *Essay on Man,* which was then appearing.

There seems to be no reason for thinking Pope was anxious about possible prosecution from the Court (Walpole) party in 1733, as the poem might seem to imply. He had been more than once attacked because of the *Epistle to Burlington,* and with many hints from Horace he here replies, defending his chosen weapon of satire and his methods of using it. He also takes occasion to satirize the government (whose cry was "Liberty") for its tendency to invoke the law in order to choke off attacks. Even Lady Mary and Lord Hervey were political as well as personal enemies; they were (so Pope wrote Swift) "certainly the top wits of the Court."

Politics largely motivate his version of Horace's poem. The poet asks his learned council, Fortescue, if there is danger of prosecution for his satires, and the cautious advice returned is to write no more—or, if writing is the only possible sedative, write Caesar's (George II's) praise. Pope then pleads the cause of satire—with darting side-thrusts that slash his foes—and happening to say that such grave epistles as his would be approved by Sir Robert Walpole himself, Fortescue shrugs his shoulders, and since thus *the case is altered,* withdraws his objections.

Lines 43-44 hit the dilemma of the personal satirist exactly: if you name the object of your satire, he alone is "corrected"; if you call him "Harpax," a score take the satire to heart, but hate the satirist. Lines 105-22 are in Pope's most eloquent and vigorous style; and their *forte* contrasts with the equally typical *piano* passage (lines 123-40) which follows. In this last passage Pope betrays a naive but excusable pride in his great friends of the Patriot group and in their visits to his grotto.

THE FIRST EPISTLE OF THE SECOND BOOK OF HORACE TO AUGUSTUS

In the absence of information in Pope's correspondence one imagines that this poem, which is really an epistle to George Augustus the Second, King of England, must have been composed in advance and, as usual, quietly put by for an opportune moment of publication. The moment came in May, 1737, when George II's treatment of the Prince of Wales had caused him considerable unpopularity. It is possible that Pope sent the poem to Swift as early as February, 1736, though Elrington Ball is probably right in thinking Swift's letter of February 9 is properly to be dated not 1736 but 1737.

The poem is Pope's most caustic attack upon George II, who was of course never regarded with enthusiasm by his subjects and certainly in the 1730's was an object of violent criticism, both because of his preference in the continental wars of the interests of Hanover to those of Great Britain—whom Walpole had so far kept out of war with difficulty—and because of his animosity towards his fractious son, the Prince of Wales, who was the idol of the Patriot opposition. The Prince had been personally friendly to Pope, who in 1736 presented His Royal Highness with a puppy born of "rare Bounce" and provided by Bounce's master with a collar inscribed:

> I am his Highness' dog at Kew;
> Pray tell me, sir, whose dog are you?

Relations between the Prince and his father were in 1737 most exasperating. In April, 1736, the King had at last permitted his son to marry, but had declined to arrange an allowance for the couple of more than £50,000, which was not sufficient for their station. In February, 1737, the 'patriotic' Pulteney moved in the House of Commons to increase the allowance to £100,000, and Walpole by a clever manoeuvre defeated the motion. The resulting *rôle* of grudging and parsimonious father rendered the King more than usually unpopular, and at this moment Pope's poem appeared. At the end of July following the Princess was brought to bed of a daughter at St. James's palace after the King and Queen had wished her to lie in at Hampton Court, and this caused further ill feeling within the royal family. On November 20 Queen Caroline died, and gossip, which Pope chose to follow in his *Epilogue to the Satires* (I, 80-82), represented her as obdurate to her son even on her deathbed.

Although Pope was fortunate in having a royal hero who could live up to such satire, the art of his "imitation" of Horace alone would have given the

poem life. In this imitation more than in any of the
others is seen his uncanny skill in applying Horace's
details to English affairs. The Roman poet wrote
at the request of Augustus, who, if in artistic ideals
somewhat "Rotarian," was the conqueror and ruler of
the world. Pope addressed a monarch who doubtless
detested him, who (except in music) had no artistic
interests, who ruled only through Walpole, and who,
though of military ambitions, had conquered nothing.
Such lines as 397 on Walpole's dear policy of buying
peace and 395 on Pope's eagerness to sing his monarch's *repose* are the height of sarcasm.

The poem follows Horace very closely, and since
the sequence of Horace's ideas is loose, and even obscure, we may expect Pope's to be so likewise. Horace
was, as Pope says, writing *"An Apology for the Poets,*
in order to render Augustus more their Patron."
Romans, Horace says, recognize contemporary merit
in Augustus, but elsewhere—in the arts—they admire
only established reputations, and admire unintelli-
gently at times. He urges the merit of the poet on
the "Rotarian" grounds of practical utility (Cf. Pope,
lines 189ff.) and urges the merit of the poet as contrasted with the dramatist. He concludes by praising the taste of Augustus above that of Alexander,
and with suspicious humility wishes he were a poet
sufficiently great to sing the imperial exploits.

Pope follows Horace, without irony for the most
part, in passages criticizing the undue and unintelligent
admiration of old writers or established reputations.
He amplifies Horace here as elsewhere with illustrations more extensive than those of the Roman poet.
English writers in general are not notably concise, but
when Pope uses 418 lines to Horace's 270, the additions represent mainly additions in substance, not
merely in verbiage. His case for neglected contempo-

rary merit is not, however, very skilfully put, and the amplifications at times give an unintentional effect of abusing earlier writers. In Queen Anne's time writers had got civic reward. Walpole, however, was contenting himself with hiring Grubstreet authors at so much a pamphlet: hence Pope had something of a case to state. Where Horace contrasts Greece and Rome, Pope contrasts France and England—or sometimes the English of the Caroline period with those of the Georgian.

In passages concerning Augustus, Pope follows Horace, but with the finest irony where Horace has none. It must be recalled that Horace, like Pope, had been an "opposition" poet, and that in his Epistle to Augustus he had in a sense made a public submission to the emperor. At first some of Pope's readers seemed to see glowing and submissive compliments by Pope to George II, but soon every one saw that lines such as those mentioned above (395, 397) were only sarcastic travesties of Horace's compliments. Lines 221-228 alone were sufficient to give a key to Pope's real attitude; for they are a tribute to Swift's achievement in his *Drapier's Letters,* and according to reports of the day nearly caused the government to take action against the poet. The Privy Council did not act because the affair of Wood's halfpence fell in the former reign. Swift thought the lines "those which are to do me the greatest honour I shall ever receive from posterity, and will outweigh the malignity of ten thousand enemies" (Letter of February 9, 1736 or 1737).

The finesse of the poem is largely a matter of detail, which can be fully perceived only after securing a thorough knowledge of the reign of George II and of Horace's poem. Coming at a moment when the none too coherent opposition against Walpole seemed to "have a chance" the poem must have been of con-

siderable political service—though in practical effect
Pope's verse never was comparable to Swift's prose
in such a situation. It is perhaps worth noting that in
dealing with the increase in refinement (263ff.) in
British arts, especially in the theatre (274-337), there
is no glance of condemnation towards the (Patriot)
farces of Henry Fielding (unless possibly in 310-11)
nor towards the Licensing Act prepared by Walpole to
curb such farces—an act that went into effect about a
month after the poem was published though probably
not yet debated when the poem was written. Pope
satirizes Cibber much in Fielding's vein (314-19),
and it is worth while to remember that these two
authors, the most eminent of the decade, were in the
'thirties both using their satire against the Walpole
government and against such "court" writers as Cibber.

EPILOGUE TO THE SATIRES

The two dialogues that constitute this poem appeared
respectively in May and July of 1738 under the title
of *One Thousand Seven Hundred and Thirty-eight*.
We have no information as to the period of composition, but internal evidence points to the year following
the *Epistle to Augustus*. The opening lines of the
second dialogue suggest that possibly Pope had once
intended it to appear under the title of "1739," but
decided not to risk its effectiveness by delay, since
anything might happen in the political world; and
some things—the total disintegration of the Patriots
or the retirement of Sir Robert, for example—would
have made poetry of so journalistic a cast sadly out
of date. We know from a letter to Fortescue (July
31, 1738) that Pope wished Walpole to appreciate the
compliments paid him in both dialogues; Pope says:
"As he shows a right sense of this, I may make him

a third, in my third Dialogue." Only a fragment of this "third" annual poetic revue exists under the title "1740."

Except for the fourth book of the *Dunciad* these dialogues are the last important poems Pope wrote. They seem, as Swift told him, "to equal almost anything you ever writ." They represent no falling off in powers, though his enemies, hoping doubtless for the time when his pen would falter, had asserted that he was "written out," that he became only duller and more sensational and scandalous with every poem. These criticisms Pope takes note of at the beginning of the poem. It may be that he abandoned "imitation" of a specific poem by Horace for imitation of the general Horatian tone and manner, so as to demonstrate to critics that he could work without a borrowed textual fabric to embroider. The poems do, as Hill wrote Pope, have something like "the acrimony of Juvenal, with the Horatian air of ease and serenity." They show Pope's exquisite tact in adapting the language of real life, the language of gentlemen, to poetry. We do not find here "unpolished, rugged verse" definitely trying to be prosaic, but rather the art of elegant sword-play, of rapier-like neatness and efficiency, that never slashes but "keeps time, distance, and proportion; rests me his minim rest, one, two, and the third in your bosom!" There is yet small trace of artificiality: the words incorporate thought as simply as ever any lines of Wordsworth did.

The tone is Pope's own; for though very like Horace, it is more serious than Horace usually is, and its seriousness is not merely acrimony. It is rather a despondent seriousness due in part to anxiety as to the path the Patriots were treading. Not all editors have shown much imagination in condemning Pope

for his unduly black and (so they have thought) doubt-
fully sincere picture of his times. They forget that
nothing is easier for a partizan than to believe his
faction one hundred per cent. in the right and the
opponents equally wrong. They do the impossible
and even forget that Pope was a partizan. As a matter of fact the position of Bolingbroke and Pope in
the Patriot opposition was unique: both were, for different reasons, debarred from political reward, and
consequently both were less suspected of selfish ends
than were other leaders. Furthermore, the recurring
absences of Bolingbroke in France frequently left Pope
alone in this position. A year or so after this poem
appeared, Sir William Wyndham, the fiery Tory leader,
was gravely ill; he wished to urge the Prince of Wales
to take personal charge of the opposition, for he feared
that the evident self-seeking of Pulteney and Carteret
would wreck the cause. To state these views to the
other opposition groups was a delicate task, and Wyndham apparently chose Pope for the duty. Pope's letter
to Lyttelton (Elwin-Courthope ed., IX, 178-81) represents a solemn and formal communication of Wyndham's last ideas, designed doubtless for the eye of
the Prince himself. Pope was also trusted to print
(and edit?) Bolingbroke's privately circulated advice
to the Prince *(The Idea of a Patriot King),* and in
other ways is shown to have been an important agent
for this opposition. He apparently maintained friendly
relations with Tories of all colors—the Jacobite Shippen, the fiery group led by Lyttelton, and the moderate group of Lord Cornbury. The apostrophe of
Prince Frederick in "1740" (line 85ff.):

> Alas! on one alone our all relies

together with lines 92-93 of Dialogue II shows Pope's

desire to follow Bolingbroke in exalting the Prince so
as to depreciate lesser leaders. The Patriots "too mean
and interested to deserve the name," upon whom he
adverts in Dialogue I, line 24 and note, and, through
the suggestion of his friend, in Dialogue II, lines
122-23, are most likely Pulteney and Carteret, though
he compliments Pulteney (II, 84-85), and believed in
using him for the cause.

Clearly Pope is a partizan, and as such he naturally
sees the corruption of the court party in dark colors.
But is he merely a partizan? He seems at times critical of the opposition, and much of his despondency
may be due to a declining confidence in his own party;
experience has taught him "how like Whig ministers
[are] to Tory" (I, 106), and if doubts are cast upon
the possibility of corrupting Patriots when in office
his only reply is,

> I only call those knaves who are so now (II, 127).

The doubts that took Bolingbroke from the fray were
beginning to affect Pope. Dimly, it is possible, he
foresaw that in the future politics must be "commer-
cialized"; he himself dealt so much in fine sentiments
that he may well have become critical of them, and
may have come to see that Walpole was the type for
the future, and Chesterfield a type from the past.
Civilization was changing subtly and rapidly in Pope's
time, and in a sense his poems, like later passages in
Burke, lament the new era — "when Truth stands
trembling on the edge of Law." The sophisters and
economists were already at the door; the earls and
colonels seemed to be passing out of mode. Is it
Voltairean cynicism that makes him advise himself at
last to take refuge in "more *Essays on Man*"?

The thought of the poems is unusually clear—though

the reader may wisely recognize that the "friend" who converses with the poet is really a hostile critic. In the first dialogue the friend urges (as some patriots were doing?) that Pope should make his satire innocuous and inoffensive. The poet replies caustically that the dignity of vice must be maintained, and that at the moment the danger of universal corruption degrades even vice (I, 141-43). Dialogue II develops further the dilemma of the satirist: he may not use names, but if he doesn't he will suffer misinterpretation; he must not go too high (24) or stoop too low; he must spare those whom satire might injure rather than correct—in fact, Jonathan Wild, a rogue hanged ten years ago (55), is the ideal object of satire. Pope urges that he has always praised where it has been possible and reiterates that in defense of truth and in punishment of vices beyond the law satire is the only weapon left. His critics have seldom wished to allow the sincerity of his avowal that his provocation is

> The strong antipathy of good to bad;

but granted that, like most partizans, he was perhaps self-deceived, I see no reason to doubt the sincerity of the deception.

After all, Swift's criticism on the poem is the soundest adverse criticism ever made. Naturally he does not doubt the reality of Pope's pessimism; but he does doubt (as he had earlier) the immortality of a poem so full of journalistic personalities: he assumes that these personal allusions "are very well known from Temple Bar to St. James's." This cuts to the heart of the matter: satire is built for a day, and not for all time. Pope's edifice survives as a towering, magnificent structure, but the ornaments and gargoyles are so eaten away as to be ruinous and unrecognizable.

THE DUNCIAD

The history of this poem is the most complex of any in Pope's career. He is thought here to have indulged a love of mystification at every turn; and every variant spelling in the many different editions has been suspected of subtle intention. There are the usual obscurities in the text incident to personalities in satire; but concerning these in his first preface Pope comforts us by saying: "I would not have the reader too much troubled or anxious, if he cannot decipher them; since when he shall have found them out, he will probably know no more of the persons than before." The perplexing difficulties are rather those external to the text of the poem found in conflicting statements inspired at times by Pope and in some cases embodied in his prefaces.

The poem is complex in nature and reflects the various states through which it passed and the varying intentions which it answered before 1743, when it reached the form in which we now have it. It is necessary to discuss, first, a hypothetical state in which parts of the poem must have existed as early as 1725 when Pope writes to Swift about its conclusion (October 15, 1725). From Book I, line 85, we learn that the action of the poem was once supposed to take place on Lord Mayor's Day (October 29) in 1719. A possible hypothesis—and nothing more—is that the poem originated as a satire on the choice of a city poet (who "functioned" on Lord Mayor's Day) in burlesque of the recent choice of a laureate (December, 1718). Elkanah Settle was the last city poet, and it is his death which in the 1728 *Dunciad* allows the choice of Lewis Theobald as prince of dulness. The idea of a succession to the throne of dulness is evidently taken from Dryden's *MacFlecknoe* (1682), and is possibly here cast in a mock-heroic form through the remote influence of the pseudo-Homeric *Margites* and the nearer influence of Thomas Brereton's *Charnock Junior: or the Coronation* (1719). Brereton's mock-heroic imitation of *MacFlecknoe* narrates the "progress" of Dr. Sacheverell from Banbury to Tyburn, where upon the execution of Charnock for treason, Sacheverell succeeds him as prince of sedition. There are many details in the *Dunciad,* like the reference to Thorold (I, 85) and the important *rôle* of Settle (d. 1724) in Books I and III, that seem to go back to this early hypothetical form of the poem. Such matters could have little interest for readers of 1728. It may be that when Pope ironically (in his first preface) declared the poem to be the labor "of full six years of his life", he was simply exaggerating the amount of labor and not the extent of time used in evolving the poem. In this early state, the poem would have been a satire on dulness in poets—a constant theme of the Scriblerus Club. As such the poem would not do, and was discarded.

Then in 1726 came Theobald's scholarly and scathing *Shakespear Restor'd,* which exploded Pope's reputation as an editor, and increased his aversion to that tribe. In the summers of 1726 and 1727 Swift was in England, and he and Pope went over various old papers, some of which were to be preserved in their *Miscellanies* (1727-32) and others to be destroyed. The "germ" of the *Dunciad* was consigned by Pope to the fire, but Swift snatched it out, having a brilliant idea how to use it. So Swift became a father to the poem, which upon publication of the later editions was appropriately dedicated to him. It is a safe guess that his brilliant idea was the making of Lewis Theobald hero. The satire now was to be directed not merely against dulness in poetry but against dulness in learning as well—and this also was a favorite Scriblerean theme, found most extensively in the prose *Memoirs of Martinus Scriblerus,* which Pope published in 1741. The name of the poem was to be "The Progress of Dulness", and Professor Griffith thinks its organizing aim was to trace the progress of dulness throughout the ages, as Gray later did that of poesy in his *Progress of Poesy.* Various facts, however, tend to make possible a view that, while progress through the ages is apparent in the 1743 *Dunciad,* in earlier forms progress may have referred (in the sense of royal "progress") to the procession of Lord Mayor's Day or some such occasion. Martinus Scriblerus in his discourse "Of the Poem" (page 275) states that the central action of progress is "the restoration of the reign of Chaos and Night, by the ministry of Dulness their daughter, in the removal of her imperial seat *from the City [i.e.,* from Bedlam (I, 29)] *to the polite world,"* i.e., perhaps to the Court of St. James's. None of these ideas of "progress" is consistently followed in any state of the poem, and as the time of publication drew on, the vision of a volume lettered on the back, "Pope's Dulness", was too much for the poet, and this projected title was dropped. Early in 1728 Voltaire had been getting public attention for a poem, formerly *La ligue,* but now published in England as the *Henriade.* Apparently at the last moment Pope imitated Voltaire's title and called his poem the *Dunciad.* In Pope's day a dunce was a person dull either because of too much intellectual lumber (as the great original, Duns Scotus) or because of a lack of mental equipment, as in the case of the simpleton. Theobald, Pope felt, belonged to the first type; Cibber had perhaps the vacuity of the simpleton, but was in no other sense dull.

The period of concentrated labor on the first form

of the poem to be printed seems to have been the second half of 1727. In this stage the poem passed with rather unusual speed from the poet's hands to those of his readers. There was much revision, but little of the intentional "delay" that some critics have written of. A letter (June 30, 1727) to Motte, printer of the *Miscellanies,* makes it clear that at first the poem was designed to conclude the Swift-Pope volume of poetical *Miscellanies* (the so-called "last" volume), but that the author decided finally to elaborate it and publish it separately. To complete the volume of *Miscellanies,* then in press, Pope added to it a prose treatise, *Peri Bathous: or, the Art of Sinking in Poetry,* which appeared March 8, 1728, ten weeks before the *Dunciad.* The *Peri Bathous* (or *Bathos*) was Pope's first known reply to many of his enemies; in a few cases (in spite of what he said) it was aggressive rather than merely retaliatory. The rejoinders from persons there satirized were instant and numerous— something over twenty in the ten weeks that elapsed before the *Dunciad.* The preface of the poem alleged these many attacks as causes of the *Dunciad*—but the causes, as everyone could see, dated from 1711 on, and became exciting only in 1726 when Theobald's book appeared.

Prudential thoughts, stimulated by retorts to the *Bathos,* aroused in Pope a desire to obscure his connection with the *Dunciad,* at least his legal connection; for it was possible the thing might prove libellous, and Theobald was an attorney. The first titlepage (May, 1728) was of course anonymous; but it suggested vaguely a Hibernian authorship by making the titlepage read "Dublin Printed, London Reprinted". The inference desired was that Swift might be coming to Pope's aid in the volume. On the last page of what seems now to be the true first edition and in certain newspaper advertisements of the *Dunciad* there were notices that "The Progress of Dulness" was soon to appear. It was probably known that Pope had been working on a poem of that name, and it might seem that if he were now about to publish it, the poem called the *Dunciad* might be by a friend of his; that is, it might seem doubtful if he would be publishing two poems at the same time. But none of these devices, and none of the others of which he has been suspected, had any success: the authorship of the poem was readily guessed, and retorts were numerous —and dull! One of the most amusing comments of Pope's dunces is that Pope offered no proofs of their dulness. In his opinion they themselves for years had been doing that!

Within a month after the first printing of the poem Pope set to work on a new edition that was to have all the "critical apparatus" of dissertations preliminary, of footnotes, indexes, etc. In fact, the poem became a burlesque on critical editions. It is this form (published in April, 1729) that shows the poem in its best light as a satire on pedantry. To be sure, there were gross inaccuracies in the statements made in the critical apparatus, and these have been offensive to very truthful persons. Pope, however, may have conceived inaccuracy as a delightful way of annoying the pedantically accurate; or he may—with his assisting friends —have written the notes with reckless abandon. Their "lies" are palpable rather than subtle. This 1729 *Dunciad,* being even more nearly libellous than that of 1728, was assigned by Pope to Lords Burlington, Oxford, and Bathurst, who reassigned the property rights to the publisher, and who themselves may have dispersed the first copies sent out to booksellers. The poem was presented to the King by Walpole on March

12, 1729, and the King is reported to have said that Mr. Pope was a very honest man.

There were other small revisions about 1735, and then came (1742-43) the great revision which dethroned Theobald and put Cibber in his place. This was a part of a general revision of Pope's works for a collected edition made in the late years of his life with Warburton's help. Warburton had been a friend to Theobald and to pedantry; he doubtless wanted Theobald "deposed." Pope, furthermore, had found no valuable allies in his attacks on the editor of Shakespeare—who though a great editor seems to have been an uninteresting person. Cibber, on the other hand, had almost as many enemies as Pope himself— all unsuccessful playwrights hated him for having refused their plays; and since he had quit the stage and set up (1730) as poet laureate, gentlefolk had taken to laughing at his bad odes for royal birthdays. For years he had seemed about the most ridiculous thing in the world to the best prose writer of the day, Henry Fielding. Details from Fielding's *Pasquin* and *Historical Register* seem to have influenced the Fourth Book of the Dunciad. So Pope, whose grudge against Cibber dated back to 1717, set to work. About March 20, 1742 appeared for the first time *The New Dunciad: As it was found in the Year 1741*. This, the Fourth Book, though published separately was obviously designed to be incorporated in the *Dunciad*. It is commonly said that Cibber's pamphlet *A Letter from Mr. Cibber to Mr. Pope Inquiring into the Motives that might induce him in his Satyrical Works to be so frequently fond of Mr. Cibber's Name* (July, 1742) angered Pope and led him to crown Cibber. But, one must first ask, why at this moment did Cibber print such a pamphlet? At first sight there seems to be no reason; for since 1738 Pope had shown no frequent fondness for Cibber's name—in fact, he had in four years mentioned it only once significantly, and that was in line 20 of the New Dunciad:

> Soft on her lap her Laureate son reclines.

Cibber, who had stood punishment for years without reply, was hardly to be exasperated into a retort by a line so innocent-seeming as this, one might say; but as a matter of fact the line places Cibber in the same intimate attitude that had previously been Theobald's in Book III, line 2; and the inference that Cibber was to supplant Theobald in the poem would from this one line alone be easy and indeed almost inevitable. The revision of the poem was probably completed long before final publication of the revised four books, which was delayed by doubts as to Pope's title in his own poem. The copyright had been sold to the bookseller Henry Lintot, and as early as January, 1741, Pope had been worrying over recovering his rights. His chancery bill of February, 1743, alleges that he had long intended to revise the poem "as soon as the property thereof should revert" to him. Not long after the case was settled, the poem, revised in the form in which we now read it, appeared. It was put on sale in October, 1743.

The action of the poem is meagre and episodic. It begins (I, 29) near Bedlam (Bethlehem Hospital for the Insane) with the goddess Dulness reflecting on the loss to her glory resulting from the lack of a City Poet; for through Settle's death the throne of dulness is vacant. Bayes (Cibber) in despair invokes the goddess' aid, and becomes laureate and King of the Dunces. In Book II we have the coronation games. (It may be remembered that George II was crowned eight months before the poem appeared.) This book contains more action than the other three—and is by all odds the foulest in images of any of Pope's writing. The hero does not appear in this book. In Book III the hero dreams that, like Ulysses and Æneas, he descends to Elysium, where Settle explains a vision of the future glories of dulness. Book IV is a picture of the gorgeous court of Dulness in its future triumphant state when Chaos and old Night are to reassume their sway.

Obviously the poem has little story; the hero—whether Theobald or Cibber—does not dominate the action. In fact, only in Book I is the hero at all prominent. The poem, furthermore, is in parts obscure, malicious, or obscene. What then constitutes its claim to greatness? It must be admitted that to tender minds it has frequently been repulsive. It was so even in Pope's own day. On the other hand, the ingeniousness and propriety in such descriptions as those of the statuesque figures at the levee of Dulness (Book IV), of Cibber in the act of poetic creation (Book I), of Lintot in the act of running (II, 63ff.), and in many other passages, are powerfully and instructively imagined. The language throughout is sparklingly trenchant; such lines as those about gentle dulness and jokes (II, 34), about the "sound divine" (II, 352), "the eel of science" (I, 280), and many others, show Pope's unsurpassed skill in verbal marksmanship. Certain things about the poet's essential attitude are also both pleasing and memorable. It is, first, a delight to see a poet throw overboard his inhibitions as to uttering frank personalities. Plain English bluntness is not always delightful; but when bluntness can be joined with finesse and polish, one forgives the rudeness or even the malice, and rejoices that wholesome truth has been told without any cant of politeness. And, in the second place, everyone of clear mind ought to see that the *Dunciad* essentially *does* tell wholesome truths. The literary historian or critic in every age needs to be reminded of the humble and ancillary—if essential—nature of his task: every doctor of philosophy might profitably ponder the *Dunciad* at least once a year. As for dull poets all one can say is that there is so much good poetry elbowed aside by the specious that no one ought ever to regret frankness about the latter sort. The good poets of Pope's day, from Prior to Thomson, were his friends. In spite of incidental bits of injustice in the poem, no one who has heard cheap critics criticize and bad poets boast, will ever be sorry that once a poet immortally turned the pitiless light of common sense on such performances, and showed their absurdity.

"THE ILIAD," BOOK IX

As a boy Pope had loved the *Iliad,* had before the age of ten made a play out of Ogilvy's translation, and among his early works had published translations of passages from Homer. He was ambitious to translate the whole *Iliad,* and was delighted in 1713 to receive the encouragement of his friends in the attempt. The chief of these encouragers were probably Sir William Trumbull, Steele, Addison, and Swift. His chief supporters in furthering the subscription for the project proved to be the painter Jervas from the Whigs, Swift from the Tories, and Caryll from the Roman Catholics. The subscription, formally announced in October, 1713, was pushed by both Whigs and Tories, and thus secured unparalleled support. The terms were six guineas for the six volumes; two guineas to be paid in advance upon subscribing, one to be paid for each of Volumes II-V upon publication, and nothing for the last volume. The volumes were to appear annually, but it turned out that none appeared in 1719 and the last two appeared together in 1720. A subscription so expensive, stretched over so many years, could have been made a success only by the energy and distinction of Pope's supporters. To be in fashion one had to subscribe: Professor Griffith finds the list of subscribers contains 17 dukes, 3 marquises, 49 earls; 7 duchesses, 1 marchioness, and 8 countesses. There were 9 generals, 10 colonels, and 19 clergymen—only one of whom was a bishop. All told there were 654 subscriptions from 574 persons. Bishop Kennet has shown us Swift at Court in the act of compelling subscribers to come in:

> Then he [Swift] instructed a young nobleman that the best poet in England was Mr. Pope (a Papist), who had begun a translation of Homer into English verse, 'for which he must have them all subscribe; for', says he, 'the author shall not begin to print till I have a thousand guineas for him.'

Pope was forced to make an enormous success or an enormous failure in view of such advertising. He was anxious to succeed both on literary and financial grounds. The family income had been considerably diminished in 1713 by an edict of Louis XIV, which had reduced the rate of interest on French annuities granted between 1702 and 1710 by twenty-five per cent. Since Pope's father had invested 8250 livres in this fashion, it behooved the son to bestir himself for money as well as for fame. Only a rank failure in the translation could prevent a financial reward that would assure the poet of a comfortable fortune. But Pope's knowledge of Greek was slight, and lesser poets, envious of the unparalleled good luck of the newly risen poetic star, began to comment orally and in print. Pope writes Caryll (May 1, 1714):

> Some have said I am not a master in the Greek, who either are so themselves or are not. If they are not, they cannot

tell; and if they are, they cannot without having catechised me. But if they can read . . . . there are fairly lying before them and all the world some specimens of my translation from this author in the Miscellanies . . . I have also encountered much malignity on the score of religion, some calling me a papist and a tory. . .Others have styled me a whig.

This was the beginning of his woes; Pandora's box was opening. The poet, however, kept up his courage, and tried to compensate for his enormous lack of sound scholarship by industry and by poetic ability. When in June, 1715, his first volume appeared and Tickell, who was a Fellow of an Oxford college, confidently brought out his *Iliad, Book I* on the following day, only Addison and the group at Button's preferred the Oxonian's translation. Edward Young tried to persuade the Oxford dons that Tickell's was the more faithful, but it was little use: "Pope was their man."

Pope was curiously systematic and astonishingly industrious in the early years of his labor on Homer. He paid little attention to the attacks that Burnet, Duckett, Dennis, Gildon, Bezaleel Morrice, Welsted, "Mr. Preston," and other pseudonymous and anonymous "critics" showered upon him. At the start he kept well ahead of the printer, but after 1717 the task became irksome—but not so irksome but that with help he was later willing to undertake the *Odyssey*. His final profits on both the *Iliad* and the *Odyssey* have been estimated usually at the unparalleled sum of from eight to ten thousand pounds. Homer was his fairy godmother.

Book IX, here used as a specimen of Pope's translation, was printed in 1717 in volume III. It is a good specimen, because Pope excels in eloquence rather than in simple, rapid narrative, and this book consists mainly in highly dramatic speech-making. Pope's ideals in translation were poetic rather than scholarly. Substantially, they had been stated by Dryden in his prefaces to his Ovid and Virgil, and more contemporaneously they had been voiced by the French modernist La Motte Houdart, whose translation of the *Iliad* (1714) was made on liberal lines explained in an ode (1711?), the substance of which was that Homer ought to be made to read as if he were an eighteenth-century poet. La Motte felt free to abridge or otherwise modify the literal meaning so long as he was

> fidele au stile héroïque,
> Au grand sens, au tour pathétique.

Pope similarly feels free to paraphrase rather than to translate; he condenses or expands, and at times quite modifies the sense of the original. He justifies this procedure only by the animation of his lines, which, if more nervous and less dignified than the original, are yet the most spirited English into which Homer has been rendered.

In order to maintain a *stile héroïque* Pope imitated, with unfortunate results, the complex and exotic style of *Paradise Lost,* and thus became responsible in the eyes of many for the "poetic diction" of his century, against which Wordsworth rebelled so strenuously. He was following a dangerous principle of his time, which frankly commended a translator for "improving" on his original. Denham, a generation or more before Pope, had remarked: "Poetry is of so subtile a spirit, that, in pouring out of one language into another, it will all evaporate; and, if a new spirit be not added in the transfusion, there will remain nothing but a *caput mortuum.*" No one has accused Pope of leaving Homer dead or dull; the criticism has rather been that the sparkle and nervous force which he transfused into the *Iliad* and the *Odyssey* savor of artifice. In the Greek Agamemnon, Achilles, Nestor, and Phoenix speak like heroes—and like men. In Pope they sound purely theatrical—and yet very effectively theatrical. The celebrated classical scholar, Richard Bentley, is supposed to have told Pope: "It's a very pretty poem, but you mustn't call it Homer." The judgment is perhaps just; but no English translation has ever given a more interesting and spirited representation of Homer than has Pope's.

USEFUL BOOKS AND ARTICLES

EDITIONS

Early "complete" editions of Pope's *Works* (negligible except for highly specialized study) were published by the following editors: W. Warburton, 1751 and later; O. Ruffhead, 1769; J. Warton, 1797; W. L. Bowles, 1806; W. Roscoe, 1824; R. Carruthers (*Poetical Works*), 1853 and 1858; etc.

The Works of Alexander Pope. Edited by Rev. Whitwell Elwin and W. J. Courthope. 10 vols. 1871-89. (The standard edition. The notes and commentaries show frequently a curious and unwarrantable hostility to Pope.)

The Poetical Works of Alexander Pope. Globe Edition. Edited by A. W. Ward. 1869. (The best annotated edition in one volume. Later dates on the title page imply little or no revision.)

The Complete Poetical Works of Alexander Pope. The Cambridge Edition. Edited by H. W. Boynton. Boston (Mass.), 1903. (This contains the translation of Homer. The "chronological" arrangement of the poems is quite unreliable.)

The Prose Works of Alexander Pope. The Earlier Works 1711-1720. Edited by Norman Ault. Oxford (Bodley Head), 1936.

The Dunciad Variorum . . . Reproduced in facsimile from the first issue of the original edition of 1729. With an Introductory Essay by R. K. Root. Princeton, 1929.

The Poems of Alexander Pope. The Twickenham Edition. 6 vols. London (Methuen), 1939- . (In process. Only Volume IV ["Imitations of Horace," etc.] of this edition has as yet appeared. Upon completion it should be standard for the poems.)

Pope's Essay on Criticism. Edited by John Sargeaunt. Oxford, 1909.

The Essay on Man. Edited by Mark Pattison. Oxford, 1869.

Pope's Rape of the Lock. Edited by George Holden. Oxford, 1909.

Pope's Satires and Epistles. Edited by Mark Pattison. Oxford, 1872.

The Iliad and The Odyssey of Homer. Translated by Alexander Pope. Edited by Gilbert Wakefield. 9 vols. 1806. Another edition (with fewer notes), 5 vols., 1817.

Pope's Own Miscellany. Being a Reprint of *Poems on Several Occasions,* 1717, containing new poems by Alexander Pope and others. Edited by Norman Ault. 1935.

BIBLIOGRAPHIES

Griffith, R. H. *Alexander Pope. A Bibliography.* 2 vols. Austin (Texas), 1922, 1927.

Wise, T. J. *A Pope Library.* London, 1931. (Valuable for its reproduction of the title-pages, but practically never to be preferred as authority to Griffith's work.)

Thoms, W. J. "A Bibliography of the Literature Connected with Pope and his Quarrels." *Notes and Queries,* 5 S XII (1879), and 6 S I (1880). (Incomplete but useful.)

Annual Bibliography of English Language and Literature. Edited for the Modern Humanities Research Association. (By E. Allison Peers and succeeding editors.) Annual volumes have appeared since 1921.

"English Literature of the Restoration and Eighteenth Century: A Current Bibliography." *Philological Quarterly* for April, annually since 1926. By Ronald S. Crane, Louis I. Bredvold, Richmond P. Bond, *et al.*

CONCORDANCE

Abbott, Edwin. *A Concordance to the Works of Alexander Pope.* 1875.

BIOGRAPHICAL AIDS

1. *Lives of Pope.*

Ayre, William. *Memoirs of the Life and Writings of Alexander Pope, Esq.* 2 vols. 1745. (Quite negligible.)

Ruffhead, Owen. *The Life of Alexander Pope.* 1769.

Johnson, Samuel. "Pope." *Lives of the Poets,* 1781. (Use the edition of G. B. Hill, 1905.)

Spence, Joseph. *Anecdotes, Observations, and Characters of Books and Men.* Edited by S. W. Singer. 1820. (A principal source of biographical data for Pope. The edition by Edmund Malone [also 1820] is less complete than Singer's.)

Roscoe, William. "Life." Volume I of Roscoe's edition of Pope, 1824.

Carruthers, Robert. "Memoir of Pope." Volume I of the *Poetical Works,* 1853. Revised edition, 1857.

Stephen, Leslie. *Alexander Pope.* English Men of Letters Series. 1880.

Courthope, William J. "Life" of Pope in Volume V of the Elwin-Courthope edition of Pope's *Works.* 1889.

"Paston, George" [E. M. Symonds]. *Mr. Pope.* 2 vols. 1909.

Sherburn, George. *The Early Career of Alexander Pope.* Oxford, 1934.

2. Allied Biographical Materials.

Dobrée, Bonamy. *Essays in Biography, 1680-1726.* 1925. (The essay on Addison bears also on Pope.)

Hillhouse, James T. *The Grub Street Journal.* Durham (North Carolina), 1928.

Jones, Richard F. *Lewis Theobald.* New York, 1919.

Nichol-Smith, David. *The Letters of Thomas Burnet to George Duckett.* The Roxburghe Club. 1914.

Straus, Ralph. *The Unspeakable Curll.* 1927.

Tickell, R. Eustace. *Thomas Tickell and the Eighteenth Century Poets.* London, 1931.

LITERARY CRITICISM FOR THE PERIOD 1688-1744.

Bredvold, Louis I. "The Element of Art in Eighteenth Century Poetry." *Selected Poems of Alexander Pope.* New York, 1926.

Clark, A. F. B. *Boileau and the French Classical Critics in England.* Paris, 1925.

Courthope, William J. *A History of English Poetry.* 1905. (Especially Vol. V.)

Courthope, William J. *Life in Poetry: Law in Taste.* 1901.

Dennis, John (of the nineteenth century). *The Age of Pope.* 1894.

Dennis, John (1657-1734). *Critical Works of John Dennis.* Edited by Edward N. Hooker. Baltimore (Maryland), 1939- . (In process.)

Havens, Raymond D. *The Influence of Milton on English Poetry.* Cambridge (Mass.), 1922.

Legouis, Emile, and Louis Cazamian. *A History of English Literature.* New York, 1935.

Nichol-Smith, David. *Some Observations on Eighteenth Century Poetry.* 1937.

Tillyard, E. M. W. *Poetry Direct and Oblique.* 1934.

Williamson, George. "The Rhetorical Pattern of Neo-Classical Wit." *Modern Philology,* XXXIII (1935), 55-81.

Vines, Sherard. *The Course of English Classicism from the Tudor to the Victorian Age.* 1930.

Literary Criticism of Pope Himself

1. *General*

Audra, E. *L'influence française dans l'œuvre de Pope.* Paris, 1931. (More than the title implies, this work is a general storehouse of information about Pope.)

Durham, Willard H. "Pope as a Poet." *Essays in Criticism, Second Series.* By Members of the Department of English, University of California. Berkeley (Calif.), 1934, pp. 93-110.

Knight, G. Wilson. "The Vital Flame: An Essay on Pope." *The Burning Oracle,* 1939.

Root, Robert K. *The Poetical Career of Alexander Pope.* Princeton, 1938.

Sitwell, Edith. *Alexander Pope.* 1930.

Tillotson, Geoffrey. *On the Poetry of Pope.* Oxford, 1938.

Warren, Austin. *Alexander Pope as Critic and Humanist.* Princeton, 1929.

Warton, Joseph. *An Essay on the Genius and Writing of Pope.* 1756 (Vol. I.) ; 1782, 2 vols. (The standard eighteenth century work on Pope's poetry.)

2. *Special Topics*

Audra, E. *Les traductions françaises de Pope, 1717-1825.* Paris, 1931.

Ault, Norman. "Pope and the Miscellanies. With a New Poem by his Hand." *Nineteenth Century,* CXVI (1934), 566-580.

Brie, Friedrich. "Pope's *Brutus.*" *Anglia,* LXIII (1939), 144-185,

Butt, John. *Pope's Taste in Shakespeare.* Oxford, 1936.

Case, Arthur E. "New Attributions to Pope." *Modern Philology,* XXXIV (1937), 305-313. Cf. Ault, *ibid.,* XXXV (1937), 179-187 ; and Case, *ibid.,* XXXV (1937), 187-191.

———. "Some New Poems by Pope." *The London Mercury,* X (1924), 614-623.

———. "Pope, Addison, and the 'Atticus' Lines." *Modern Philology,* XXXIII (1935), 187-193.

Chandler, W. K. "The First Edition of the *Dunciad.*" *Moaern Philology,* XXIX (1931), 59-72.

———. "Pope's Self-Plagiarism." *Modern Philology,* XXX (1932), 98-100.

Chesterton, G. K. "Pope and the Art of Satire." *Varied Types.* 1908.

Dilke, Charles Wentworth. *The Papers of a Critic.* 2 vols. 1875.

Griffith, R. H. "The *Dunciad* Duodecimo." *Colophon,* III (1938), 569-586.

————. "The Progress Piece of the Eighteenth Century." *The Texas Review,* V (1920), 218-233.

————. "News for Bibliophiles." *The Nation* (New York), XCIII (20 July 1911), 52-53. (Shows how Pope revised the conclusion to the *Dunciad.*)

Havens, Raymond D. "Romantic Aspects of the Age of Pope." *PMLA,* XXVII (1912), 297-324.

Hazen, Allen T. "Crousaz on Pope." *Times Literary Supplement,* 2 November 1935, p. 704. Cf. also Davidson Cook, *ibid.,* 9 November, p. 728.

Hodges, John C. "Pope's Debt to One of his Dunces." *Modern Language Notes,* LI (1936), 154-158.

Lounsbury, T. R. *The First Editors of Shakespeare.* London, 1906. (Identical, except for the title, with the following item:)

————. *The Text of Shakespeare.* New York, 1908.

Mack, Maynard. "The First Printing of the Letters of Pope and Swift." *Library,* XIX (1939), 465-485.

MacClintock, W. D. *Joseph Warton's "Essay on Pope": A History of the Five Editions.* Chapel Hill (North Carolina), 1933.

McLean, L. Mary. "The Riming System of Alexander Pope." *PMLA,* VI (1891), 134-160.

Mead, William E. *The Versification of Pope in its Relation to the Seventeenth Century.* Leipzig, 1889.

Ratchford, Fannie E. "Pope and the *Patriot King.*" *University of Texas Studies in English,* No. 6. Austin (Texas), 1926.

Sherburn, George. "Timon's Villa and Cannons." *The Huntington Library Bulletin,* VIII (1935), 131-152.

————. "Two Notes on the *Essay on Man.*" *Philological Quarterly,* XII (1933), 402-403.

————. "Walpole's Marginalia in *Additions to Pope, 1776.*" *The Huntington Library Quarterly,* I (1938), 473-487.

Simpson, Percy. *Proof-reading in the Sixteenth, Seventeenth and Eighteenth Centuries.* Oxford, 1935.

Stephen, Leslie. "Pope as a Moralist." *Hours in a Library,* I (1873), 113-168.

Sutherland, James R. "The *Dunciad* of 1729." *Modern Language Review,* XXXI (1936), 347-353.

Tillotson, Geoffrey. "Lady Mary Wortley Montagu and Pope's 'Elegy to the Memory of an Unfortunate Lady.'" *Review of English Studies,* XII (1936), 401-412.

Tupper, James W. "Pope's Imitations of Horace." *PMLA,* XV (1900), 181-215.

Williams, W. H. "Pope and Horace." *Temple Bar Magazine,* XV (1898), 87ff.

Winslow, Ann "Re-evaluation of Pope's Treatment of Nature." *University of Wyoming Publications,* IV (1938), 21-43. (Incisive and interesting.)

Wyld, H. C. "Observations on Pope's Versification." *Modern Language Review,* XXV (1930), 274-285.

POPE'S BACKGROUNDS

1. *Political*

Feiling, Keith. *History of the Tory Party, 1640-1714.* Oxford, 1924.

―――. *The Second Tory Party, 1714-1832.* 1938.

Hanson, Laurence. *Government and the Press, 1695-1763.* Oxford, 1936.

Laprade, William T. *Public Opinion and Politics in Eighteenth Century England to the Fall of Walpole.* New York, 1936.

Leadham, I. S. *The History of England* (1702-1760). 1921.

Morley, John. *Walpole.* 1889.

Realey, Charles B. *The Early Opposition to Sir Robert Walpole, 1720-1727.* Lawrence (Kan.) and Philadelphia, 1931.

Robertson, John M. *Bolingbroke and Walpole.* 1919.

Taylor, G. R. S. *Robert Walpole and his Age.* 1931.

Trevelyan, George Macaulay. *History of England.* 1926.

———. *England under Queen Anne.* 3 vols. 1932-1934.

2. *Social and Artistic*

Allen, B. Sprague. *Tides in English Taste (1619-1800):* A Background for the Study of Literature. 2 vols. Cambridge (Mass.), 1937.

Allen, Robert J. *The Clubs of Augustan London.* Cambridge (Mass.), 1933.

Ashton, John. *Social Life in the Reign of Queen Anne.* 1882.

Grundy, C. Reginald. *English Art in the Eighteenth Century.* 1928.

Irving, William Henry. *John Gay's London.* Cambridge (Mass.), 1928.

Trevelyan, George Macaulay. *The England of Queen Anne.* Reprinted from *Blenheim.* 1932.

Turberville, A. S. *English Men and Manners in the Eighteenth Century.* 1926.

3. *Intellectual*

Becker, Carl L. *The Heavenly City of the Eighteenth Century Philosophers.* New Haven, 1932.

Bond, Donald F. " 'Distrust' of Imagination in English Neo-Classicism." *Philological Quarterly,* XIV (1935), 59-69.

———. "The Neo-Classical Psychology of the Imagination." *Journal of English Literary History,* IV (1937), 245-264.

Bundy, Murray Wright. *Theory of the Imagination in Classical and Medieval Thought.* Urbana (Ill.), 1927.

Evans, A. W. *Warburton and the Warburtonians.* Oxford, 1932.

Fairchild, Hoxie N. *Religious Trends in English Poetry (1700-1740): Protestantism and the Cult of Sentiment.* New York, 1939.

Lovejoy, Arthur O. *The Great Chain of Being: a Study of the History of an Idea.* Cambridge (Mass.), 1936.

———. "Nature as Aesthetic Norm." *Modern Language Notes,* XLII (1927), 444-450.

———. "Optimism and Romanticism." *PMLA,* XLII (1927), 921-945.

———. "The Parallel of Deism and Classicism." *Modern Philology,* XXIX (1932), 281-299.

———. "Pride in Eighteenth Century Thought." *Modern Language Notes,* XXXVI (1921), 31-37.

MacLean, Kenneth. *John Locke and English Literature of the Eighteenth Century.* New Haven, 1936.

Moore, Cecil A. "Did Leibniz Influence Pope's *Essay on Man?*" *Journal of English and Germanic Philology,* XVI (1917), 84-102.

———. "Shaftesbury and the Ethical Poets in England, 1700-1760." *PMLA,* XXXI (1916), 264-326.

Stephen, Leslie. *English Thought in the Eighteenth Century.* 2 vols. Third Edition, 1902.

Whitney, Lois. *Primitivism and the Idea of Progress in the Eighteenth Century.* Baltimore, 1934.

Willey, Basil. *The Eighteenth Century Background.* 1940.

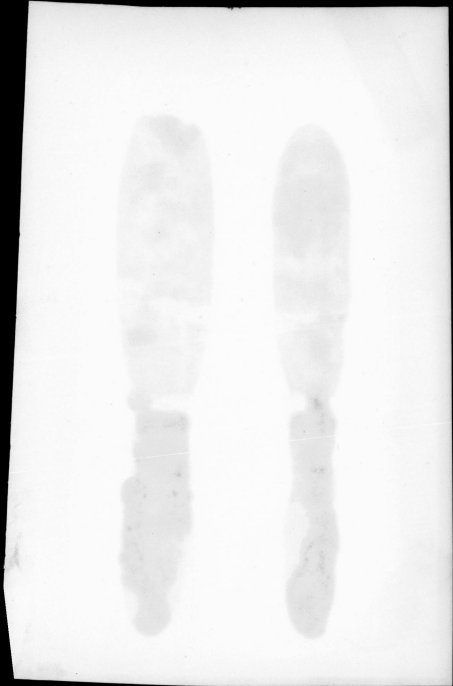

DATE DUE

GAYLORD   PRINTED IN U.S.A.